Latvia

THE BRADT TRAVEL GUIDE

PUBLISHER'S FOREWORD

The first Bradt travel guide was written in 1974 by George and Hilary Bradt on a river barge floating down a tributary of the Amazon. In the 1980s and '90s the focus shifted away from hiking to broader-based guides covering new destinations – usually the first to be published about these places. In the 21st century Bradt continues to publish such ground-breaking guides, as well as others to established holiday destinations, incorporating in-depth information on culture and natural history with the nuts and bolts of where to stay and what to see.

Bradt authors support responsible travel, and provide advice not only on minimum impact but also on how to give something back through local charities. In this way a true synergy is achieved between the traveller and local communities.

*

It's lovely to welcome a fourth edition of Latvia by my old friends Stephen Baister and Chris Patrick. They were responsible for one of the first Bradt best-sellers, a guide to East Germany published when this was a separate country and independent Latvia didn't exist. When The Wall came down we lost one title but gained many others, notably Estonia, Latvia and Lithuania. There are few remnants of the old Soviet Union in this now vibrant country, but Stephen and Chris can justifiably claim to have helped put Latvia on the tourist map when their guide was first published in 1995.

Hilary Bradt

Hilary Bradt

19 High Street, Chalfont St Peter, Bucks SL9 9QE, England
Tel: 01753 893444 Fax: 01753 892333
Email: info@bradtguides.com
Web: www.bradtguides.com

Latvia

THE BRADT TRAVEL GUIDE
Fourth Edition

Stephen Baister
Chris Patrick

Bradt Travel Guides Ltd, UK
The Globe Pequot Press Inc, USA

Fourth edition 2005
First published 1995

Bradt Travel Guides Ltd
19 High Street, Chalfont St Peter, Bucks SL9 9QE, England
www.bradtguides.com
Published in the USA by The Globe Pequot Press Inc,
246 Goose Lane, PO Box 480, Guilford, Connecticut 06437-0480

Text copyright © 2005 Stephen Baister and Chris Patrick
Maps copyright © 2005 Bradt Travel Guides Ltd
Illustrations © 2005 individual artists and photographers

The authors and publisher have made every effort to ensure the accuracy of the
information in this book at the time of going to press. However, they cannot accept any
responsibility for any loss, injury or inconvenience resulting from the use of
information contained in this guide.

All rights reserved. No part of this publication may be reproduced, stored in a retrieval
system, or transmitted in any form or by any means, electronic, mechanical,
photocopying, recording or otherwise without the prior consent of the publishers.
Requests for permission should be addressed to Bradt Travel Guides Ltd, 19 High
Street, Chalfont St Peter, Bucks SL9 9QE in the UK; or to The Globe Pequot Press Inc,
246 Goose Lane, PO Box 480, Guilford, Connecticut 06437-0480
in North and South America.

British Library Cataloguing in Publication Data
A catalogue record for this book is available from the British Library

ISBN-10: 1 84162 121 8
ISBN-13: 978 1 84162 121 0

Photographs
Front cover Statue by Indulis Ranks at the Sculpture Park, Turaida (SC)
Text Stephen Baister & Chris Patrick (SC), Tricia Hayne (TH), Rachel Russell (RR),
Mark Wadlow (MW)

Illustrations John Baister, Carole Vincer
Maps Alan Whitaker, Matt Honour

Typeset from the authors' disc by Wakewing
Printed and bound in Italy by Legoprint SpA, Trento

Authors

Stephen Baister studied modern languages at Oxford and London universities and worked as a publisher before becoming a solicitor. While in practice, he represented a number of clients with interests in eastern and central Europe. He was co-author of the *Bradt Guide to East Germany*, published in 1990, a contributor to *Eastern Europe by Rail* (Bradt Travel Guides 1994) and co-author of the *Riga: The Bradt City Guide*. He has a doctorate in East European law from University College London. He is now a Registrar in Bankruptcy in the High Court.

Chris Patrick has a degree in French and German from Oxford University. After graduation she lived and worked in Japan and travelled extensively in the Far East. She works now in international research and consultancy. She has assisted a number of organisations from eastern Europe in doing business in the Far East. She first visited Latvia in 1989 and has returned many times since. She was co-author of the *Bradt Guide to East Germany*, published in 1990, a contributor to *Eastern Europe by Rail* (Bradt Travel Guides 1994) and co-author of *Riga: The Bradt City Guide*.

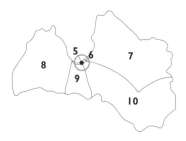

Contents

LIST OF MAPS

For key to map symbols, see page 228.

Acknowledgements

The authors would like to thank the following people for their generous help in the preparation of this book:

- Ināra Punga, William Hough and Karlis Cerbulis who produced the first edition. Although the current edition has been substantially re-written as a result of all the changes which have taken place recently in Latvia, we have built on their original format.
- Irēna Hamilton of the Embassy of Latvia for advice on language and culture.
- Neil Taylor of Regent Holidays for invaluable suggestions, in particular on travel and practical information.
- Eva Staltmane, Director of the Latvian Tourism Development Agency in London, for providing local knowledge and information.
- Clifford Baister for help on birds and birdwatching.
- James Charters for information on Jelgava and eating possibilities near the Daugava.
- Vieda Skultans for hotel recommendations.
- Mareks Ameriks of the Jelgava City Museum for historical information.
- George Spodris of the Bristol Latvian Society for his helpful suggestions.
- The many people in the Latvian tourist offices in Latvia who provided advice and local information.
- All the staff at Bradt Travel Guides Ltd.

Introduction

WHY GO TO LATVIA?

Many people are vague about the location of Latvia. Even those who know where it is often have no idea what is there. This is not surprising; very little was heard of Latvia during the period from the end of World War II until 1991 when it was part of the Soviet Union, and before then it had only a brief period of existence as a unified and independent country. As an ethnic cultural area, Latvia is very old, but as a nation it is young. The story of the past 150 years, as revealed time and time again during a visit to Latvia, is the fascinating tale of the creation of a nation.

So why go to Latvia? Perhaps the main reason for most people would be to see the capital, Riga. Of the three Baltic capitals, Riga is the largest and the most cosmopolitan. Its Old Town area is picturesque, well restored and contains many historic churches and museums. Whether walking around the cobbled streets, viewing the many art nouveau buildings, or eating at one of the many good restaurants and cafés, just being in Riga is a pleasure. For visitors with more time to spare, a number of interesting day trips can be made from Riga. The historic towns of Cēsis, Sigulda and Bauska, with castles dating from the Middle Ages, the seaside towns of Jūrmala overlooking the Gulf of Riga, and the palace at Rundāle, built by the architect of St Petersburg's Winter Palace, are all within easy reach of the capital. For countryside enthusiasts, longer trips are possible, for example to the Gauja National Park, to the Latgale Uplands, close to the Russian border, or to the gently rolling landscape of Kurzeme, west of Riga. Birdwatchers may be particularly interested in seeing the thousands of migratory birds which daily fly over Cape Kolka in April.

A few words of warning are, however, necessary. While Riga is in most respects a modern capital and visitors will find everything they want or expect there, outside Riga many towns and villages are less developed. Good hotels are relatively few outside the capital (although increasing); many people in the country speak little or no English; many roads are not of a high standard – some are unmade, and most have no markings; restaurants too are relatively few, although, together with shops, on the increase. While the countryside is often attractive, it is not generally spectacular; large areas consist of dense forests, and many of the small towns and villages have little of specific interest.

It is important to remember too that Latvia only left the communist world in 1991. Many changes have occurred and many more continue to occur. The economic system, social conditions, business practices and almost every other aspect of Latvian life are still subject to change. Within this book we have made every effort to provide the latest information, but visitors should be aware that restaurants can disappear overnight, opening hours can vary, and buses can be renumbered. It is always wise to check up-to-date conditions locally.

To get the most out of a trip to Latvia, a little reading will pay more than usual dividends. An understanding of the long and frequently tragic history of the country and of the people's struggle to create a nation with its own language, its own literature, its own way of life and now finally its own government, will greatly increase visitors' appreciation of the country's achievements and of Latvia's many unsung charms. What is more, you will become one of the growing number of people who not only know where Latvia is, but also know what is there – and why.

A NOTE ON NAMES AND SPELLING

In general the spellings used in this guide are native Latvian ones. In the case of names of people this means adding an 's' to all male names and an 'a' to all female ones. Because nouns decline, noun endings vary according to context; do not be misled into thinking that slightly different names refer to two different people or places (you may come across Rainis or Raiņa, for example, depending on the context). A further complication is that Latvia's history means many people and place names were originally German. Generally we have used the Latvian spelling for the names except in the case of Riga (Rīga in Latvian). Where a word refers to a place or person from this era, we have generally used the German spelling; when referring to the history of Kurzeme when Germans dominated the area, we have, for example, used Kurland, the German equivalent. However, within Latvia you will find that German names are sometimes Latvianised; the German philosopher Herder, for example, sometimes becomes Herders. Finally, as a relatively new written language, Latvian is not always consistently spelt; accents are sometimes used and sometimes omitted. In this book we have tried to be consistent and to use the most frequent spellings, but do not be alarmed to find variations within Latvia.

Part One

General Information

LATVIA AT A GLANCE

Location On the eastern shore of the Baltic Sea, opposite Sweden. One of the Baltic states, bordering Estonia, Lithuania, Belarus and Russia.
Size 64,589 km^2 – about the size of the Irish Republic.
Climate Mild summers, cold winters. Average temperature in July 18°C. Average temperature in January –3°C. Coastal area humid, inland more continental, drier.
Government Parliamentary democracy
Population 2.32 million (2004), of whom around 58% are Latvian, 30% Russian, 4% Belarussian, 3% Ukrainian, 3% Polish, approximately 2% others (Lithuanians, Estonians, Germans, Livs etc).
Regions Kurzeme, Zemgale, Latgale, Vidzeme
Capital city Riga
Other major cities Daugavpils, Liepāja, Jelgava, Ventspils
Language Latvian is official language; Russian widely spoken
Religion Lutheran, Catholic among Latvians and Poles; Russian Orthodox and Old Believers among Russians and Belarussians
Currency Lat and santīm; 1 lat = £0.99/US$1.87/€1.44 (March 2005)
International telephone code +371
Time GMT +2
Electricity 220 volts, 50 Hz
Weights & measures Metric
National flag Horizontal stripes of maroon-white-maroon
National anthem *Dievs Svētī Latviju* ('God Bless Latvia')
National holidays January 1 (New Year's Day), Good Friday, Easter Monday, May 1 (Labour Day), 2nd Sunday in May (Mother's Day), June 23 (Līgo Holiday), June 24 (Midsummer's Day – Jāņi), November 18 (Independence Day), December 25 & 26 (Christmas), December 31 (New Year's Eve)

The Country

GEOGRAPHY

Latvia is one of the three Baltic Republics, located on the eastern side of the Baltic Sea, east of Sweden. It is bordered to the north by Estonia, to the south by Lithuania, and to the east by Russia and Belarus. The capital, Riga, lies on the Gulf of Riga in the centre of the country.

Latvia is one of the smaller countries in Europe. With an area of 25,400 square miles (64,589 km²) it is approximately the same size as the Irish Republic. The size of the country means that, from the capital, any part of the country can easily be reached by car within a day. Most of the country is flat or gently rolling. An aerial photo of the whole country would show large areas of forests, many lakes and rivers, a largely unspoilt coastline, meadows and farmland, and, with the exception of Riga, no large cities.

Latvia has a very long coastline, more than half of it around the Gulf of Riga, which sweeps inland from the Baltic Sea. Several of its largest rivers, including the Daugava which cuts through the centre of the country, flow out into the Gulf of Riga.

Regions

The country is divided into four regions: Kurzeme in the west, Zemgale in the centre and south, Latgale in the southeast and Vidzeme in the north. Each region is sub-divided into districts (*rajons*), a total of 26 (see map page 4), and each *rajon* is further divided into *pagasts* (parishes/municipalities). Each region has its own history and its own distinct characteristics.

Kurzeme (English: Courland; German: Kurland)

Kurzeme, in western Latvia, has two large ports on its Baltic Sea coastline, Ventspils and Liepāja, but is otherwise a largely rural and underpopulated area. The northern part is heavily forested; it also has hilly areas, including the area around the Abava Valley known as the Switzerland of Kurzeme. In the tiny villages around Cape Kolka there is still a small community of Livs, ancient inhabitants of this area.

Zemgale

This region covers the centre of the country, running along the west bank of the Daugava from the Gulf of Riga in the north to Lithuania in the south. It is a low-lying, flat area, and one of the most fertile parts of the country. The River Lielupe (literally 'big river') and its many tributaries criss-cross much of the region.

Latgale

This southeastern region of the country is the most Russified and also the poorest area of Latvia. It includes Latvia's second largest town, Daugavpils, and the River Daugava flows through the region towards Riga. The Latgale Upland area contains many lakes and rivers, and is largely unspoilt and rarely visited.

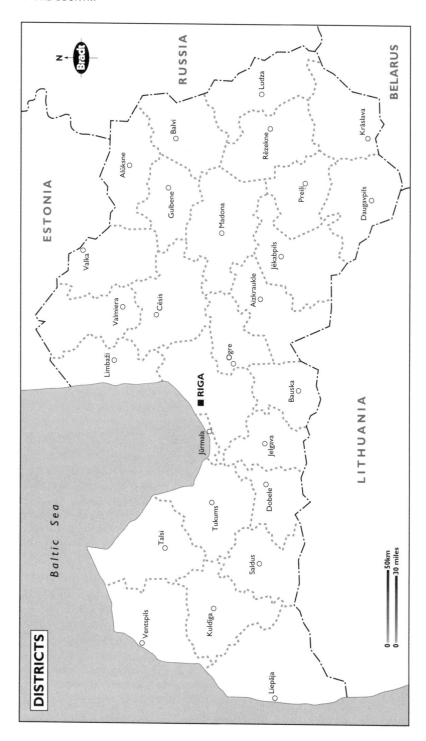

Vidzeme
The northern region of Latvia is mostly hilly and includes the country's highest point, Gaiziņškalns (Gaizins Hill – 1,017ft/310m) in the Vidzeme Uplands. The Gauja River winds through the region, and the Gauja National Park occupies a large area along its banks. The historic towns of Cēsis and Sigulda are also within the national park area.

Natural features
Lakes
Latvia has around 5,000 lakes. The largest concentration is in Latgale, although wherever you are in the country you will never be far from a lake. The largest lake is now Rāzna, southeast of Rēzekne in Latgale, covering an area of 55km^2, although until it was drained to half its original size of 90km^2 during the Soviet occupation, Lake Lubāns, northwest of Rēzekne, was the largest. It is now overgrown wetland and a good site for ducks, terns and reed-bed birds.

Most of Latvia's lakes are shallow. In winter they freeze over for several months, and in summer it is possible to swim in most of them. Some also have facilities for boating.

Rivers
Almost 1,000 rivers and streams flow in or through Latvia. The largest, the Daugava, has its source in Russia, and flows through the centre of Latvia from the border near Daugavpils to the Gulf of Riga. Other major rivers include the Gauja in Vidzeme, which both starts and ends in Latvia, the Lielupe in Zemgale and the Venta in Kurzeme.

The Baltic Sea
The coastline stretches 307 miles (494km) along the Baltic Sea and the Gulf of Riga. In earlier centuries the Baltic Sea froze over in winter and travellers could walk across from Latvia to Sweden, stopping overnight in temporary inns set up on the ice. Today, the Baltic remains ice-free. One of the main attractions of Latvia for the Soviet Union was access to its ice-free ports.

NATURAL HISTORY
Although most Latvians now live in towns, the countryside is never far away, and most Latvians feel a strong sense of identity with the land, where their not-so-distant ancestors almost certainly lived as peasants. Many town dwellers have country *dachas*, small houses on a private plot of land, or allotments. During the Soviet period these were often a welcome source of vegetables and fruit. Gardens in the country are usually well kept and full of flowers, and many flats in town have window-boxes or plants on a balcony (see page 33 for more details).

Latvian literature too is full of evocations of and references to nature. Folk stories often include birds and animals and make much of their setting in forests or meadows. A favourite theme of Latvian poetry is nature: the transience of the seasons in Latvia, the welcome to spring after long, hard winters, and the beauty of the trees and flowers in the country.

Wildlife
Latvia has a large variety of animals, birds and insects, although this will not be obvious unless you travel to certain areas of the country, and even then you may need an expert guide – and some determination.

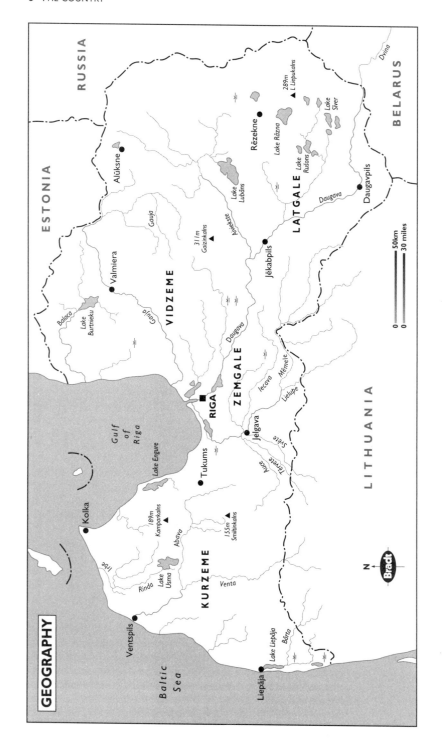

Birds

The very visible star of Latvian birds is the white stork (see box). Its relative, the black stork (called *melnais stārķis*), is also found in Latvia, notably in the Slītere Reserve in Kurzeme and at the Ķemeri Reserve near Riga, but numbers are relatively small (around 1,000 breeding pairs compared with 10,000 pairs of white storks).

The huge areas of forest provide an ideal habitat for woodpeckers. Latvia has seven species: the great spotted, middle spotted, white backed, lesser spotted, green, grey headed and black. If you spend some time in the forest, you would be unlucky not to hear the hammering of their beaks or to see their bright plumage.

Water birds which can be seen on Lake Engure and elsewhere, include mute swans, a protected species whose numbers have been growing, the relatively rare grey heron, cranes, bitterns, grebes, oystercatchers and various gulls. Birds of prey, particularly buzzards and kestrels, are a familiar sight in the countryside. Owls are more often heard than seen. Latvia is even estimated to have some 100–300 breeding pairs of hoopoes, although sightings are relatively rare.

In towns, hooded crows, with their black heads and grey backs and underparts, are common. On the edge of towns and flitting by the side of roads, large flocks of chaffinches, sometimes as many as hundreds strong, can be seen.

The best and most accessible places for birdwatching are Lake Engure and the Slītere Reserve in Kurzeme. At Cape Kolka large flocks of migratory birds gather in spring (see page 187 for more details). The Ķemeri National Park also attracts a large number of birds, including rare species such as sea eagles, eagle owls and whimbrel (see page 141 for more details). More remote spots include Lake Pape,

STORKS

White storks (in Latvian *baltais stārķis*) are happily a common sight in Latvia: there are six times as many storks here as in all of western Europe, and around 5% of the whole world population of white storks nest here. Unmistakable with their white plumage, jet-black flight feathers and long, bright-red bills and legs, storks are summer visitors to Latvia and build their large nests at the top of telephone poles, on farm buildings and in other conspicuous places. Every year in April around 10,000 pairs of birds arrive from their winter homes in Africa, rebuild their nests, lay and hatch two to six large, pale eggs and then migrate south again in August.

During their migration storks use air currents to aid their soaring flight. These currents are plentiful over land, but not over water. Storks, therefore, take account of this in the routes they instinctively choose to head south and north. Birds which nest in Latvia fly south to Romania, then cross the Bosphorus and fly towards the Gulf of Suez, on to the Nile Valley and finally to East Africa where they spend the winter. Flocks have been spotted in the Gulf of Suez, with up to 40,000 birds flying in a ribbon 30m wide, 1–3m above the sea, and extending in a line up to 40km. Interestingly, the storks you may see in France and Spain fly south through Spain, cross the Mediterranean at Gibraltar (again minimising the passage over water) and then head to West Africa for their winter quarters.

Storks are regarded as bringing luck, and are welcomed by Latvian farmers. Some even try to attract the birds by putting an old cartwheel in a tree or on a pole where they can build a nest. It is thought that the faithfulness of storks to their partners was traditionally admired in the Baltics.

NATURE RESERVES AND NATIONAL PARKS

Latvia has three national parks: Gauja, Ķemeri and Slītere. All three are easily accessible from Riga. There are also a number of nature reserves and other natural areas under protection. Gauja National Park is an area of the country open to visitors all year round and can be visited without prior arrangement. Ķemeri can also be visited easily. The other reserves listed below can be visited only by prior arrangement. If you wish to enter the reserves, you should therefore contact the relevant organisations listed below, preferably well in advance.

Gauja National Park (Gaujas Nacionālais Parks GNP) Set up in 1973 as Latvia's first national park, it focuses on environmental protection but is also a major tourist and educational attraction. A few small areas identified as containing particularly rare wildlife are closed to the public, but most of the area offers visitors good opportunities for walking, driving or cycling on empty roads, horse riding etc. The historic towns of Sigulda and Cēsis are within the area, as is the **Līgatne Educational and Recreational Park** with its collection of wild animals. For further details, see page 152.

Contact: 3 Baznīcas iela, LV 2150 Sigulda; tel: 297 4006; fax: 297 1344.

Ķemeri This is a nature reserve, planned from 1992 and opened in 1997, at the western end of Jūrmala, and just 40km from Riga. It has more birds than any other reserve in Latvia (237, of which 188 nest in the area), including black storks, a large population of corncrakes and many water and marsh birds. It also contains a wide variety of plants, mosses and mushrooms, and a large beaver population. Around 50% of the area is forested, 30% marsh and 10% water, including several small lakes.

Contact: 'Meza maja', LV 2012 Ķemeri; tel: 776 5386; fax: 776 5040; email: kemeri@vdc.lv.

Krustkalns Located in the Madona district in eastern Vidzeme. It contains many freshwater springs, nine lakes and 48 protected species of flora. Around 90% of the area is wooded; an oak tree in the reserve is a commemorative tree in memory of Kārlis Ulmanis, president during the first period of independence.

south of Liepāja near the Lithuanian border, and the Nagļi Ponds, near Lake Lubāns, northwest of Rēzekne.

Other sites closer to Riga include Lake Babīte, frequented by wildfowl, particularly in spring and autumn, and Lake Kanieris, north of Ķemeri, where the white-tailed eagle can sometimes be seen.

For further information, consult *Putni Latvijā* (*Birds of Latvia*), a colour guide in Latvian but with bird names in Latin and English too. See also Subbuteo Natural History Books, *List of Latvian Bird Species 1992 with Comments on Distribution and Number* and the excellent website www.putni.lv. A few companies specialise in birdwatching holidays, including Eastbird (see page 53).

Mammals

Latvia, in common with the other Baltic States, has a considerable number of large mammals, including deer, wild boar, wolves, wood marten, elk, lynx and a few brown bears, which make occasional forays into Latvia from Estonia. With the exception of deer, most of these animals are difficult to spot. If you would like to see them in a semi-wild situation, a good spot is the nature park in Līgatne

Contact: 3 Aiviekstes iela, LV 4862 Ļaudona, Madona; tel: 484 8291; fax: 484 8161; email: teichi@madona.lv.

Moricsala Located in the Ventspils district of Kurzeme, is Latvia's oldest nature reserve, established in 1912; it is made up of several islands in Lake Usmas, and is 90% wooded.

Contact: As for Slītere.

Pape Located just 10km north of the Lithuanian border in the southwest of Latvia. During migration periods it is one of Latvia's best areas for birdwatching: 271 bird species have been recorded. It has an ornithology station, where birdwatchers can exchange information, as well as two nature trails, one of 9km and one of 26km. Between August and November it is also possible to stay here overnight, although conditions are very basic.

To book a visit to the ornithology station, contact Dr Janis Baumanis; tel: 920 3235; email: jbaumanis@email.lubi.edu.lv. For other information on Pape, contact the 'Nature House', Pape, Rucava, LV 2377 Liepāja district; tel/fax: 349 3859; email: wwf@com.latnet.lv.

Slītere This reserve covers an area bordering the Baltic Sea in northern Kurzeme. It is rich in forests, woods and, along the coast, dunes and beaches. Pines, birch and yew are particularly plentiful. Animals include deer, wild boar, elks and wolves. The reserve is particularly well known for migratory birds: in April each year around 150,000 birds are estimated to pass over Cape Kolka every day. In summer 1992 one of the largest forest fires in Latvia's history destroyed over 20% of the trees in the reserve; in line with the country's environmental policy, the area is being left to recover naturally.

Contact: 3 Dakterlejas iela, LV 3270 Dundaga; tel/fax: 324 2542; email: slitere@mail.bkc.lv.

Teiči In the Madona and Jēkabpils areas of southeast Latvia. This is the largest protected marsh area in the Baltics, and is important in protecting the population of birds, such as cranes, which thrive in this type of habitat. Within the reserve are 19 large lakes; a settlement of Old Believers remains on an island in one of the lakes.

Contact: As for Krustkalns.

(see page 152). Common European mammals including squirrels, mice, rabbits, foxes, weasels, bats, hedgehogs and moles are also present in Latvia in quite large numbers.

Some species have been introduced quite recently. These include the American mink and the Norwegian rat, which were introduced accidentally; beavers, now numbering around 50,000, and red deer, which have been reintroduced to counter the threat of extinction. In addition to beavers, Latvia has a large otter populationof around 4,000. Seals can also sometimes be seen around the coast.

Other wildlife

In the countryside you may come across grass snakes and adders, as well as lizards, newts, frogs and toads. Latvia also has a large number of freshwater and sea fish within its territory. Freshwater fish include bream, pike, perch, trout, eel and carp. The best-known sea fish is the Baltic pilchard, more likely to be seen canned than live. Cod and plaice are also common.

Summer visitors will rapidly become aware of the large number of mosquitoes which proliferate in the heat, particularly along the coast and close to inland water.

Beware in summer too of the ticks found on the edge of forests and in long grass which may bear encephalitis (see page 58).

Flora

Today around 40% of Latvia is covered by forests. Unusually in 21st-century Europe, the area of land covered by forest has increased since World War II as some farms, abandoned under collectivisation, returned to their previous wild state. Two-thirds of the forests are coniferous, mainly pine, and a familiar sight to anyone travelling in the countryside will be long straight roads lined on both sides with pine trees. Some of these pines survive for as long as 500 years. Inland, forests may often consist of deciduous trees or a mixture of species such as spruce and birch. Other common trees include oak, ash, lime, juniper and yew. In the undergrowth and at the edge of forests berries grow, including raspberries and blueberries. Forests are also ideal places for mushrooming, a popular Latvian pursuit. It is common to see people in markets selling the small quantities of mushrooms they have gathered; some of the most widespread varieties are the dark-capped boleti, cep, chanterelles, russulas and saffron milk cap.

Around 25% of the country consists of grassland meadow, although only a small part of this is now natural, uncultivated meadow. In summer the meadow land is covered with wild flowers. A wide variety of species flourish, including clover, caraway, lady's mantle, milfoil, timothy and meadow foxtail.

A further 10% of the land area is marshland. Much of this is covered with moss, but heather, rosemary and other flowering species are also common. The marshlands attract large populations of birds and insects, and several marsh areas, notably Teiči, have become nature reserves.

ENVIRONMENTAL ISSUES

During the Soviet occupation Latvia industrialised quickly. Large manufacturing and industrial centres were set up in and around Riga and in towns such as Liepāja and Daugavpils. Environmental issues were not addressed, and air and water pollution was often high. Dams were built across the Daugava to provide hydro-electricity, destroying some of Latvia's historic sites. Lake Lubāns was partially drained, destroying important wildlife habitats. All of these grievances were widely publicised in the 1980s when Latvia was fighting for independence.

Since independence, the Latvian government and various associations and individuals have worked to put the environment higher on the agenda. The Gulf of Riga is now much cleaner, thanks to new sewerage facilities in Riga, and some of the industrial centres have received financial assistance from other European countries, notably Scandinavia and Germany, to help them clean up their operations. Agricultural practices have also changed, and there is now considerably less use of mineral fertilisers.

As a result of these measures, there has been a significant improvement in the pollution situation. Swimming in the Gulf of Riga is now safer than it was, although it is still not advisable to swim in some areas. The Blue Flag has been awarded to Jūrmala, Ventspils and Liepāja. The local press gives warnings of where it is best to avoid in summer. The air quality has generally improved. Still, however, according to the Municipal Air Control Management office in Riga, the air in the capital is unhealthy, particularly in winter when sulphur dioxide pollution, caused by energy production, can be high. Traffic pollution can also be bad in the morning and evening rush hours. Pollution-induced damage to some of Old Riga's historic buildings is starting to be tackled.

A high proportion of Latvia's energy (40%) already comes from renewable sources, and this figure is set to rise to approaching 50% by 2010. Most of this comes from hydro-electric energy, although the dams situated in various parts of the country have proved controversial due to the flooding which they sometimes cause, as well as the damage to fish stocks. More recently, wind power has become more important. You can see a park with 33 wind turbines just outside Liepāja and two others in Ainaži near the Estonian border. Although more turbines are planned for Liepāja, the lack of profitability of this type of energy is dampening enthusiasm.

EU entry has imposed new environmental obligations on the country: the government is committed to full enforcement of all EU environmental directives by 2010.

Silver birch, Betula pendula

Pocket an expert!
City guides from Bradt

Comprehensive coverage of a range of European cities,
complemented by full-colour street maps.

Dubrovnik Piers Letcher

Piers Letcher brings his in-depth knowledge of Croatia to
this historic walled town, fast becoming a popular short-
break destination. Here is everything for that idyllic break,
from nightlife and the best local restaurants to island
retreats and nearby national parks.

Ljubljana Robin & Jenny McKelvie

Slovenia's capital blends Austro-Hungarian and Italian
influences, with both a lively nightlife buzz and classical
attractions like art galleries, museums, classical music and
opera. Travellers are provided with a range of places to
stay, from new five-star luxury hotels to family-run
guesthouses that retain their typical Slovenian charm.

Riga Stephen Baister & Chris Patrick

The Latvian capital is rapidly increasing in popularity as
travellers tour the new map of Europe. Features in this
guide include a list of the best cafés, restaurants and bars,
as well as a city walking tour to allow the visitor to
explore Riga's rich history and culture.

Tallinn Neil Taylor

Take a walking tour through the cobbled streets of Old
Tallinn with Estonia expert, Neil Taylor. With details of
local excursions and cosmopolitan bars, cafés and
restaurants this is the essential guide to Estonia's beautiful
medieval capital.

Available from all good bookshops, or by post, phone or internet direct from:

Bradt Travel Guides Ltd
Tel: +44 (0)1753 893444 www.bradtguides.com

History and Economy

HISTORY

The history of the area of land now known as Latvia is long and complex, particularly to visitors not familiar with the Baltic area. Some appreciation of this history is, however, extremely helpful for visitors wanting to understand present-day Latvia or trying to grasp the significance of some of the buildings and places mentioned in this guide.

Several important points emerge from Latvia's historical development:

* The area currently known as Latvia has only existed as a single country within its present borders (more or less) since just after World War I; Latvia as a political entity was not even thought of until the middle of the 19th century;
* Latvia has only been governed as an independent state for two short periods (1918 to 1940 and since 1991);
* Throughout the rest of its history since the 13th century the whole area was subjected to foreign rule: all or various parts of the country were governed at different times by Germany, Sweden, Poland, Russia and the Soviet Union;
* Before the 13th century the area was inhabited by various Baltic and Finno-Ugrian tribes, the forebears of many present-day Latvians.

In short, as a nation state, Latvia is young; as an area inhabited by peoples with some communality of identity, a shared history and a common struggle for independence, it is old.

Early Baltic peoples

Archaeological evidence suggests that the area of the Baltic States was inhabited as early as 9000BC, although the ancestors of the current inhabitants arrived somewhat later. Two groups of tribes inhabited what is now Latvia and became the ancestors of many present-day Latvians. The first group to arrive, the Finno-Ugrian tribes, came as hunters from the east and settled in Estonia and northern Latvia between 3000 and 2000BC. These tribes included the Estonians and also the Livs, most of whom are now extinct, but a few of whom still live in the Kurzeme area of Latvia. These tribes are related to the Hungarians and Finns, among many others. The second group of tribes, which came to the area from the south around 2000BC were the Baltic tribes, including the Latgals, Zemgals and Cours (or Kuronians), the ancestors of most present-day Latvians. According to the earliest written records referring to the Baltic tribes, they were 'farmers living on the coast of the amber sea' (Cornelius Tacitus, 100BC).

Amber (known in later centuries as 'Latvian gold' – see also page 97) is a stone formed from the fossilised resin of pine trees embedded for millions of years in the floor of the Baltic Sea. From early times amber itself, as well as amber jewellery, was sought after by the Roman Empire, and the Baltic tribes began to trade not only with the Romans but also with German and Russian tribes and the Vikings.

From these early times the strategically important location of the Baltic States brought benefits but also strife. One of the main trade routes from Scandinavia to Byzantium passed through present-day Kurzeme, along the River Daugava to Kievan Rus (the area around present-day Kiev) and continued further south across the Black Sea to Constantinople. This made Kurzeme a rich trading area, but also made other peoples want to control it. From the 11th century armies from Kievan Rus invaded parts of Latvia, although mostly unsuccessfully. The Orthodox Christianity they brought with them did, however, penetrate parts of eastern Latvia, and some of the castle mounds scattered around this area date from the 11th and 12th centuries.

Knights of the Sword
The greatest change in medieval Latvia came from the introduction of Catholicism, not Orthodox Christianity. Although the crusades to the Holy Land are well known, few people know of the crusade to the Baltics. At the time the Pope initiated the Baltic crusade, however, it was considered as 'equal before God to the crusade to Jerusalem'. Missionaries from Germany arrived in Riga, and in 1202, under Albert von Buxhoevden, the first Bishop of Riga, the Knights of the Sword (*Kreuzritter*) were founded to convert the region. Known as Knights of the Sword because of the red swords and crosses on their white cloaks, the crusaders encountered strong resistance. Despite the avowed religious nature of the crusade, it quickly became apparent that economic motivation was paramount, and subjugation rather than conversion the aim. Subjugation was achieved relatively quickly in most of Latvia. The Livs were conquered by 1207 and most of the Latgals by 1214, although the Zemgals and Cours held out until later in the century.

The new German rulers called the area they had conquered around the Gulf of Riga by the name of Livonia. Alongside the Germanic state, a number of small city states were formed, usually headed by a bishop. These included towns which became important trading centres, such as Riga, Cēsis, Ventspils and Kuldīga. The ruling classes in these towns were all German, while the artisans and farmers were the indigenous Latvians. Throughout the Baltic area, this division on ethnic lines could not be crossed: whatever their social status, people from the Baltic tribes could not become Germans. For this reason the ethnic identity of the Baltic nations remained strong throughout centuries of domination. This is in contrast to the territory of Prussia, where native farmers were able to become Germans, and former tribal identities were lost over the years.

The Livonian Order
In 1237, after a catastrophic defeat by the Lithuanians, the Knights of the Sword were reorganised into another military order, the Teutonic Order, and became known as the Livonian Order. Although soundly defeated by Alexander Nevsky in a battle on the frozen Lake Peipus in eastern Estonia, the Livonian Order subsequently defeated the Cours during the 1260s, and in 1290 overcame the only remaining resistance in Latvia, the Zemgals. The Livonian Order set up its headquarters at Cēsis (then known by its German name of Wenden). By the 16th century, almost all the tribes in what is now Latvia had been assimilated into one group – the Latgals or Letts; only a small group of Livs remained in the west with their own culture and language.

Under German rule Latvia's major trading centres, Riga, Ventspils (then known as Windau) and Cēsis (Wenden), thrived as members of the Hanseatic League, the group of trading cities which dominated commerce in the Baltic and North Sea.

Invasions and rule by Sweden, Poland-Lithuania and Russia

By the middle of the 16th century, however, the Livonian Order and the system of semi-autonomous town states were weakening. The Hanseatic League was also weakening in the Baltic area, and elsewhere in Europe the Reformation was beginning to threaten Catholic states. In 1554 Walter von Plettenberg, the Master of the Livonian Order, declared Protestantism, rather than Catholicism, the state religion. Encouraged by growing peasant discontent and the loosening hold of the Livonian Order, Muscovy (forerunner to the Russian state), under the legendary Ivan the Terrible, invaded the eastern part of Latvia and Estonia. This was the beginning of the Livonian War, 25 years of great bloodshed and misery for the Baltic States (1558–83), during which large numbers of towns and villages were

DUKE JAKOB OF KURLAND

Duke Jakob of Kurland (Duke James of Courland) ruled the duchy of Kurzeme (present-day Kurzeme and Zemgale) from 1642 until his death in 1681. Although the territory was a fief of Poland-Lithuania, the duke was recognised as a free and independent prince, and made full use of this freedom to build up the strength of Kurzeme both at home and overseas.

Duke Jakob himself was well educated and widely travelled. He was a godson of King James I of England and during his reign had a number of significant encounters with England. Although tiny in area and in population (around 200,000 people), Kurland built up one of the world's largest maritime fleets. During the civil war in England, Duke Jakob was able to send ships to the aid of Charles I. Ironically, only a few years later Oliver Cromwell became one of the duke's greatest allies, supporting Kurland's colonial ambitions by signing a treaty of neutrality between the two countries in 1654.

At a time when many European nations, including England and France, were trying to enrich themselves by establishing colonies, Duke Jakob believed Kurland should do the same, if on a smaller scale. Accordingly he sent a ship, *Das Wappen der Herzogin von Kurland* (*The Coat of Arms of the Duchess of Courland*), to Tobago with the express purpose of colonising the island and establishing a base for exporting tropical products to Europe. The captain of the ship, Willem Mollens, proclaimed Tobago the property of Kurland, and renamed it New Kurland. The soldiers built a fort, Jekabforts, in the southwest of the island, and gave Kurland names to other towns and areas on the island (Liepāja Bay, New Jelgave etc).

Once established, the colony acted as a base for exports from all over the Caribbean. Tobacco, cotton, ginger, rum, cocoa, tropical birds, tortoise shells and many other items were shipped to Poland, Sweden, Muscovy, Britain, Spain and the Netherlands to satisfy the increasingly demanding tastes of the rising middle classes. Ships returning to the Caribbean took with them European timber, glassware, beer, salted meat, fish and amber. The ships, with the duke's distinctive flag depicting a black crab on a red background, were well known throughout the trading world.

The duke's ambitions were not limited to the Caribbean. For a time he also controlled a small island at the mouth of the River Gambia in West Africa.

SWEDEN AND THE BALTIC STATES

Accustomed as the 21st century is to thinking of Sweden as a relatively small, peace-loving European country, it can come as something of a surprise to remember it once had an empire. Its army penetrated into Muscovy (Russia), what is now Germany and even Hungary, and occupied parts of the Baltic States, including Riga and north Latvia, for almost a century.

The story of Sweden's development into a great European power and its subsequent decline, all within the span of around 200 years from 1523 to 1721, makes fascinating reading. In short, and somewhat simplistically, it is the story of a country anxious to overcome its geographical weakness as a state located along the Baltic coast, and to protect itself from territorial and trading threats from a variety of neighbouring states. At the beginning of the period Sweden had enemies to the west, with Norway and Denmark controlling its only access out of the Baltic; as time went on, its access to the east was threatened by the rise of Muscovy, instability in the Baltic states in the wake of the collapse of the Livonian Order, and the hostile actions of Poland and even of the Habsburg Empire.

Sweden's imperial adventure began with the first king from the Vasa family, Gustav, who at the start of his reign made Sweden independent from Denmark, but it was his grandson, Gustavus Adolphus, who ruled from 1611 to 1632, who took Sweden to the Baltic states. Gustavus Adolphus, known during his lifetime as 'the Lion of the North' and 'the Lion from Midnight', is a great hero of Swedish history. Well-versed in languages, theology and history, as well as in the strategy of war, he is widely recognised as an inspired ruler, who worked in close partnership with a gifted administrator, Axel Oxenstierna, his chancellor. Together they sought to maintain Sweden's control of the Baltic Sea, in the face of threats from Muscovy. When in 1617, after many years of fighting, Sweden signed a peace treaty with Muscovy, the country gained Estonia as part of the settlement. However, Poland considered Estonia to be part of Polish Livonia, and fighting soon broke out between Sweden and Poland. In 1621 Gustavus Adolphus acted by invading Livonia and capturing Riga. Four years later he followed up this victory with a second invasion, and captured the whole of Livonia. Swedish rule in the area was formalised in 1629 when Sigismund of Poland gave up Poland's claims as part of a peace treaty.

Swedish rule of Livonia (Riga and what is today Vidzeme) tends to be viewed as a period of progress and enlightenment. The local peasants, ruled as serfs by the German-speaking nobility, were oppressed, uneducated, frequently starving and forced into warfare. Paganism was rife in many areas, since the Church had no interest in the peasantry. As early as 1627 Gustavus Adolphus sent a

damaged or destroyed and thousands of people lost their lives.

To prevent Russian rule the local aristocrats, except in Riga and Kurzeme, sought the protection of Poland-Lithuania. A separate Duchy of Kurland, owing its allegiance to Poland, was formed in 1561, and it remained a separate duchy until 1795. Riga was independent from 1561 to 1582, when it became autonomous under Polish rule.

Meanwhile, across the Baltic Sea Sweden had developed ambitions for foreign territory, and from 1592 this Protestant state began a war against Catholic Poland-Lithuania, fought mainly on Latvian soil. Sweden's victories led to almost a century commission to Livonia and began to force the nobility to agree to improvements. Perhaps the most enduring legacy was the Swedish king's commitment to education, which led to the setting up of schools throughout the area, and the establishment of a university at Dorpat (now Tartu in Estonia). Improvements were also made to trade, agriculture and the judicial system.

Charles XI (1660–97) continued the reforms Gustavus Adolphus had initiated, ensuring that a primary school was set up in every parish in Livonia, introducing Swedish law and banning torture. During this period, the Bible was also translated into Latvian for the first time (see page 173). In areas directly controlled by the Swedish crown, serfdom was abolished, although it continued in the areas of land given by the crown to Swedish nobles.

Unfortunately for Livonia, this betterment of conditions was threatened from 1700 onwards by Charles XII's involvement in the Great Northern War, and progress came abruptly to an end in 1709–10 with Sweden's defeat at the hands of the Russians, under Peter the Great (a giant in deed and also in size: he was 6ft 7in tall).

Charles XII came to the Swedish throne in 1697 at the age of 15. Keen to take advantage of his inexperience and to press their various claims to ownership of the Baltic ports, Denmark, Poland and Muscovy united against Sweden, and in 1700 attacked simultaneously from east and west. After defeating Denmark, Charles sailed to Estonia and there defeated Peter the Great. He then marched south to Livonia, crossed the River Daugava, defeated an army of Russians and Saxons near Riga in June 1701 and occupied Kurland. The occupation was short-lived. As Charles went on to fight in Poland and Saxony leaving the Baltic provinces inadequately defended, Peter re-formed his army, invaded Kurland and devastated large areas of Livonia. Charles's defeat at Poltava, east of Kiev, in May 1709, effectively meant Sweden's loss, not only of the Great Northern War (which actually continued until 1721), but also the end of Sweden's imperial experience. The Russian army moved quickly to take over the Baltic ports. Riga capitulated in 1710, and Russian troops were sent to garrison Kurland in the same year.

Sweden's defeat in the Great Northern War meant the loss of all its colonies, and a withdrawal to the Scandinavian peninsula, albeit to a larger territory than a century earlier. It was also the end of rule by the Vasa family: Frederick I gave up the absolutist claims of Charles XI and XII and conceded to the demands of the *riksdag* (parliament) that it should become the supreme authority. Swedish historians therefore see 1720 as 'the end of the Age of Greatness and the beginning of the Age of Liberty'; for Latvia, history was however set on a divergent course – away from liberty.

of Swedish rule in Livonia (see box above for details), until the Russians finally took control of northern Latvia in 1710.

Over the same period in Kurland, the economic situation improved rapidly. The rule of Duke Jakob (1642–81) was a time of great expansion when industries such as shipbuilding and metallurgy flourished, and this tiny Baltic duchy even won overseas colonies in Tobago and the present-day Gambia (see box on page 15 for details). The strength of Kurland meant that it held out longer against the Russians, but after the third and final partition of Poland-Lithuania in 1795 the tsarina, Catherine II, annexed Kurland.

Throughout Latvia there followed a period of Russian rule but with the German gentry overseeing the day-to-day administration. Baltic Germans tended to fill all the prestigious places in the Russian army, as well as the government. For a portrait of what was considered a typical Baltic German, see Tolstoy's none-too-flattering depiction of Vera's husband, Lieutenant Berg, in *War and Peace*. While the Baltic Germans flourished, the Latvian population remained as serfs. The relatively liberal measures that the Swedes had tried to introduce were buried under Russian landowners' more brutal attitudes to peasants. The Baltic nobility finally put an end to serfdom in the early 19th century (1811–19), some 40 years earlier than in Russia; serfdom remained, however, in the Latgalian areas. Although the serfs were liberated without land, unlike in Russia, by the middle of the 19th century peasants were given the right to own land and to move freely.

The National Awakening

During the same period, agriculture became an increasingly commercial activity, the absence of war, famine and plague led to an overall growth in the rural population, the emergence of independent peasant farmers and a small rural professional class drawn, for the first time, from native Latvians, rather than Germans. As education spread and the economy of the towns also improved, many Latvians were attracted to the towns. For the first time since their foundation, often 600 years previously, the population of towns once again included a sizeable proportion of Latvians (sometimes even a majority), rather than a large majority of Baltic Germans.

It was against this background of increasing national prosperity and growing opportunities for the native Latvian population, that the Latvian national movement arose, led initially mostly by the Latvians who had come to work in the towns, often as teachers, and who formed the new Baltic intelligentsia. The National Awakening Movement was formed in 1856 with the aim of strengthening Latvia's national identity by studying the country's history and culture and by promoting the use of the Latvian language.

Throughout much of the second half of the 19th century the local Latvian population allied itself more with their Russian overlords than with the Baltic Germans. Although this uneasy alliance did lead to a weakening of German influence in cities such as Riga, the relationship was put under increasing strain by the policy of tsars Alexander III and Nicholas II to Russify the Baltic provinces completely. This included taking over the local school system which Latvian nationalists saw as the key to strengthening national identity.

The 1905 revolution

The cities of Latvia, principally Riga and Liepāja (known as Libau at the time), were developing rapidly as industrial ports during the same period and, as in most parts of northern Europe, the workers in these cities were becoming increasingly involved in class politics. The close ties between the Baltic region and Germany meant that political ideas from German intellectuals such as August Bebel were at least as strong as Russian influences. The Latvian poet, Jānis Rainis, was among those involved in popularising German political texts in Latvia at this time.

All these factors meant that when the 1905 revolution began in Russia ('the great dress rehearsal' for 1917, as Lenin later called it), it was quickly taken up in the Latvian provinces. Military uprisings occurred in Daugavpils, strikes in Riga, Jelgava and Liepāja, and peasant disturbances in many areas throughout the country. Some sources even claim that the social democratic movement in Latvia in 1905 was larger than the Russian Bolshevik and Menshevik organisations. During the revolution around 650 Germans and Russians were killed by the

LATVIAN PROVINCES OF THE RUSSIAN EMPIRE BEFORE WORLD WAR I

Tallinn (Reval)
ESTLAND
ST PETERSBURG
NOVGOROD
DAGÖ
Lake Peipus (Peipsi)
Lake Ilmen
Pärnu (Pernau)
Tartu (Dorpat, Iurev)
ÖSEL
Pskov (Pleskau)
LIVLAND
PSKOV
Ventspils (Windau)
Riga
KURLAND
Jelgava (Mitau)
VITEBSK
Liepaja (Libau)
Dünaburg
0 — 100km
0 — 50 miles
KOVNO
VILNA
N

Latvian rebels, and 184 manor houses were burnt down. When order was restored by the Russian Imperial Army, with the support of the Baltic Germans, the losses on the Latvian side were even greater. Estimates vary, but between 900 and 2,000 Latvians and local Russians were executed or killed, and over 2,000 deported to Siberia. In an attempt to discourage further unrest, around 20,000 Germans from Russia were resettled in Latvia and Russian immigration was stepped up. The nationalist movement lost members, but continued to grow in influence.

World War I

As part of the Russian Empire, Latvia was immediately involved when Germany declared war on Russia in August 1914. Many Latvians joined the Russian army and thousands were killed early in the war at the Battle of Tannenberg in Prussia. The Russian army was no match for the Germans in terms of training, equipment or leadership, and as early as spring 1915 German troops entered Kurzeme. Shortly after this, the Latvians were given permission to organise their own military units led by their own Latvian officers. Eight battalions, known as the Latvian Riflemen (*Latviešu strēlnieku bataljoni*), were quickly established and went into action against the Germans at the end of October 1915. To the surprise of many inside and outside Latvia, the Riflemen forced the German units to retreat, albeit only for a few months. By April the following year the German army was once more ready to launch a fierce attack on Riga. Russians and Latvians fighting together outside Riga fended off the attack, but many lost their lives when the Germans used gas. The area of land where so many died is still known as the Island of Death (*Nāves Sala*). Encouraged by this success, the Russian commanders decided to go on the attack and to try to drive the Germans out of Kurzeme. This battle, known as the

Battle of Christmas because it began on December 23 1916, lasted for 25 days and cost the lives of thousands of Latvian soldiers. Although the German front line was broken, the refusal of Russian units to join the attack meant the advantage was lost; some commentators have even claimed that the Russians wanted the Latvians to lose. Whatever the truth, the battle left the Latvians feeling betrayed, and led to the exile over the next few months of a very large proportion of the Latvian population. Later that year the German army finally managed to capture Riga, but was prevented from capturing most of Vidzeme when German troops were withdrawn to bolster the western front in France.

Meanwhile events were moving quickly in Russia. In February 1917, Tsar Nicholas was forced to abdicate, and Kerensky became leader of the provisional government, quickly replacing the imperial governor of Livonia with a Latvian commissioner. Latvian nationalists lost no time in seizing the opportunity to replace the institutions of the Baltic-German nobles with their own provisional councils. Despite this move, most Latvians at the time did not have full independence in mind, but were hoping to achieve autonomy within a Russian federation.

During 1917 the Bolsheviks became more powerful within the Baltic States, gaining 41% of the vote in the city elections in Riga that summer and assuming control of much of the Baltic area after the October revolution. The extreme measures directed at the Baltic Germans and non-communist politicians by the Bolsheviks led to a strengthening of the desire for full independence among the remaining Latvian population. In March 1918 the Russian government surrendered the Baltic States to the Germans in the Treaty of Brest-Litovsk. Eight months later Germany surrendered to the Western allies, and within a week a coalition of Latvian political parties, the Democratic Block, came together to form a government under the leadership of Kārlis Ulmanis. Independence was formally declared on November 18 1918.

War of Independence

Latvia's declaration of independence was accepted neither by the Bolsheviks in Latvia nor by the Germans who remained in Latvian territory. As the majority of the Germans retreated, Soviet troops, including some native Latvian soldiers from the Riflemen, marched in and set up a provisional government in Valka before capturing Riga in January 1919. A new Bolshevik government was established under Pēteris Stučka.

The national government under Ulmanis fled to Liepāja where it received some support from the British navy and, initially, from German land forces. These German forces were organised by a German general, von der Goltz, and led by Bermondt, and were keen to avoid both native Latvian and Bolshevik rule. After helping to force some Bolshevik troops into retreat, they staged a coup against the Ulmanis government in April 1919, which only escaped capture by fleeing to a British warship off Liepāja. The Germans were finally forced to retreat under heavy pressure from the western powers. They headed north through Latvia, suffering defeat at Cēsis, and the Latvian government was able to return to Riga. Even then, however, the situation was not secure. Von der Goltz rearmed his forces and mounted a surprise attack on Riga in October. He was defeated by the Latvians, with help from British and French ships, and was forced to withdraw for the last time, although once again Latvian territory was subjected to plundering and burning as the German troops retreated.

This left only Latgale under foreign domination. Late in 1919 the Latvian army, helped by Polish forces, drove the Bolsheviks from Latgale; it was incorporated into Latvia by the Riga Treaty, signed in August 1920 with the Russians. Western recognition was slow to come; only on January 26 1921 did the European powers recognise Latvia and the Baltic states officially, with admission to the League of Nations following in September that year. The first Saeima (parliament) formally elected Jānis Čakste as president (see page 205) in 1922.

The first independence

The new Latvia came into existence with formidable disadvantages. During World War I and the War of Independence the population had fallen by 28%, industrial output by 83%; the country had been devastated by the advances and retreats of army after army; many children had had no formal teaching; the population was extremely mixed racially and by religion; and the majority of the new politicians had little or no experience of government. At the same time, at least three countries, Germany, Russia and Poland, were looking with envy at the country's seaports and the opportunities they would give them for building up their power.

Despite these problems, this period was marked by considerable economic success. One of the most important early changes was the land reform, which broke up the large estates previously owned mainly by Baltic Germans and distributed them among the 66% of the population who were farmers and peasants. Whereas under the old regime one hereditary estate had been over 170,000 acres, the average now became 55 acres for arable farms and under 25 acres for horticulture. The growth in agriculture which followed in the wake of these reforms proved vital to counterbalance the decline in economic activity in other sectors. Until 1914, for example, the Baltic ports had accounted for over 30% of Russia's European trade. After independence, the proportion fell heavily, and by the mid 1930s only around 3% of Latvia's trade was with Russia. By the end of independence, Latvia had made a very successful recovery, with exports in 1938 over five times higher than in 1922.

This period of independence saw great progress in education, the arts and overall living standards. At the beginning of the 1930s, 0.3% of the Latvian population received a university education, the highest level in Europe at that time. Visitors tended to be impressed by living conditions there, which were often considered higher than in other parts of Europe: indeed it is reported that some 'Latvian students visiting Britain in the 1930s, were appalled at conditions in the port of Hull.'

Politically, despite democratic beginnings, Latvia was unable to resist the fascist tendencies sweeping through much of continental Europe in the early 1930s. Against a background of growing economic depression and political instability fostered by a multiplicity of small parties, the prime minister, Kārlis Ulmanis, dissolved parliament in 1934, imprisoned many of his political opponents and two years later became president of the Government of National Unity.

World War II

As far as foreign policy was concerned, Latvia endeavoured to steer a course between the major powers. The Baltic Entente signed in 1934 between Latvia, Lithuania and Estonia was an attempt to form a united front against Nazi Germany, but it remained without teeth and largely without influence. When Germany and the Soviet Union signed the Molotov–Ribbentrop Pact in 1939, Latvia was assigned to the Soviet Union, under the 'secret protocol'. The Red Army occupied Latvia in June 1940, and in July the Latvian government was replaced by deputies put forward by Soviet and local communists. Ulmanis and other leading figures were arrested and deported to the Soviet Union where Ulmanis died in prison two years later.

During the next year, between 30,000 and 35,000 Latvians were murdered or deported, mainly to Siberia. On June 13–14 1941 alone, very shortly before the Germans marched into Latvia, tens of thousands were rounded up by the NKVD (the forerunner to the KGB); those who were not murdered were deported. These Soviet actions encouraged many Latvians to support the Nazis as liberators, and predisposed some to turn a blind eye to the persecution of the Latvian Jews, who were accused of having supported the Soviets. The Nazis built several concentration camps in the Baltics, including the one at Salaspils near Riga (see page 141), where over 100,000 people from all over Europe, including many Latvian Jews, Russians, Poles and Belarussians, were killed. They also formed local SS legions who fought against the Russian front line.

By 1944 the Germans were beginning to retreat and the Red Army once more to advance. The Baltic States prepared to form their own national governments again, but they were unable to resist the Soviet forces despite fierce opposition. Latvia was incorporated into the Soviet Union. A guerrilla movement in Kurzeme, known as the 'Forest Brothers', continued its armed opposition until as late as 1957. The arrival of the Soviet forces once again meant deportations (between 1945 and 1949 around 150,000 Latvians were killed or deported to Siberia); other Latvians, particularly intellectuals, fled to the West and finally emigrated, many to the United States.

Soviet rule

Under Soviet rule migrant workers, mainly from Russia but also from the Ukraine and Belarus, were brought into Latvia to build and operate new factories and enterprises. Within the Soviet scheme of planned industrialisation, Latvia was chosen as a centre for investment in light industry, consumer goods and food processing, but steel manufacturing was also supported. Shipbuilding was a major industry for Riga, and large trawler fleets were based both in Riga and in Liepāja. Huge dams and electrification projects were instigated along the Daugava River, and blocks of flats erected everywhere, mainly to house the immigrants. All Latvia's larger towns were dominated by Russian-speaking majorities, despite the influx of Latvian farmers, many of whom left the countryside when collectivisation was introduced in the late 1940s.

Despite environmental and social problems, the industrialisation of Latvia meant that, like the other Baltic States, its economy fared better than most other parts of the Soviet Union and its people lived relatively well, in what became known as 'the Soviet West'.

Throughout the period of Soviet rule most Latvians continued to hope for independence and a revival of Latvian culture. For a brief period in the 1950s, during Soviet President Khrushchev's 'thaw', this seemed a realisable aim: Deputy Prime Minister Eduards Berklavs made great efforts to replace Russian managers and officials, to re-Latvianise the educational system and generally to stem the tide of Russification. His efforts were short-lived, however, halted by the intervention of Khrushchev, but he continued to be widely praised and became leader of the National Independence Party in the 1990s.

During the Brezhnev regime in the 1980s, it became clear in Latvia, as elsewhere in the Soviet Union, that economic planning was not working. Nonetheless, industrialisation speeded up in Latvia, and many more immigrant workers were sent into the country, particularly to work in plants processing raw materials imported from elsewhere in the Soviet Union. At this time the Staburags cliffs, a natural feature of mythological significance to Latvians, were flooded by a dam, reinforcing the feelings of deep bitterness within most Latvians towards the Soviet

Union. Active opposition was difficult and dangerous and networks of KGB spies operated throughout the country. Despite this a spirit of resistance was maintained, particularly through theatre and literature, and through the various churches, which still functioned despite Soviet disapproval and persecution of priests and clergy.

Towards independence

On June 14 1987, the first protest since the war, commemorating the 1941 deportations to Siberia, took place around the Freedom Monument in Riga. In the new climate of relative openness which prevailed under Mikhail Gorbachev's policies of *glasnost* and *perestroika*, more protests occurred over the following months. In June 1988 anti-Soviet feeling was heightened by the revelations made by the Latvian Writers' Union of the secret protocols of the Molotov–Ribbentrop Pact of 1939, under which the Baltic States had been given to the USSR. The Latvian flag with its maroon and white bands, which had been outlawed for many years, became a common symbol at rallies and on November 11 1988 was raised on Riga Castle.

During the summer of 1988 new political organisations began to emerge. The Popular Front of Latvia (PFL) quickly became a major force, speaking for the interests of many of Latvia's social and political groups and commanding huge grass-roots support. On May 31 1989 the Popular Front called for full independence for Latvia.

On August 23 of the same year, to commemorate the 50th anniversary of the Stalin–Hitler Pact, some two million Latvians, Estonians and Lithuanians joined hands to form a human chain stretching from Tallinn to Vilnius, along the 650km Baltic Way.

Demands for independence were intensifying all the time, with almost unanimous backing from native Latvians and growing support from Russians living within Latvia. Following elections in March 1990 in which Popular Front candidates won 124 of the 201 seats in the Supreme Council, the Council voted to re-establish an independent Republic of Latvia.

Throughout the period from 1987 to the declaration of independence in May 1990 the atmosphere throughout Latvia was calm. Protests were peaceful and reactions from Moscow were muted. In January 1991, however, the Soviet Union finally decided to intervene in the Baltics. Soviet forces attacked the TV tower in Vilnius, Lithuania. In anticipation of similar action in Riga, Latvians from all over the country came to Riga two weeks later and erected barricades to protect parliament and repel Soviet attacks. When a special police unit of Soviet troops did attack the interior ministry building on January 20, they were forced to retreat. Five Latvians were killed and many others injured in the struggle.

In early March a national referendum was held in which 73.7% voted for independence from the Soviet Union. As a result, the Popular Front adopted a plan for transition to independence by spring 1992. Moscow had not yet given in, however, and on August 21 1991 OMON (Black Beret) personnel carriers approached the Latvian parliament across Cathedral Square, driving back protesters as they advanced. Just as the troops were about to take control, they stopped, turned back and retreated. The coup to overthrow President Gorbachev's government in Moscow had failed, and with it the attempt by Moscow hardliners to take over the Baltic States. The Latvian parliament declared independence the same day. The USA recognised Latvia's independence on September 2, and the USSR followed suit on September 6.

The second independence

Latvia consolidated its independence more strongly than many people thought possible in 1991. The forecast short-lived independence and violent confrontations with Moscow fortunately never materialised, although there were some tense moments.

There have been many landmarks since independence. On March 5 1993, after a period of transition, a national currency, the lat, was introduced to replace the Latvian rouble. Financially the country managed to remain fairly stable until a banking crisis in June 1995 resulted in the Banka Baltija, the largest commercial bank in the country, being declared insolvent. Overall, however, the economy has performed relatively well (see below).

On the political front, in 1993, the first completely free parliamentary elections were held, and Guntis Ulmanis (great-nephew of Kārlis Ulmanis) was elected president of Latvia. In April 1994 the Latvian president and Boris Yeltsin signed an agreement timetabling the withdrawal of Soviet troops, resulting in all Soviet troops leaving Latvian soil by August of that year, with the exception of 500 officers operating the early-warning radar system at Skrunda. On August 31 1998, the last Russian military personnel left Skrunda.

Since 1998 Latvia has had a succession of coalitions and prime ministers: in the latest changes in early 2004 the government led by Einars Repše collapsed and Indulis Emsis was elected prime minister, Europe's first Green prime minister. In June 1999 Latvia elected its first female president, Vaira Vīķe-Freiberga. In May 2003 she was re-elected for a second term. In March 2004 Latvia joined NATO and on May 1 2004 became a member of the European Union.

A remaining area of tension is the rights of people of Russian origin within Latvia. Since independence, automatic citizenship has only been given to pre-World War II citizens and their descendants. Russians and other nationalities who have come to Latvia since the war have to pass examinations in Latvian history and the Latvian language in order to gain citizenship. Following a referendum, these rules have been relaxed to some extent, but there is still bad feeling about language qualifications. The number of Latvian speakers has increased in the last few years: according to the 2000 census 79% of the population now know Latvian. The number of stateless citizens, however, remains high at almost half a million people. These people, who are resident in Latvia but not Latvian citizens, are now considered as third-country nationals of the EU; they can work in Latvia but not elsewhere in the EU and cannot travel freely within the EU.

GOVERNMENT AND POLITICS

Latvia is governed by the Saeima (parliament), a single-chamber legislative body headed by the prime minister. It is made up of 100 members directly elected by Latvian citizens in regular elections. The role of the president as head of state is largely ceremonial. The current president is Vaira Vīķe-Freiberga, a Canadian Latvian. Born in Riga in 1937, before becoming president Ms Vīķe-Freiberga spent most of her adult life in Canada, where she was a professor of psychology at the University of Montreal from 1965 to 1998. Her wide command of languages (she speaks Latvian, French, English, German and Spanish) has been a key advantage during her presidency.

In the early years following the restoration of independence a large number of parties competed for seats, resulting in broad but fragile coalitions and many changes of government. More recently, there has been some consolidation of the party structure: in 1998 only six parties obtained seats in the Saeima. Governments have remained short-lived, however. In parliamentary elections in October 2002, following a short period of government by a four-party coalition led by former Riga mayor Andris Berzins, the New Era Party, led by Einars Repše gained most seats and formed another four-party coalition. Repše, however, resigned in early 2004, and on March 9 a minority government, led by Indulis Emsis from the Greens and Farmers Union, and including the People's Party and the First Party, came to power. This government was able to lead Latvia into NATO at the end of March 2004 and then into the European Union on May 1, both of which had been goals for successive governments.

Riga has its own city council with 60 deputies and its own mayor, since 2001 Gundars Bojars, a former deputy chairman of the Saeima. Currently the mayor is elected by the Saeima but there is discussion as to whether future mayors should be directly elected by the citizens of Riga.

ECONOMY

Despite predictions that after independence Latvia would never be able to survive, the country has made good progress towards developing a stable economic environment. Although the country remains poor in comparison with most of western Europe and North America, in common with the other two Baltic Republics it is well in advance of Russia and most of the other ex-Soviet republics. Real growth is currently averaging around 5.9% per year and inflation in 2003 was 2.9%. Unemployment, however, is still relatively high, at around 8.7% of the labour force (mid 2004).

Wages are low by Western standards: the average annual wage in 2003 was only Ls2,304 (around US$4,042). Since independence, the main beneficiaries of high wages have been young people and entrepreneurs, particularly those in urban areas. There are clear differences in wealth between different parts of the country, and between different parts of major cities such as Riga. It is now extremely rare to see beggars, but many people are living very much on the breadline. The lowest unemployment rate is in Riga (4.8%), and the highest rates tend to be in rural areas, particularly in Latgale. In the Rēzekne region, for example, unemployment in 2004 stood at 26.6%.

Within the economy, the most important industries are timber, engineering, metal-working, textiles and the food industry. Other significant activities include chemicals, paper, telecommunications and petrochemicals. Wood, wood products and textiles are the most important export items, and Germany and the UK Latvia's largest markets: in 2003 17% of exports went to Germany and 16% to the UK. Since independence, the importance of these industries within the economy has fallen, as the service sector has grown rapidly, accounting for over 60% of jobs by 2003. Economic policy has concentrated on trying to create a stable currency, on privatising land and state-owned companies, and on attracting foreign investment. The Latvian lat was introduced in March 1993, after a transitional year during which the Latvian rouble was used. In the wake of the economic crisis in Russia, Rīgas Komercbanka (now back in operation as the Pirma banka) and some other Latvian banks were declared insolvent. However, Latvia's overall monetary stability is now good. From January 1 2005, the lat has been pegged to the euro at a rate of €1 = 0.703 lats. It is aiming to enter the eurozone in 2008.

By early 1993 around 50,000 private farms, accounting for some 20% of agricultural land, had been created; the vast majority of farms are now privately owned. Since 1994 most small companies have been privatised. Latvia has also been selling shares in some of the country's largest industries with the result that the government now has a stake in only a handful of large enterprises.

Latvia has worked hard to attract foreign investment and many international companies are now active in the country. The business climate is increasingly favourable, and is expected to improve further as a result of Latvia's entry into the EU.

Baltic Holidays

Since starting out as Lithuanianholidays.com in 2000, we have branched out to become Baltic Holidays, a specialist tour operator to the Baltic States of Lithuania, Latvia & Estonia.

Specialists in:
- City breaks to Vilnius, Riga & Tallinn
- Baltic Tours and country tours
- Tailor-made travel throughout the Baltics
- Family holidays
- City & Spa breaks
- City & Coast breaks
- Family research

Why use us ..?
- We are the only specialist UK travel company to deal solely with the Baltic States
- We visit Lithuania, Latvia & Estonia regularly
- Regular updates with our hotels and suppliers
- Up to date information on the best places to go
- We are fully ATOL bonded, ABTA bonded and members of AITO.

ABTA
W5202

"Our travel through the Baltic States with your company went without a hitch and your wealth of local knowledge ensured we saw most of what there was to see and gain a rewarding insight to these wonderful countries."

Mr & Mrs South, tailor-made Baltic trip, May 03

Go with the leaders not the followers. You won't be disappointed.

Contact details:
Baltic Holidays, 40 Princess Street, Manchester M1 6DE
Tel: 0870 757 9233 Fax: 0870 120 2973
info@balticholidays.com www.balticholidays.com

People and Culture

ETHNICITY

Fewer than 60% of the 2.32 million people now living in Latvia can be called ethnic Latvians. The remaining population consists of Russians (30%), Belarussians (3%), Ukrainians (3%), Poles (3%) and small populations of Lithuanians, Estonians, Germans and Livs. In all the major towns, Latvians are outnumbered by Russians and other non-Baltic people; in Riga only around 42% of the population is Latvian. This situation is in marked contrast to the period just before World War II when most of the major towns had majority Latvian populations. Two factors have caused the reversal: firstly the large-scale loss of Latvian lives as well as emigration during and just after World War II, following on from similar events before and during World War I; and secondly the influx of people from Russia and other Soviet states during the period of Soviet occupation.

Although accurate figures are not available, it is estimated that around 200,000 Latvians were killed or deported during World War II and that a further 150,000 to 200,000 left Latvia to avoid death or deportation by the Soviets. As a result of emigration to Western countries, around 200,000 Latvians live in countries such as the USA (around 100,000), Australia, Canada, Germany and Britain.

During the Soviet occupation, troops and workers were brought in to Latvia from the other Soviet states. By 1989 around 1.2 million workers had settled in the country, mainly from Russia, Belarus and the Ukraine. They lived mostly in the big industrial centres, such as Daugavpils (where around 85% of the population is Russian-speaking), Liepāja and Ventspils, as well as Riga and Jūrmala. Around 200,000 Soviet military personnel also lived in Latvia during the occupation, many of them remaining in Latvia after retirement. During this time, Jūrmala was also a major tourist destination for Soviet workers, and the whole Jūrmala area seemed almost entirely Russian.

The co-existence of various ethnic groups in Latvia is nothing new. The changing power structure within the country over the last 150 years has meant huge changes in the populations, particularly in the larger towns. In Liepāja, for example, in 1863 79% of the population was German; by 1943 very few Germans remained and 85% of the population was Latvian; by 1996 Latvians had been outnumbered by non-Latvians (54% of the population). In Daugavpils, the largest single ethnic group in 1897 was Jews (46%); by 1935 the largest group was Latvians (34%), but by 1996 over 85% of the population was Russian speaking.

Given these huge shifts in population, it is surprising that the people of Latvia today manage to live in such relative harmony. Although there are tensions, and at a political level moments of conflict, on a day-to-day level the various ethnic groups largely co-exist peaceably. One issue which remains contentious is the question of Latvian citizenship (see page 24).

At present the number of people living in Latvia is declining. This is due in part to the departure of the Soviet troops (the remaining few left in August

FAMOUS LATVIANS

Latvia is particularly good at commemorating its outstanding citizens: few countries can have proportionately so many memorial museums, plaques and statues. Latvians have of course excelled in many fields and throughout this guide you will find references to well-known figures in the fields of art, literature, politics, music etc. The list below focuses on six people born in Riga who have made an impact in the world outside Latvia during the 20th and 21st centuries. Among those born outside Riga, Mark Rothko (see page 223) stands out.

Mihail Barishnikov (now Mikhail Baryshnikov; born in Riga in 1948)
The ballet dancer Mikhail Baryshnikov trained in Riga and at the Kirov Ballet in Leningrad before emigrating to the USA in 1974. In the USA he danced with the New York City Ballet and the American Ballet Theatre and during the 1980s was artistic director of the American Ballet Theatre. He has danced with many famous troupes, including the UK's Royal Ballet, and has appeared in films, Broadway productions and HBO's *Sex and the City*.

Isaiah Berlin (born in Riga in 1909)
The political philosopher Isaiah Berlin lived in Riga at 2a Alberta iela (see page 118ff) until 1915. His adult life was spent in Britain, where he was a fellow of All Souls College and the first president of Wolfson College, Oxford. He died in Oxford in 1997.

Gunars Birkerts (born in Riga in 1925)
Birkerts is a highly respected architect, resident in the USA since 1949. Major projects include the Federal Reserve Bank in Minneapolis, the Corning Museum of Glass and the IBM Building in Southfield. His plans for a new national library in Riga, to be known as Gaišmaspils ('the castle of light'), have been awaiting funding for several years.

Valters Caps (also known as Walter Zapp; born in Riga in 1905)
Caps invented the Minox camera, the tiny camera used by spies, real and imaginary (including Sean Connery as James Bond in *You Only Live Twice*). The cameras were made in Latvia from 1938 to 1943. Zapp, who subsequently lived in the USA, died at the age of 97 in 2003.

Mariss Jansons (born in Riga in 1943)
Known to classical music fans throughout the world as a conductor of intensity and imagination, Jansons has worked as music director of the Oslo Philharmonic Orchestra and of the Pittsburgh Symphony Orchestra, and since 2004 has been the principal conductor of the Royal Concertgebouw Orchestra in Amsterdam and of the Bavarian Radio Symphony Orchestra.

Mihails Tāls (born in Riga in 1936)
Known as the 'Magician of Riga' because of his legendary tactical skills, Tāls won the World Chess Championship in 1960 at the age of 24, the second youngest World Chess Champion of all time. He died in Riga in 1992. In 2001 a monument to the chess player was erected in Vērmanes Park.

LATVIA: BETWEEN ESTONIA AND LITHUANIA

Latvia is situated between the other two Baltic states, Estonia and Lithuania, in more senses than one. Geographically it is sandwiched between Estonia to its north and Lithuania to its south. Both its population and its land area are larger than Estonia but smaller than Lithuania. In terms of religion, Latvia includes both Catholics (the majority religion in Lithuania) and Lutheran Protestants (the majority religion in Estonia). The Latvian language is related to Lithuanian, but historically much of the area that is now Latvia was linked to Estonia as part of Livonia. It is even said that the typical Latvian character is less emotional than the Lithuanians but more flamboyant than the notoriously unemotional Estonians.

Small wonder that a long-standing joke in the Baltics is that Latvians are able to support two opposite opinions at the same time!

1998) and the relatively low birth rate, particularly among the Latvian-speaking population. The number of live births fell from 31,569 in 1992 to 21,070 in 2003, a decline of 33.3%, and at 7.29 per thousand population in 1997, Latvia's crude birth rate was the lowest in the world that year. The 2003 rate of 9.04 is no longer the lowest but is still very low by international standards. Life expectancy is also low compared with that in most European countries. At present women can expect to live for an average of 75 years (compared with 80 years in the UK) and men for 63 years (compared with 74 years in the UK). As a result of these factors, the population in all the major towns has declined over the last few years.

National characteristics

It is always difficult to identify national characteristics, but it is a particular problem in the case of Latvia where the population is made up of people of different ethnic backgrounds and of families who have been subject to so many different influences over the years. Latvia, and in particular Riga, has long had a reputation for being cosmopolitan: pre-World War I, Riga was said to be one of the most ethnically, religiously and linguistically diverse of all the major cities of Europe; between the wars Riga had the largest Russian emigré population after Paris. It may be possible, however, to outline a few characteristics first of ethnic Latvians and then of Baltic Russians living in Latvia.

Ethnic Latvians are often said to be reserved, sometimes even cold. Visitors may have the impression that Latvians, like other northern people, are pessimistic and frequently depressed. Certainly the history of the country has left people with plenty to be depressed about, and the long, cold and dark winters do not encourage a carefree lifestyle. Manners are generally not good. In the street people frequently tend to push and shove and rarely say thank you. Most people who stay longer in Latvia, however, find that once the ice is broken, friendships are warm and long lasting.

Baltic Russians, it must be said, do not generally have a good reputation among Latvians, although in Riga, where Russian intellectuals and business people play a major role, attitudes tend to be more positive. According to some commentators, many Baltic Russians themselves see Latvians as more assiduous, neater and better organised than they are, but Russians claim for themselves a greater humanity.

RELIGION
Animist beliefs

Before the arrival of Christianity, the native beliefs of the Latvians were animist: they believed in the divinity of all living things, from people to animals, birds or trees. Although these beliefs have long disappeared, some folk songs still contain references to tree spirits. Occasionally too in remote country areas, an oak tree may be left standing in the middle of an otherwise cultivated field, a symbol of Latvia's ancient respect for the oak.

During the first period of independence, as Latvia was trying to establish a clear national identity, neo-pagan beliefs experienced a revival. During the 1930s President Ulmanis quite frequently made allusions to neo-pagan beliefs in his speeches. In the same period a movement, known as *Dievturība* (from the Latvian for god, *Dievs*), was formed to rediscover Latvia's pre-Christian religion and mythology. Under the leadership of the writer Ernests Brastiņš, the group gained a certain popularity but was too closely associated with extreme fascist groups to enjoy widespread appeal. After the arrival of the Red Army in 1944, the movement was strongly persecuted and its leaders repeatedly imprisoned.

Recently, however, the movement has again enjoyed a revival. In 1989 *Dievturība* proclaimed itself a religion, and although it has very few members and its right-wing ideology is disapproved of by the majority of Latvians, elements, including its rendering of Latvian folk songs, are more widely respected.

Dievturība beliefs centre around a trinity of gods, although some 5,000 deities exist. The three principal gods are Dievs, the creator of the universe, who lives in heaven and represents all that is spiritual; Māra, the Mother Earth Goddess; and Laima (meaning 'happiness' or 'fortune' in Latvian), who is responsible for the spiritual well-being of humans. Among the lesser gods, Kārta and Dekla are Laima's assistants, while Saule ('sun'), Pērkons ('thunder') and Jumis ('eternal life') are also prominent. Dievs's adversary is Velns, who originally created the universe with him, and is a rather likeable rogue, in contrast to the devil of the Christian tradition.

Also connected with pagan traditions is Jāņi, the midsummer holiday still celebrated in Latvia. In early times, the year was governed by the cycles of the sun and the moon, and the summer solstice on what is now June 24 was and remains today a major festival. Fires were lit to keep away winter, and priests and priestesses danced around them in celebration.

ICONS

Icons are an important part of Orthodox worship. Large churches will have an iconostasis, a screen covered with icons, which separates the main part of the church from the sanctuary. Icons will also often be hung on the walls, and frescoes, painted in the manner of icons, may be on the ceiling and in the dome. When entering a church, Orthodox believers often go straight to an icon, kiss it and light a candle in front of it. The purpose of icons is to create an atmosphere of spirituality, to make believers feel they are actually in the midst of a heavenly gathering. For this reason, the characters portrayed on the icons – frequently Christ, Mary and saints – are not naturalistic. They are different from people still on earth: their bodies are often elongated, the hands held symbolically, the eyes staring and the nose long and thin. The perspective and the colours of the icon, including the frequent use of gold which pours out light, draw onlookers to the icon and are intended to transport them into the realms of spirituality.

OLD BELIEVERS

Old Believers share the beliefs of the Eastern Orthodox Churches but reject the reforms to the practices introduced by the Russian Orthodox Church in the 17th century. These reforms (for example a ruling that the sign of the cross should no longer be made with two fingers but with three) were ordered in 1666 by the Patriarch of Moscow, Nikon, but were opposed by a group of priests in Moscow. Some of the leaders of the opposition group were executed but their followers kept alive their beliefs, splitting into two groups: the Popovtsy (priestly sect) and the Bezpopovtsy (priestless sect). The first group established a church based around a priestly hierarchy, while the second group rejected the priestly hierarchy and all sacraments, with the exception of baptism. Rejected by the Church and persecuted by the State, many Old Believers fled to the remoter corners of the Russian Empire and to surrounding territories, including Latgale. Old Believers were not allowed to practise their religion freely in Russia until 1905, and it was not until 1971 that the Russian Orthodox Church revoked the anathemas of the 17th century. Despite attempts to bring the Russian Orthodox Church and Old Believers back together, the two groups remain largely in opposition, and many Old Believer communities continue to live rather isolated lives.

Today, there are estimated to be at least one million Old Believers, living mainly in the Russian Federation and Lithuania as well as in Latvia, although there are some communities in the USA, Brazil and elsewhere. The majority of Old Believers in Latvia belong to the Bezpopovtsy (priestless sect) and live in the Latgale area, although there is also a community in Riga. Jēkabpils was founded as a settlement by Old Believers who fled there in the late 17th century. In the mid 1990s, 56 of Latvia's 811 parishes were categorised as Old Believers' parishes. Old Believer prayer houses can be seen in Riga, Daugavpils and Moskvina (near Preiļi), and in other parts of Latgale, including a small community at Teiči. They are typically full of icons and decorated with huge candelabra covered with candles. Men and boys can still be seen in the traditional long Russian shirt, or *rubashka*, girded with a belt.

Christianity

Orthodox Christianity was introduced into parts of eastern Latvia by Russian invaders in the 12th century, but it was not until the arrival from Germany of the Knights of the Sword in the early 13th century that the **Catholic faith** reached the area. Willing converts were initially few and far between, and the Knights frequently resorted to violence to try and force their religion – and their commerce – on the local population. The fact that services were held in Latin, a language which the Latvian population did not understand, did not encourage conversion.

Protestant beliefs were introduced into Latvia in 1521 and gained ground rapidly, particularly in Riga. Again the reasons were not necessarily religious: the new beliefs were politically useful in opposing the influence of the Pope and the Knights of the Sword. The Lutherans made efforts to reach the local population: they held their services in Latvian, and before too long the Bible was translated into Latvian (1685-89, see page 173). Lutheran churches gradually supplanted Catholic churches in most of Latvia, although Catholicism remained strong in Latgale.

Aglona, in particular, became an important Catholic centre after a church was built there in 1699.

By the time of Latvia's first period of independence 55% of the population were Lutheran, 25% Catholic, 9% Orthodox and 5% Jewish. World War II saw the annihilation of the Jewish population and during the Soviet occupation religious adherence was strongly discouraged. Many priests and clergy were deported or killed, and many churches were turned into museums, concert halls, sports halls, warehouses or cinemas, while others were either pulled down or left to deteriorate.

As the Soviet grip loosened, the churches began to reassert their power, and during the 1980s membership of both the Lutheran and Catholic churches increased rapidly. A core policy of the Popular Front was the demand for religious freedom. Since independence, many churches have been restored and re-opened for religious services, although many still need funds to continue the restoration work. The number of Christians in Latvia is currently estimated at around 800,000–900,000, around one in three of the population. There are thought to be around 370,000 Lutherans and almost the same number of Catholics, 350,000. Other groups, including the Baptists, are growing in number. Russian Orthodox churches have also been restored and re-opened. Particularly among the older Russians in Latvia, there are many Orthodox Christians, and some Old Believers (see page 31). A few Jews have returned to Riga and there is one functioning synagogue.

Although many of Latvia's churches have interesting interiors, it is often difficult to see them, as Catholic and Lutheran churches tend to be locked except for services. Increasingly, however, churches that have been restored, not only in Riga but in towns such as Bauska and Jēkabpils, now have set opening hours when you can visit them. Alternatively you may find a note on the door indicating where you can go to ask for a key. Orthodox churches, in contrast, are nearly always open, and visitors are free to enter. Typically the atmosphere will appear heavy and mystical; candles will be burning, icons glowing in their flickering light. The Russian Orthodox cathedrals in Riga and Daugavpils are both typical, and worth a visit.

LANGUAGE

The three major Baltic languages (Estonian, Latvian and Lithuanian) are of great antiquity: it is believed that there may have been up to ten languages in the Baltic branch of the Indo-European languages, although now only Latvian and Lithuanian are widely spoken (Estonian is a Uralic language, distantly related to Finnish). Although known through writing dating back to the 16th century, the literature is largely modern. The languages existed in a number of dialects: Latgalian (spoken in the east), Vidus (spoken in central Latvia) and Tamnieku (spoken in the west); the so-called Curian dialect, spoken only by a fishing population in East Prussia, died out in the 15th–16th centuries. The modern language is believed to have originated mainly in the Latgalian dialect.

The survival of the Latvian language has been no small achievement. For many years Latvia (together with Estonia) formed the Duchy of Livonia, part of the Russian Empire. Before that it had been under German rule in the Middle Ages and had also been ruled at various times by Poland and Sweden. From the 17th century onwards the German language enjoyed considerable influence. However, it was the work of German Lutheran clergymen, who wrote dictionaries and religious tracts in the local language, that helped to preserve it until the National Awakening movement of the mid-19th century revived national pride in the Latvian language and its cultural traditions.

LATVIAN THROUGH STREET NAMES

One easy way to learn some simple Latvian words, and also to learn about Latvia's heroes and history, is to take note of the names of streets. Streets themselves tend to be called:

iela	street	*laukums*	square
bulvāris	boulevard	*prospekts*	avenue

The most popular names divide into common words, places and people.

Common names

Brīvības iela	freedom street
Fabrikas iela	factory street
Kalna iela	hill street
Lielā iela	big street (high street; main street)
Pasta iela	post street
Rūpniecības iela	industry street
Smilšu iela	sand street
Tirgus iela	market street
Vēstures iela	history street

People's names

Note that in the Latvian language even people's names change their endings to agree with the word which follows. Raiņa iela, for example, would be Rainis Street in English.

Aspāzija	Latvian poet and wife of Rainis
Kr Barona	Collector of folksongs (see page 148)
K Ulmaņa	One of Latvia's presidents during the first period of independence
Lāčplēša	Legendary hero (see pages 216–17)
Puškina	The Russian poet Pushkin, whose name is retained in Riga, Daugavpils and other towns
Rainis	Latvian poet (see page 218) and husband of Aspāzija
Valdemāra	A leader of Latvia's Great Awakening (see page 184)

The language enjoyed a period of strength during Latvia's brief independence between 1918 and 1940 but suffered a setback when Latvia became part of the USSR, and Russian became the official language. Latvian children were obliged to learn Russian, and in many areas Russian became the principal means of communication, forcing Latvian into a secondary position. All signs and official notices were in Russian as well as Latvian.

When Latvia became independent again in 1991 the native language of the country began to reassert itself. As early as 1989 legislation was passed making Latvian the official language in place of Russian, and since independence almost all traces of Russian have been gradually eliminated from signs and public places, and steps have been taken to minimise the Russian influence. Anyone seeking Latvian nationality must pass a language test, as must anyone seeking employment in the public sector. However, Latvians have yet to re-acquire full confidence in their native tongue: what constitutes 'proper' Latvian is the subject of much debate, and there are radio programmes and newspaper articles devoted to the promotion of the language.

Modern Latvian inevitably reflects the languages of the countries which have dominated Latvia from time to time. Many words show the extent of the influence of Russian (*cilvēks*, person; *sirds*, heart; *krēsls*, chair), others the influence of German (*torte*, cake; *aptieka*, pharmacy – although probably via Russian); yet others are part of the modern global mainstream (*biļete*, ticket; *bagāža*, luggage). Foreign influences can also be seen in many place names: the River Daugava is the Dvina in Russian; Windau and Mitau are the old German names for Ventspils and Jelgava.

Unfortunately, Latvian is not an easy language to learn. The vocabulary bears little resemblance to that of other languages. Nouns decline (there are six cases), and the verbs conjugate (there are three conjugations). Even names of non-Latvians are generally Latvianised, by adding 's' to male names and 'a' to female names, for example Džordžs Bušs and Tonijs Blērs. A number of grammatical constructions used in Latvian do not exist in English. Although the pronunciation is regular, the intonation is fairly sing-song, and words tend to be run together, making everyday speech difficult to understand without a great deal of practice. The majority of signs are in Latvian only, and the same applies to much of the information in museums and other places of interest.

In Riga, English and German are widely spoken, and menus are often available in English, German and Russian as well as Latvian. English is increasingly spoken outside the capital, too, although in remote spots you cannot necessarily rely on this. In *Appendix 1*, you will find a guide to pronunciation and some basic words and phrases which will help you to get by.

NATIONAL CUSTOMS

Latvians have retained many customs whose roots reach into pre-Christian times. Some come from rituals placating the deities and other supernatural forces. For example, it was believed that the spirit of the dead might follow one home unless all living footprints were erased. To this day in Latvian cemeteries the sandy paths around the gravestones are carefully raked after each visit. Other customs come from Christian practices. Among family traditions, name days are as important as birthdays. Every Latvian name is assigned its special day, a custom deriving from the Christian practice of giving each saint a feast day.

One of the most ancient and popular traditions is the celebration of Midsummer's Day, or Jāņi, which has retained nearly all its pre-Christian rites and rituals. Preparation for Jāņi begins weeks before June 23. Gardens are weeded, ale brewed, farms tidied, clothes washed. The day before is Grass Day, when Jāņi grasses, flowers, leaves, oak and birch branches are gathered and strewn about the house, in barns and stables, and around the necks of farm animals. Women weave crowns of flowers to wear on their heads, while men make crowns from boughs of oak .

The evening begins with the singing of traditional Jāņi songs, short four-lined *dainas* with a refrain of *līgo* or *rota*. Still singing, families pack up beer, freshly baked bread, bacon rolls, and Jāņi cheese, and visit neighbouring farms. As dusk falls, and it falls slowly in this country of seemingly endless summer twilight and short nights, torches of wooden barrels tied to the end of a tall pole are lit. Their flames dot the countryside. Huge bonfires crackle through the night. Around them people sing, dance, eat, drink and jump over the flames. It is said the fern blossoms only once a year, on Midsummer's Eve, and finding it ensures you a lifetime of happiness.

Nature and folklore

Like most societies where many people's recent forebears were farmers and peasants, Latvians retain close associations with nature.

Flowers are particularly close to the hearts of many Latvians. If you travel around the country, you will notice how beautiful the graveyards are. Cemeteries are not confined to a flat field with a headstone over a plot, but are usually in wooded areas where many plots are tiny gardens. Often green hedges mark the boundaries between plots, and gravel is present around the grave – always neatly raked. Sometimes there's a bench by the gravestone, many of which show a picture of the deceased – a Russian custom. In general, graveyards have a tranquil, park-like atmosphere.

Gardens too are generally tended with care: a particularly pleasing sight is the small but generally picturesque gardens outside signal boxes at railway crossings in the countryside. In summer, country gardens are full of phlox, Michaelmas daisies and roses, and few town houses or flats are without brightly flowering window-boxes. Late spring too is an attractive time in gardens; in the words of the Latvian poet Plūdonis: 'I love a leafy garden / Green with the light of May'. Flowers are the most common gift when welcoming home friends or relatives. If you arrive in Riga on a flight with Latvians, you are likely to emerge into an arrivals' hall full of Latvians bearing flowers, waiting to greet their returning loved ones.

If you plan to give flowers to someone in Latvia, there is one important thing to remember: make sure you give an odd number. Bunches with even numbers are reserved for funerals, cemeteries and other sad occasions.

Trees also have a special meaning within Latvian culture. The oak was traditionally regarded as a sacred tree and also as a symbol of masculine virtues, whereas the lime is associated with feminine virtues. Traditionally, when a baby was born, oak or lime branches would be burnt to give the baby the male or female strengths he/she would need in life. At weddings oak leaves can still be seen decorating the approach to the church. Oak and lime trees are also frequently planted in cemeteries and other important national sites.

Sun, moon and stars: According to Latvian folklore, whenever a child is born a new star appears and stays bound to the child with invisible ties throughout his/her life. When the person dies the star falls to earth – a symbol of a soul disappearing. It is also said that children born when the sun is shining are destined to be particularly lucky. The colour white, associated with the sun and with light, is a particularly sacred symbol. White signifies not only lightness, brightness and cleanliness, but also everything that is good and holy.

Animals and birds: Latvian folk stories are full of animals and birds, often with human attributes. Cats, mice, pigeons, frogs, bears and wild boars all make frequent appearances alongside the human characters. Storks too have long been regarded as a sign of luck if they decide to nest close to a Latvian house.

Pirts

Like other Scandinavians, Latvians have traditionally enjoyed saunas, or *pirts* as they are known in Latvian. As you can see at the Open Air Museum outside Riga (see *Chapter 5* page 126), traditional farms had their own bath house, where stones were heated and water poured on top to produce the necessary steam. The bathers sat on benches in the steam and used birch twigs to open up the pores and aid circulation. In winter, after the hot steam bath, people would rub themselves with snow in order to cool down.

In the towns, *pirts* were also introduced from early times; by the 14th century Riga apparently had six public saunas. Today there are very few of these remaining, but many hotels have their own saunas, which visitors can enjoy.

TRADITIONAL LATVIAN HOLIDAYS AND EVENTS

As **Christmas** celebrations were forbidden during the Soviet occupation, and New Year festivities were played up. Father Frost came on New Year's Day giving gifts to those who deserved them. Today, Christmas has regained its former glory. In Latvian towns, food is at the centre of the celebrations; traditionally people eat pork, including pigs' trotters, brown peas and rolls with special fillings, washed down with beer. In the countryside older traditions persist. A burning log may be dragged around the house at New Year, symbolising the death of the old year's misfortunes. In other areas, groups of women go from house to house singing traditional songs in return for small gifts.

Some people say that the Christmas tree originated in Latvia. Journals from Riga dating from 1510 mention the practice of gathering around a tree on Christmas Eve, and guild members carrying the decorated tree to the market place before setting fire to it. It may be that this custom was taken back to Germany by the German knights.

January 6 is **Zvaigžņu Diena** (Star Day) or **Trijkungu Diena** (literally 'Three Kings Day') celebrating the Epiphany. If the sky is clear that night, it is said there will be a good harvest.

February 2 is **Sveču Diena** (Candlemas Day). In the past this was the day devoted to paying homage to nature, particularly fertility, when women were supposed to avoid work and men to make candles. Candles made on this day were said to be able to protect the house and, magically, act as a weathervane. Traditionally, Candlemas Day also marked the beginning of spring – an optimistically early date.

Metenis falls on the seventh Tuesday before Easter. In pagan times, it marked the beginning of the new year. It was the last day of winter, and feasts, usually including pork, barley-based dishes and beer, were prepared. Special ceremonial dances were performed: one by farmers' wives was supposed to encourage healthy and plentiful livestock and corn. Folk bands still preserve the tradition.

Pelnu Diena or **Ash Day** followed Metenis. Farmers took the ashes of the previous day's fire and sprinkled them on their new fields. Sons left home to start their own farms.

Lieldienas, today's **Easter**, replaces the pagan celebration of the Great Day, or Day of Light. Lieldienas used to celebrate the spring equinox. As in much of northern Europe, the Easter bunny is omnipresent. In the shops you will find chocolate bunnies; in the country and in town squares you will see straw bunnies and other similar scenes. Eggs are also part of the celebrations: traditionally Latvians dye eggs using saffron, beetroot, grass or onion skins to produce yellow, purple, green and brown shells. In Riga, an Easter Market takes place in Doma laukums (Cathedral Square).

May 1 is **Labour Day**, a 20th-century international holiday celebrating work. It was initiated in 1920, when Latvia's new government was called upon to create a new democratic constitution.

Second Sunday in May, Mother's Day, was first celebrated in 1922.

Jāņi is perhaps Latvia's most popular holiday. It falls on June 24 (see page 34). Accompanying it is Līgo Diena, June 23. In pagan times Jāņi celebrated the summer solstice when sunlight dominates darkness.

PICNICS IN THE RAIN

If you thought the British were the only people to brave bad weather and pretend to enjoy picnics in rainy lay-bys, you would be wrong. Latvian families can frequently be spotted on public holidays, and at weekends, on beaches and in forest clearings, spreading out rugs, setting up tables and enjoying their picnic food – even in the rain, wind and cold. Stoicism is said to be part of the Baltic character – what more everyday proof could there be?

September 23 Mikeli, harvest festival.

November 18 marks Latvia's Independence Day. Latvia first declared independence on November 18 1918, in Riga's grand National Theatre.

Memorial days

March 25 In Memory of the Victims of the Communist Terror. Between March 20 and March 30 1949, the Communists deported more than 50,000 Latvians in railway cars to Siberia. The largest round-up occurred on March 25 1949.

May 4 The Re-declaration of Latvia's Independence. On May 4 1990, members of Latvia's *Augstākā Padome* (Supreme Council) voted to restore Latvia's lost independence.

May 9 In Memory of the Victims of World War II. On May 8 1945, Nazi Germany surrendered and World War II was officially over.

June 14 In Memory of the Victims of the Communist Terror. June 13 and 14 1941 marked the beginning of the Communists' organised effort to deport Latvians. Over 15,000 Latvians were separated from their families and deported to Siberia and the *gulags*.

July 4 In Memory of the Jewish Genocide. On July 4 1941 the Nazis burnt down nearly all Jewish synagogues in Riga.

November 11 *Lāčplēša Day*. On November 11 1919, after a bloody fight, Riga's army rid the city of the Germans. On this day war heroes from World War I and those who fought to liberate Latvia are honoured. Lāčplēsis is a Latvian epic hero (see pages 216–17).

National costume

Traditional Latvian folk costume can still be seen at song and dance festivals and at other traditional events. The main colours are dark grey, brown and green, embroidered with colourful symbols and patterns, although in some areas of Latvia brighter materials tend to be worn.

Women's clothes were made from linen or wool. Long, unpleated, multi-coloured skirts were the norm. In Latgale, for example, black or brown material with yellow, red or green stripes was worn, while in Kurzeme skirts were often red or purple. Blouses were generally embroidered with traditional patterns and held together by a silver brooch (*sakta*). Men generally wore trousers fastened with a woven woollen belt, sometimes with bone buttons also at the waist. Long, dark capes were worn by both men and women, although men also wore long sheepskin coats in winter.

Accessories such as mittens, socks and belts with traditional patterns were also worn. Young women would often knit these items as a declaration of their love for the man they wanted to marry. Very poor peasants would wear simple foot coverings made of the bark of lime trees, tied round with rope; richer people had footwear resembling moccasins tied with straps around the lower leg up to the knee.

For special occasions, including weddings, people normally wore white. Young girls also wore wreaths as a symbol of virginity and honour. Although married women did not normally wear wreaths, the one exception was on Jāņi night, when women, men and even cattle all wore wreaths made of oak leaves or flowers.

At the Open Air Museum outside Riga you can still see people wearing, and making, traditional folk costumes (see *Chapter* 5, page 126).

ARTS
Music

Music has always been an important element in Latvian culture, much of which has its origins in traditional folksongs, or *dainas* (see pages 42 and 148). However, the concept of Latvian music as a formal art form did not evolve until the second half of the 19th century.

In 1869 Jānis Cimze began collecting folk melodies, some of which were over 1,000 years old. Approximately 20,000 such melodies were collected and preserved. Cimze's songs eventually found their way into the repertoire of school choirs and gradually became popular. His collected works formed the basis of Latvia's first Song Festival, where thousands of singers gathered in huge choirs. This festival, the first of many, played a major role in forging the strong sense of national identity which eventually led to Latvia's independence.

One of Latvia's greatest composers was Jāzeps Vītols, also known as Joseph Wihtol. Composer of numerous choral works, Vītols replaced Nikolai Rimsky-Korsakov as teacher of composition at the St Petersburg Conservatory. Among his students were Sergei Prokofiev and Nikolai Myaskovsky. On returning to Riga after the Bolshevik Revolution, Vītols founded the Latvian National Opera and the State Conservatory of Music.

Another well-known Latvian composer is Alfreds Kalniņš. Kalniņš wrote several hundred choral works for solo and choir performance and composed many ballads. He also wrote the first Latvian opera, *Baņuta*, based on an old Latvian myth.

When the Soviets occupied Latvia, numerous composers fled to the West. Those who remained had to toe the party line if they wished to compose. Latvian music and the Latvian song festivals became russified. Yet Latvia retained some world-class choirs, such as Ave Sol, which travelled regularly throughout Europe, Asia and, later, the United States.

Today, song and dance festivals are held periodically in Riga. These are huge events attended by up to 20,000 participants from around the world. The programme includes works for large choirs, soloists, operas and musicals, as well as folk dancing, theatre and art.

Whilst few Latvian composers are known outside the country, except perhaps Pēteris Vasks (born in Aizpute in 1946), whose Symphony No 2 received its London debut at the Proms in 1999, Latvia has provided a home and platform to a number of famous musicians. Wagner (after whom one of the concert halls in Riga is named) lived in Riga between 1837 and 1839 and conducted there. It had considerable influence on him, and the opera house there became, to some extent, a model for Bayreuth (specifically the idea that the orchestra should be sunk in an orchestra pit, and the raking of seats is said to have been adopted from his experiences in Riga). He conducted over 40 operas during his time in Riga and

Above Sunset over Riga's Old Town across the Daugava River (TH)

Below View of Riga from St Peter's Church tower, including the Central Market and the TV tower (RR)

Above Buildings of Riga (SC)
Below St Peter's Tower (TH)
Below right The Powder Tower,
or Pulvertornis, Riga (SC)

wrote a large part of *Rienzi* while he was there; it is said that he conceived some of the motifs for *The Flying Dutchman* on a journey from Riga to Copenhagen. While in Latvia he also wrote a song, *Der Tannenbaum*, which had elements of Latvian/Livonian melodies in it and which can be discerned in *The Ring*. Eventually Wagner was compelled to leave Riga because of debts.

Robert and Clara Schumann also visited Latvia in 1844, and Clara gave piano recitals and concerts in Königsberg (now Kaliningrad), Jelgava, Riga, Dorpat, St Petersburg and Moscow. Robert Schumann wrote a letter home complaining that the people in Riga were not really interested in music but only in food.

Bruno Walter, Carlos Kleiber, Otto Klemperer and many other world-class conductors performed in Riga, and the quality of the opera and orchestras continues to attract musicians from around the world. The well-known conductor Mariss Jansons originally came from Latvia.

Rock

Rock music came to Latvia in the late 1950s. Though frowned upon by the Soviet authorities, it filtered into Latvia via radio, relatives from the West, and sailors returning from foreign ports. Elvis Presley was popular in the 1950s, and in the 1960s the Beatles and Rolling Stones predominated. Young Latvian musicians imitated American and English rock bands and even performed in English.

All groups had to register with the official Soviet Orchestra Bureau. In order to gain the Bureau's approval, every group had to include Soviet songs in its repertoire, and officials regularly appeared at concerts to check on what was being performed. Lack of Russian or Soviet content could entail paying a fine, instruments being confiscated, and even being prohibited from giving public concerts. Officially outlawed groups were the norm, not the exception. For a long time officials outlawed rock festivals in Latvia as well as Estonia and Lithuania even though they were allowed in the Soviet republics.

Following independence, many new rock groups have sprung up and several singers have emerged. Modern groups such as Perkons, Linga, Līvi (from Liepāja) and the Reggae group Pchely (The Bees) perform regularly in clubs in Riga and elsewhere. Prata Vetra (Brain Storm) came second in the 1999 Eurovision Song Contest, which was won in 2002 by Marie N. In 2003 the Eurovision Song Contest was held in Riga and evoked considerable interest.

An interesting phenomenon is the rock opera/musical *Lāčplēsis*, written by Māra Zālīte and composed by Zigmars Liepins. A combination of Latvian myth and modern music, *Lāčplēsis* was first performed in 1988 and is still performed today. A new popular rock-opera is Jānis Litsens's *Noterdame*.

Art

It has only recently become widely known that one of the 20th century's best-known artists, Mark Rothko, was born in what is now Latvia and spent the first ten years of his life in Daugavpils, where the museum has now set up a Rothko Hall (see page 223).

If one read only standard accounts of Latvian art history, whether in scholarly texts or in typical guides, one could conclude that serious art in Latvia came to an end in about 1945. The permanent exhibitions in the State Art Museum in Riga reinforce the perception that Latvian painting, graphics and sculpture flowered in the mid-19th century, passed through a golden age of Impressionism at the turn of the century, then the brief, explosive modernist experiments of the 1920s and early '30s, after which there are few examples strong enough or, more importantly, connected enough, to that evolution to warrant wall space in the museum. In fact,

Latvian art since 1945 provides some of the most dramatic evidence of shrewd accommodation and heroic resistance that ultimately enabled the Baltic peoples to regain political independence.

Well into the 1960s, the Kremlin imposed severe restrictions on artists regarding acceptable subjects (they were to be socialist) and style (they had to be realistic or representative). Socialist Realism was practised in Latvia, of course, but the relative physical and psychological distance between the Baltics and the Kremlin allowed possibilities for greater artistic liberty than elsewhere in the former USSR. Some teachers at the Academy in Riga continued to teach officially discouraged techniques; museum workers quietly preserved nationalist artworks in their collections, and even the Riga-born dean of Socialist Realist sculptors, Vera Muhina, supposedly interceded, on aesthetic grounds, on behalf of the *Brīvības piemineklis*, the Latvian Freedom Monument, which some officials wanted to remove from the centre of Riga in the Soviet era.

Even though past traditions were carefully maintained, Latvian art developed, often taking its cues from progressive Western art. By the late 1950s, painters such as Kurts Fridrihsons and Jānis Pauļuks had begun to work in idiosyncratic, highly expressive manners. In increasingly abstract compositions, Fridrihsons took advantage of the capacity of watercolour to blur and run, while Pauļuks splashed paint freely over his otherwise realistically drawn portraits and landscapes, indicating some knowledge of Abstract Expressionism. Oļģerts Jaunarājs became Latvia's first truly abstract artist in the mid 1960s with glorious colour patch gouaches. Uldis and Ilze Zēmzari began articulating distinctive interpretations of Surrealism, the latter having a particularly inventive protofeminist vision. Also working privately – and never displaying their most revolutionary efforts – Zenta Logina constructed fibre-sculptures on great cosmological themes, and Georgs Šēnbergs painted extraordinary Symbolist canvases. Throughout the 1970s, Andris Grīnbergs resisted the conventions separating art and life with his courageous experiments in performance and body art.

These six artists remain neglected by most art historians in Latvia, but as we examine art of the Soviet era from a greater distance and more objectively, opportunities to view their work increase significantly. At the same time, it is easier to find exhibitions by contemporaries of these innovators, men and women who challenged official norms by working imaginatively within the system. Prominent among them are Ojārs Ābols, Ilmārs Blumbergs, Džemma Skulme and Maija Tabaka. The Arsenāls exhibition hall frequently mounts thoughtful retrospective exhibitions from this aspect of Soviet era art.

Most readily available to the visitor, however, is art created by the generation that emerged from the Academy during *perestroika*. These artists were perfect voices for the cultural discontent of the age, their work demonstrating both respect for local tradition and fluency in the latest international trends. Artists like Ieva Iltnere, Dace Lielā and Ivars Poikāns maintain superb standards of craftsmanship in traditional areas such as painting and graphics; others like Juris Boiko, Hardijs Lediņš and Miervaldis Polis have investigated postmodern media like video, installation and performance art. A well-known and active local sculptor is Igor Dobičins, born in Riga in 1958, an enthusiastic explorer of the qualities of different types of stone. Travellers are as likely to see the work of artists such as Kristaps Gelzis, Ojārs Feldbergs, Leonards Laganovskis, Ivars Mailītis, Ojārs Pēteršons, Oļegs Tillbergs and Aija Zariņa in exhibitions abroad as in Latvia, attesting to the appeal and vitality of the new art. Within Latvia the most likely venues to find cutting-edge art is the exhibition hall Arsenāls (1 Torņu iela), and galleries such a

Birkenfelds (6 Amatu iela), Carousell (2 Kaļķu iela) and Ivonna Veiherte (9 Pils iela) (see page 96).

Ballet

Though the former Soviet Union damaged Latvia in many ways, Latvian ballet is one artistic form that owes its existence, success and quality to the Soviets. It began as a small group of dancers whose work was confined to operatic performances. Now and then one-act ballets with guest soloists were staged. Riga was a halfway house between the great dancing centres of western Europe and St Petersburg.

That changed in 1925, when the Latvian National Opera called on soloist Alexandra Feodorova-Fokine of the St Petersburg Mariinsky Theatre to be Riga's resident ballet mistress. A prima ballerina and choreographer herself, she soon opened a school, and through her teaching and vigorous practice sessions she brought on a talented generation of dancers. She staged classic ballets such as *Swan Lake* and *The Nutcracker* – 18 in all.

It is not easy to get into the Riga Ballet. All dancers are chosen from graduates of the Riga Ballet School, founded in 1933. Entrance to the school is via a competition among nine to ten year olds, with about 25 students chosen from 200 applicants. They graduate after ten years, though the drop-out rate is high due to stiff competition.

Latvian ballet also flourished at the Liepāja Opera, which staged grandiose ballet productions for many years. After the Soviet occupation of Latvia in 1944 the Riga Ballet School was renamed 'The Opera and Ballet Theatre'. The Riga Ballet was considered the third finest behind the Kirov and Bolshoi ballets and the Riga school has consistently produced star dancers, among them Alexander Gudonov, Mikhail Baryshnikov (see page 28), Māris Liepa, and his son, Andrejs Liepa. A Baltic Ballet Festival is held every year in Riga, presenting ballets of all types from classical to avant-garde. See www.ballet-festival.lv.

Literature

Early Latvian literature was entirely oral, a spontaneous tradition of folk songs and stories. It is probable that nothing was written down until about the 13th century, when the Teutonic tribes migrated to the east disseminating the Christian religion. However, the position remains uncertain, since no texts from this early period have survived. The earliest printed folk song was written down by Fredericus Menius in 1632, but it was only in the 18th and 19th centuries that the folk tradition began to attract serious attention: the German writers Herder and Hamann were among the first to recognise the significance of this ancient Baltic tradition. Ancient folk songs were only systematically researched and collected in the 19th century by Krišjānis Barons (1835–1919), who opened up the 'choked sources' of Latvian song and collected some 35,000 original songs and numerous variants in eight large volumes. The song written down by Menius still existed in the same form, an indication of the reliability of the oral tradition. As might be expected, the folk songs deal with the seasons, the passing stages of life, and the work of those who sang them: many preserve the rhythms of work in their metre.

The first records of written Latvian come in the form of the accounts in the books of the porters' guild of Riga dating back to the 16th century. The oldest text in Latvian is, however, the Lord's Prayer in the Chronicle of Simon Grunau (c1530). In fact most of the writing of this early period was religious, inspired by Luther and the Reformation and the idea that the word of God should be accessible to all in the vernacular. Georgius Mancelius (1593–1654) published works on folklore and custom and the first Latvian dictionary, thereby establishing a Latvian

DAINAS

The traditional Latvian folk song, *dainas*, is a short song consisting of four lines. They deal with basic themes, the passing of the seasons, the stages of human life, in particular birth, marriage and death, work, war and peace, love and the loss of love. They are simple and unsophisticated since they are rooted in the lives of ordinary people centuries ago. As the German historian Johann Kohl wrote in 1841, 'Every Latvian is a born poet, everyone makes up verse and songs and can sing.' The 'father' of the *dainas* is Krišjānis Barons, whose work in collecting and preserving them is honoured throughout Latvia (see pages 148, 152). The example below is typical. Note the common image of the garden as a place of refuge and a vision of heaven.

Dziedot dzimu, dziedot augu,	Singing I was born and grew,
Dziedot mūžu nodzīvoju;	Singing lived my whole life through;
Dziedot gāja dvēselīte	Singing when my place I won
Dieva dēla dārziņā.	In the garden of God's Son.

prose style for the first time. Christoforus Füreccerus (born c1615) began to write poetry in Latvian and established a new poetic tradition; he also compiled a dictionary and grammar book and translated parts of the Bible into Latvian.

The first full translation of the Bible was made by Ernst Glück (1652–1705, see page 173), a German who studied in Wittenberg and Leipzig, and whose New Testament appeared in 1685 followed by the Old Testament in 1689. It had a colossal influence on the development of the language and on the style of writers in Latvian for generations to come. At the same time, Latvian literature was being enriched by the work of Jānis Reiters (c1632–c1695). Born in Riga and educated at Dorpat University, Reiters was a clergyman and advocate of the Latvian language who also translated parts of the Bible and campaigned for church services in the vernacular in the face of opposition from Rome. The establishment of Latvian as a literary language and a cultural vehicle can largely be attributed to the work of Reiters, Mancelius, Füreccerus and Glück.

Although for some time Latvian writing remained largely religious in character, the clergyman Svante Gustav Dietz (1670–1723) also wrote poetry dealing with the devastation caused by the Northern War; another clergyman, Vilis Steineks (1681–1735), found himself in conflict with the German landowners and clergy in Tukums where he worked and he also gave vent to his concerns in his poetry. Through them, and others writing at the time, a tradition of secular writing began to emerge.

This process was developed in the 18th century with the growth of rationalism, the main proponent of which could be said to be Gotthard Friedrich Stender (1714–96). Stender's *Augusta gudrības grāmata no pasaules un dabas* (*A Book of High Wisdom concerning the World and Nature*) was the first scientific work to be published in Latvian. His grammar book and dictionary again strengthened the language and influenced usage by future writers.

The Latvian literary tradition (and in particular the folk tradition) was enhanced further in the 18th century as a result of the work of Herder and Merkel, both Germans, who undertook research on the Latvian folk song. Herder learned Latvian and championed the cause of folk literature; Merkel published (in German) an influential article in *Der neue teutsche Merkur* in 1797 claiming that the folk songs were part of an ancient epic tradition. The folk song, which was being ignored by native Latvian writers, acquired a new status that was to be influential in the National Awakening movement.

The National Awakening was a period of political and literary revival of Latvian nationalism. The main literary figures of the movement were Krišjānis Valdemārs (1825–91) and Kronvalda Atis (1837–75). They set in motion the revival of the folk song and folk tale which was ultimately taken up so vigorously by Krišjānis Barons. This in turn inspired others to write original work in Latvian, drawing on this tradition: poets such as Auseklis (1850–79) and Andrejs Pumpurs (1841–1902) pioneered a new genre in which nationalism asserted itself through culture, perhaps most famously in Pumpurs's epic, *Lāčplēsis* (*The Bear-slayer*), in which Lāčplēsis' fight against the Black Knight is a clear symbol of Latvia's struggle against foreign domination.

The 19th century also saw the birth of the Latvian novel. Perhaps the most influential was *Mērnieku laiki* (*The Times of the Land Surveyors*) by the brothers Reinis and Matīss Kaudzīte. Published in 1879 it deals with the life of ordinary people in the Piebalga district. The majority of prose writing of this time was similarly parochial in its concerns, dealing with childhood reminiscences or peasant life on the land.

The *Jaunā strāva* (New Movement) of the late 19th century sought to open Latvia to mainstream European influence. Literature was to become the vehicle for exploring major questions about life and the cosmos, not just the detail of everyday life. The poet Eduards Veidenbaums (1867–92) sought to explore such themes in the hundred or more poems he wrote in his short life (see page 42 for an example). Jānis Poruks (1871–1911), in his poetry and short stories, explored the new world of ideas opened up by Wagner and Nietzsche and delved into the nature of the human spirit.

One of Latvia's most influential writers, Jānis Rainis (1865–1929), was a product of this period. In his poetry, and in his most famous work for the theatre, *Jāzeps un viņa brāļi* (*Joseph and his Brothers*), Rainis explores in depth the relationship between the individual and the society in which he lived, always endeavouring to produce a creative synthesis from the tension between the two. In style, too, he attempted a synthesis of old forms and modern modes of expression. Rūdolfs Blaumanis (1863–1908) wrote in similar vein. His novels depict the life of the peasantry of Vidzeme and verge on naturalism; his verse belongs firmly in a modern age.

Two women writers were also influential in the development of Latvian poetry at this period: Elza Rozenberga (1868–1945), who wrote under the name Aspāzijas, and Anna Brigadere (1861–1933) contributed significantly to the poetic output of the New Movement period.

The period of independence between 1918 and 1940 saw a flowering of Latvian literature, and this continued after World War II, although often from abroad, many of Latvia's leading writers having gone into exile in Germany, the USA, Canada, Sweden and elsewhere. This resulted in a great deal of work being published and read abroad. Much of the literature written by Latvian exiles appeared in two periodicals, *Jaunā Gaita* (*The New Path*), which was published in Canada, and *Ceļa Zīmes* (*Signposts*), which appeared in London. At home, poets such as Arvids Grigulis, Vilis Lācis (1903–66) and, perhaps the best, Andrejs Upīts (1877–1970) continued to be published even in the Soviet era. Mārtiņš Zīverts contributed to the work of the modern theatre, while novelists such as Alberts Bels became popular for their novels.

During the 1960s the 'Hell's Kitchen' school of Latvian writers which flourished in New York (which included Linards Tauns and Gunārs Saliņš) maintained a

FOR GLORY...

Pēc goda, pēc varas, pēc mantas	For glory, for power, for riches
Bez atpūtas ļautiņi skrien,	Men ceaselessly labour in vain,
Tie dzenās, tie cīnas, tie pūlas,	They strive and they chase and they struggle,
Ar rūpēm tie kapenēs lien.	Then crawl with their cares to the grave.
Gan lauri tiem kapenēs pušķo,	Though their graves may be covered with laurel,
Gan varoņu dziesmās tos min, –	And their lives praised by every man's breath,
Ne greznumu mana, ne dziesmas,	No pomp and no singing can banish
Ko miroņu tumsība tin.	The darkness that comes with their death.

Eduards Veidenbaums

Latvian identity but embraced American modernism; the publication of Agate Nesaule's *A Woman in Amber* in 1996 in the USA brought Latvian literature to the attention of a wider readership for the first time. Modern Latvian literature now flourishes both in Latvia and overseas. Latvian poets, for example, read their poetry at the Edinburgh Festival in 2004, and the spring 2004 issue of the Canadian literary quarterly *Descant* was devoted entirely to Latvian literature. Whilst some classical and modern works have been translated into various languages, relatively little Latvian literature is available in English translation, so that, like much of Latvia's culture, it remains relatively unknown. Poems from *Nakts Saule* by Latvian poet Guntars Godiņš are being translated into English as part of Cork's celebrations as the European Capital of Culture 2005. The Latvian Literature Centre aims to promote translations of Latvian literature; see www.literature.lv for more information.

Theatre

The first theatrical performances in Latvia are believed to have taken place in Riga in 1205. In early times, religious plays were performed and sometimes a guest dramatist from western Europe would put on a play.

In the late 1700s, the ruling German élite, lovers of theatre, set up a permanent German theatre in Latvia. Through the first half of the 1800s, theatre remained in German hands and the German language. In 1863 they built a new theatre in Riga, the building that is known today as the National Opera House. At about this time, in the province of Vidzeme, a Latvian peasant, J Peitāns, translated and staged Schiller's play *Laupītāji* (*The Robbers*), which is believed to be the first modern theatrical work to have been staged in Latvian.

Latvia developed a strong middle class and with it came the National Awakening of 1850–80, and intellectuals interested in theatre and trends in western Europe. The Latvian Society of Riga was born, and one of its many projects was to produce drama. In 1883 the Riga Russian Theatre was founded and also proved successful.

One of the greatest playwrights of Latvian realistic drama, Rūdolfs Blaumanis, emerged, as well as Aspāzija, writer of romantic, poetic tragedies. She was the wife of writer and playwright Jānis Rainis, a master at using Latvian folklore and medieval history in symbolic works that clearly spoke of a Latvian nation, independent and self-sustaining.

The major theatre companies of this time were the National Theatre, set up in 1919 under director A Amtmanis-Briedītis, and the Art Theatre, set up in 1920, under director E Smilǧis. The National Theatre specialised in the plays of Rūdolfs Blaumanis, which dealt with the everyday lives of ordinary people and their complex inner problems. At the Art Theatre the plays of Rainis prevailed, with their grandiose, colourful stage settings and design. Both theatres achieved a grandeur never before seen in Latvian drama. They each employed over 40 actors, as well as resident technical personnel, set designers and others. In addition to the works of Latvian playwrights, many translations of international contemporaries such as Brecht and O'Neill were performed.

In the 1970s new directors and actors turned to modern theatre and experimentation. Rising and falling curtains were banished, actors performed in the aisles amongst the audience, the traditional raised stage gave way to a circular, closer one. Latvia's Youth Theatre has also dramatised poetry, which has led to a revival of verse drama. See www.theatre.lv for details of current theatre projects and festivals.

Cinema

Latvia's first domestic film was shot in 1910. The first films using live actors came in 1913 and 1914. Throughout Latvia's first independence, regular newsreels, documentaries and feature films were popular. Latvian film-maker J R Doreds was the only foreigner who managed to film Lenin's funeral without permission. During the 1920s Latvian stars M Lia and M Leiko were well known throughout Europe.

The Riga Film Studio was built in 1961. It produces full-length feature films as well as puppet stories, cartoons, documentaries and newsreels. During the occupation it co-produced films with France and other nations. Today it works with a number of European countries. Latvian documentaries have been shown at the international film festivals of Lyon and Berlin, and have received awards in Cannes and Glasgow.

During the late 1980s, Latvian documentaries received international attention. Juris Podnieks, in his thirties, became known for his film, *Vai viegli būt jaunam?* (*Is it Easy to be Young?*), a penetrating, often surrealistic look at the various ways young Latvians dealt with the problems of youth under communism. In *Hallo, vai jūs mūs dzirdat?* (*Hello, Can You Hear Us?*) he examined the state of the various republics of the former Soviet Union and their desire for independence. When the Black Berets attacked several buildings in Riga in January 1991, he was present filming the events unfold. One of his cameramen was hit by bullets and later died (see page 116 for details of the monument that commemorates the incident). Podnieks drowned while scuba diving during a study of Latvia's lakes in June 1992.

The 1990 European cinema prize, the Felix, was awarded to *Sķērsiela* (*Side Street*), the work of Latvian producer I Seleckis. In 1998 the Latvian feature film *Kurpe* (*The Shoe*), directed by Laila Pakalniņa, was a candidate for the Golden Camera award. In 2000 *Nocturnal*, directed by Anna Viduleja, was screened at the Cannes International Film Festival.

VHS videos of Latvian films with English subtitles can be bought at the Jumava bookshop, Dzirnavu iela, Riga, or by contacting Anna Apsite (tel: 638 8760; email: pipars@mailbox.riga.lv).

Architecture

Traditionally Latvians lived in rural areas in wooden houses with thatched roofs, built to a variety of designs depending on the area of the country. Farmsteads and settlements often consisted of several buildings grouped together, including a building for eating and sleeping, a bath house (*pirts*), sometimes a smoke-house (for smoking fish), and a barn (for storing grain or fish). Many households also had their own beehives, often consisting of hollowed-out trees (known as *dores*) and hollowed logs (*auļi*), protected from evil spirits by sacred signs. Some examples of traditional houses, windmills and barns, as well as long one-storey inns (*krogs*), can still be seen in rural areas. An excellent collection can also be seen in the Open Air Museum just outside Riga.

Riga

In contrast, Riga offers a wealth of urban architectural styles: a mixture of old Germanic, Swedish, modern Baltic and Soviet-style monoliths. Many buildings have been, or are, in the process of being restored. In other towns, notably Ventspils, restoration work is also well under way, although it will be some time before the historic architecture of towns such as Daugavpils and Liepāja can be appreciated in its original splendour.

The earliest buildings in Riga date from the 13th century. St Peter's Church (Pētera baznīca) was built in wood in 1209, before being rebuilt two centuries later in stone. Work on the Cathedral of the Archbishop (Riga's Dome), started in 1211, in a mixture of Romanesque and Gothic styles. By 1225, the Church of St James (Jēkaba baznīca) was built in the form of a basilica.

In the course of the next few centuries wooden residential buildings also began to be replaced by brick structures. One of the 'Three Brothers' (three houses in Mazā Pils iela in the Old Town) is the earliest remaining brick house in Latvia, and dates from the 15th century.

Renaissance styles came to Riga in the 16th century. A good surviving example is the Ekke's Convent building at 22 Skārņu iela, built in 1592. Under Swedish control, baroque buildings became fashionable. The castle was built during this time as well as some well-to-do citizens' homes, such as the Reiter House at 2–4 Mārstaļu iela built in 1685 and Dannenstern's House at 21 Mārstaļu iela built in 1696. When Latvia was incorporated into the Russian Empire, Russian classicism made its appearance.

Riga got a major facelift in 1856, when city architect J Felsko and engineer O Dice tore down its fortifications and built a ring of boulevards and a canal. Now Riga was ranked on a par with other culturally élite European cities. Art nouveau buildings proliferated at the end of the 19th century and the beginning of the 20th, and are today perhaps the most striking aspect of Riga's architecture. Many extravagant examples can be seen in the New Town area (see page 115).

During the Soviet occupation nearly all of Latvia's well-known architects fled. The Soviets eliminated the Faculty of Architecture at the University of Latvia and designed buildings in the new utilitarian Soviet style. Many examples of these high-rise apartment complexes ring the city. Western-style buildings were also constructed in Riga (Riga's TV buildings, for example).

Sinc the restoration of independence a number of modern buildings have been erected, both in Riga and in other large cities, although in general they are not particularly noteworthy: in fact Latvia runs the same risk of being overrun by inferior supermarket buildings and retail malls as the rest of Europe. Modern buildings of note include the Saules Akmens (Sun rock) Hansa Bank building on the left bank of the Daugava in Riga (see page 129), and the business centre near the castle in Ventspils. The projected new national library (see page 68), if built, should be an outstanding landmark. Over the last ten or so years, much work has also gone into restoring old buildings in many parts of the country and there are numerous examples of impressive renovations and complete reconstructions, including the Blackheads' House in Riga (see page 110) and the Free Port of Ventspils Authority Building (see page 190).

Outside Riga
Churches
Brick and stone churches began to be built as early as the 13th century, but wooden structures were more common until the 18th century. One of the earliest stone churches is the Jāņa baznīca (St John's) in Cēsis (1281). Most surviving Catholic churches date from much later than this. Richly decorated examples can be seen in Latgale, for example in Krāslava (1767) and Aglona (1699). Lutheran churches are more common throughout the country and although Lutheran doctrine advocates simple buildings, some churches, particularly those built in Kurzeme at the time of its economic development, have rich baroque interiors. Some early examples of Lutheran churches include Tukums (1670), Kuldīga (1655), Bauska (1591) and Talsi (1567). Russian Orthodox churches can also be found in all Latvia's larger towns. Riga and Daugavpils have some of the most interesting examples.

Castles
Latvia abounds in castle mounds (*pils kalns*) where castles once stood. Surviving or restored castles are less plentiful. Some of the most interesting examples, in addition to Riga Castle, are Bauska (prettily situated at the confluence of two rivers, with sections dating from 1451), Cēsis (the first stone castle, dating from 1209), Turaida (begun by the archbishop of Riga in 1214) and the newly restored Ventspils castle.

Palaces
Rundāle, near Bauska, is without doubt Latvia's grandest palace. Built by Rastrelli, the architect of Russia's Winter Palace, in the mid 18th century, it compares favourably with many of Europe's most outstanding palaces. Another palace by Rastrelli in Jelgava is also worth visiting.

Manor houses
The Latvian countryside abounds in manor houses (sometimes translated as castles – *pils* in Latvian), mostly the former homes of Baltic-German families. Some have been or are being restored, and some are open to the public as museums. Notable examples include Mežotne near Bauska, Dundaga in Kurzeme, and Jaunmoku and Durbes, both near Tukums.

Wooden buildings
Although still not very well known internationally, Latvia's wooden buildings, many from the 19th century and the beginning of the 20th, have aroused a great deal of interest locally in recent years, and with justification. In the post-war period, when wooden buildings in many countries were destroyed, buildings in Latvia were frequently left intact, mainly because of the lack of housing under Soviet occupation. Since the restoration of independence there has been a trend to restore some of these houses and 'old town' areas. There are several examples in Riga (see pages 126–7), as well as in many other cities and towns, for example in Ventspils, Tukums and Jūrmala.

REGENT HOLIDAYS

a world apart

Group Tours
Individual Arrangements
Hotels Throughout the Country
Tailor-made Itineraries
Year Round Weekend Breaks
Experienced, Knowledgeable Staff

Regent Holidays
15 John Street
Bristol BS1 2HR
Tel: 0117 921 1711
Fax: 0117 925 4866
e-mail: regent@regent-holidays.co.uk
www.regent-holidays.co.uk

Baltic Specialists Since 1980

Part of Western & Oriental

Practical Information

WHEN TO GO

May to September is probably the best time to visit Latvia, although if you are planning to visit only Riga, the winter months, though cold, are often picturesque in the snow. November to March can be very cold and wet; summer is warm, even hot, but can also be rainy, especially in July and August; spring and autumn are temperate. The average annual temperature in Riga is 6.6°C, but it can rise to 30°C in summer and go as low as minus 23–25°C in December. Even the Germans thought Baltic weather notoriously foul, and 'Courland weather' used to be a byword for wind and rain, according to Anatol Lieven in *The Baltic Revolution*.

Average monthly temperatures (°C) are as follows:

January	–3.0	July	18.1
February	-0.6	August	18.2
March	-0.4	September	11.2
April	2.7	October	4.5
May	9.0	November	1.4
June	15.5	December	-4.5

If you have any special interests, such as opera, you should check festival times. Riga holds a ballet festival, for example, every spring, an opera festival in June and a sacred music festival in August. Sigulda has an opera festival in July and Cēsis a beer festival also in July. Other events can be found on the websites in *Appendix 3*.

GETTING THERE AND AWAY
By air

From the UK, British Airways and AirBaltic both operate direct flights from London Heathrow to Riga. AirBaltic flies daily except Saturdays and BA every day except Mondays and Wednesdays. The flight takes about two and a half hours. In August 2004 AirBaltic started direct flights from Manchester to Riga. From November 2004 Ryanair has operated a daily service from Stansted to Riga. The flight leaves Stansted at 14.40 and arrives in Riga at 19.15. The return flight, however, is less convenient. It leaves Riga at 22.50 arriving at Stansted at 23.25. There are also regular flights to Riga from Amsterdam, Berlin, Brussels, Copenhagen, Dublin, Frankfurt, Hamburg, Helsinki, Kiev, Milan, Minsk, Moscow, Munich, Oslo, Prague, Stockholm, Tallinn, Vienna, Vilnius and Warsaw. Fares fluctuate frequently and for short-break visitors it is often cheaper to book a package than flights and hotels separately. The lowest fares are usually available in winter, spring and autumn, but invariably increase over Christmas and Easter. To secure reasonable prices in the summer, it is important to book well in advance. While Riga has not yet become as popular a weekend destination as Tallinn in Estonia, it has the potential to do so, and with the entry of Latvia into the EU in 2004 it is likely that low-cost carriers will lead to an increase in visitors.

For travellers from the USA, SAS and Finnair offer good connections via Copenhagen and Stockholm, but given the very low fares usually available to London from the USA and Canada, it may often be cheaper to break the journey in London and take a separate package from there. Via London is always the best route for tourists from Australia and New Zealand, as well as from South Africa.

Airport transfer

The airport (Lidosta Riga) is about 8km from Riga. A taxi from the airport to the capital should cost a maximum of Ls10. There is also a bus service (the A22 leaves from a bus stop in front of the terminal slightly to the right and on the far side of the airport car park) between the airport and the central bus station. At present it runs every half-hour from 05.50 to 23.15. Buy your ticket (Ls0.20; Ls0.40 for large cases) from the information booth in the terminal building or on board. The journey from the airport to the centre of Riga should take no more than about 20 minutes by taxi, and about 30 minutes by bus.

Liepāja Airport

Liepāja claims to be Latvia's second international airport. It is currently small and little used, although it is likely to develop in the future. There are no scheduled flights at present but it is possible to organise direct flights for groups to and from Liepāja and other cities in Europe; tel: 340 7592; email: air_liepaja@anet.lv.

Airline addresses/telephone numbers (in Riga)

Aeroflot Airport; tel: 720 7472; city centre; 6 Ģertrūdes iela; tel: 727 8774
AirBaltic Airport; tel: 720 7777; email: reservations@airbaltic.lv; www.airbaltic.lv; city centre; 15 Kaļķu iela; tel: 722 9166
British Airways Airport; tel: 720 7097; www.britishairways.com; city centre; 4/111a Torņa iela; tel: 732 6737
CSA Airport; tel: 720 7636; email: csa-riga@apollo.lv; www.czech-airlines.com
Estonia Air 22 Aspāzijas bulvāris (Hotel Riga); tel: 721 4860; email: riga@estonian-air.ee; www.estonian-air.ee
Finnair Airport; tel: 720 7010; www.finnair.lv
KLM Airport; tel: 766 8600; www.klm.com
LOT 5 Mazā Pils iela; tel: 722 7234; email: lotrix@lot.com; www.lot.com
Lufthansa Airport; tel: 750 7711; email: lufthansa@apollo.lv; www.lufthansa.com
SAS 15 Kaļķu iela; tel: 720 7777

By train

It is less likely that you will choose to travel to Latvia by train unless you are coming from Moscow or St Petersburg. The train journey from Moscow to Riga takes about 12½ hours, from St Petersburg to Riga 12 hours. All trains to Riga arrive in Riga Central Station (Centrālā stacija) which is a short walk from the Old Town. International trains arrive at platform 2. There are automatic luggage lockers below the Central Hall (Centrālā zāle). The price is Ls0.50 to Ls1.00 per day; it is open 04.30–midnight. There are currency exchanges in tunnels A and B and banks to the left and right of the Central Hall, as well as several money withdrawal machines.

By coach

Buses and coaches are cheap. Coaches run daily between Riga and Kaliningrad, Kaunas, Klaipeda, Minsk, Moscow, St Petersburg, Tallinn, Tartu, Warsaw and Vilnius. There are also regular buses to Berlin, Bonn, Bremen, Brussels, Frankfurt,

London, Munich and Prague. Coaches leave London on Mondays and Wednesdays at 06.15, arriving in Riga at 21.30 the following day, and at 08.30 on Tuesdays and Saturdays, arriving at 21.30 the following day. They leave Riga on Fridays and Sundays at 07.15, arriving in London the following day at 20.30; and on Wednesdays and Saturdays at 07.15, arriving the following day at 18.00. The London–Riga buses are operated by **Ecolines** (Bus Station, 1 Prāgas iela, Riga; tel: 900 0009; email: ecolines@ecolines.lv; www.ecolines.lv).

The bus station in Riga is next to the railway station. The left luggage office is open 05.30–midnight (Ls0.20/0.40 an hour, and Ls0.10 per extra hour). The bus station is quite close to the Old Town. Follow signs to Vecriga – Vaļņu iela.Tram 7 stops in front of the bus station and is only one stop from the centre. Pay Ls0.20 to the conductor on the bus.

By sea
There are regular ferries from Lübeck and Stockholm to Riga: **Rigas Jūras Līnija**, 3a Eksporta iela; tel: 720 5460; email: booking@rigasealine.lv; www.rigasealine.lv. The ferry terminal is around 1km to the north of the Old Town. There is a money exchange bureau in the terminal, open 09.00–18.00. To get to the Old Town, take tram numbers 5, 7 or 9 from Ausekļa iela for two stops.

There are also ferries from Nynäshamm (Stockholm, Sweden) and Travemünde (Germany) to Ventspils (see page 188), and from Karlshamn (Sweden) and Rostock (Germany) to Liepāja: **Terrabalt Company**, 46 Brīvostas iela; tel: 342 7214; note that the ferries to and from Liepāja often have limited passenger space.

By car
If you decide to drive you will have to cope with the border crossings, which may still entail a wait of up to one hour. You should take an international driving licence and contact your insurers about any special requirements and any extra premium you will almost certainly have to pay. Seek advice from your local motoring organisation for up-to-date requirements. It is probably wiser to hire a car locally. For details of the major car hire companies operating in Latvia see page 54.

All the Baltic states are trying to promote the Via Baltica as a tourist route. The Via Baltica (Baltic Way) is the name that has been given to the 1,500 miles of road from Tallinn, leading through Pärnu (in Estonia), Riga, Kaunas (in Lithuania), Suwałki (in Poland) and ending in Warsaw. From Tallinn you can also take the extended route east to St Petersburg or the ferry to Helsinki. The route is being promoted mainly in Scandinavia and in Germany because of the relatively easy access to the route from Berlin and elsewhere in Germany to Warsaw. For more information contact the Riga tourist office (see page 67).

TOUR OPERATORS
The following specialise in the Baltic States (among other destinations):

UK
Baltic Holidays 40 Princess St, Manchester M1 6DE; tel: 0870 757 9233; fax: 0870 120 2973; email: info@balticholidays.com; www.balticholidays.com

Bridge Travel Bridge House, 55–59 High St, Broxbourne, Herts EN10 7DT; tel: 0870 191 7270; fax: 01992 45609; email: info@bridgetravel.co.uk; www.bridgetravel.co.uk

Martin Randall Travel Voysey House, Barley Mow Passage, Chiswick, London W4 4PH; tel: 020 8742 3355; email: info@martinrandall.co.uk; www.martinrandall.com. Specialises in art, music and architecture, including trips to the Riga Opera Festival.

Operas Abroad The Tower, Mill Lane, Rainhill, Prescot, Merseyside L35 6NE; tel/fax: 0151 493 0382; email: info@operasabroad.com; www.operasabroad.com
Regent Holidays (UK) Ltd 15 John St, Bristol BS1 2HR; tel: 0117 921 1711; fax: 0117 925 4866; email: regent@regent-holidays.co.uk; www.regent-holidays.co.uk. Organises weekend and longer trips to Latvia and all the Baltic states.
Scantours 47 Whitcomb St, London WC2H 7DH; tel: 020 7839 2927; fax: 020 7839 5891; email: info@scantours.com; www.scantours.com
Specialised Tours 4 Copthorne Bank, Copthorne, Crawley, West Sussex RH10 3QX; tel: 01342 712785; fax: 01342 717042; email: info@specialisedtours.com; www.specialisedtours.com
Traveleditions 69–85 Tabernacle St, London EC2A 4BD; tel: 020 7251 0045; fax: 020 7251 7399; email: tours@traveleditions.co.uk; www.traveleditions.co.uk
Travelscene 11–15 St Ann's Rd, Harrow, Middlesex HA1 1LQ; tel: 0870 777 9987; fax: 020 8861 4154; email: admin@travelscene.co.uk; www.travelscene.co.uk

USA
Amest Travel 16 Ocean Parkway #19, New York 11218; tel: 718 972 2217; fax: 718 851 4175; email: info@amest.com; www.amest.com
Value World Tours Plaza del Lago Building, Suite 203, 17220 Newhope St, Fountain Valley, CA 82708; tel: 714 556 8258; fax: 714 556 6125; email: travel@vwtours.com; www.vwtours.com
Vytis Tours 40–24 235th St, Douglaston, New York 11363; tel: 800 778 9847 or 718 423 6161; fax: 718 423 3979; email: tours@vytistours.com; www.vytistours.com

Canada
Valhalla Travel and Tours 120 Newkirk Rd, Unit 25, Richmond Hill, Ontario C4C 9S7; tel: 800 265 0459 or 905 737 0304; email: info@valhallatravel.com; www.valhallatravel.com

Special-interest holidays
Country holidays
A number of organisations can provide information and bookings for homestay holidays and country holidays, including country sports. Details of countryside accommodation and holidays can be found in *Lauku Ceļotājs* (*Country Traveller*), available at bookshops in Riga, or by contacting tel: 761 7600; email: lauku@celotajs.lv; www.celotajs.lv. Walking, cycling and fishing (see below) are all possible in most parts of the country. Latvia is endeavouring to promote 'ecological' tourism, that is to say tourism in areas of natural beauty responsibly undertaken in a manner sensitive to the environment. The following claim to organise 'green' tours and trips:

Gandrs 28 Kalnciema iela, Riga; tel: 761 4775; fax: 761 4927; email: veikals@gandrs.lv; www.gandrs.lv
Latvia University Tourist Club c/o Travel Agency LUTK, 51 Dzirnavu iela; tel: 724 2347; email: inara@lutk.lv; www.lutk.lv

Fishing
Latvia has many rivers and lakes that are rich in fish, including pike, perch, carp, bream, tench, roach and chub. Fishing from small boats, from the shore, or in winter under-ice fishing are all popular. To fish, you must buy a fishing permit. These cost Ls3–5 and are available from any post office. In some areas a special licence may also be needed. This is available from the local municipal office in the area where you intend to fish. All local tourist offices can provide more information on particular

sites, but Vidzeme is particularly active in this area. Contact: Vidzeme Tourism Association, 1 Pils laukums, Cēsis; tel: 412 2011; email: info@vta.apollo.lv.

Birdwatching
Although Latvia is good for birdwatching, there are few specialist tours. Two possibilities are Eastbird, Box 1603, 1050 Riga; tel: 616 1077 (Agris Celmiņš); email: eastbird@latnet.lv, and Ibisbill Tours, 7 Holders Hill Gardens, London NW4 1NP; tel/fax: 020 8203 4317; email: ibisbill@talk21.com. The main places for birdwatching are Lake Engure, Lake Pape, Cape Kolka and the Nagļi ponds. For information contact the Institute of Biology, 3 Miera iela, 2169 Salaspils; tel: 794 4988; email: biolog@tesla.sal.lv; www.lza.lv.

Winter sports
Winter sports are popular in Latvia. There is skiing on the Reiņa Trase in Krimulda (just by Sigulda), a 200m-long artificial ski run in Baiļi near Valmiera, and eight tracks at Ezernieki in the Krāslavas district. Gaiziņškalns, the highest mountain in Latvia, near Madona, was a well-known ski resort in Soviet times, but nowadays skiing there is limited, although Latvia's first snowboard park is here. Sigulda is well known as the site of one of Latvia's most famous winter sports facilities, the bobsleigh track used by the former Soviet bobsleigh team (see page 148). There is also a large skating rink in Riga. For further information contact the Information Centre of the Latvian Sports Committee, Tērbatas iela, Riga; tel: 728 0515 or local tourist offices.

Railways
Latvia provides a number of areas of interest for railway enthusiasts, including the narrow-gauge railway between Gulbene and Alūksne, and the railway museums in Riga and Jelgava. See the relevant city information for more details, and www.banitis.lv for the development of railways in Latvia.

For tours that focus on the arts, architecture or music, see pages 51–2.

GETTING AROUND
By rail
There are good and frequent train services between Riga and Jūrmala and Riga and Jelgava. There are also regular trains along the Daugava as far as Daugavpils, towards Valka, stopping at Sigulda and Valmiera, and to Tukums, but all these places can be reached more quickly by bus. Prices on the other hand are a little lower than the buses. For information on rail travel enquire at the Central Station (*Centrālā stacija*) in Riga, Stacijas laukums, Riga; tel: 583 2134. Alternatively consult the Latvian Railways website: www.ldz.lv. Timetables for main bus and train services are listed in *Riga in Your Pocket*.

By bus
There are bus services between most major towns and cities and these are more frequent than the train services. For information go to the central bus station (*autoosta*), 1 Prāgas iela, Riga; tel: 721 3611. The main destinations with details of frequency and approximate journey times are as follows:

Bauska	Every 30–40 minutes from 06.00 to 22.30	1½ hours
Cēsis	Every hour from 08.00 to 20.30	2 hours
Daugavpils	7 a day from 10.00 to 20.20	4 hours
Kuldīga	7 or 8 a day from 08.10 to 20.00	3½ hours
Liepāja	14 a day from 06.45 to 19.40	4 hours

Sigulda	Every 30 minutes from 07.00 to 21.30	1 hour
Valmiera	Every 30–40 minutes from 07.30 to 22.20	2½ hours
Ventspils	14 a day from 06.40 to 22.35	4 hours

Prices are low and never exceed Ls3 for the longest one-way journey.

In towns

In Riga itself there is a good system of public transport: trolley buses, trams and buses operate throughout the capital from about 05.30 to midnight. You can only buy tickets on board from the *konduktors*. You should keep your ticket until you finish your journey. To get to grips with the bus and tram network, buy the Riga city map. There are also buses and trams in Latvia's other major towns such as Daugavpils. Apart from the normal bus services, in Riga there are small buses (called *taksobuss* or *mikroautobuss*) that serve nearby towns and the outer suburbs. They leave from a special stand opposite the central railway station.

Riga, and most other cities and large towns, now have taxis. They are generally reliable and cheap by Western standards. Official taxis have signs and meters and charge Ls0.30 per kilometre during the day and Ls0.40 per kilometre between 22.00 and 06.00. Unofficial ones can be dangerous; they operate more like minicabs, so it is essential to agree a fare in advance and beware of being overcharged.

Car hire

Almost all the major international car hire companies now have offices in Riga. Car hire is relatively expensive, drop-off charges in Estonia and Lithuania are high, and cars cannot be taken into Russia or Belarus.

Avis 3 Krasta iela; tel: 722 5876; fax: 782 0441; email: avis@avis.lv; www.avis.lv, and at Riga Airport; tel: 720 7353

Baltic Car Lease – Sixt franchisee 28 Kaļķu iela (Hotel de Rome); tel: 722 4022, and at Riga Airport; tel: 720 7121; fax: 720 7131; email: car.rent@carlease.lv; www.e-sixt.lv

Budget Rent A Car Riga Airport; tel: 720 7327; fax: 720 7627; email: budget@delfi.lv; www.budget.lv

Easyrent 52 Daugavpils iela; tel: 919 3198; email: office@easyrent.lv; www.easyrent.lv

Europcar 10 Basteja bulvāris; tel: 721 2652; fax: 782 0360; email: europcar@europcar.lv; www.europcar.lv, and at Riga Airport; tel: 720 7825

Hertz 24 Aspāzijas bulvāris; tel: 722 4223, and at Riga Airport; tel: 720 7980; fax: 720 7981; www.hertz.lv

National Car Rental Riga Airport; tel: 720 7710

Car hire can be organised through local tour operators and their agents abroad, often more cheaply. It is advisable to take an international driving licence.

Driving

Latvian roads are of variable quality. Major roads are fairly good, and traffic is light. Minor roads can be bad, and some tend to degenerate into mud in bad weather and in spring when the snow is melting. Pot-holes are common. Special care should be taken when the weather is bad: allow a greater braking distance than you would on more advanced European roads.

Generally the speed limit is 50km/h in towns, 70km/h in suburban areas, 90km/h on open roads and 110km/h on motorways. Seat belts are compulsory. On the spot fines for speeding and other minor offences are common. Be ready to produce your driving licence and car registration and insurance documents. Drinking and driving

BUYING PETROL – LATVIAN-STYLE

If you drive in and around Riga, buying petrol will be much the same as in London, Berlin or Paris. Travel into more remote country areas, however, and a true Soviet experience awaits. In old-style petrol stations – recognisable by a complete lack of any structure except two or three old pumps, a broken concrete forecourt and a small and apparently abandoned shed-like building at the back – you have to pay for your petrol before you fill up. This of course means you have to guess how much you might need. Once you have decided how much you would like to pay, take your money (preferably the correct change) to the assistant, who will generally be completely invisible in the small building at the back of the forecourt: you speak and pass your money through a small hole. After paying, you can then fill up your car: the pump may stop automatically once you have used up your credit.

should be avoided: the legal blood/alcohol limit is 0.05%, equivalent to half a litre of beer. If you are driving in towns, give way to trams and be careful of passengers getting on and off, since trams often operate in the centre of the road. Pay attention to give way signs (a white triangle with red border): often there is only a sign and no road markings to make clear that you should stop and give way. The yellow diamond sign, still found in many parts of Europe, means you have right of way in accordance with the bold black line which shows the direction of the main road. Traffic lights are small and not always easy to see. They flash green before turning amber and then red, and some go directly from red to green without passing through an amber phase. If you are turning right or left after traffic lights watch out for pedestrians who have right of way. Many traffic lights also have a separate green filter light for right-hand turns. Road markings are generally scarce.

All cars in Latvia must now drive with headlights on irrespective of the time of day or weather conditions.

Parking is not a problem in most places, but there are parking meters in the centre of Riga and Liepāja. Note too that access to the Old Town in Riga is restricted for cars. To enter the Old Town you need a special pass (*viedkarte*), which costs a minimum of Ls5 per hour. If necessary, you can buy the pass at Statoil (1c Eksporta iela; open 24 hours) or at Centrs shopping centre (from the information desk) at 16 Audēju iela (open 08.00–22.00).

Signs to towns and cities are scarce and often hard to read. A good road map is essential. The best are Bartholomew's *Latvia* in the European Travel Map series (1: 400,000), and the Jāņa Sēta yellow town and area maps which contain detailed local information.

Petrol is now widely available, although in the major cities petrol stations (which are often signposted) tend to be located on the outskirts. Not all take credit cards, so make sure you have cash. Petrol is cheap: about Ls0.46 per litre for 92 octane petrol, Ls0.47 per litre for 95e petrol and Ls0.49 per litre for 98e petrol. A full tank of petrol is likely to cost about Ls14–17 for a medium-sized saloon car.

RED TAPE
Passports and visas

To visit Latvia you need a valid full passport. No visa is needed for EU, US, Canadian, Australian, New Zealand or Japanese citizens visiting Latvia. Citizens of these countries may stay up to 90 days within a period of six months to one year, depending on nationality. If you want to stay in Latvia for more than 90 days you will need a residence permit or special visa. Persons who need a visa may obtain one for ten days or 30 days, and it can be extended for a maximum of 90 days in total in any one year. The cost of a visa can vary depending on your country of origin, as can the time it will take you to get one. You are advised to seek advice from your nearest Latvian embassy (see below).

Obtaining a residence permit can be a lengthy process, and may entail a wait of up to three months. The application must be made before your visa expires. For further and up-to-date information contact your nearest Latvian embassy or the Foreigners' Service Centre of the Citizenship and Migration Board in Riga, at 1 Alunāna, Riga; tel: 721 9656; email: aad@pmlp.gov.lv; www.pmlp.gov.lv.

Embassies and consulates

Australia (Consulate) 8 Barr-Smith St, Tusmore, SA 5064; tel: 8833 33 123; fax: 8833 33 227; email: fsvilans@ozemail.com.au

Canada 280 Albert St, Suite 300, Ottawa, Ontario; tel: 613 238 6014; fax: 613 238 7044; email: consulate.canada@mfa.gov.lv; www.ottawa.am.gov.lv

Denmark Rosbaeksvej 17, DK-2100 Copenhagen; tel: 39 27 60 00; email: embassy.denmark@mfa.gov.lv

Estonia 10 Tõnismägi Str, 10119 Tallinn; tel: 627 7850; fax: 627 7855; email: embassy.estonia@mfa.gov.lv

France 6 Villa Said, Paris 16; tel: 01 53 64 58 10; fax: 01 53 64 58 19; email: embassy.france@mfa.gov.lv; www.paris.am.gov.lv

Germany Reinerzstrasse 40/41, 14193 Berlin; tel: 308 260 0222; fax: 308 260 0233; email: embassy.germany@mfa.gov.lv; www.botschaft-lettland.de

Ireland 14 Lower Leeson St, Dublin 2; tel: 1 662 1610; fax: 1 662 1599; email: embassy.ireland@mfa.gov.lv

Lithuania 76 M K Čiurlionio Str, 2009 Vilnius; tel: 5213 1260; fax: 5213 1130; email: embassy.lithuania@mfa.gov.lv

South Africa (Consulate) 4 Lafayette, 39 Harrow Rd, Sandhurst, Sandton 2916; tel: 11 783 9442; fax: 11 783 9450; email: neishlos@icon.co.za

United Kingdom 45 Nottingham Pl, London W1U 5LY; tel: 020 7312 0040; fax: 020 7312 0042; email: embassy.uk@mfa.gov.lv; www.london.am.gov.lv

USA 4325 17th St NW, Washington DC 20011; tel: 202 726 8213; fax: 202 726 6785; email: embassy.usa@mfa.gov.lv; www.latvia-usa.org

Customs

It is forbidden to import arms, explosives, drugs or pornography. On leaving Latvia, you should declare any large quantities of jewellery or other valuables you are taking out of the country. If you export any item over 50 years old it may be subject to duty. There are no restrictions on bringing in or taking out currency. For up-to-date information you should contact your local embassy, and for enquiries on works of art, the Ministry of Culture, 22 Pils iela (1st floor), Riga; tel: 721 4100; fax: 722 7916; the relevant department is open on weekdays 08.30–17.00.

Local time

Latvia is in the eastern European time zone, as are Estonia and Finland, ie: time is two hours ahead of GMT/BST. When it is midday in Riga it is 10.00 in London, 11.00 in Paris, 05.00 in New York, 13.00 in Moscow and Lithuania, and 20.00 in Sydney.

MONEY
Currency
During the Soviet era, the currency in Latvia was the rouble, the currency used throughout the USSR. The rouble was abolished in April 1993 and replaced by a transitional currency, the Latvian rouble, which in turn was replaced by the lat, which is now the official currency of Latvia (the singular is *lats*, the plural *lati*). There are 100 santīmi to the lat (the singular is *santīms*, the plural *santīmi*). The lat comes in notes in denominations of 5, 10, 20, 50, 100 and 500 lats, and in the form of 1 and 2 lat coins. The lat is relatively strong and stable. In mid 2004 the exchange rate was about Ls0.53 to the dollar, Ls0.66 to the euro and Ls0.99 to the pound.

Changing money
You can change money easily; there is a bureau de change at Riga Airport, though with a poor exchange rate, and you can change money at most banks, hotels and, most conveniently, at exchange booths/shops around Riga. Look for the sign *Valūtas Maiņas*. Note that if you are arriving late in the evening, the bureau de change at the airport may occasionally be closed, so it is a good idea to change at least a small amount of money before you leave your home country. You can buy lats in some (but not all) exchange bureaux at London Heathrow (try Travelex). In Riga itself, you will get a better rate at exchange booths than at the hotels or banks, but even here the rates of exchange can vary enormously, so it is best to check around. There are several 24-hour bureaux de change in Riga, including Marika at 14 Basteja bulvāris, 14 Marijas iela and 30 Brīvības iela. Many bureaux stay open until late at night. Exchange bureaux do not accept travellers' cheques, and they can be difficult and time-consuming to change in banks; it is better not to bring them.

Try to carry a certain amount of money in small change since museum entrance charges are cheap (usually no more than Ls1), as are most things you are likely to need on a day-to-day basis (drinks, bus fares and so on); large denomination notes are rarely welcome. As prices are low, avoid changing large sums. Street crime is rare in Latvia, and the atmosphere is generally relaxed. However, you should avoid carrying large sums in cash, and it is wise to leave money and valuables in a hotel safe; carry some cash in a money belt.

Credit cards
For major purchases and in hotels and restaurants, credit cards are widely accepted, and cash dispensers (which take major credit cards, in particular MasterCard and Visa) are common in Riga.

HEALTH
with Dr Felicity Nicholson
For an emergency ambulance, phone 03.

Hospitals and medical care are of a reasonable standard but not up to Western standards. You are advised to take out health insurance. If you are unlucky enough to contract a major illness while in Riga, it is probably best to fly home (although your insurance will not cover this). If you do need treatment in Riga, however, there are a number of places where you can be guaranteed help from English-speaking professionals:

ARS 5 Skolas iela; tel: 720 1001 or 720 1003: medical practice
A&S Health Care 60 Lāčplēša iela; tel: 728 9516: a private dental clinic
Latvian-American Eye Centre 93 Tallinas iela; tel: 727 2257

Pharmacies can help too. They are easy to find. Look for the word *aptieka* (pharmacy). In Riga many have extended opening hours and several pharmacies are open 24 hours, including:

Kamēlijas Aptieka 74 Brīvības iela; tel: 729 3514
Saules Aptieka 230 Brīvības iela; tel: 755 3368
Tallinas Aptieka 57b Tallinas iela; tel: 731 4211
Vecpilsētas Aptieka 20 Audēju iela; tel: 721 3340 or 722 3826

Standards of hygiene are generally good, but you should avoid drinking tap water: it is advisable to stick to bottled water.

No vaccinations are required for travel to Latvia. That said, travellers here, as anywhere, should be up to date with tetanus and diphtheria, and hepatitis A vaccine is also recommended as standard. If you are camping or staying by the sea, for example in Jūrmala, from May to September there is a small risk of encephalitis from ticks found in the forests. Injections are available, and now can be done within three to four weeks of travel. Whether you opt for vaccination or not, simple precautions such as using tick repellents and wearing hats and long trousers tucked into boots should suffice.

CRIME AND PERSONAL SAFETY
To call the police in an emergency, dial 02.

Crime has increased in all the Baltic States since they gained their independence, but by and large they are pretty safe places for travellers. Avoid leaving money or valuables in your hotel room, and make sure you carry only modest sums of money on you at any time. Make sure you have a contact number to telephone your credit card company to cancel your account if your card is stolen. Street robbery remains relatively rare, but avoid flaunting large amounts of money or valuables. In particular, be careful when you leave clubs or bars late at night and try not to walk back to your hotel unaccompanied. As in most countries, it is best to avoid parks and streets next to parks after dark. Cars are the most vulnerable objects of crimes: crook locks and other devices are in common use and should be used on hire cars if you leave them for long periods of time. Try to park in guarded and well-lit spots overnight.

The police are well trained and unobtrusive, although they do carry out spot checks on cars. If you run into trouble with the police remember that officers must produce their identification, they must tell you why you have been detained (if you have been arrested) and you cannot in any event be held by the police for longer than 72 hours (in the case of a serious offence) or three hours (for a minor, administrative offence). As in most countries, you are entitled to have a lawyer present when the police question you. Contact your embassy or consulate if you need legal help (see page 67 for embassy details).

Women are unlikely to be subject to any dangers in Latvia that they would not experience elsewhere in Europe. It is wise to take the usual precautions on personal safety, especially when travelling alone, but no special measures are needed.

COSTS
If you take a package holiday to Latvia, you are not likely to need to change much money at all – just enough for drinks and souvenirs and so on. If you are travelling independently, you are advised to change money as you go, changing as little as possible at one time (although there is no problem in changing larger notes back into your domestic currency). There is a big difference in costs between Riga and other parts of Latvia. In Riga allow about £60–110 (US$110–210) a night for

accommodation in a double room in a good hotel, or £30–50 (US$55–90) for a tourist-class hotel. A good restaurant meal (two courses and wine for two) will cost about £25–35 (US$45–65). An overnight stay in a more modest hotel is likely to cost about £15 (US$28) per person per night. You can eat out in the cheaper restaurants for as little as £3–5 (US$5.50–9) per person. Outside Riga and Jūrmala, costs are much lower. Apart from in the Amrita Hotel in Liepāja, it is impossible to spend more than Ls45 for a double room in the best hotel available. Other costs are correspondingly low.

The following prices may give you some idea of the cost of living:

Snickers bar	Ls0.23
Loaf of white bread	Ls0.25
Bottle of vodka (1 litre)	Ls4.50
Bottle of local beer (0.5l)	Ls0.40
20 Marlboro cigarettes	Ls0.75
Cup of coffee	From Ls0.50 for a basic cup to over Ls1 for a latte or cappuccino in a coffee house in Riga
Petrol	Ls0.47 (95e) and Ls0.49 (98e) (see comments on page 55)

TIPPING
Tipping is not compulsory but is common. It is usual to acknowledge good service by leaving an extra 10%. In some restaurants menus will indicate whether service is included.

LANGUAGE
The official language of Latvia is Latvian, an Indo-European language similar to Lithuanian. Russian is still widely spoken. In Riga, English is also widely spoken, less so in smaller towns and in the country. Take a phrase book and even a small dictionary since signs are generally only in Latvian – even Russian has been largely eliminated. The *Baltic States Phrase Book* (Lonely Planet) is small and cheap but covers all three Baltic languages (Estonian and Lithuanian as well as Latvian) so is fairly restricted. The yellow *Latvian–English Phrase Book* (published by Jumava) is more comprehensive and has a cassette. If you want to buy a phrase book or dictionary see the recommended bookshops on page 96. For some Latvian words and phrases see *Appendix 1*.

ACCOMMODATION
There is now plenty of hotel and other accommodation in Riga, and rooms are generally available; however, it may be wise to book in advance during the summer. Outside Riga accommodation of any kind remains scarce, although there is a steady increase in the number of guesthouses.

Hotels fall into three broad categories. First, there are the modern purpose-built luxury hotels that can now be found in Riga, some built with money from Germany or Scandinavia. Many of these offer lower rates in holiday times when business travellers are absent. Next, there are the old Latvian hotels which have now been refurbished, again often with foreign investment. The final category is the small private hotel or guesthouse, often no more than a part of or a few rooms in a private house. Hotels in the first two categories can cost £60–110 (US$110–210) or more a night for a double room. The older, Soviet-style hotels are likely to charge about £20–30 (US$35–55) a night for a double room (most are now modernised). Rooms in the last category can cost anything from £6 (US$11) to about £20 (US$35) a night. Prices are normally quoted in lats. Prices outside Riga are considerably lower than in the capital.

There is a small number of youth hostels in Riga. Contact Hostelling Latvia, 17–2 Siguldas prospekts; tel: 921 8560; email: info@hostellinglatvia.com; www.hostellinglatvia.com. Campsites are available, and are usually well signposted.

Homestays can be organised through Patricia, 22–26 Elizabetes iela, 1011 Riga; tel: 728 4868; fax: 728 6650; email: tourism@parks.lv; www.rigalatvia.net, at rates of £10–15 (US$19–28) per person per night. Farmstays are also possible and can be arranged through the Country Tourism Association, Lauku Ceļotājs, 11 Kuģu iela, 2 Stāvs, 1048 Riga; tel: 761 7600; email: lauku@celotajs.lv; www.celotajs.lv.

FOOD AND DRINK

Latvian cuisine has evolved from the agricultural lifestyle that typified (and to some extent still typifies) Latvian life. It is basic, hearty fare, created for the sustenance of hard-working farmers and fishermen. Dairy products, fish and meat, especially bacon, vegetables, and fruits and berries are the mainstay of the Latvian diet.

Background

During the first period of independence Latvia's dairy industry expanded greatly, and soon the country ranked fourth among European countries in the export of butter. Cereal crop production improved greatly and Latvia went from a grain importing to an exporting country.

The commercial fishing industry evolved from the 75 fishing centres along the coastline. Fish and seafood were delivered fresh to markets and processing plants in the cities: in Riga alone, nine canning factories exported to the rest of Europe, the United States, Australia, Africa and Asia. *Rigas Sprotes* (Riga Sardines) was a well-known brand around the world. The Soviet method of collective farming and fishing changed Latvia's traditional economy, and the very products Latvia was known for became scarce or unavailable within the country. As a result of major economic reforms this position has been reversed, and local goods are now available everywhere, as are food products from abroad.

Meals

Breakfast (*brokastis*) is similar to that of many east and northern European countries. It generally consists of bread and cheese, cold meat and smoked fish. Eggs and pancakes (sweet or savoury) are often served, although a full cooked breakfast of the traditional British kind is rare outside the big international hotels. Coffee and tea (the latter often served without milk) and juice (not always of the best quality) are the norm. Yoghurt and milk-based drinks are also quite common, as is cereal.

Lunch or dinner (*pusdienas; vakariņas*) is from one to three courses, a first course of hors d'oeuvres (*uzkožamie*) or soup, a main course of fish or meat and vegetables and salad, and finally a dessert (*saldie ēdieni*), often ice-cream or fruit. Meals are eaten at any time: you can find Latvians having lunch at any time from about 11.30 onwards, and dinner from as early as 17.00 to 23.00 or even later. Some restaurants serve vegetarian food, often pasta or omelettes.

Restaurants and cafés

You can eat in restaurants, cafés and many bars. The restaurant (*restorāns*) tends to be fairly upmarket and expensive; the Latvian café (*kafejnīca*) can simply serve drinks and light snacks, but many serve full meals and are more like restaurants than anything else; many bars, especially in Riga and the larger towns, also serve full meals. The only way to tell is to go in and look at the menu. Sometimes the way in which the tables are laid gives a clue to what is on offer.

In Riga, in large hotels and in the more expensive eating places, the menu will come in Latvian, Russian and English (occasionally German too). In small cafés and outside Riga English and other foreign languages are less commonly used, so take a phrase book or dictionary. Some cafeterias are self-service and sell food by weight, each portion being separately weighed and charged accordingly.

About the food

Dairy products – in the form of *biezpiens* (cottage cheese), *siers* (cheese) and *rūgušpiens* (curdled milk) – are used extensively in Latvian cooking. The same is true of *putras* (cooked wholemeal porridge), including *griķi* (buckwheat), *grūbes* (barley) and *auzas* (oats). *Rupjmaize* (rye bread) and *saldskāba* maize (sweet/sour rye bread) are both common (see box), and no holiday or celebration would be complete without *pīrāgi* (a Russian speciality – small pies or pasties filled with bacon or other meat and onion).

Zivis (fish) is a popular staple. It comes in the form of *kotletes* (filets), *galerts* (aspic), *zupa* (soup), with *tomātu mērce* (tomato sauce), *žāvēta* (smoked), *pildīta* (stuffed), and as *salāti* (salad). *Siļķe* (herring), *līdaka* (pike), *lasis* (salmon) and *zutis* (eel) are among the most common.

When it comes to *gaļa* (meat), you will encounter *vērša* (beef), *teļa* (veal), *cūkas* (pork), *jēra* (lamb), *vistu* or *cāļu* (chicken), *pīle* (duck) and *zoss* (goose), or in the form of *desa* (sausage). *Cūkas galerts* (pork in aspic) is especially tasty and is generally served with *etiķis* (vinegar) and *sinepes* (mustard) or *mārrutki* (horseradish). Meat is served *cepetis* (roast), as *karbonāde* (chops, although often made of minced meat), *frikadeles* (meatballs), *galerts* (aspic), *sautējums* (stew) or *salāti* (salad). Boiled peas with bacon and onions is a common home-made dish (*pelēkie zirņi ar speķi*). Although it is often described as a soup, it is generally thick and could equally be considered to be a stew. It is often described as the national dish of Latvia.

LATVIAN BREAD

Bread in all its forms, from sweet varieties to sour dough, is a great favourite with Latvians. Many areas of the country have their own special bread recipes, and although the baking trade is currently undergoing some consolidation you can still find many regional variations. Jelgava Maiznieks (the bakery of Jelgava, a town to the west of Riga), for example, has branches in Riga, and in the central market you will find many more local breadmakers.

If you would like to try something different, look out for dark rye bread (*ista rupjmaize*), a traditional Latvian bread, baked in a wood-fired oven and containing no additives. The long fermentation process means that the bread can be kept for up to three weeks and also that the vitamins in the bread are better for you than additives. It is often known now as Lāči (bears), the name of one farm bakery which has revived the traditional method of making the bread, and which now even exports large loaves (at 8kg this gives a new meaning to the concept of a large loaf) to the USA. The bread can be found in most food shops and at the central market in Riga (Centrāltirgus). With local caraway cheese, Ķimeņusiers, it makes a filling lunchtime snack.

A RECIPE: PĪRĀGI

Pīrāgi are little pies or pasties and are common in Latvia, although they probably originated in Russian cuisine (the Russians call them pirozhki). They have many fillings, but cabbage and boiled egg is traditional (it tastes better than it sounds).

Pastry

250g flour	3tbsp water
250g margarine	salt

Mix the flour and margarine with a little salt in a mixing bowl and knead the mixture to make pastry. Leave to stand for an hour. Roll the pastry out (it should be as thick as you would make it for a traditional pasty).

Filling

1kg white cabbage, finely chopped	oil or fat
2–3 large onions, finely chopped	2 hard-boiled eggs (chopped into
1 tbsp salt	small pieces); 1 egg

Melt the fat or heat the oil in a pan and add the chopped cabbage and onion. Add salt (according to taste). Brown until the cabbage and onion are soft. Allow to cool.

Roll out the pastry. Use the pastry to make small pouches, filling each with some of the mixture of cabbage and onion, to which you should add the chopped boiled egg. Use the remaining egg (which should be beaten) to seal the pouches; any left over can be used to brush the tops of the completed pīrāgi. Put the pīrāgi on a greased baking tray and bake in the oven (180°C/350°F/gas mark 4) for 20 minutes or until the pīrāgi are golden brown.

Serve on their own or with a bouillon.

The most commonly served vegetables are *bietes* (beetroot), *kāposti* (cabbage), *kartupeļi* (potatoes), *skābie kāposti* (sauerkraut), *burkāni* (carrots), *redīsi* (radishes), *rutki* (black radish), *svaigi gurķi* (cucumbers) and *skābi gurķi* (pickles), *zirņi* (peas), *puķu kāposti* (cauliflower), *sēnes* (mushrooms), *sīpoli* (onions) and *tomāti* (tomatoes). Green vegetables you will often find are *skābenes* (sorrel), *špināti* (spinach), *lociņi* (green onions) and *lapu salāti* (lettuce). Vegetables and greens are prepared in a variety of ways. *Salāti* (salads) are most often dressed with *skābais krējums* (sour cream). *Kartupeļu salāti* (potato salad) is a delight, and when beet, herring and apple are added it becomes *rasols*. Potatoes are also used to make *pankūkas* (pancakes), and are a meal in themselves.

Native fruits include *cigonijas*, quince, which are excellent for making syrups and jams.

Zupas (soups) are popular in Latvia, and appear in numerous variations. *Buljons* (bouillon) often accompanies the meat course or is served with *pīrāgi*. It becomes a full meal when *frikadeles* (meatballs) are added. *Svaigu kāpostu zupa* (cabbage soup) and *zivju-piena zupa* (a milk-based fish soup) make use of local products. For a refreshing summer soup, try *skābeņu* (sorrel), or *biešu* (beetroot). An ancient recipe handed down through the generations and still popular today is *skāba putra* (sour barley soup). It is made with cracked barley, buttermilk, milk and sour cream. It sounds more like a porridge, and indeed *putra* means just that, but it is actually a cold, refreshing soup.

Latvian desserts make extensive use of fresh berries and fruits. In summer, *upenes* (blackcurrants), *dzērvenes* (cranberries), *ērkšķogas* (gooseberries), *jāņogas* (redcurrants), *avenes* (raspberries) and *brūklenes* (red bilberries) are often made into a *ķīsels* (thickened fruit soup) and served cold, either alone or with *buberts* (crème caramel).

Fruit juice, usually cranberry or redcurrant, whipped up with *manna* (a kind of semolina) is a traditional dessert called *debess manna* (manna from heaven), which is usually served with *vanilas mērce* (custard). In winter, dried apples, pears and plums are stewed to make *kompots* (compote) and served with *putu krējums* (whipped cream).

A Latvian birthday, or other celebration, would not be complete without a *kliņģeris*. This rich, yeast coffee bread is shaped in the form of a pretzel, studded with *rozīnes* (raisins) and *mandeles* (almonds), and flavoured with *safrans* (saffron), and/or *kardamons* (cardamon).

Finally, of course there are all manner of *tortes* (cakes), with fillings of jam and buttercream, as well as countless variations of *kūciņas* or *cepumi* (biscuits or cookies).

Drinks

Apart from all the usual drinks, you may come across an unusual concoction called *kvass*, especially in the summer. This refreshing, fermented drink is made from either rye bread or fruit, water, yeast and sugar or honey. It is drunk cold, is not sweet, and is non-alcoholic. A similar drink is *Veselība*, not generally for sale in restaurants but sold in half-litre bottles that make it look like beer, which is also made out of bread and is marketed as a vitamin drink. Another typical Latvian

TIME FOR A BEER?

For a small country Latvia has an awful lot of breweries, and it is not difficult to find many of the local brands at cafés and restaurants in Riga. Two of the most common beers, Aldaris and Cēsu, are now owned by foreign companies, Aldaris by Baltic Beverages Holdings, a joint venture between Scottish and Newcastle and Carlsberg, and Cēsu by the Finnish brewer Olvi, but most of the rest are pure Latvian, produced in local breweries in different parts of the country.

Beer (*alus*) is a traditional Latvian drink. There are many records of beer drinking in medieval times, when hop growing was also common. Over the last few years beer consumption has risen rapidly in Latvia: in 2003 average per capita consumption stood at 53 litres, almost double the level of the early 1990s, but even this level fades into insignificance in comparison with Finland, not to mention Europe's heaviest beer drinkers, the Czech Republic.

Aldaris is the brand leader in Latvia. Its Aldaris Zelta is widely available and has a taste similar to international brands such as Budweiser and Heineken. Cēsu Gaišais, from Latvia's oldest brewery in Cēsis, has a similar taste. If you'd like to try something a little different, you could look for Bauskas, Lāčcplēsis, Piebalgas, Rigas, Tērvetes or Užavas. All of these brands are considered among the best in Latvia and all have distinctive tastes. Note that most brewers produce light (*gaišais*) and dark (*tumšais*) beer, so choose the brand and the type you would like. The Piebalga brewery also produces the Minhauzena (Munchhausen) brand, which is slightly fruity and rather sweet.

drink is *bērzu sula* (birch juice). Birch trees are tapped for their sap in the spring, which is then combined with rye bread crusts, and blackcurrant bush twigs. The mixture is left in a cool place until it reaches the desired degree of tartness. It is then bottled with raisins and stored in a cool place for six weeks.

When it comes to alcoholic drinks, there is no lack of choice in Latvia. Latvians are among the heaviest drinkers in Europe, and traditionally have been the heaviest spirits drinkers. Drinking habits are changing, however: Latvians are now drinking less vodka and liqueurs and more beer (see box, page 63), wine and brandy.

For something that is uniquely Latvian, be sure to pick up a bottle of *Rigas Melnais Balzāms* (Black Balsam), a thick, black drink with a bitter taste, marketed as a medicinal tonic. Supposedly it calms the nerves and is good for an upset stomach. Production of *Melnais Balzāms* was begun in the 1700s in Riga. To this day the exact recipe is a closely guarded secret, but the ingredients (over 25 in all) include: 16 grasses, ginger, oak bark, bitter orange peel, lime blossom, iris roots, nutmeg, peppermint, valerian, brandy and sugar. It is sometimes mixed with vodka or (more recently) Coca-Cola. The distinctive brown ceramic bottle in which it is sold is as well-known in Latvia as the drink itself.

Allažu ķimelis is a caraway-flavoured liqueur. The Latvian government sends the queen of the United Kingdom a case of *Allažu ķimelis* every year, a tradition which began during Latvia's first period of independence. The dessert liqueur *Kursa* is fruit based. You will also come across *Kristal Dzidrais*, a locally made vodka.

Wine is imported, much of it from conventional wine-producing countries, but you will also come across wine from more unusual countries such as Georgia and other parts of the former USSR. Latvia itself is not known for its wine with the exception of its champagne, which is cheap and widely available in restaurants and in supermarkets.

WHAT TO TAKE

Winter can be very cold, so make sure you take enough warm clothes if you are going to Latvia between October and May. June, July and August are usually warmer, but even so you will probably need a jacket or similar most of the time. You should also always take something rainproof, even in summer, since the weather is unreliable, and July and August often have heavy rain. Weather forecasting can be difficult in Latvia due to the closeness to the sea and the frequently changing wind directions, so it is always worth checking an internet weather service just before you leave. See for example www.wunderground.com/global/stations/26422.html.

In Riga you can now buy virtually anything you would expect to find in the shops in any major city. Smaller towns are likely to have less choice. The only special items you might like to consider taking are mosquito repellent (mosquitoes can be a problem in summer – Latvia's lakes and marshlands are ideal breeding grounds) and specialist film or camera equipment.

ELECTRICITY

The electric current in Latvia, as in most of continental Europe, is 220 volts AC, 50 Hz. Plugs are the standard European two-pin variety so take an adaptor from the UK.

MEDIA AND COMMUNICATIONS
Telephones

The country code for Latvia, for calls from outside the country, is 371. To call Riga or Jūrmala from abroad therefore dial 371, plus 2 (the city code) and then the seven-digit number. For all other areas in Latvia, dial 371, followed directly by the seven-digit number.

To make an international call from Latvia, dial 00 followed by the country code and the local number.

Australia	61	France	33	Lithuania	370
Canada	1	Germany	49	UK	44
Estonia	372	Ireland	353	USA	1
Finland	358	Italy	39		

To use a public payphone in Latvia you normally need a phonecard (Telekarte). These can be bought at kiosks, stores, post offices and wherever you see the sign Telekarte, and are available for Ls2, 3 or 5. Some phones also take coins. In Riga, the post office at 1 Stacijas laukums and Plus Punkts kiosks also sell Interkarte, an international pre-paid telephone card that can also be used with mobile phones; tel: 707 3434; www.baltia.net.

Mobile phones
More Latvians now have mobile phones than landlines. To call mobile phones in Riga, just dial the seven-digit code. Contact your service provider before leaving in order to set up international roaming. If your own mobile phone does not operate in Latvia, it is possible to rent one from many shops in the centre of the town or from the better hotels.

For further information on telephoning contact Lattelkom; tel: 800 80 40; www.lattelkom.lv.

Useful telephone numbers
Fire	01
Police	02
Ambulance	03
Directory enquiries	118 (Lattelkom) or 117 (private directory service)
Tourist information	703 7900

Internet
All major hotels in Riga have a business centre offering a full range of services including internet access but the charges are high. An alternative in Riga is internet cafés, including those listed below. Most offer internet access for Ls0.45-0.50 per hour. Outside Riga you will find some internet cafés in cities such as Daugavpils, Liepāja and Ventspils, but very few elsewhere. See the *Riga* chapter (page 90) for internet café addresses.

WiFi
The number of wireless hotspots in Riga is growing all the time. If your laptop is equipped with a Wireless LAN card, you should be able to go online at most large hotels and many cafés/restaurants.

Post
There are post offices in most towns. Look for the sign *Pasts*. The most convenient post office (Latvijas Pasts) in Riga is at 19 Brīvības bulvāris; www.pasts.lv and is open 07.00–22.00 Monday–Friday, 08.00–20.00 on Saturdays and Sundays.

Local media
The *Baltic Times*, published weekly on a Thursday, is the best English-language source of news for all three Baltic republics. It also lists exhibitions and concerts.

In addition no fewer than five bi-monthly guides are widely available at no cost. At the airport you can usually pick up the latest *Riga This Week* while you are waiting for your luggage to be delivered. If not, your hotel will certainly provide a copy and/or a copy of *Riga in Your Pocket, Riga Guide, Welcome* or the *City Paper* (which also covers Tallinn and Vilnius). Of these the most informative are *Riga in Your Pocket*, an independent review, and *Riga This Week*. These can be accessed online if you need information prior to your trip to Riga: www.inyourpocket.com and www.rigathisweek.lv.

European editions of British and American newspapers are on sale in Riga at the larger hotels on the day of publication.

Although there are no local radio or television stations that transmit in English, if you have access to FM radio you may be interested in:

96.2	Radio Naba	A student station playing all types of non-classical music
99.5	Russkoje Radio	Easy listening Russian channel
100.5	BBC World Service	
103.7	Klassika	Classical music
105.2	Radio SWH	Popular Latvian music

DOING BUSINESS IN LATVIA

The Latvian government is keen to attract foreign business. Details of specific help available can be obtained from the Latvian Development Agency, 2 Pērses iela, Riga LV 1442; tel: 703 9400; fax: 703 9401; email: invest@lda.gov.lv; www.lda.gov.lv, from the Latvian Chamber of Commerce, 21 Brīvības bulvāris, Riga LV 1849; tel: 722 5595; fax: 782 0092; email: info@chamber.lv and from city councils such as Riga City Council, 3 Kr Valdemāra iela, Riga LV1539; tel: 800 0800; fax: 702 6337; email: dome@rcc.lv; www.rcc.lv.

Many major international accountants have offices in Riga and can assist with investment and business. They include:

Deloitte & Touche 2 Bīskapa gāte; tel: 781 4160; www.deloitte.com
KPMG Latvia 33 Valdemāra iela, Riga; tel: 703 8000; email: kpmg@kpmg.lv; www.kpmg.lv
PriceWaterhouseCoopers 19 Valdemāra iela; tel: 709 4400; email: riga.general@pwcglobal.com; www.pwcglobal.com

Lawyers with English-speaking staff include:

Hough, Vilcinš, Seppala & Palubinskas 34–38 Valdemāra iela; tel: 731 5396; email: latlaw@apollo.lv
Skudra & Udris Law Offices 13 Marijas iela (in the Berga bazārs); tel: 781 2078; email: attorneys@su.lv; www.su.lv

There is a **business centre** in the Radisson Hotel: Amberland, 24 Kuģu iela, Riga; tel: 706 1111; and at the Maritim Park Hotel, 1 Slokas iela; tel: 706 9000.

Translation services are offered by a number of agencies in Riga, including: Baltija NS, 33-201 Raiņa bulvāris; tel: 721 0046; Roberts Līsmanis, 8 Laipu iela; tel: 950 6192; Strombus, 28 Aspāzijas bulvāris; tel: 722 4376; fax: 722 4283; email: strombus@com.latnet.lv; www.strombus.lv.

Photocopying shops and services are widely available in Riga and can be found in all major city centres. Prices range from Ls0.03–0.05 per page. Fax delivery services are available at the Central Post Office, 19 Brīvības bulvāris; tel: 701 8740. Mobile phones can be hired from a wide range of shops in central Riga.

OTHER PRACTICALITIES
Toilets
Men's toilets are often marked **t**, women's **s**. V (*vīrieši*) or K (*kungi*) are also used for men, and S (*sievietes*) or D (*dāmas*) for women.

Smoking
Despite recent government efforts, smoking continues to be popular in Latvia. Smoking is illegal in public buildings but allowed in restaurants and bars. A recent attempt by Jūrmala to ban smoking on its beaches has been declared illegal although the government has said that in future it intends to allow cities and towns to decide for themselves whether to ban smoking or not. As around 33% of the total population and about 50% of Latvian men smoke (compared with 28% in the UK and 25% of adults in the USA), businesses fear that a ban on smoking could ruin their trade.

USEFUL ADDRESSES
Foreign embassies in Latvia
Many countries now have an embassy in Riga, but some countries are represented from elsewhere. Below is a list of the major countries which have embassies or similar representation in Riga:

Belarus 12 Jēsusbaznīcas iela; tel: 722 2560; fax: 732 2891; email: latvia@belembassy.org; www.belembassy.org
Canada 20–22 Baznīcas iela; tel: 781 3945; fax: 781 3960; email: Riga@dfait-maei.qc.ca; www.dfait-maeci.qc.ca
Estonia 13 Skolas iela; tel: 781 2020; fax: 781 2029; email: embassy.riga@mfa.ee; www.estemb.lv
Finland 1 Kalpaka bulvāris; tel: 707 8817; fax: 707 8814; email: rii.sanomat@formin.fi; www.finland.lv
Ireland (Consulate) 54 Brīvības iela; tel: 702 5259; fax: 702 5223
Lithuania 24 Rūpniecības iela; tel: 732 1519; fax: 732 1589
Russia 2 Antonijas iela; tel: 733 2151; fax: 783 0209; email: rusembas@delfi.lv; www.latvia.mid.ru
UK 5 Alunāna iela; tel: 777 4700; fax: 777 4707; email: british.embassy@apollo.lv; www.britain.lv
USA 7 Raiņa bulvāris; tel: 703 6200; fax: 782 0047; email: pas@usaembassy.lv; www.usembassy.lv

Tourist information offices
All Latvian tourist offices produce detailed brochures with local and national information for visitors, nearly always in English. For further suggested reading see *Appendix 3*.

To telephone or fax the numbers given below, dial your local international code followed by 371, the country code for Latvia. The tourist office in Riga can supply information about the whole of Latvia: 7 Rātslaukums; tel: 703 7900; email: tourinfo@rcc.lv; www.rigatourism.com (the office is in the House of the Blackheads – see page 110).

Other tourist information offices include:

Bauska 1 Rātslaukums; tel: 39 23797; email: tourinfo@bauska.lv; www.bauska.lv
Cēsis 9 Pils laukums; tel: 41 21815; email: info@cesis.lv; www.tourism.cesis.lv
Daugavpils 22 Rigas iela; tel: 54 32916; email: tourinfor@daugavpils.apollo.lv; www.daugavpils.lv
Jēkabpils 3 Vecpilsētas laukums; tel: 52 33822; email:jektic@apollo.lv; www.jekabpils.lv

Jelgava 37 Pasta iela iela; tel: 30 22751; email: rica@jrp.lv; www.jrp.lv
Jūrmala 42 Jomas iela, Majori; tel: 776 4493; email: jurmalainfo@mail.bkc.lv; www.jurmala.lv
Kuldīga 5 Baznīcas iela; tel: 33 22259; email: tourinfo@kuldiga.lv; www.kuldiga.lv
Liepāja Hotel Līva, 11 Lielā iela; tel: 34 80808; email: ltib@apollo.lv; www.liepaja.lv
Sigulda 6 Pils iela; tel: 797 1335; email: info@sigulda.lv; www.sigulda.lv
Talsi 19–21 Lielā iela; tel: 32 24165; email: talsutic@apollo.lv; www.talsi.lv
Tukums 3 Pils iela; tel: 31 24451; email: tuktic@tukums.park.lv; www.tukums.lv
Valmiera 2 Lāčplēša iela; tel: 42 07177; email: tic@valmiera.lv; www.valmiera.lv
Ventspils 7 Tirgus iela; tel: 36 22263; email: tourism@ventspils.lv;
www.ventspils.tourism.lv

For tourist offices in other towns in Latvia, see www.rigatourism.com

Other addresses
American Chamber of Commerce 1–2 Torņa iela, Riga; tel: 721 2204; email:
amcham@amcham.lv; www.amcham.lv
British Chamber of Commerce Office 605, 21 Valdemāra iela, Riga; tel: 703 5202
British Council 5a Blaumaņa iela, Riga; tel: 728 5361; email: mail@britishcouncil.lv;
www.britishcouncil.lv
Goethe Institute 1 Torņa iela, Riga; tel: 750 8200; email: rigainfo@goethe.lv;
www.goethe.de/riga
Latvian Chamber of Commerce 21 Brīvības iela, Riga; tel: 722 5595; email:
info@chamber.lv

LOCAL CHARITIES
Over the past ten years the amount of voluntary work and the number of NGOs
(non-governmental organisations) has expanded rapidly in Latvia. Most NGOs are
small and around two-thirds work in small towns and villages. The most common
activities are education and training, and environment-related work.

UNESCO is looking for support to build a new national library, the Castle of
Light. The library has been designed by the Latvian-born architect Gunars Birkerts
(see page 28) and a site found, but funds are needed to make the project a reality.
A foundation has been set up backed by UNESCO. To contact the foundation: 85
Brīvības iela, LV 1001 Riga; tel: 784 3767; email: inbaf@inbaf.lv.

FCO TRAVEL ADVICE
know before you go
fco.gov.uk/travel

Bradt Travel Guides is a partner to the 'know before you go'
campaign, masterminded by the UK Foreign and Commonwealth
Office to promote the importance of finding out about a destination
before you travel. By combining the up-to-date advice of the
FCO with the in-depth knowledge of Bradt authors, you'll ensure
that your trip will be as trouble-free as possible.

www.fco.gov.uk/knowbeforeyougo

Part Two

The Country

Bradt Travel Guides

Africa by Road Charlie Shackell/Illya Bracht
Albania Gillian Gloyer
Amazon, The Roger Harris/Peter Hutchison
Antarctica: A Guide to the Wildlife
 Tony Soper/Dafila Scott
Arctic: A Guide to Coastal Wildlife
 Tony Soper/Dan Powell
Armenia with Nagorno Karabagh Nicholas Holding
Azores David Sayers
Baghdad Catherine Arnold
Baltic Capitals: Tallinn, Riga, Vilnius, Kaliningrad
 Neil Taylor et al
Bosnia & Herzegovina Tim Clancy
Botswana: Okavango, Chobe, Northern Kalahari
 Chris McIntyre
British Isles: Wildlife of Coastal Waters
 Tony Soper/Dan Powell
Budapest Adrian Phillips/Jo Scotchmer
Cameroon Ben West
Canada: North – Yukon, Northwest Territories,
 Nunavut Geoffrey Roy
Cape Verde Islands Aisling Irwin/
 Colum Wilson
Cayman Islands Tricia Hayne
Chile Tim Burford
Chile & Argentina: Trekking Guide
 Tim Burford
Cork Linda Fallon
Croatia Piers Letcher
Dubrovnik Piers Letcher
East & Southern Africa: The Backpacker's Manual
 Philip Briggs
Eccentric America Jan Friedman
Eccentric Britain Benedict le Vay
Eccentric California Jan Friedman
Eccentric Edinburgh Benedict le Vay
Eccentric France Piers Letcher
Eccentric London Benedict le Vay
Eccentric Oxford Benedict le Vay
Ecuador: Climbing & Hiking in
 Rob Rachowiecki/Mark Thurber
Eritrea Edward Denison/Edward Paice
Estonia Neil Taylor
Ethiopia Philip Briggs
Falkland Islands Will Wagstaff
Faroe Islands James Proctor
Gabon, São Tome & Príncipe Sophie Warne
Galápagos Wildlife David Horwell/Pete Oxford
Gambia, The Craig Emms/Linda Barnett
Georgia with Armenia Tim Burford
Ghana Philip Briggs
Hungary Adrian Phillips/Jo Scotchmer
Iran Patricia L Baker
Iraq Karen Dabrowska
Kabul Dominic Medley/Jude Barrand

Kenya Claire Foottit
Kiev Andrew Evans
Latvia Stephen Baister/Chris Patrick
Lille Laurence Phillips
Lithuania Gordon McLachlan
Ljubljana Robin & Jenny McKelvie
Macedonia Thammy Evans
Madagascar Hilary Bradt
Madagascar Wildlife Nick Garbutt/
 Hilary Bradt/Derek Schuurman
Malawi Philip Briggs
Maldives Royston Ellis
Mali Ross Velton
Mauritius, Rodrigues & Réunion Royston Ellis/
 Alex Richards/Derek Schuurman
Mongolia Jane Blunden
Montenegro Annalisa Rellie
Mozambique Philip Briggs/Ross Velton
Namibia Chris McIntyre
Nigeria Lizzie Williams
North Cyprus Diana Darke
North Korea Robert Willoughby
Palestine, with Jerusalem Henry Stedman
Panama Sarah Woods
Paris, Lille & Brussels: Eurostar Cities
 Laurence Phillips
Peru & Bolivia: Backpacking and Trekking
 Hilary Bradt/Kathy Jarvis
Riga Stephen Baister/Chris Patrick
River Thames, In the Footsteps of the Famous
 Paul Goldsack
Rwanda Janice Booth/Philip Briggs
St Helena, Ascension, Tristan da Cunha
 Sue Steiner
Serbia Laurence Mitchell
Seychelles Lyn Mair/Lynnath Beckley
Slovenia Robin & Jenny McKelvie
South Africa: Budget Travel Guide Paul Ash
Southern African Wildlife Mike Unwin
Sri Lanka Royston Ellis
Sudan Paul Clammer
Svalbard Andreas Umbreit
Switzerland: Rail, Road, Lake Anthony Lambert
Tallinn Neil Taylor
Tanzania Philip Briggs
Tasmania Matthew Brace
Tibet Michael Buckley
Uganda Philip Briggs
Ukraine Andrew Evans
USA by Rail John Pitt
Venezuela Hilary Dunsterville Branch
Your Child Abroad Dr Jane Wilson-Howarth/
 Dr Matthew Ellis
Zambia Chris McIntyre
Zanzibar David Else

Bradt guides are available from all good bookshops, or by post, fax, phone or internet direct from:
Bradt Travel Guides, 19 High Street, Chalfont St Peter, Bucks SL9 9QE, UK
Tel: +44 (0)1753 893444   Fax: +44 (0)1753 892333
Email: info@bradtguides.com   Web: www.bradtguides.com

Riga

Riga is the largest and most cosmopolitan of all the Baltic capitals and is by a long way the most interesting town or city in Latvia. It is located on the Daugava River about 15km from the point where the Daugava meets the Baltic Sea in the southeastern corner of the Gulf of Riga. Riga can trace its history to the beginning of the 13th century, but it was in the course of the Middle Ages that it developed into a Hanseatic city, and by the 18th to 19th century it had grown into one of Europe's leading ports and industrial centres. By the late 19th/early 20th century it had also become a cultural centre, famous for its opera, theatre and music. It celebrated its 800th anniversary in 2001.

The modern city is divided into two main parts by the city canal that flows through the elegant parks which separate the historic Old Town from most of the New Town, with its shops, offices and suburbs. The air of elegance and spaciousness created by the area of open space in what is otherwise the centre of a busy capital has led to Riga being compared to Paris by a number of guidebook and travel writers. There is some justification in the comparison. Even when Latvia was part of the Soviet Union, Riga was more sophisticated than Russian Soviet cities and towns, since it had better shops and the odd decent restaurant and café. Now its medieval and art nouveau architecture and well-kept parks allow the comparison to continue. There are several modern, international hotels, many good cafés and restaurants, and small and pleasant shops stocking local art and international brands. In 1992–93 the local authority privatised about 90% of Riga's shops, from the large GUM (State Universal Store) in the Old Town, to the small bookshops and tobacconists.

Between 1945 and 1991 Riga grew enormously, largely as a result of Soviet expansion, which generally took the form of building enormous, drab, low-quality blocks of flats in the suburbs. One of the first, called Kengarags, can be seen along the Daugava and plenty can also be seen on the trip from the airport to the city centre. Since Latvia regained independence in 1991 an immense amount of restoration work has gone on in central Riga, and the city is well on the way to being one of the most attractive capitals in Europe.

The present population is estimated at 739,232, down from its peak of over 900,000 at the end of the period of Soviet occupation. Even now only about 42% is Latvian and about 43% Russian (the balance is made up mainly of Poles, Belarussians and Ukrainians). Over half the population (about 54%) is female.

Until Latvia's independence from the Soviet Union in 1991 Russian was the predominant language heard in Riga. Over the past 13 years Latvian has been regaining ground, but Russian is still widely spoken.

HISTORY
Foundation

Archaeological excavations indicate that the area now occupied by Riga was probably inhabited and operated as a trading centre as early as the 2nd century BC. The first mention of the modern city can be traced to 1201 when Bishop Albert von Buxhoevden (or Buksherden) of Bremen established the *locus Riga* and the first German fortress. In 1202 Albert founded the *fratres militiae Christi*, the Knights of the Sword, whose aim was to win over the territories occupied by the Livs, Latgals, Zemgals and Cours to Christianity. Thus Riga celebrated its official 800th anniversary in 2001. The *Chronicles of Arnold of Lübeck*, for example, refer to the founding of an episcopal see of Livonia in a place called Riga in 1186. However, whether 1201 was really the date of its foundation is doubtful since Albert had been preceded by Abbot Berthold (who in turn had taken over from the Augustinian Meinhard) whose death in battle in 1198 marked the initial repulsion of German invaders. Albert had come to restore German rule with the aid of 23 ships of merchants, sailors and armed men. By 1207 Livonia was established as part of the German Empire, when Albert was formally given it by Philip of Swabia as an imperial fief.

In 1201 the Cours attacked Riga but failed to defeat the Germans who held the town firmly; however, it was primarily in the towns (notably Riga, as well as Reval – now Tallinn – and Tartu – then Dorpat – both of which are in what is now Estonia) that the Germans were strong, not the surrounding countryside. Riga was constantly under attack from hostile outside elements. A major setback in German domination occurred in 1236 when the Knights of the Sword were defeated by an army of Zemgals and Samogitians (a tribe in what is now Lithuania) at the Battle of Saule. However, in 1237 the weakened Knights of the Sword amalgamated with a stronger order of knights, the Teutonic Order, to form the Livonian Order. As a result, German control of Livonia was firmly established. It was to last for the next three centuries.

In spite of the fact that during the 13th century Riga suffered from no fewer than five major fires (in 1215, 1264, 1272, 1293 and 1297), which eventually gave rise to a law prohibiting the construction of wooden houses inside the town walls, the town prospered as a trading centre, joining the Hanseatic League in 1282.

Despite the prosperity, there was constant tension between the citizens and their rulers, giving rise to numerous battles and reprisals. In 1300 the Pope was obliged to intervene and promise that no more than ten knights would be stationed in Riga at any one time. However, the knights simply took control of the shipping on the Daugava. A battle ensued, entailing a 13-month siege at the end of which Riga capitulated (March 18 1330) again to the German knights, promising them a new castle.

The foundations of the new castle were laid in 1330 but building continued until 1353. In 1483–84 the castle was again stormed by the people of Riga who tore it down stone by stone; however, by 1491 the knights had reasserted themselves and again a new castle was built.

The Reformation

In 1521 St Peter's Church began to operate as a centre for Reformation doctrine; in 1524 the first Latvian Evangelical Lutheran congregation was formed at St James's Church. In 1525 Walter von Plettenberg secured permission for the Lutheran doctrine to be taught, and preachers such as Andreas Knopken and Silvester Tegetmeyer preached the new Reformation theology so that Lutheran teachings gained a foothold in Riga. Catholicism retreated: Catholic churches were demolished, and religious paintings and carvings were destroyed. In 1562 the last master of the Livonian Order left the castle, and the Livonian state gradually shook off the German influence. By the end of the Livonian wars (1558–83) Riga had fallen to the Russians.

The end of the 16th century marks a period of instability, and Russia (under Ivan the Terrible), Poland, Denmark and Sweden all laid claim to the city. An attempt by the Polish king, Stephen Bathory, to stage a counter-reformation in 1582 failed, although a Polish-Lithuanian kingdom prevailed for a short period until the Polish–Swedish war.

The Polish–Swedish War

The Polish–Swedish War of 1599–1629 ended as far as Riga was concerned when it fell to Gustavus Adolphus II in 1621. Following the Peace of Oliva of 1660, Riga became the second capital of Sweden. Again there was a period of commercial success and prosperity. In 1663 a water supply was established using wooden pipes. In 1681 Riga's first newspaper, the *Rigische Nouvellen*, was established. In 1685 the first Bible was printed in Latvian. In the same year a number of large rocks that blocked navigation of the Daugava were removed by explosion. In 1701 a pontoon bridge was built over the Daugava – it was the longest in the world.

The Northern War

The year 1700 saw the beginning of the end of Swedish rule. This was the year in which the so-called Northern War started between Russia, Poland, Denmark and Sweden. The Northern War lasted until 1721 when Sweden ceded Estonia, Livonia and Karelia to Tsar Peter I of Russia under the terms of the Treaty of Nystadt. However, the war ended much earlier for Riga. In 1709 the city's food supplies were severely depleted as a result of unprecedented flooding (most food was stored in cellars). In July 1710, after an eight-month siege, the Russian general, Count Sheremetyev, was able to enter the city, which was forced by plague and hunger to present him with the keys. Under the terms of the Treaty of Nystadt, Peter I guaranteed to leave the rights of Riga and the surrounding provinces intact, so the people continued to enjoy freedom of religion and education, and the guilds and livery companies remained unaffected.

Riga in the 18th century

This period was by no means a bad one for Riga. Peter I married the fourth daughter of Ernst Glück, the Lutheran pastor who translated the Bible into Latvian. She became Catherine I of Russia. Writing in German of the time he spent in Riga between 1764 and 1789 Johann Gottfried Herder (see page 108) wrote 'I lived, taught and behaved in such a free and such an unrestrained way in Livonia that I can hardly imagine living and behaving like that again.' In 1743 street lighting was introduced. In 1782 a theatre was established (where Wagner conducted from 1837–39). Riga was also a place of intellectual and scientific enlightenment in the 18th century. In 1798 Dr Otto Herr introduced vaccination against smallpox, and in 1802 the Latvian pharmacist Grindels founded the Society of Pharmacy, which started a trend for the formation of a whole range of medical and scientific associations. In 1801 torture was abolished as part of the legal process, as was public execution.

The 18th century also saw a growth of Latvian cultural awareness. Whilst Herder wrote his *Fragmente über die neuere deutsche Literatur (Fragments on Recent German Literature)* while in Riga, in 1774 he published a number of Latvian folk songs in German translation, and in 1796 G H Merkel published his *Latvians, particularly in Vidzeme, at the end of the Philosophical Century* in which he described the misery of serfdom.

The role of the Baltic Germans in the commercial development of Riga is discussed under *History* (see *Chapter 2*).

Riga in the 19th century

Riga avoided the effects of the Napoleonic Wars; although Napoleon had threatened to attack 'this suburb of London', he never reached it. As Napoleon's troops under the leadership of the Prussian field marshal, Jork, approached Riga in 1812, the governor-general of Riga set the wooden houses of the Riga suburbs on fire to deflect the invaders. In the wake of the French Revolution, the wave of liberation that swept across Europe made itself felt in Riga too, and in 1817 serfs were emancipated, 40 years before Russia. In 1830 farmers gained the right to live in the cities. In 1840 a rural education law was passed. Soon an educated rural class grew up, starting up trade in Riga and other towns. Jews were only given rights of residence in Riga in the mid 19th century, before which most were itinerant traders. By the outbreak of World War I in 1914, their numbers in Riga had reached about 100,000 and they were active both in commerce and in the academic world.

In 1857–58 the town walls were dismantled to allow expansion. In 1861 the railway came and the postal service was expanded. Riga gradually developed into a major industrial centre and the first shipyard opened in 1869. Telephones arrived in 1877; horse-drawn trams appeared, and a major bicycle factory was established. In 1887 an electric power generation station was built. This industrialisation also brought a huge increase in the population of Riga: in 1767 the town had 16,300 inhabitants; 100 years later the population had grown to 102,590 (of whom about 20–25% were Latvian). By 1897 the population doubled to 255,879, but the Latvian population now accounted for almost 50%. A prosperous Latvian working class and middle class began to emerge.

Parallel to this industrial expansion came a growth in Latvian nationalism. Latvian newspapers, notably *Tas Latviešu Ļaužu Draugs* (*The Friend of the Latvian People*), had appeared since the 1820s and 1830s, but Russian remained the language of education, government and the legal system. However, Krišjānis Barons's work in collecting Latvia's *dainas* and the establishment of a folk song festival in Riga in 1873 gave impetus to the movement called the Latvian Awakening, which grew out of the Riga Latvian Association. The Latvian Association published a Latvian encyclopaedia, founded a national opera and a national theatre. The folk song festival gave birth to a national anthem, *Dievs Svētī Latviju* ('God Bless Latvia').

The thrust of the National Awakening Movement was, however, primarily anti-German and somewhat pro-Russian. It turned its back on the architecture of Germany (manifest in the castle, the cathedral and the churches of St Peter and St James) yet did not object to the construction of Orthodox churches. It did, however, demand equality of treatment for the Latvian language.

Riot and revolution

The end of the 19th century was also a time of growing working-class political awareness. In 1899 women workers at the Džuta textile mill went on strike. The police intervened, and before long demonstrations began in the course of which five workers were shot dead and 31 wounded. A full-scale riot soon ensued.

In 1900 Lenin set up his revolutionary magazine *Iskra* (*The Spark*) in Zürich, and in 1904 the Latvian Social Democratic Party was formed, the most significant movement of its kind in imperial Russia.

On January 13 1905 a demonstration of the poor and working classes was put down with force in Moscow. The demonstrators had wanted to show solidarity with demonstrators who had gathered four days earlier in front of the tsar's palace in St Petersburg to hand in a petition seeking political reform. A demonstration in support also began in Riga, but again it was put down by force of arms and over 70 people were killed. The Social Democratic Party began to organise resistance, and by October Riga was in the grip of a general strike. Armed peasants attacked German landowners, and other strikers attacked the prison, aiming to free a number of political prisoners.

Before the end of the year Russian troops moved to regain control, putting the revolution down with particular brutality in which over 900 peasants and teachers were executed under martial law, and thousands were exiled to Siberia. The Russian authorities aimed their vengeance especially at teachers who were known for their social-democratic leanings.

Many Latvian intellectuals only escaped by fleeing to the West. The writer, Jānis Rainis, fled to Switzerland, Kārlis Ulmanis, the chairman of the peasants' party, who was later to become president of Latvia, sought refuge in the United States.

A new 1906 Latvian constitution gave limited recognition to Latvian nationalist aspirations by allowing, for example, Latvian to be used for teaching in schools.

World War I

The outbreak of World War I drove Latvia into the arms of the Russians with whom they allied themselves against the German foe. In 1915 German forces were approaching Riga. In a manic evacuation, the Russians moved Riga's industry and about 96,000 workers to Russia. Even the power station was dismantled and moved. In all, about one-third of the total population of Latvia was forced to leave the country. In 1917 German troops crossed the Daugava, and the capital surrendered to the Germans.

In the same year, however, the Russian Revolution was making its consequences felt. Whilst some political elements in Riga sought the annexation of Latvia to the German Empire, others were looking to Soviet power to free their country from the Germans. In spring 1918 Latvia was split into three: Kurzeme and Riga went to Germany, Latgale to Russia, and the rest of Vidzeme (other than Riga) was left unmolested. However, following the defeat of Germany, on November 18 1918, in the Riga national theatre an independent republic of Latvia was proclaimed, and Kārlis Ulmanis was given the task of forming a provisional government. A period of what amounted to civil war ensued, the Russians supporting Latvia against the persistent exercise of German military force. Only on August 11 1920 was a peace treaty signed between Latvia and the Soviet Union following the final expulsion of German troops from Latvia in December 1919.

The first Latvian independence

The period between the two world wars is often referred to as the first period of Latvian independence. The 1920 treaty provided for the Soviet Union and Latvia to recognise each other as states. In 1922 Latvia adopted its own constitution and issued its own currency. Jānis Čakste was elected as the first president (see page 205).

Riga was not immune to the depression that gripped most of Europe during the 1930s and unemployment rose to high levels. On May 15 1934 Ulmanis mounted a coup and formed an authoritarian administration. Democratic socialists were imprisoned, political parties of both left and right were banned, and freedom of the press was curtailed. In 1935, the Freedom Monument was erected in the centre of Riga.

World War II

Under the terms of the pact between Hitler and Stalin of August 23 1939 it was agreed that the Baltic States would fall under the sphere of influence of the Soviet Union. By the end of that year the Soviet Union had already begun to establish a military presence in Latvia.

On June 17 1940 Soviet troops marched in to take over the country and establish a pro-Soviet regime. On July 21 'elections' were held under Soviet auspices and a new government and parliament declared Latvia to be a republic of the USSR. Ulmanis was deported, as were thousands of citizens from Riga and elsewhere in Latvia, many of them to Siberia or central Asia.

In June 1941 the USSR was forced to join in the war when they were attacked by Germany. Latvia was unprepared, and on July 1 1941 Hitler's troops arrived in Riga to 'liberate' it from Stalin's USSR, causing the Russians to retreat, leaving devastation in their wake. Stalin had murdered or deported a substantial proportion of the Jewish population in Riga as enemies of the people; Hitler imposed his anti-Semitic policies, massacring Jews at Rumbula and Biķernieki, and establishing concentration camps.

Riga was 'liberated' on October 13 1944. The German occupation of Kurzeme continued until May 1945 when the Red Army arrived again to 'liberate' Riga from the Germans. The retreating Germans destroyed houses, factories, roads and bridges, and thousands of Latvians fled to the west.

The USSR

After the end of World War II the USSR provided economic assistance to Latvia, and Russian immigrants took the places left by the fleeing or slaughtered native Latvian population. However, the Soviet 'liberators' were not welcomed: many Latvians formed resistance groups and fighting ensued until Stalin intervened with his usual brutality.

However, Latvian nationalism whilst repressed was not extinguished. In 1988, 5,000 demonstrators gathered in Riga on June 14 to commemorate the deportations, and on August 23, 10,000 demonstrators gathered to mark the anniversary of the Hitler–Stalin pact. In the meantime in June at a meeting of the Latvian Writers' Union a resolution was passed that led to the founding of the Popular Front of Latvia in October 1988 that was to campaign for political, cultural and economic independence.

Liberation/independence

In 1989 Latvia experienced its first free elections of deputies to the Supreme Soviet of the USSR. This event was followed by the passing of laws in the Latvian Supreme Soviet proclaiming the sovereignty of the Latvian Soviet Socialist Republic and declaring Latvian the official language of the country. Latvia was again on the road to independence. On November 18 1989 over 500,000 people gathered on the banks of the Daugava in Riga to mark the 71st anniversary of Latvia's independence.

On May 4 1990 the Supreme Soviet of Latvia met in the pre-war Saeima building and passed a resolution on 'the renewal of Independence of the Republic of Latvia'.

A period of instability followed as the Latvian Communist Party endeavoured to take back the helm of government, staging a coup in January 1991 which, however, failed. A plebiscite held in March 1991 resulted in three-quarters of the population voting to secede from the Soviet Union. On August 25 1991 Iceland became the first country to recognise the new independent Baltic state, but others soon followed, and by the end of the year the Republic of Latvia had been granted admission to the UN.

A new constitution proclaiming Latvia as an independent democratic republic was adopted in 1992. Riga was once more the capital of an independent democratic state.

Since then Riga has made huge efforts to establish itself not only as a vibrant capital of Latvia but also as the major city in the Baltics. Although in terms of size it is the largest of the Baltic capitals, in terms of influence it faces tough competition from the other Baltic capitals. Even within Latvia, its trading status is frequently under threat from the port of Ventspils. Major strides have, however, been made in improving the city. Many buildings have been restored or rebuilt (most notably the Blackheads' House, see page 110), infrastructure has been improved and the economy expanded. Since its accession to NATO and the European Union in 2004, the city looks forward to consolidating this progress and establishing itself as a major European capital.

GETTING AROUND
Seeing Riga
It is best to see Riga on foot. The Old Town is a relatively small area, and if pushed for time, you could walk round most of it in a day, although that will only give you a superficial impression. To see the Old Town more thoroughly and to see something of the New Town, you should allow two days. A car is not much use: access to the Old Town is restricted for cars (see page 55), and parking in the New Town can be hard to find. There are, however, some guarded car parks, including 2 Prāgas iela (close to the bus station), 8 Basteja bulvāris, and 31 11 Novembra krastmala. Parking areas are signposted with the word *Autostāvvieta*.

A number of firms offer city tours by coach. It is probably best to organise these through your hotel if you are staying in one that offers this facility. Otherwise you can contact one of the agencies below:

Latvia Tours 8 Kaļķu iela; tel: 708 5057; and 13 Marijas iela; tel: 724 3391. Does city tours from 10.00–13.00 Mon and Sat May–Sep, and also offers regular trips to the Open Air Museum and Motor Museum (see page 126), Rundāle (see page 206) and Sigulda. Trips to Cēsis, Jūrmala and Liepāja can also be arranged.
Patricia LTD 22 Elizabetes iela; tel: 728 4868; email: tour@balticguide.net. Various tours for groups – minibus tours, walking tours, Jewish Riga tours etc. Also offers trips to Sigulda.
Riga Sightseeing (Amber Way); tel: 703 7900; email: amberway@inbox.lv. Daily departures from the Latvian Riflemen's Monument and individual sightseeing around Latvia and the Baltic States. Walking tours as well as tours by bus.

Public transport
Buses and trams
Riga has a well-developed transport system of eight tram lines, 24 trolleybus lines and 39 bus lines. The fare is charged at a flat rate of 20 santīmi (Ls0.20) a journey. Different tickets are needed for each mode of transport and can only be bought on board from the *konduktors*. In addition to the bus, tram and trolleybus, there is another form of transport, the *taksobuss* or *mikroautobuss*, which covers longer distances and costs more, depending on the length of the journey.

The maps in *Riga in Your Pocket* and the yellow Jāņa Sēta Riga map contain information showing public transport routes. There are no route maps at bus/tram stops or inside the buses and trams, but the driver normally announces the name of the approaching stop and other passengers are generally helpful if you ask for directions.

The bus station (*autoosta*) is in Rīgas iela, close to the main market and on the other side of the railway station (under the bridge) away from the city centre. You

THE RIGA CARD

The Riga Card provides access without further charge to trams, buses and trains in Riga and Jūrmala, as well as entitling the holder to free admission or a discount at certain museums. The card costs Ls8 for 24 hours, Ls12 for 48 hours and Ls16 for 72 hours (half price for children under 16). It can be purchased from most hotels, the airport (arrivals hall) and the tourist information office. Although it is convenient, most tourists do not spend this amount of money per day if they pay for individual journeys and tickets as they go.

can telephone for information (tel: 900 0009), but may find it advisable to attend in person: timetables are on display, otherwise apply to window 1 for information. Some ticket sellers also speak English.

Trains

Riga has a brand-new, sparkling railway station (Stacijas laukums; tel: 583 2134 for information, or 583 3397 for advance booking; see www.ldz.lv for timetables and fares), although the same cannot be said of the local trains. Tickets can be bought in the main ticket hall from counters 1 to 13. Most staff selling tickets speak English. The timetables show the track (*ceļš*) the train leaves from. When you go to your train, you will also see the word *perons* (platform) with a number. Ignore this and look for the right track (*ceļš*).

Taxis

Taxis are plentiful. You can flag them down anywhere in Riga but in the Old Town there are normally several waiting at both ends of Kaļķu iela, just near the Hotel de Rome and just beyond the Riflemen's Monument. Licensed cabs (these all have yellow licence plates) are fairly reliable provided you check that the meter is on. Rates are 30 santīmi per kilometre during the day, rising to 40 santīmi per kilometre between 22.00 and 06.00. If you want to save money, avoid using taxis waiting outside hotels, as these tend to charge above average rates. To book a taxi, use one of the following free 24-hour numbers: Bona Taxi 800 5050; Riga Taxi 800 1010; Rigas Taksometru parks: tel. 800 1313.

Car hire

See page 54.

Local information

If you need detailed information, suggestions for particular trips or other specialist information, the staff at the tourist office will be pleased to help. The tourist office can also arrange guides. It is located in the Old Town in the Blackheads' House at 7 Rātslaukums; tel: 704 4377; fax: 704 4378; email: tourinfo@rcc.lv; www.rigatourism.com. Open 10.00–18.00.

Riga is also exceptionally well provided with regularly updated and free city guides, which will answer many of your queries. See page 66 for details.

ACCOMMODATION

Riga offers a wide choice of accommodation. If money is no object, you can choose from an ever- growing number of luxury hotels, many conveniently situated in the Old Town. For budget travellers there are some very acceptable options too: some of these are located away from the centre but most are on tram routes, which makes getting into the Old Town an easy and relatively quick matter.

Particularly in the summer period, it is definitely advisable to book well ahead if you want a room in a particular price range or location. You will always find somewhere to stay in Riga, but it may not be exactly what you want, if you have not arranged it in advance. There is currently no tourist information service at the airport, although there are plenty of telephones if you want to find a hotel yourself before going into town.

An alternative to staying in Riga, particularly in summer, is to book a hotel in nearby Jūrmala, Riga's seaside resort. Jūrmala is about 20 minutes from Riga by car and about 40 minutes by train (see page 133). Jūrmala has some attractive and recently restored small hotels, as well as larger hotels with views over the Gulf of Riga. However, if you have only a few days in Riga, you probably will not want to travel backwards and forwards every day.

Prices of Riga hotels are often quoted in US dollars and/or euros on websites and brochures but you will always need to make payment in lats. The rates quoted by hotels generally include a buffet breakfast and VAT, unless otherwise specified. All the quality hotels take credit cards. In practice, there tends to be little difference between prices for single rooms and prices for doubles, and single travellers will often be given a double room anyway.

If you book directly, a double room in a luxury hotel will cost from £90/US$170 upwards, from £60/US$115 in a first-class hotel, and from around £30/US$55 in a tourist-class hotel. Rooms in budget hotels can be found for £12/US$22 upwards, while dormitory beds in hostels can be found from £4/US$7 per person. As one UK pound is currently roughly equivalent to one lat, the prices in UK pounds give a guide to the prices in lats.

Note that the prices quoted for luxury hotels are maximum rates. If you book your holiday through a tour operator you may benefit from lower package rates. Discounts are also offered by some chains if you book hotels in Riga and Vilnius or Tallinn at the same time. As ever, it is always worth checking internet booking agencies for special offers.

Luxury hotels

Grand Palace Hotel 12 Pils iela; tel: 704 4000; fax: 704 4001; email: grandpalace@schlossle-hotels.com; www.schlossle-hotels.com. Superbly located near the Dome cathedral, this luxury hotel opened in 2001 and is probably the most expensive in the Old Town, with rooms at Ls130–172 and suites at Ls263–367. Although the building is old, the hotel has all modern facilities, including a fitness centre, sauna and steam room.
Hotel Bergs 83–85 Elizabetes iela; tel: 777 0900; fax: 777 0940; email: reservation@hotelbergs.lv; www.hotelbergs.lv. One of Riga's most recently opened hotels, the Hotel Bergs is in the Berga Bazārs shopping area on the edge of the New Town. The hotel is suitable for tourists, many of whom will also enjoy the hand-made chocolates and other exclusive products on sale in the adjoining shopping area, but the hotel also has some of Riga's most comprehensive business facilities, as well as an elegant and acclaimed restaurant. Prices for suites range from Ls89 to Ls199. Lower rates may be available at the weekend.
Hotel de Rome 28 Kaļķu iela; tel: 708 7600; fax: 708 7606; email: reservation@derome.lv; www.derome.lv. At the edge of the Old Town, this German-run 4-star hotel is one of the best in Riga. The location, overlooking the Freedom Monument and surrounding parks on the edge of the Old Town but within easy reach of the New is ideal for the tourist. The German Otto Schwarz restaurant offers an excellent breakfast and first-class meals at other times of day. It has 90 rooms (10 single, 60 doubles and 20 luxury suites). Prices start from about Ls91 for a single room, and Ls100 for a double, including breakfast.

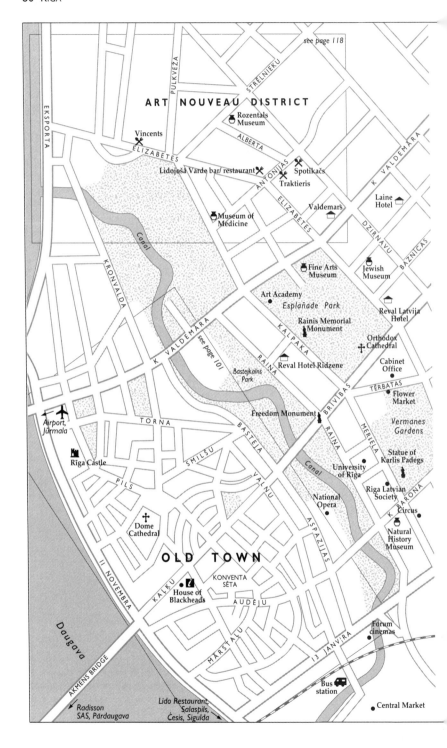

see page 118

ART NOUVEAU DISTRICT

Rozentals Museum

Vincents

Lidojušā Varde bar/ restaurant
Spotikačs
Traktieris

Valdemars

Laine Hotel

Museum of Medicine

Fine Arts Museum

Jewish Museum

Art Academy
Esplanade Park

Reval Latvija Hotel

Rainis Memorial Monument

Orthodox Cathedral

see page 101

Bastejkalns Park

Reval Hotel Ridzene

Cabinet Office

Flower Market

Freedom Monument

Vermanes Gardens

Airport, Jūrmala

Riga Castle

University of Riga

Statue of Karlis Padegs

National Opera

Riga Latvian Society

Circus

Dome Cathedral

Natural History Museum

OLD TOWN

House of Blackheads

KONVENTA SĒTA

AUDĒJU

Forum cinemas

Daugava

Bus station

Radisson SAS, Pārdaugava

Lido Restaurant, Salaspils, Cēsis, Sigulda

Central Market

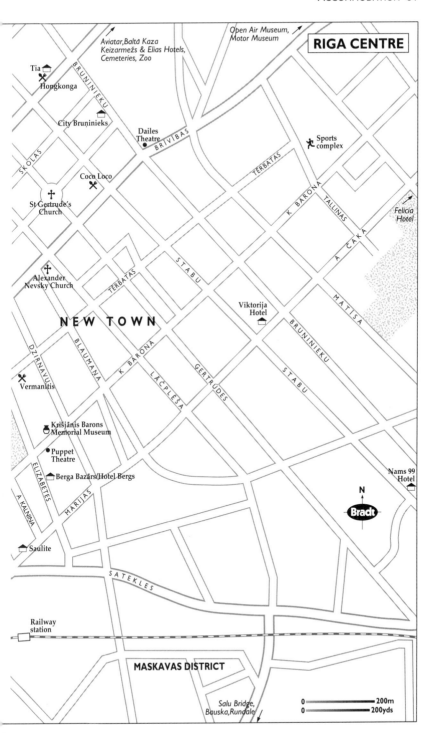

Park OK Hotel 43 Mazā Nometņu iela; tel: 789 4860; fax: 789 2702, email: parkhotel@okhotel.lv; www.okhotel.lv. Not to be confused with the OK Hotel (see page 85), this is a super-luxurious and super-expensive hotel on the far side of the River Daugava, set in parkland around 4km from the town centre. Suites start at Ls270 and go up to Ls650 for the presidential suite.
Radisson SAS Daugava Hotel 24 Kuģu iela; tel: 706 1111; fax: 706 1100; email: info.Riga@RadissonSAS.com; www.radissonSAS.com. This is one of the leading business hotels in the Baltics. It is a rather unimaginative white block of a building and is on 'the wrong side' of the Daugava away from the main part of the city, but is quiet and has good views over the river. It offers free transfers from the airport and an hourly shuttle bus to the Old Town. Prices are from Ls76 for a single room to Ls82 for a double.
Reval Hotel Ridzene 1 Reimersa iela; tel: 732 4433; fax: 732 2600; email: ridzene@revalhotels.com; www.revalhotels.com. Formerly a Soviet hotel, the Ridzene has been elegantly refurbished and is now part of the Reval group. It is located at the side of the Esplanade Park in the New Town, close to many embassies and international businesses, whose visitors are among the hotel's main clients. Room prices range from Ls112 for a single room to Ls123 for a double.

First-class hotels
Ainavas 23 Peldu iela; tel: 781 4316; fax: 781 4317; email: reservations@ainavas.lv; www.ainavas.lv. This hotel, opened in 2001, has only 22 rooms but each has a different colour scheme and décor based on the browns or greens of Latvia's countryside ('Ainavas' means landscape). The tone is set in the lobby bar, which is decorated with wood and flowers and where a welcoming fire burns in the hearth. Located in a quiet street in the south of the Old Town, the hotel is suitable for both tourists and business people. Singles Ls60; standard doubles Ls77.
Centra Hotel 1 Audēju iela; tel: 722 6441; fax: 750 3281; email: hotel@centra.lv; www.centra.lv. The hotel opened in 2000 and is wonderfully situated near St Peter's. It is decorated in a minimalist style with furniture and fabrics which all come from Latvia. Although the area nearby can be noisy at night, the rooms are well sound-proofed. Rooms on the higher floors offer unusual views of the Old Town. The hotel is excellent value, with rooms at prices below those in similar hotels in the same area. A double typically costs around Ls60.
Eurolink 22 Aspāzijas bulvāris; tel: 722 0531; fax: 721 6300; email: eurolink@metropole.lv; www.metropole.lv. This is actually the third floor of the Riga Hotel (see below) but is run as a separate hotel under joint Latvian–Swedish management. It is conveniently located, opposite the Opera House and within easy reach of the Old and New Towns. Doubles are available from Ls48.
Hotel Gutenbergs 1 Doma laukums; tel: 721 1776; fax: 750 3326; email: hotel@gutenbergs.lv; www.gutenbergs.lv. Located in one of the Baltic States' first publishing houses, hence the name, in a quiet street next to the Dome cathedral, this hotel has proved very popular since its opening in 2001, and often needs to be booked well in advance. An attraction in summer (which the hotel thinks begins in April) is the rooftop terrace, where you can eat, drink and admire the view. Prices are from Ls60 for a single and Ls70 for a double room.
Konventenhof or **Konventa Sēta** 9–11 Kalēju iela; tel: 708 7501–5; fax: 708 7506; email: reservation@konventa.lv; www.konventa.lv. The Konventa Sēta stands out from other hotels in Old Riga in that it is housed on the site of the old city walls in a complex of restored buildings, some dating back to the 13th century. See page 111 for an account of the restoration of the Konventa Sēta. The complex includes a Latvian restaurant, Raibais Balodis, and Melnais Balodis (a bar). Single rooms cost Ls46 per night; double rooms and suites from Ls55–70 a night.

Man-Tess 6 Teatra iela; tel: 721 6056; fax: 782 1249; email: info@mantess.lv; www.mantess.lv. This charming hotel in the centre of Old Riga is an elegant 18th-century house once owned by H Haberland, a Riga architect. It has only 10 rooms, each one in a different style (the so-called white room is light and modern, the 18th-century room is furnished in the style of the Hanseatic period). The ground-floor restaurant is exotically decorated (marble, a pond with goldfish, and even caged birds) and is one of the best in the Old Town. Prices range from Ls60 for the only single room to Ls100 for a suite.

Maritim Park 1 Slokas iela; tel: 706 9000; fax: 706 9001; email: reservations@maritim.lv; www.maritim.com. A large (240 room) hotel across the river from the Old Town, the location may put off some people, but it is quiet and you can reach the Old Town in about half an hour on foot or by taking the number 2, 4 or 5 trams. On the positive side, the rooms and the Bellevue restaurant on the 11th floor have wonderful views of the Old Town. Standard rooms cost Ls59–101 for a single, Ls68–110 for a double.

Metropole 36–38 Aspāzijas bulvāris; tel: 722 5411; fax: 721 6140; email: metropole@brovi.lv; www.metropole.lv. Run by the same Latvian–Swedish management team as the Eurolink, the Metropole is suitable for both tourists and the business traveller. It is conveniently located on the edge of the Old Town and only a short walk away from the New Town. Single rooms cost from Ls37, doubles from Ls44 and suites from Ls75, including breakfast. All rooms are equipped with cable TV.

Nams 99 (House 99) 99 Stabu iela; tel: 731 0762; fax: 731 3204; email: nams-99@delfi.lv; www.nams99.lv. Located in a renovated art nouveau building, the Nams offers 8 apartments and a restaurant. Intended mainly for business users, the rates range from Ls90–150 for an apartment.

Reval Hotel Latvija 55 Elizabetes iela; tel: 777 2222; fax: 777 2221; email: latvija@revalhotels.com; www.revalhotels.com. Two advantages are its location in the New Town but just 5 minutes from the Old Town and the views from its upper storeys, and its 2 glass-sided lifts and the skyline bar on the 26th floor. All rooms include satellite TV with games and email possibilities, and minibars with drinks, chocolate and condoms. Rooms cost from Ls77 a night for a single and Ls88 for a double.

Riga Hotel 22 Aspāzijas bulvāris; tel: 704 4222; fax: 704 4223; email: info@hotelriga.lv; www.hotelriga.com . On the edge of the Old Town, the Riga is one of the largest and oldest hotels in central Riga. Fully refurbished in 2002–03, all the rooms are pleasantly decorated and spacious. Some have internet dataports. To see what the staff got up to before 1991, visit the Occupation Museum (see page 110) which displays the bugging devices they used to monitor phone calls. Singles cost around Ls60 and doubles Ls75.

Rolands 3a Kaļķu iela; tel: 722 0011; fax: 728 1203; email: info@hotelrolands.lv; www.hotelrolands.lv. Named after Riga's patron saint and located in the heart of the Old Town close to the Blackheads' House and Roland statue (page 110), this hotel was opened in 2002. The rooms make extensive use of Latvian birch wood and are equipped with full business facilities, including a bouncy, ergonomic desk chair. The restaurant in the cellar has a medieval décor and pleasantly warmed table-tops and often offers a range of local game specialities. Single rooms cost around Ls60 and doubles Ls100. (Temporarily closed, 2005)

Vecriga 12–14 Gleznotāju iela; tel: 721 6037; fax: 721 4561; email: vecriga@inet.lv. A small hotel with only 10 double rooms, in a renovated 18th-century house in a quiet street in the Old Town, next to the Palete restaurant. Spacious bedrooms are fitted out with comfortable antique-style furniture, although the bathrooms tend to be small. The hotel has an intimate atmosphere but with all modern facilities, and an elegant restaurant. The ten double rooms cost from Ls55–65.

Tourist-class hotels

Avitar 127 Valdemāra iela; tel: 736 4444; fax: 736 4988; email: avitar@apollo.lv; www.avitar.lv. A modern hotel a few kilometres away from the centre but on public transport routes. A shuttle service is also available to the airport and to the train and bus stations. Rooms are clean and spacious, and have cable TV, a telephone and bathrooms with showers. A double is Ls36–52.

Best Western Hotel Mara 186 Kalnciema iela; tel: 770 2718; fax: 770 2708; email: mara@mailbox.riga.lv. Part of the Best Western chain, the Mara has 24 rooms at prices from Ls55 for a single room and Ls65 for a double room. It is out of the centre on the way to the airport, and is the only 3-star hotel near the airport. It operates a shuttle bus to both the airport and the city centre. More of a business hotel than one for tourists. Singles cost Ls45 and doubles Ls50.

City Hotel Bruņinieks (The Knight) 6 Bruņinieku iela; tel: 731 5140; fax: 731 4310; email: hotel@bruninieks.lv. Originally known just as Bruņinieks, the hotel changed its name to City in 2003. It is sufficiently far from the town centre for the neighbouring shops all to offer Latvian rather than Western prices and for peace and quiet to be assured in the evenings, although a wide range of buses are available on nearby Brīvības iela. The hotel caters in particular for families, with adjoining rooms available and – for those with smaller children – triple rooms with a roll-up bed. Doubles cost Ls50.

Felicia Hotel 32b Stirnu iela; tel: 759 9942; fax: 754 8145; email: mail@hotelfelicia.com; www.hotelfelicia.com. Take trolleybus number 11 or 18 from the city centre to the Ūnijas iela stop. The hotel is good value for money if you do not mind the 15-minute ride from the town centre. It offers single and double rooms, and also 'minis', very small singles for tourists watching their budget. In addition to a restaurant, two bars and a nightclub, it has billiards, saunas, a swimming pool, and even indoor tennis courts. Rates from Ls30–40. Very small singles for just Ls8.

Forums 45 Vaļņu iela; tel: 781 4680; fax: 781 4682; email: reservation@hotelforums.lv; www.hotelforums.lv. On the edge of the old city, near the train station, the hotel has large rooms, with a bath and satellite TV. Despite the modest exterior, it offers elegantly decorated accommodation. Some of the rooms on the upper floors have good views. Breakfast is served, but there is no bar or restaurant, so evenings are quiet. Double rooms cost Ls37–48.

F-Villa 9 Skanstes iela; tel: 751 9922; fax: 751 9921; email: hotel@miests.lv; www.meists.lv. This is a newly built hotel, located in a quiet area a few kilometres away from the Old Town. Rooms are comfortable, the environment green and friendly, and the prices relatively modest. The hotel has a restaurant and bar, and in summer opens a beer terrace. Double rooms cost around Ls24.

Karavella 27 Kātrinas dambis; tel: 732 4597; fax: 783 0187; email: hotel@karavella.lv; www.karavella.lv. With 80 rooms this is a fairly large hotel situated about 10 minutes by car (2km) from the centre of Riga towards the harbour (it is 1km from the marine passenger terminal). You can also reach the hotel on trams number 5 or 9, alighting at Katrinas iela. Some rooms overlook the harbour; all have cable TV, a refrigerator and telephone. The hotel has a café, which serves snacks and drinks, and a bar. Single rooms from Ls35 and doubles from Ls41.

Ķeizarmežs 30 Ezermalas; tel: 755 7576; fax: 755 7461. Situated on Lake Ķīšezers, near the zoo and Mežaparks, this is a modern complex which may appeal to sports lovers, particularly in summer. There is a well-equipped fitness centre, with a swimming pool, squash court, billiards and sauna. Rooms have satellite TV, phone and a private shower or bath. To get there takes around 25 minutes from the Old Town: take trolleybus number 2 to the terminus. Doubles cost from Ls30–38.

Laine Hotel 11 Skolas iela; tel: 728 8816 or 728 9823; fax: 728 7658; email: info@laine.lv; www.laine.lv. A small hotel (28 rooms), the Laine has the advantage of being centrally located in the New Town, not far from the Reval Hotel Latvija. With rooms at prices ranging from Ls30–40 for a single room to Ls40–60 for a double room (the cheaper rooms require you to use communal showers) in an elegant art nouveau building, the Laine is exceptionally good value. Most rooms now have satellite TV and a minibar. Do not be put off by the entrance through an unprepossessing courtyard.

OK Hotel 12 Slokas iela; tel: 786 0050; fax: 789 2702; email: service@okhotel.lv; www.okhotel.lv. The OK opened in 2001 and is modest but good value with rooms at Ls45–80. Rooms are adequately furnished and include telephone and cable TV. The disadvantage is its location, over the river from the Old Town. It is a 30-minute walk from the Old Town, but the hotel can also be reached quickly by taking tram number 4 or 5 from the Grēcinieku stop to the Kalnciema stop, just over the river. Doubles cost Ls36–55.

Radi un Draugi (Relatives and Friends) 1–3 Mārstalu iela; tel: 782 0200; fax: 782 0202; email: radi.reservations@draugi.lv; www.draugi.lv. This 76-room hotel right in the centre of the Old Town is comfortable and affordable, as well as being in a superb location. Recently modernised and extended, the hotel has only one drawback: the proximity of two pubs means it can get noisy late at night. Singles cost Ls35 and doubles Ls44.

Tia 63 Kr Valdemāra iela; tel: 733 3918, 733 3035 or 733 3396; fax: 783 0390; email: tia@mail.bkv.lv. A clean and comfortable hotel near the centre with rooms from Ls29 for a single to Ls51 for a suite.

Valdemārs 23 Kr Valdemāra iela; tel: 733 2132 or 733 4462; fax: 733 3001. Centrally located in an art nouveau building, the Valdemārs is clean and spacious. Room prices range from Ls25 for a single, Ls35 for a double.

Viktorija 55 A Čaka iela; tel: 701 4111; fax: 701 4140; email: info@hotel-viktorija.lv. This small hotel in a lovely art nouveau building has been partially renovated. The rooms in the renovated area are comfortable and have cable TV. Although not quite central (about 10 minutes by car from the central station and a bit further to the Old Town) it is not too far to walk. Singles are Ls30 and doubles Ls40.

Budget hotels

Baltā Kaza 2 Ēveles iela; tel: 737 8135. The name means 'White Goat'. Located some way out of the centre of Riga, this small and simple hotel looks grim but is clean, with 35 rooms (it also has dormitories and bunk-bed accommodation) at prices from Ls25 for a double to Ls4 in a dormitory (4 beds to a room). To get there take tram number 3 from Barona iela.

Elias 14 Hamburgas iela; tel: 751 8117. A small hotel with only 7 double rooms near Lake Ķīšezers reached by taking the number 11 tram from Kr Barona iela or the number 9 bus from the station. The location in the Mežaparks is pleasant, and the rooms have private bathrooms and TV. Rooms are Ls16 a night; breakfast not included.

Lidosta at the airport; tel: 720 7149 or 720 7375. A hotel next to the airport (look for the Soviet-style building beyond the car park outside the terminal), and therefore unprepossessing in location as well as appearance. Rooms from Ls9–23; breakfast not included.

Saulīte 12 Merķeļa iela; tel: 722 4546; fax: 722 3629, email: hotel_saulite@one.lv; www.hotel-saulite.lv. Located just opposite the station, the hotel offers basic accommodation at very low prices. Singles Ls8–25; doubles Ls12.

Hostels

Riga is not bursting with hostels for backpackers.

Old Town Hostel 50 Kalēju iela; tel: 614 7214; fax: 727 8809; email: oldtown@hostel.lv; www.oldtownhostel.lv. Offers mainly dormitory accommodation, but a few doubles, quads and 2 apartments. Located close to the bus station. Prices include free internet access, washing machines, a kitchen and a common room with TV. Also has baggage storage, a bar and sauna. Dormitory beds Ls10 per person.

Posh Backpackers (Centrāltirgus, Central Market) 5 Pūpolu iela; tel/fax: 721 0917; email: posh@hostel.lv; www.poshbackpackers.lv. Located in one of the old warehouses at the

edge of the Central Market, the hostel has spacious single and double rooms, as well as small dormitory rooms. There is no kitchen, only a fridge. Dormitory beds Ls8 per person.
RPRA Hostel 26 Nīcgales iela; tel: 754 9012. Clean rooms at cheap prices, but quite a distance from the centre of Riga. The hostel is a member of the International Hostelling Association. To reach the hostel, take trolleybus number 11 or 22 and get off at the Purvciems stop. By taxi the ride from central Riga will cost around Ls3.
Turība 68 Graudu iela; tel: 761 7543; fax: 761 9152; email: viesnica@turiba.lv; www.turiba.lv. Around 250 beds, a kitchen, café, minigolf course and internet access. The hostel is part of a business school campus about 20 minutes by public transport from the centre of Riga. To get there, take a *taksobuss* from the railway station or trolleybus number 8 from the Town Hall Square. Get off at the Graudu stop and you will find Turība 100m to the right. Singles Ls12, doubles Ls5.50, triples/quads Ls3–4 per person.

Camping
In 2004 a campsite opened on Ķīpsala island. It offers 63 places for tents and 20 places for trailers. It is also possible to play tennis and volleyball, rent roller-skates and bikes, and have a meal. The campsite is around 20 minutes' walk from the Old Town. Lodging costs Ls1 per adult per night, Ls0.50 per child. See www.bt1.lv/camping for more details.

EATING OUT
Eating has been transformed in Riga over the past few years. Whatever your taste and whatever your budget, you should have no difficulty finding something to tempt you. Riga offers an immense selection of restaurants, cafés and bars, many up to the best international standards. In both the Old Town and the New Town Japanese and Chinese restaurants compete for custom with Italian, Russian, Ukrainian and, of course, Latvian restaurants. And if you just want a coffee or a snack, you will not need to walk far to find one of the many new coffee shops or teahouses. Wine is widely available in restaurants but is all imported and therefore not cheap. Beer is good quality and good value for money (see page 63).

In general you do not need to book in advance, although if you want to make absolutely certain of a table in a particular restaurant at peak times you should do so. Tipping has become increasingly the norm in recent years. At least 10% is considered about right for good service. Menus are nearly always available in English.

Prices tend to be low by western European standards but perhaps on the high side compared with some other eastern European cities. Main courses cost on average between £4–8/US$7–15 in upmarket restaurants, although more expensive dishes are also offered. A good two-course meal with wine for two therefore costs around £25–35/US$45–65. You can have a pizza for £2–3/US$4–6, or in some restaurants a small one for under £1.50/US$3. An ordinary coffee will cost you around £0.50/US$1, although a latte or cappuccino could go up to £1.40/US$2.60. Many restaurants and cafés offer special lunch menus at very reasonable prices.

Latvian cuisine, if eaten regularly, is not for the weight-conscious (see page 60). Once or twice on a weekend trip to Riga, however, is an enjoyable and fun thing to do.

Upmarket
Most of Riga's upmarket restaurants are in hotels. All of them are pleasantly decorated and all serve food to high standards, but the ambience depends very

Above Memorial to the Latvian Riflemen, Riga (SC)

Above right Detail of the reconstructed Blackheads' House, Riga (TH)

Below Art nouveau building (RR)

Below right Art nouveau or Jugendstil door, Riga (SC)

Above A tranquil park in Riga (SC)

Right Traditional wooden building at the Ethnographic Open Air Museum, near Riga (SC)

much on the clientele. On a wet Monday out of season it is by no means unusual to eat alone in the evening in some of these restaurants, and although the staff do their best, it may be you would be happier in a livelier Old or New Town restaurant. On other occasions, the atmosphere might be just right, and there could be little more pleasant than the elegant dining these Riga restaurants offer.

Bellevue Maritim Park Hotel, 1 Slokas iela; tel: 706 9000. The 11th-floor restaurant looks out over the river on to the Old Town and is an ideal place for a sunset dinner in summer. Fish and seafood are often among the highlights, and there are frequently local game dishes too.

Bergs Hotel Bergs, in Berga Bazārs, 83–85 Elizabetes iela; tel: 777 0957. The atmosphere is relaxed and the food includes a wide range of original dishes. As well as serving lunch and dinner, there is a breakfast buffet from 07.00–11.00, and in the afternoon you can drop in for tea and cakes on the terrace.

Otto Schwarz Hotel de Rome, 28 Kaļķu iela; tel: 708 7623. Located on the top floor of the hotel, this is a restaurant in the international mould but with an emphasis on German cuisine, including even a special asparagus menu in season. Prices are international, but at lunchtime there is a business menu for Ls8 (2 courses) or Ls10 (3 courses). A good choice of vegetarian dishes is always available too.

Rolands Hotel Rolands, 3a Kaļķu iela; tel: 722 0011. Game dishes are what the restaurant has become known for, but it also serves fish, including eel, pork and other meat dishes. If available, try the *confit* of duck with vanilla potato mash and Cumberland sauce, or one of the dishes with a Japanese influence (shiitake mushrooms, udon etc). (Temporarily closed, 2005)

Skonto Zivju Restorāns 4 Vāgnera iela; tel: 721 6713; www.zivjurestorans.lv. Riga's best fish restaurant is commensurately expensive and generally used by expense-account diners. Fish is a mixture of local catch (try, for example, the Baltic pike perch rolls as a starter) and of more exotic origins, and is always a pleasure to look at as well as to eat. Main courses go up to Ls17.

Vincents 19 Elizabetes iela; tel: 733 2634 or 733 2830; fax: 783 0206; www.vincents.lv. Vincents is one of Riga's best-known restaurants. Situated in the New Town, like many restaurants it is making increasing use of high-quality local products, for example chicken from the Dobele region in western Latvia, but also has an impressive range of meat and fish dishes based on the best-imported ingredients. Its prices are very high by Riga standards, but both the food and the service are excellent.

International

Melnie Mūki (The Black Monks) 1–2 Jāṇa Sēta; tel: 721 5006. Dark and rather formal, this highly respected restaurant in what used to be a cloister in the Old Town is rapidly gaining popularity for international food at prices that, if high for Riga, are by no means off the scale for the overseas visitor. The cuisine is genuinely international – Turkish kebabs alongside dishes with Asian influences.

Palete 12–14 Gleznotāju iela; tel: 721 6037. Located in an elegant building in a narrow street in the Old Town, the Palete is worth a visit. Despite its central location, it is often missed by tourists, so even in summer it tends to be uncrowded. Atmospheric and elegant with unobtrusive piano music and good value at about Ls12 per person for a full meal with wine. The name means 'palette' and comes from its location in Painter Street.

Raibais Balodis (Colourful Dove) 9–11 Kalēju iela; tel: 708 7580. Part of the Konventa Sēta hotel. Although the name may suggest a Latvian restaurant, the food here is definitely international. Menus change to make use of seasonal produce such as asparagus. The setting in the 13th-century convent is a definite plus, as are the fresh flowers and helpful service.

Latvian

Dzirnavas (The Mill) 76 Dzirnavu iela; tel: 728 6204. One of the most popular of Riga's restaurants among locals, this Latvian farmhouse-style restaurant is not the place for a quiet tête-à-tête. The service is buffet-style: choose from a vast array of food laid out in several rooms, take it back to your table, across the stream in the centre, and enjoy it to the strains of Latvian country music. The food is decent, the atmosphere fun, and the prices very affordable. If you want a quick initiation into Latvian food and at the same time to observe local life, this is a good place to start.

Lido Atpūtas Centrs (Lido Recreation Centre) 76 Krasta iela; tel: 750 4420. This is undoubtedly one of Riga's recent success stories in the restaurant world. Family groups are the main target, as large play areas are available, and service is cafeteria-style with trays along the counter. More and more foreigners are now coming too; they enjoy, as the Latvians do, the space, the light and the wooden tables, not to mention the variety and quality of food available in the bistro, express restaurant and beer cellar with its own micro-brewery. They enjoy the broad clientele too; Latvia mixes here in a way it hardly does elsewhere. The centre also has the largest skating rink in the Baltics. To get there take tram 7 or 9 to the Dzērvju stop. It is then a 10-minute walk towards the windmill. Alternatively take a short taxi-ride (Ls2–3).

Livonija 21 Meistaru iela; tel: 722 7824. There are few restaurants in Riga where an identical review could be written year after year. For the Livonija, this is the case and it has always been positive. A broad international menu, with a wine list to match, is offered, although there is a good choice of Latvian dishes. Acclaimed dishes include local venison, pork knuckle, smoked eel and lamprey. Its cellar location shelters it not only from noise but also from the climate: it stays cool in summer and warm in winter.

Russian

Arbat (named after an area in Moscow) 3 Vāgnera iela; tel: 721 4056. This is probably the most upmarket Russian restaurant in Riga, although the prices, for the quality of the food, are not at all unreasonable. Caviar, sturgeon and vodka feature prominently on the menu and blend well with the richly ornate interior. The dishes are attractively presented by staff who are unusually keen to please.

Krievu Sēta/Russkij Dvor (Russian Yard) 3 Ķengaraga iela; tel: 713 4930. This is the Russian equivalent of the Latvian-food Lido restaurant (see above), and owned by the same group. A huge building in an unfashionable part of the city, off Maskavas iela, the interior resembles a theme park, with its painted wood and traditional *matryoshka* dolls. Like the Lido it offers a self-service restaurant with a massive choice of dishes and a recreational area outside. The food includes Russian favourites such as *borshch*, *blini*, *solyanka* and pork, all at low prices. Trams number 7 or 9 from opposite the opera will take you there. Alight at the Ķengaraga iela stop.

Traktieris 8 Antonijas; tel: 733 2455. Hearing Russian and Ukrainian spoken here by other diners is clearly a good sign. Although in the heart of the art nouveau area, the décor is from rural Russia, as are the costumes worn by the staff. The menu is from aristocratic St Petersburg and includes staples such as *blini* and *borshch* as well as more unusual dishes, but the prices appeal to quite a range of classes.

Ukrainian

Spotikačs 12 Antonijas iela; tel: 750 5955. Unless you visit Ukraine there are not so many opportunities to sample the cuisine. This restaurant will give you a good idea of what is eaten in Kiev: straightforward, tasty dishes, with plenty of meat, potatoes and *vareniki* (dumplings). The floral friezes and puppets give the décor a childish feel and, added to the friendly service, should make your visit here a happy experience. If you need any further help, try the chilled home-made vodka. A branch has also opened in Jūrmala (see page 137).

Italian
Da Sergio 65 Terbātas iela (entrance from Matīsa iela); tel: 731 2777. A very Italian Italian restaurant, with a chef from Venice, many ingredients imported directly from Italy, Italian music and Italian food and wine. The atmosphere is warm and welcoming and puts you in the mood to enjoy everything from the bread, baked daily on the premises, to the excellent desserts, via an interesting range of pizza, pasta, meat and fish main courses. Prices are very accessible.

Pomodoro 81 Vecpilsēta iela; tel: 721 1044. Turn off Audēju iela with its crowds of shoppers into the peace of Vecpilsēta iela and you will shortly find yourself at Pomodoro, a bar, café and restaurant. The restaurant is on the ground floor of a 17th-century warehouse, and the décor is a mixture of traditional and modern, but the mood is definitely contemporary. Pizza and home-made pasta are the specialities, and the Italian owners ensure authenticity. Prices are very reasonable, and a special children's menu is also available. Another branch has recently opened at the Domina shopping centre, 2 Ieriķu iela; tel: 787 3648.

Pizza
Pizza Jazz 15 Raiņa iela; tel: 721 1237. The pizzas offered by this Lithuanian chain are very acceptable and eminently affordable. The menu has a large choice of pizzas, available in large or small size (and small really is quite small), as well as pasta and salad. Even large pizzas are only a little over Ls2. For dessert, try the *biezpiena štūdele*, cottage cheese strudel, if you fancy something with a Latvian flavour. Other branches are at 76 Brīvības iela, 19 Šķūņu iela and at the railway station.

Chinese
Hongkonga 61 Valdemāra; tel: 781 2292. What a relief to find a Chinese restaurant in the Baltics where what you see is what you get. The ambience is straightforward but the cooking more elaborate. It is clear that Chinese are in control of the whole operation and are catering for their colleagues; if others wish to come, they are welcome to have a meal that makes no concessions to so-called Western tastes.

Japanese
Planeta Sushi 16 Šķūņu iela; tel: 722 3855. The quality of the vast range of Japanese dishes in this chain comes as a very pleasant surprise. From miso soup to sushi (Japanese and Californian), teppan steaks or shabu shabu, the taste is first rate, and the prices quite reasonable too, with shrimp or squid sushi at only Ls1.20 per portion and teppan steaks at Ls5. The overall ambiance is pleasant, unhurried and comfortable, and the location, close to Dome Square, makes this a convenient and highly recommendable spot.

Indian
Sue's Indian Raja 3 Vecpilsētas iela; tel: 721 2614. The food is authentically Indian and includes tandoori and tikka dishes as well as curries. Thai dishes are also available. The camels that feature on the door are possibly a reference to the fact that Indian spices, transported by camel on part of their journey, used to be stored in a warehouse here. Prices are not low, but the quality of food and service are worth paying for. There is also a branch of the restaurant in Jūrmala.

Vegetarian
Kamāla, 14 Jauniela; tel: 721 1332. An Indian ambiance suffuses the restaurant: you will notice the incense before you enter, and once inside the colourful table and wall decorations will transport you beyond Riga. The menu too features Indian food fairly

strongly, but a range of other dishes is also available. Recommendations are difficult as the menu changes from day to day but you will always find a number of very appealing, and rather different, options.

Jamaican
Coco Loco 6 Stabu iela; tel: 731 4265. The only Jamaican bar and restaurant in Riga (although there is now also a branch in Jūrmala), Coco Loco is a colourful and lively venue, offering Jamaican and other Caribbean dishes in generous portions and at very affordable prices. If you like reggae music, this will be paradise: reggae plays every day but on Friday and Saturday nights from 20.00 the restaurant becomes a club with DJs putting on the music. There is also a choice of trendy cocktails. Although slightly out of the centre, this area around Stabu iela is enjoying something of a renaissance. Close to Coco Loco is the **Sarkans** restaurant, a branch of Zen café and also of Double Coffee.

Quick snacks
Blinoff 30 Brīvības bulvāris. If you want to replenish your energy between the Old Town and the New Town, call in at Blinoff. This small but welcoming café offers a long list of *blini* (Russian-style pancakes) for Ls1–2. Choose from sweet or savoury *blini*, with coffee or a soft drink.
Pīrādziņi 14 K Barona iela; tel: 728 7824. A *pīrāgi* (pasties) shop offering pasties with a wide range of fillings from cabbage to meat. An excellent snack if you're in a hurry in the New Town.
Sievasmātes Pīrādziņi (Mother-in-law's *pīrāgi*) 10 Kaļķu iela. *Pīrāgi* (pasties) and cakes are baked here on the premises and sold for as little as Ls0.08. Good quality and very popular. You can afford several, and a juice (no alcohol available) as well, and still have plenty of money left in your pocket.

Cheap and filling
Olé 1 Audēju iela; tel: 722 9563. Another buffet-style café, which, despite the name, serves international, not Spanish, food. Take as much as you can eat and you should still have change from Ls3.
Pelmeņi XL 7 Kaļķu iela; tel: 722 2728. It is not sophisticated, but it certainly will not leave you either hungry or bankrupt. *Pelmeņi* are rather like ravioli, but their Russian origin means they are more substantial. You can fill up your plate with an XL portion from a choice of 6 different types (chicken, pork, vegetarian etc), and accompany the main dish (Ls1.50) with soup and salad. There is a similar ambiance, but bigger choice, at **Pelmeņi**, 38a Čaka iela.

Internet cafés
Riga has a generous sprinkling of internet cafes, including the sample listed below. Most offer internet access for Ls0.45–0.50 per hour.

In the Old Town
Dualnet café 17 Peldu iela (next to the Ainavas hotel); tel: 781 4440. Open 24 hours.
Virtual Travel Bureau 20 Kaļķu iela; tel: 722 8228; email: café@iec.lv. Open Mon–Sat 09.30–00.30.

In the New Town
C&I Internet Club 11-308 Merķeļa iela; tel: 721 2040; email: club@icc-info.lv. Open Mon–Fri 08.00–20.00, Sat 09.00–17.00, closed Sun.
Elizabete 75 Elizabetes iela; tel: 728 2876. Open Mon–Fri 09.30–22.00, Sat and Sun 10.00–21.00.

Cafés

Café Opera Aspāzijas bulvāris. There has been an ornate café inside the Opera House since it opened in 1995, with plenty of marble and wood. It never advertises, which suits the regulars who prefer the peace and quiet and the absence of tourists even in July and August. A thick soup followed by a light salad makes a good lunch here. The café has an outside terrace too – with parasols to ward off showers.

Lidojošā Varde 31a Elizabetes iela at the corner of Antonijas iela; tel: 732 1184. 'The Flying Frog' serves simple food (omelettes, pasta, salad, hamburgers) at very affordable prices, as well as drink. Popular both in summer, when you can sit on the terrace, and in winter, when a fire glows in the hearth. Handy when exploring Riga's art nouveau buildings.

Coffee and tea

A new generation of coffee and tea houses has arrived in Riga in the last few years. Gone are some of the traditional Viennese-style cafés, to be replaced by an ever-growing choice of cappuccino bars and tea houses. Wherever you are in central Riga, you will never have to go far for a high-quality coffee or a mouth-watering cake. Chains of coffee shops have emerged, but they have not (yet) been joined by the international chains so well known elsewhere. An unusual feature in most coffee shops is that take-away coffee costs a little more than drinking in the café.

Coffee houses

Double Coffee 11 Vaļņu iela, on the corner of Kaļķu iela; tel: 712 3522. Also at 40 Brīvības iela, 25 Raiņa iela, 15 Stabu iela and 52 Barona iela. Always busy, with good reason. The cafés offer an immense choice not only of coffee, tea and chocolate, but also of sandwiches, cakes, omelettes and even sushi. Prices are very reasonable, with a single cappuccino available for well under Ls1.

Emihla Gustava Shokolahde 13/VI Marijas iela (in Berga Bazārs); tel: 728 3959. Also at 24 Aspāzijas bulvāris (in Valter & Rapa bookstore). Essentially hand-made chocolate shops, but you can also have coffee, or chocolate, watch Belgian-style chocolates being made (at the Berga Bazārs) and enjoy a chocolate or two with your coffee. The cappuccinos are large and extremely frothy, the service very friendly, and the prices rather on the high side for Riga.

Kafijas Veikals (Coffee shop) 6 Mazā Pils iela; tel: 722 4216. Now an exception in Riga, this Viennese-style café is small, popular and one of the best for coffee and cakes. Unfortunately it is closed on Sat and Sun as well as in the evenings. Open Mon–Fri 08.30–18.00.

Monte Kristo 18–20 Kalēju iela; tel: 722 7443, close to Konventa Sēta. Also at 27 Ģertrūdes iela and 10 Elizabetes iela. At once spacious but cosy, this high-class coffee house offers a very wide choice not only of coffee but also of tea. Cakes include an enticing berry tart, excellent warm and with cream.

Tea houses

Aspara Tea Rooms 22 Skārņu iela; tel: 722 3160. In the historic Ekke's Convent built in 1435 as a guesthouse for travellers (page 113), this tea house offers a relaxing ambience in the heart of the Old Town. In the basement you can sit on cushions and choose from a vast array of Japanese, Chinese and Indian teas, while upstairs the décor is European medieval. Another branch is located in a small wooden house in the Vermānes Garden (opposite house Number 75 on Elizabetes iela). Other branches also at 10 Šķūņu iela, 77 Valdemāra iela and 2 Terbātas iela.

Zen 6 Stabu iela; tel: 731 6521; www.zen.lv. This will definitely not be your cup of tea if you are just looking for a refuelling stop. Enter Zen and you enter a slow-motion world which you will need some time to enjoy. Chinese tea is prepared in ceremonial style and, authentically, takes at least 20 minutes. The décor is oriental too: tatami, cushions, candles and lanterns, though – slightly out of keeping with the rest of the place – waterpipes are also available.

NIGHTLIFE

Riga's night scene has blossomed in the last few years. It now offers a huge variety of venues and entertainments to suit all tastes and most pockets. The venues below are only a very small selection of what is on offer. For up-to-date listings in this rapidly changing area, see one of the bi-monthly Riga guides.

Bars and clubs

La Habana 1 Kungu iela; tel: 722 6014 (entrance from Rātslaukums, Town Hall Square). On the upper floor this is a quiet restaurant serving Tex-Mex dishes. The basement is quite different. From Thu to Sat, it turns into a popular disco hosted by local DJs. The rest of the week Latin music predominates.

Paldies Dievam Piektdiena Ir Klāt (Thank God it's Friday) No 9, 11 Novembra krastmala; tel: 750 3964. Closed on weekdays until the eponymous Friday, this weekend bar offers a taste of the Caribbean on the banks of the River Daugava.

Pulkvedim Neviens Neraksta (Nobody Writes to the Colonel) 26–28 Peldu iela; tel: 721 3886. One of the longest-established clubs in Riga, this is also one of the city's trendiest venues, regularly crowded with young locals and visitors. If you like sitting in a warehouse listening to alternative music, this is for you. If you prefer something more colourful, go down to the **Baccardi Lounge** in the basement of the same building, and enjoy cocktails to the accompaniment of disco house, but be warned that if you're over 20 you may well be the oldest there.

Rigas Balzāms Building 1b at 4 Torņa iela in the Jēkaba Kazarmas row of shops near the Powder Tower; tel: 721 4494. If you would like to try Riga's distinctive alcoholic drink, *Rigas Melnais Balzāms* (Black Balsam, see page 64), this is a good bar to visit.

Skyline Bar (in the Reval Hotel Latvija) 55 Elizabetes iela; tel: 777 2222. One of the best views in Riga can be had from the Skyline Bar on the 26th floor of the Reval Hotel Latvija. Take one of the 2 glass-sided lifts up to the top and enjoy a beer or a cocktail with all Riga spread below you.

Vairak Saules Cocktail Bar (More Sun) 60 Dzirnavu iela; tel: 728 2878. One of the longest cocktail menus in Riga (around 90) will not prevent your being stunned by the brightness of the décor in this trendy bar. The music is mostly rhythm and blues and the service better than in many bars.

Voodoo (part of Reval Hotel Latvija) 55 Elizabetes iela; tel: 777 2355; www.voodoo.lv. This revamped club is open Thu–Sat 20.00–05.30. It offers several dancefloors, quieter areas for drinking and a lively atmosphere. It attracts many Russians, partying in Riga, as well as locals. Admission Ls3–5.

Gay Riga

Although the legal restrictions imposed by the Soviet authorities have long since disappeared, the gay scene is not yet well developed in Riga. Open affection in public is rarely seen and may attract hostility. Only two gay clubs are widely advertised:

Purvs (The Swamp) 60–62 Matīsa iela; tel: 731 1717; www.purvs.lv. Generally well reviewed, if you can find it – there is no sign. It offers dance performances, sometimes including transvestite shows. Open Sun, Mon, Wed, Thu 22.00–midnight, Fri and Sat 22.00–06.00; closed Tue. Admission Ls1–4.

XXL 4 A Kalniņa iela; tel: 728 2276; email: xxl@xxl.lv; www.xxl.lv. XXL started life as a small bar but has now expanded into a larger club and restaurant, with shows on Friday and Saturday at 03.00. Video cabins and dark rooms are also available. Open 18.00–07.00 every day, but men only on Sundays. Admission Ls1–10.

For further information, contact Gays and Lesbians Online; tel: 727 3890; email: gay@gay.lv; www.gay.lv (in Latvian only). A new website is also currently under construction: www.gaybaltics.com.

ENTERTAINMENT
Opera
The Latvia National Opera (3 Aspāzijas bulvāris; tel: 722 5803; fax: 722 8240; email: boxoffice@opera.lv; www.opera.lv) has an extensive programme of opera, ballet and recitals. Ticket prices are extremely reasonable by international standards, tending to range from Ls2–30, although international stars may sometimes dictate higher prices. Tickets can easily be booked from outside Latvia via email, and then collected at the ticket office (slightly behind the main building, towards the park) on arrival in Riga. Even if you do not book in advance, it is often possible to buy tickets once you are in Riga. Performances are normally in the original language but surtitled in English and Latvian where necessary. An opera festival is held every year in June. This can be booked directly or as part of an opera tour (page 51). Tours of the Opera House are available in summer, from Monday–Friday, at 12.00 and 14.00; tel: 707 3777. Unfortunately the opera is closed in July, August and much of September. Café Opera is a peaceful haven of wood and marble, which offers a pleasant venue for a snack and is open even in July and August when the theatre is closed.

Classical concerts are held in a variety of venues, including the **Wagner Hall** (Vāgnera Zale, 4R Vāgnera iela; tel: 721 0817), where many great artists including Clara Schumann have performed and which is sometimes open for visits; the **Great Guildhall** (Lielā Ģilde, 6 Amatu iela; tel: 721 3798); and the **Small Guild Hall** (mazā Ģilde, 3–5 Amatu iela; tel: 722 3772). Organ and other chamber recitals are given regularly at the **Dome Cathedral**, Doma laukums, usually on Wednesdays and Fridays. Tickets can be purchased just inside the porch of the main entrance. In all these cases, there is generally no need to book, unless the artist is extremely well known. Other venues also host occasional performances: if you keep your eyes open when walking around Riga you will see adverts for up-coming events. The free city guides also give a selection of concerts with details of time and place. Information on music in Riga generally can be found at www.lmic.lv.

Venues for non-classical music are more varied. For blues, one of the most highly recommended places is **Bites Blūzs Klubs** (34a Dzirnavu iela; tel: 733 3125), which frequently attracts singers from the USA and elsewhere. **Sapņu Fabrika** (Dream Factory, 101 Lāčplēša iela; tel: 729 1701; email: info@sapnufabrik.com) is a large hall which puts on a variety of world music, jazz and rock concerts. **The Hamlet Club** (5 Jāņa Sēta; tel: 722 8838) hosts jazz concerts, and also serves as a small theatre, putting on plays which often have a strong political content. For a genuine Latvian experience, try **Četri Balti Krekli** (Four White Shirts, 12 VecpilSētas iela; tel: 721 3885; www.krekli.lv), which specialises in Latvian musicians, including for example Ainars Mielavs (page 96).

Cinema and theatre
Riga offers a number of state-of-the-art cinemas, all of which show films in the original, rather than dubbed, so visitors will have no problems viewing missed Hollywood films. Seat prices are low by international standards at an average of

Ls2–2.70, but even so discounts are offered on weekday showings before 17.00. Information on what is showing can be found at www.filmas.lv (in Latvian but comprehensible to English speakers: click Afiša on the top horizontal for film times and locations), on the individual websites indicated below, by phoning 722 2222 or checking one of the city guides.

With 14 screens, **Forum Cinemas** (www.baltcinema.lv) is the largest cinema in Riga and the second largest cinema complex in the whole of northern Europe. It is located at 8 Janvāra iela, more or less at the end of Aspāzijas bulvāris, and has all the modern facilities you would expect. Other possibilities include: **Daile** (31 Barona iela; tel: 728 3843; www.baltcinema.lv), which shows older films for just Ls1.20 per person; **K Suns** (83–85 Elizabetes iela; tel: 728 5411), which tends to show European, rather than Hollywood films; **Kinogalerija** (24 Jauniela; tel: 722 9030), which specialises in classics; and **Riga** (61 Elizabetes; tel: 728 1195), the first cinema to open in Riga and recently renovated in its original style but with modern equipment.

Riga has a number of theatres but most of these are inaccessible to visitors who do not speak Latvian or Russian. For those who do, the **New Riga Theatre** (25 Lāčplēša iela; tel: 728 0765; www.jrt.lv), tends to perform avant-garde plays in Latvian, while the **Russian Drama Theatre** (16 Kaļķu iela; tel: 722 4660) does what it says. The **National Theatre** (2 Kronvalda bulvāris; tel: 732 2759; www.teatris.lv: Latvian only), housed in a classical building close to the canal, performs a primarily classical repertoire. It was here that Latvia declared independence on November 18 1918. A concert is held here every year to commemorate the event. For more information, see www.theatre.lv, which gives information in English as well as Latvian.

Of possible interest is the **State Puppet Theatre** (16 Kr Barona iela; tel: 728 5418; email: info@puppet.lv; www.puppet.lv). The puppet theatre is a strong Latvian tradition and performances are generally well acclaimed. They are in Latvian or Russian, but visitors with a particular interest may appreciate the artistry.

Health and sports
Bowling
Toss 6 Ķengaraga iela; tel: 713 900; email: info@toss.lv; www.toss.lv. 24 bowling lanes, as well as pool tables, darts and a restaurant. Open Mon–Fri 11.00–02.00, Sat and Sun 10.00–02.00.

Gym – general fitness
City Fitness 55 Elizabetes iela; tel: 724 0888. Open Mon-Fri 07.00–23.00.
Reaktors 27 Rūpniecības iela; tel: 732 5348. Open Mon–Fri 07.00–23.00, Sat and Sun 09.00–20.00.

Saunas
The Latvian for sauna is *pirts*. Many hotels have saunas. Otherwise, there are saunas in Riga as follows. Prices range from Ls5–10 per hour.

Antīkās Pirtis 62–66 Lāčplēša iela; tel: 728 8972. Russian and Roman baths, sauna – and Greek restaurant.
Baltā pirts 71 Tallinas iela; tel: 727 1533
Lana 15 Pulkveza Brieza iela; tel: 731 3099

Skating
Olympia Skating Rink 5 Arzenes iela (Olympia shopping centre, 2nd floor); tel: 706 5607. Ls2 per hour, including hire of skates. Open daily 10.00–19.00.

Swimming pools
Radisson SAS Daugava Hotel 24 Kuğu iela; tel: 706 1111. Open Mon–Fri 06.30–23.00, Sat and Sun 08.00–22.00. Swimming pool and sauna. Admission Ls6.
Riga Technical University 5 Ķīpsalas iela; tel: 761 6989. The university has a pool that is open to the public; also a children's pool. Open Mon–Fri 08.00–21.30, Sat and Sun closes 20.00
VEF 197 Brīvības iela; tel: 727 1735. Open Mon–Fri 07.00–21.00, Sat and Sun 08.30–21.00.

Tennis
Riga Technical University 3 Kronvalda bulvāris; tel: 732 5379. Open Mon–Fri 08.00–21.30, Sat and Sun closes 20.00.

SHOPPING
Shopping in Riga is good: you can buy almost anything you are likely to need. Below, however, are the names of some shops selling things peculiar to Latvia. Amber and jewellery are popular purchases, as are traditional wooden toys and linen. Some shops also sell traditional Russian goods (wooden spoons and dolls and so on). Latvian art is also popular. Consult *Riga in Your Pocket* and the other Riga city guides for details of local commercial galleries and what they are showing. Other possibilities include *Laima* sweets and chocolates, and the traditional Black Balsam drink (see page 64) in its distinctive bottle.

Many, but not all, small shops close on Sundays, but the shopping centres are open seven days a week. During the week small shops tend to be open from 10.00 or 11.00 until 18.00 or 19.00, while most of the shopping centres are open from 10.00 to 22.00.

Antiques
Note that generally a licence from the Inspection Board for History and Culture and the Protection of Monuments is needed before you can export antiques or valuables. There are no customs duties if goods are exported to EU countries, and reduced rates are payable on export to certain designated countries (for example, Australia, Canada and Russia). For further information, consult the Board at 22 Pils iela; tel: 721 4100. Most shops will also help you with the paperwork.

Whilst antiques are available in the Old Town, most shops are off Brīvības iela fairly near to the Reval Hotel Latvija.

Antikvariats 8 Baznīcas iela. Mainly deals in paintings and clocks but also has a few books.
Antiqua 20 Kr Valdemāra iela; tel: 728 4377. Paintings and other fine art.
Doma Antikvariats 1a Doma Laukums (Dome Square); tel: 722 1056. Furniture, paintings, porcelain and other high-priced items. If you can read Russian, more information is available at www.antikvariats.lv.
Galerija 53 Dzirnavu iela; tel: 728 2978. Not really antiques – more mementoes of the Soviet era, plus books, coins and similar small items.
Konvents 9–11 Kaļķu iela (in Konventa Sēta); tel: 708 7542. Paintings, icons, porcelain and antique furniture.
Raritets 45 Čaka iela; tel: 727 5157. Interesting selection of porcelain, furniture, paintings and icons.
Volmar 6 Šķūņu iela; tel: 721 4278. Two floors of paintings, icons, furniture, old musical instruments and other antique items. Also at 46 Brīvības iela; tel: 728 3436 and at 9–11 Kalēju iela; tel: 708 7542

Art

Riga has a large number of contemporary art galleries with regularly changing exhibitions where it is possible to purchase local art works. Most are in the Old Town.

Birkenfelds 6 Amatu iela; tel/fax: 721 0073
Carousell 2 Kaļķu iela; tel: 721 0487
Ivonna Veiherte 9 Pils iela; tel: 722 2641
XO 8 Skārņu iela (in Konventa Sēta); tel: 948 2098

Books

Globuss and **Valters un Rapa** are almost side by side, opposite the Riga Hotel and with just the post office in between. Valters un Rapa is probably the largest bookshop in the Baltics. It also sells CDs, plus films (including Fuji Velvia). A branch of Emihla Gustava Shokolahde is located on the ground floor, where you can buy coffee, tea or hot chocolate, and choose hand-made chocolates to accompany them. Globuss concentrates on travel books. **Jāņa Sēta** are best known for their maps that cover the whole Baltic area. They produce country maps, town plans and atlases. Prices for their own publications tend to be cheaper at their shop than elsewhere. Their catalogue can be consulted on www.kartes.lv. **Jumava**, close to the Konventa Sēta hotel, has a wide selection of antiquarian books in German, English and French, many about Latvia and Riga. The **War Museum** in the Powder Tower has a wide selection of books, many in English, about the build-up to independence in the late Soviet period. The **Museum of the Occupation** also sells books in English relating to the occupation.

Globuss 26 Vaļņu iela; tel: 722 6957. Specialises in travel books.
Jāņa Rozes 5 Kr Barona iela; tel: 728 4288; www.jr.lv. Also in the Dole shopping centre at 90 Brīvības iela; tel: 727 4556; in the Centrs shopping centre at Audēju 16; tel:701 8092; at Basteja iela12; tel: 721 0080; in the Mols shopping centre at 46 Krasta iela; tel: 703 0331; and in the Origo shopping centre at the railway station; tel: 707 3169
Jāņa Sēta 83–85 Elizabetes iela; tel: 724 0892
Jumava 73 Dzirnavu iela; tel: 728 2596; www.jumava.lv. Has a café and a good stock of foreign-language books. A branch at 12 Vāgnera iela sells second-hand books. Also videos of Latvian films with English subtitles.
Valters un Rapa 24 Aspāzijas bulvāris; tel: 722 9294

Music

CDs and cassettes are cheap, but watch out for pirated and counterfeit products. If you would like to take home something distinctively Latvian, look for folk music, organ music from the Dome cathedral or perhaps the music of Imants Kalniņš, a contemporary Latvian composer who has worked in a wide variety of forms from symphonies to rock and roll, or of Ainars Mielavs (see below).

Randoms 4 Kaļķu iela; tel: 722 5212. Claims to be the largest music shop in the Baltics. Two floors of Latvian, world and pop music (ground floor) and heavy metal (basement).
Upe (River) 5 Vāgnera iela. Sells traditional Latvian instruments and cassettes and CDs of Latvian music. Upe is owned by Ainars Mielavs, a well-known figure in the Latvian music industry, who has worked with the Latvian band Jauns Mēness (New Moon), and who appears frequently on local TV and radio.

Souvenirs

Many amber sellers have stalls in the Old Town, notably near the Dome and in Vaļņu iela. Products are of variable quality, so you need a good eye for genuine value if you decide to shop here.

AMBER

Amber is formed from the resin that oozed from pine trees some 30 to 90 million years ago and gradually fossilised. It is found in several parts of the world, but the oldest source, some 40 to 50 million years old, is in countries around the Baltic Sea, including Latvia. The use of Baltic amber goes back a very long way: amber of Baltic origin has been found in Egyptian tombs from around 3200BC, and Baltic amber was regularly traded in Greek and Roman times. Animal figurines made of amber have also been found in Latvia dating back to the 4th millennium BC. After the Teutonic Order conquered Latvian territory, local people were forbidden to collect it on pain of hanging and only in the 19th century could inhabitants of the coast once again begin amber-working.

Traditionally Latvian folk costumes made use of three items made from amber: beads, brooches and *kniepkeni* (fastening for women's blouses). All of these items, and many others, can be found in shops in Riga. Are they all real natural amber? Definitely not. Unfortunately the only recommended test to establish authenticity is hardly a practical shopping tip: make a solution of water and salt and drop in your amber. Only real amber will float.

Dzintars, the Latvian word for amber, can be seen and heard all over Riga. It is the name of Latvia's main perfume company, a brand name for a cheese spread, the name of a well-known choir, a children's dance group, and is also a common first name (Dzintars for men and Dzintra for women).

A & E 17 Jauniela; tel: 722 3200. Specialists in amber, particularly designer jewellery. Visiting dignitaries such as Hillary Clinton are always taken here. Prices reflect this customer base, but you can rely on the quality.

Domiņa 3 Maiznīcas iela; tel: 921 9032. Wooden toys and games for children and adults. Custom orders also taken.

Grieži 1 Mazā Miesnieku iela; tel: 750 7236. More than just a shop selling linen, ceramics and jewellery. Demonstrations of craft-making (Mon) and traditional cooking (Thu). Best to telephone in advance to check.

Koka Varde (Wooden Frog) 31 Lāčplēša iela; tel: 728 2063. A good place to go for wooden souvenirs, many from the Sigulda area north of Riga, as well as for linen and other souvenirs.

Laipa 2–4 Laipu iela; tel: 722 9962. Hand-made linen table cloths, napkins and towels, plus woollen items, jewellery and other souvenirs. Weaving demonstrations too.

Livs 7 Kalēju iela; tel: 722 9010. Like Laipa, specialises in linen and jewellery, often fashioned on traditional Baltic designs. Weaving demonstrations.

Māra 9–11 Kalēju iela (in Konventa Sēta); tel: 708 7541. A wide choice of amber products, as well as linen. If you are visiting Māra you can also have a look at **Rota**, also in Konventa Sēta; tel: 708 7546, which sells amber, ceramics and a range of small Latvian gifts.

Nordwear 7 Kaļķu iela; tel: 784 3546; www.nordwear.com.lv. Advertises itself as 'amber-free'. In this mode, it has a number of humorous souvenirs (mugs, T-shirts etc), but its main speciality is hand-knitted sweaters, based on traditional Latvian symbols. You can obtain a 5% discount card from many hotels, so there is no need to pay the full price. See the website for the shop's full catalogue.

Sakta (Brooch) 32 Brīvības bulvāris; tel: 728 0868. This was Riga's first souvenir shop and dates back to Soviet times. Offers a wide variety of gifts, including amber, linen and *Rigas*

Balzāms. Prices tend to be lower here than in some of the Old Town shops. There is another smaller branch between the Riga and Metropole hotels at 30 Aspāzijas iela; tel: 722 7751.
Senā Klēts 13 Merķeļa iela; tel: 724 2398. Specialises in folk costume from the different regions of Latvia. If they do not have one that fits you, they are happy to make one.
Vecpilsēta 7–9 Kaļķu iela; tel: 722 5427. Amber jewellery, ceramics and some paintings.

Chocolates
Laima chocolates have been made in Riga since 1870. You can find them at speciality shops at 22 Miera iela, 16 Smilšu iela, 16 Marijas iela and other branches in Riga, and also in supermarkets, where they tend to be cheaper. See also www.laima.lv. The classic *Luxs* bar with the red rose design is a long-standing favourite. For a more indulgent present, try the cranberry liqueur chocolates (*Prozit*) or the beautifully presented Riga selection.
    Emihla Gustava Shokolahde 13 Marijas (in the Berga Bazārs), in Valters un Rapa bookshop (café and shop) and in many shopping centres around Riga. These hand-made Belgian-style chocolates are a relatively new, and very welcome, arrival in Riga.

Flowers
Flowers are particularly close to the hearts of most Latvians: you will see people welcomed at the airport with flowers, and people walking to work or going home, clutching small bunches. They are on sale in markets and on the street throughout Riga, generally at very low prices. The main **Flower Market** is at the side of Vērmanes Garden on Tērbatas iela, but you will make one of the many people standing on the street selling their own flowers very happy if you buy a small bunch for your hotel room.

Speciality shops
Ballera Kanceleja 13 Marijas iela (in Berga Bazārs). Hand-made paper and stationery.
Latvijas Balzāms 1 Marijas iela, and other branches in Riga; tel: 722 8715. More than 50 different types of Latvian alcoholic drinks, including the well-known Black Balsam.
Latvijas Bite 13 Ģertrūdes iela; tel: 727 9495. The honey shop of the Latvian Association of Beekeepers specialises in honey and related products. Branches also at 34b Dzirnavu iela and 1a Kalniņa iela.

Shopping centres
The last few years have seen an explosion of shopping centres in Riga. Centrs, which has survived many rebirths since the 1920s, is now one of a large range of malls which can stand comparison to those to be found in most capitals anywhere in the world.

Centrs 16 Audēju iela; tel: 701 8018. In the heart of the Old Town, since renovation in the 1990s, this old department store has been reborn with a Rimi supermarket on the ground floor, plus 4 other floors with clothes shops, restaurants, cafés and a pharmacy.
Mols 46 Krasta iela; tel: 703 0300. An American-style mall with clothes shops, supermarket, coffee shops and sushi bar. Located on the banks of the Daugava, a short walk in time, but at least a century in mood, from Maskavas iela. A free minibus service (clearly marked Mols) operates to and from the station.
Origo 2 Stacijas laukums; tel: 707 3030. This huge shopping centre engulfs the new railway station to such an extent that you may have difficulty finding the platforms. A massive choice of shopping and eating possibilities of a far higher quality than that often to be found around stations.

Supermarkets
Rimi In Centrs at 16 Audēju iela in the Old Town; tel: 701 8020, and in most shopping centres.
Stockmann No 8 13 Janvāra iela. On the ground floor of this recently opened Finnish department store is a large supermarket with an extensive and much-praised delicatessen.

Markets
Riga's indoor and outdoor markets are great fun to walk round. The largest by far is the Central Market (Centrāl tirgus), but if you are passing, the Vidzeme market in the New Town is also worth a quick look. The central market sells a huge array of food of all types, as well as clothing, hardware and more or less anything you can imagine. It is open 08.00–18.00, and makes an interesting pre-breakfast walk.

Centrāl Tirgus (Market) 1 Prāgas iela; tel: 722 9981, close to the railway station.
Vidzemes Tirgus (Market) 90a Brīvības iela; tel: 731 1796

24-hour shops
Avots 22 Čaka iela; tel: 728 1828. Food, drink and a delicatessen.
Delikatesen 7 Šķūņu iela; tel: 722 2706
Kalissa 4 Ģertrūdes iela
Visbija 68 Brīvības iela; tel: 727 5190. Small supermarket.

PLACES OF WORSHIP
The majority of churches are Lutheran, Orthodox churches coming in second place. Few offer services in languages other than Latvian or Russian.

Church of England St Saviour's, 2a Anglikāņu iela (service in English 11.00 on Sun).
Lutheran The Dome (12.00 on Sun); St John's (08.00, 09.00 and 11.00 on Sun); other Lutheran churches abound.
Old Believers Grebenščikova Church, 73 Krasta iela (services in Church Slavonic at 08.00 and 17.00 on Sun).
Orthodox The Orthodox Cathedral, 23 Brīvības iela (services in Church Slavonic at 08.00 and 17.00 Mon–Fri, 07.00, 09.30 and 17.00 on Sat, and 08.00, 10.00 and 17.00 on Sun).
Roman Catholic St Jacob's/St James's (page 105), 7 Jāņa iela (the Roman Catholic cathedral – service in English 10.00 on Sun); Our Lady of Sorrows, Lielā Pils iela.
Synagogue 6–8 Peitavas iela (Hebrew service at 09.30 on Sat).

There is currently no **mosque** in Riga.

MONEY AND POST
Changing money
See page 57.

Post office
The most convenient post office (*Latvijas Pasts*) is at 19 Brīvības bulvāris (www.pasts.lv) and is open Monday–Friday 07.00–22.00, Saturday and Sunday 08.00–20.00. It sells phonecards and postcards, and can help with international calls. Other post offices are at Stacijas laukums (station square) and 41–43 Elizabetes iela.

WALKS IN RIGA

The majority of sights are in the Old Town (Vecriga), the area of the city located between the Daugava River and the city canal (pilsētas kanāls). If your time is limited, this is the place to start. If you have more time, you could include a look at the art nouveau area in the New Town (see page 118). For visitors with still more time or other interests, a number of other walks in and around the centre are described below.

Old Town walks

The Old Town contains a wealth of historic buildings from the medieval town walls dating back to the 13th century to a number of buildings including the Occupation Museum built when Latvia was part of the Soviet Union. Between the two extremes there are buildings of almost every period and style, classical, Gothic, art nouveau and modern. Much of the Old Town suffered neglect when Latvia was part of the USSR, but a great deal of restoration and reconstruction has been undertaken in the years following independence (the reconstruction of the Blackheads' House and Townhall Square being perhaps the best examples).

The best way to see the Old Town is on foot: the area is relatively small, but in any event, large parts of the Old Town have been made traffic-free zones (there is access for vehicles, but you have to buy a pass), while other parts consist of narrow streets, making vehicle access impractical. Many of the streets are cobbled and others suffer from lack of maintenance, so you have to keep your eyes open for holes and uneven road and pavement surfaces. Wear sensible walking shoes.

The main sights of the Old Town are described below by reference to two suggested walking routes covering the Old Town sights on either side of Kaļķu iela.

Old Town: Walk one

Our first walk starts from the Hotel de Rome at the corner of Kaļķu iela and Aspāzijas bulvāris, not far from the Freedom Monument. Take Kaļķu iela, the road leading away from the Freedom Monument and the parks along the side of the hotel, and you will find yourself almost immediately at Vaļņu iela, a pedestrianised street of shops, bars and cafés. Turn right into Vaļņu iela. At the end of the street you will see one of the major landmarks of the old town, the Powder Tower.

Powder Tower

The Powder Tower (Pulvertornis) is one of the oldest buildings in Riga. Its name is derived from the fact that it was once used to store gunpowder, although at times it was also referred to as the Sand Tower after Smilšu iela (Sand Street), the road that leads past the tower and which was once the main road to Pskov in Russia. Records of the tower can be traced back to 1330. The tower is the sole survivor of what used to be 18 towers that formed part of the city fortifications. Because it was used to store gunpowder it had to be dry, well ventilated and secure, hence the walls which are 2.5m thick. They were relatively effective: nine cannonballs are said to be embedded in the walls, relics of the Russian invasions of 1656 and 1710. Only the lower parts of the tower are original. The tower was substantially destroyed by Swedish forces in 1621 and restored in 1650.

Since it ceased to have any military significance, the Powder Tower has been put to various uses. In 1892 it was used as the headquarters of a German student fraternity called Rubonia. After World War I it was turned into a war museum. In 1957 it became the Latvian Museum of the Revolution and functioned as such until independence. Now it houses the War Museum.

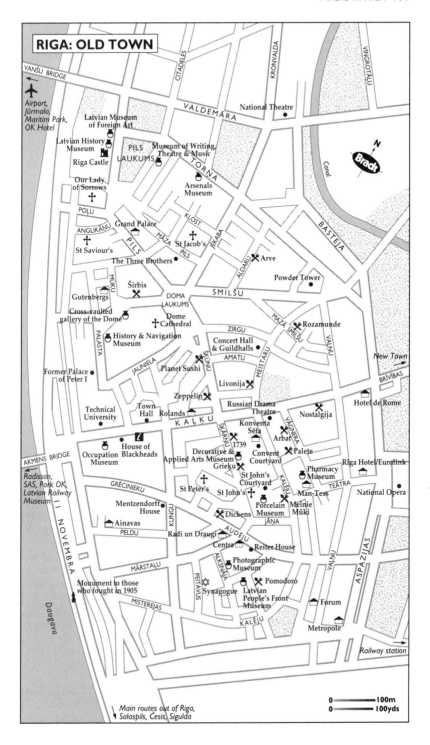

RIGA: OLD TOWN

VANŠU BRIDGE

Airport,
Jūrmala,
Maritim Park,
OK Hotel

CITADELES

VALDEMĀRA

KRONVALDA

VINGROTAĻU

National Theatre

Canal

N
Bradt

Latvian Museum
of Foreign Art

Latvian History
Museum

Riga Castle

PILS
LAUKUMS

Museum of Writing,
Theatre & Music

TORŅA

Our Lady
of Sorrows

Arsenals
Museum

BASTEJA

POLU

ANGLIKĀŅU

Grand Palace

KLOST

PILS

MAŽA

St Jacob's

JEKABA

ALDARU

Arve

St Saviour's

The Three Brothers

Powder Tower

MUKU

Širbis

Gutenbergs

DOMA
LAUKUMS

SMILŠU

MAŽA SMILŽU

Cross-vaulted
gallery of the Dome

Dome
Cathedral

Rozamunde

VAĻŅU

PALASTA

History & Navigation
Museum

ZIRGU

Concert Hall
& Guildhalls

New Town

JAUNIELA

SĶUŅU

AMATU

MEISTARU

BRIVIBAS

Former Palace
of Peter I

Planet Sushi

Livonija

Hotel de Rome

Technical
University

Town
Hall

Zeppelin

Rolands

KALĶU

SKĀRŅU

Russian Drama
Theatre

VAGŅEBA

Nostalgija

AKMENS BRIDGE

Konventa
Sēta

Arbat

Radisson,
SAS, Park OK,
Latvian Railway
Museum

House of
Occupation Blackheads
Museum

1739

Decorative &
Applied Arts Museum
Grieķu

Convent
Courtyard

Palete

Riga Hotel/Eurolink

GRĒCINIEKU

St John's
Courtyard

Pharmacy
Museum

KAĻEŽU

TEĀTRA

National Opera

11 NOVEMBRA

Mentzendorff
House

KUŅGU

St Peter's

St John's

Man-Tess

Porcelain Melnie
Museum Mūķi

JĀŅA

Ainavas

PELDU

Radi un Draugi

AUDĒJU

Dickens

Centra

Reiter House

MĀRSTALU

ALKSŅAJA

Photographic
Museum

Daugava

PEITAVUS

Monument to those
who fought in 1905

MISTEREJAS

Synagogue

Pomodoro

Latvian
People's Front
Museum

VALŅU

Forum

ASPAZIJAS

KALĒJU

Metropole

Railway station

0 ———— 100m
0 ———— 100yds

Main routes out of Riga,
Salaspils, Cēsis, Sigulda

VIEWS OF RIGA

The city of Riga itself is a most disagreeable one: the buildings being crowded together, and surrounded by fortifications which prevent a possibility of alteration, or amendment in this respect. The houses are all high, and the streets very narrow, ill paved, and very dirty. The suburbs are as large as the place itself, and are possessed by native Russians; the municipal privileges of Riga, which are highly maintained, excluding them from the capacity of exercising any trade within its walls.

Sir N W Wraxall, *A Tour Round the Baltic* (1775)

There was something decayed 'Parisian', rather shocking in an old fashioned way about the place … a kind of aristocratic Brighton to which one slipped away from a Duchess's bed with someone from the theatre, someone to be described in terms of flowers and pink ribbons, chocolates and champagne in the slipper, of black silk stockings and corsets. All the lights in Riga were dimmed by ten: the public gardens were quite dark and full of whispers, giggles from hidden seats, excited rustles in the bushes. One had the sense of a whole town on the tiles. It was fascinating, it appealed immensely to the historical imagination, but it certainly wasn't something new, lovely and happy.

Graham Greene, *Journey without Maps* (1936)

Smilšu iela

Smilšu iela itself is one of Riga's oldest streets. Some say it got its name from the sand of which the road was made; others say the name comes from the Kubes Hill and nearby sand-dunes which were levelled in the 17th century. If you stand in Smilšu iela with your back to the Powder Tower and look across Basteja bulvāris you can see the remains of Bastion Hill (*Basteja kalns*), one of the fortification towers dating back to the 17th century.

Torņa iela

Behind the Powder Tower is Torņa iela (Tower Street), a well-restored, traffic-free street. Next to the tower is the entrance to what is now again the **War Museum** (Latvijas Kara Muzejs). The museum is devoted to the military history of Latvia and concentrates on recent history with permanent exhibitions devoted to World War I, the 1905 revolution and the liberation struggle of 1918–20, and the fate of Latvia during World War II. Open May–September 10.00–18.00 except on Monday and Tuesday; October–April 10.00–17.00.

Further along Torņa iela you come to part of the city wall (best seen from the parallel Trokšņu iela). Riga was protected by a wall from the early 13th century. Eventually it extended to a length of over a mile. By the 14th century the walls were 1.83m thick. The arches between the pillars would be filled with stones and sandbags to provide reinforcement when the city was under siege; in peacetime they were emptied again and used for storage or as stables or even accommodation. The income derived from letting the arches was used to raise money to pay for the upkeep of the city's defences.

Swedish Gate

At the corner of Torņa iela and Aldaru iela (Brewer Street) is the Swedish Gate (Zviedru Vārti), so called because it was built when Riga was under Swedish rule and because it was the gate through which the Swedish king, Gustavus Adolphus, entered the city in 1621. It is the only city gate still left intact. According to legend, the citizens of Riga abducted a young Latvian woman who had unwisely fallen in love with a Swedish soldier and was meeting him secretly near the gate, and walled her up in the gate as a warning to others. The Swedish Gate is unusual in that it passes through a whole house (Number 11 Torņa iela). The house at Number 11 is the first recorded house in private ownership in Riga. It is recorded as belonging to Ivan Martin Serpentin who acquired it on April 2 1679. The first floor was let to a man called Kordu, the town lamplighter, who paid a rent of six talers per annum.

Executioner's House
Although it is not possible to visit them, there are several attractively restored historic houses on Torņa iela of which the most notorious is the one now at Number 7, a large pink house that was once occupied by the city executioner until the position was abolished in 1863. Number 5 Torņa iela was the site of the prison built in 1685 by Rupert Bindenschu, the architect who also worked on the reconstruction of St Peter's Church.

Jēkaba laukums and the Arsenal
At the end of Torņa iela you come to Jēkaba iela (Jacob or James Street) and to the right Jēkaba laukums (Jacob's or James's Square), where concrete barricades were erected during the struggles of January 1991. The square, which was first laid out in the 18th century, was once used for military parades and exercises.

On the side of the square closest to Jēkaba iela is a row of low buildings. The middle building, taller than the others, is the former Arsenal. Built from 1828–32 to designs by I Lukini and A Nellinger on the site of what was once part of the town wall, the arsenal that stood here was replaced by a customs house. Now the building is a gallery (the Arsenals Museum of Fine Arts, Mākslas Muzejs 'Arsenals') where modern painters exhibit. Open 11.00–17.00 every day except Mondays.

Castle Square and Riga Castle
Close to the end of Torņa iela is a green which forms part of **Pils laukums** (Castle Square). The large building on the corner on your right is the Bank of Latvia, built in 1905 to designs by the Latvian architect, Reinbergs. Number 2 Pils laukums was formerly a Red Army museum but is now the **Museum of Writing, Theatre and Music** (Rakstniecības, Teātra un Mūzikas Muzejs). Permanent exhibits include photographs, manuscripts and texts relating to the history of Latvian literature from its earliest times right up to the 20th century, although unfortunately very little information is available in English. Open 10.00–17.00 every day except Mondays and Tuesdays.

The main building on Pils laukums, at the other side of the square, is **Riga Castle** (Rīgas pils), a large cream building with a red roof, where the president of Latvia now lives. The present structure is the last of three that have stood here. Its predecessors were two Livonian castles, the first of which was built in 1330, the second in 1515. The leader of the Livonian Order lived in Riga Castle up to 1470 when his residence was moved, eventually to Cēsis. The people of Riga destroyed the castle in 1487 but were forced to build a replacement by Walter von Plettenberg, the last head of the Livonian Order. It was completed in 1515 and included the so-called Lead Tower (Svina tornis), which still stands. The castle was extended in the 18th century by the addition of a new wing which became the residence of the Russian governor, and between 1918–40 that of the president of Latvia. It also underwent substantial restoration in 1938, which included construction of the 'three stars tower', easily recognised by the three stars on its top. In the early part of the 19th century Wilhelm von Kester built an observatory on the main tower from which Alexander I of Russia observed the solar eclipse of April 23 1818.

The castle also houses two museums: the **Latvian History Museum** (Latvijas Vēstures Muzejs) and the **Latvian Museum of Foreign Art** (Latvijas Ārzemju Mākslas Muzejs), the biggest collection of foreign art in Latvia. The History Museum traces the history of Latvia and Latvian culture from 9000BC to the present day. Each room takes a different and unrelated theme. Do not judge the museum by the gloomy entrance to the building or by the torn signs on the stairs. One room concentrates on archaeology but sadly the labels are only in Latvian; another covers religious statues in both stone and wood which have been rescued from churches all over the country. Turning to more modern history, there are models and original tools to display 19th-century farming, a school room from the 1930s and a costume room from the same period. When the European Bank for Reconstruction and Development met in Riga in May 2000, a permanent coin room was set up in the museum. The coins on display go back to the 9th century but of most interest, perhaps, are those from 1914–20 when German and Russian ones circulated side by side. A hat exhibition opened in 2002. Open daily 11.00–17.00 except Mondays and Tuesdays.

The Foreign Art Museum consists of three floors of paintings, sculptures, drawings and ceramics by artists from Germany, Holland, France and Belgium. It is a rather odd museum: many of the oldest exhibits (sculptures from Greece and Rome and artefacts from ancient Egypt) are mixed up with modern works; the more conventional galleries exhibit paintings by 17th-century Dutch artists, German works dating from the 16th–19th century and Belgian paintings of the 20th century. There are almost no works of great distinction. Open daily 11.00–17.00 except Mondays.

To the right of the castle, in the direction of Kr Valdemāra iela, is the old stable block, recognisable by horse-head designs on the wall.

Our Lady of Sorrows

Leaving Castle Square (Pils laukums) and crossing the cobbled area of the square (the opposite end to the one at which the stables are located, in the direction of Lielā pils iela) you come to a church, the Roman Catholic Church of Our Lady of Sorrows (Sāpju Dievmātes baznīca). The location was already the site of a humble Catholic chapel in the 18th century, but the present building owes its existence to the Austrian emperor, Joseph II, who persuaded the Russian tsar, Paul I, and the king of Poland, Stanislav August, to donate money for the construction of the present church which was built in 1784–85.

St Saviour's Church

Just beyond the Catholic church is Riga's only Anglican church, St Saviour's, which stands in Anglikāņu iela, just off Lielā pils iela. This red-brick church, the largest Anglican one in the Baltic States, was built in 1857–59 to cater for the spiritual needs of the English seamen and merchants who came to Riga. The main door leads on to a small porch that overlooks the Daugava. The bricks used to build the church were imported from England, as was a layer of soil on which the church was built, although construction was supervised by the Riga architect, Johann Felsko. During the Soviet era the church was used as a discothèque by the students of the Technical University, but it was returned to the Church of England when the Archbishop of Canterbury visited Riga in 1994.

The Three Brothers

Returning to Pils iela and going back to the corner of the square, turn right into Mazā pils iela, heading away from the tower of Riga Castle. The three houses at Numbers 17, 19 and 21 Mazā pils iela are known collectively as 'the three brothers' (Trīs brāļi). The oldest is the right-hand house with the Germanic step-gable and dates back to the 15th century. It is claimed that it is the oldest domestic building in Riga. Little is known about its history except that in 1687 it is recorded that it was used as a bakery. Numbers 19 and 21 were built later in the 17th and 18th centuries respectively. In 1966 repair work began with a view to restoring the buildings after years of neglect. Number 17 is set back from the street: when it was built there was less pressure on building land in Riga so a small area was left for stone benches to be installed by the main entrance; but by the time the other houses were built land had become more expensive, so they were built closer to the road and with more storeys so as to maximise land use.

Note also the house at 4 Mazā pils iela where the Baltic historian Johans Kristofs Broce worked from 1742–1823 as rector of what was then Riga's imperial lycée.

St Jacob's (or St James's) Church

Opposite the three brothers is Klostera iela (Monastery Street) which leads to St Jacob's, or St James's, church (Jēkaba baznīca), the Roman Catholic cathedral of Riga. (Jacob and James are alternative translations of Jēkabs.) Originally built outside the city walls from 1225–26, the church has been rebuilt several times, although the sanctuary and naves are original. The church has changed hands on several occasions: after the Reformation it became a Lutheran parish church (the first Lutheran service in Latvia was held here in 1522); but in 1582 it was handed over to the recently formed Society of Jesus (the Catholic Jesuit order founded by Ignatius Loyola in 1540); in 1621 it became a Swedish garrison church; it was finally returned to the Roman Catholic Church in 1922, and is now the Roman Catholic cathedral of Riga.

The 73m-high tower shows traces of restoration work carried out in the 16th and 17th centuries. The heavy buttresses are unusual for Riga churches: shortage of land meant that most churches were built with internal buttresses. The church is open daily 07.00–20.00 except Saturdays.

Parliament Building

At the corner of Jēkaba baznīca, if you turn right, you come to a formidable brown building with a coat of arms and a balcony over the main entrance. This is the building where the Supreme Soviet of Latvia used to sit. From 1919–34 it was the seat of the Latvian national parliament. Now it functions once again as the parliament building, the seat of the Saeima. It was here on May 4 1989 that parliament passed a resolution on the independence of Latvia. The building itself is in the style of a Florentine palace. Note the decoratively carved double doors and heavy lanterns. In the outbreak of crime that followed independence in the early 1990s, the bronze plaque on the front of the building was stolen.

National Library

Turn right into Jēkaba iela and walk along the back of the cathedral. Numbers 6–8 Jēkaba iela is a substantial stone building which houses the Latvian National Library. Designs by the Riga-born architect Gunars Birkerts for a new national library, to be known as Gaišmaspils (the 'Castle of Light', see page 68), so far remain on the drawing board.

Turning left back into Smilšu iela, the house at Number 6 has a modern front and is now a bank. The upper storeys are good examples of the art nouveau style of architecture for which Riga is so famous. Next to it is Aldaru iela (Brewer Street) with its view back to the Swedish Gate. The large brown building that dominates the rest of Smilšu iela is occupied by ministries and government offices.

House of the Cat
Here the road forks. Take Mazā Smilšu iela (Little Sand Street) and turn right into Meistaru iela (Master Street). On your left is a large yellow building called the House of the Cat: perched on each of the building's two pointed towers is an arched cat looking down on the city. The origins of this piece of architectural caprice are uncertain but inevitably there is a story. Apparently a Latvian businessman sought admission to the city guild but was refused. To spite the guild he bought the nearest property he could find to the guildhall, built the house that still stands and had two cats put on top so that each directed its backside towards the guildhall. According to the same story the spurned merchant was eventually forced to move them, hence their present position.

Guildhalls
If you continue down Meistaru iela you come to what used to be the Guild Square but is now known as the Philharmonic Park (Filharmonijas Parks). On a wet day it can look fairly grim but in better weather it is enlivened by kiosks selling ice-cream and drinks, and by pavement artists. The Great Guildhall (Lielā ģilde) is the large, dull-yellow building at one edge of the square, at the corner of Meistaru iela and Amatu iela (Commercial Street). The Small Guildhall is right next to it on Amatu iela itself. These buildings represent the centres of Riga's former glory as a Hanseatic City. The Great Guildhall was the council chamber of the merchants; the smaller one housed the council of the less influential craftsmen's guilds. The Great Guildhall was originally established in the 14th century, but has undergone substantial changes over the years. From 1853–60 it was reconstructed in English Tudor style according to designs by Beine and Scheu. The Old Guild Chamber dates back to the 16th century and is decorated with the emblems of the 45 Hanseatic towns. The so-called 'Brides' Chamber' dates back to 1521: until the 19th century it was still used on the wedding night of children of members of the guild or members themselves. However, a great deal of damage was done by a fire in 1963. Now the building is used as a concert hall. The smaller hall was built (in its present form) from 1864–66. It is also sometimes called the St John's Guild – notice the statue of St John with a lamb in one corner of the façade under the tower. The interior is richly decorated in Gothic style, and is sometimes open for visits or small concerts (see www.gilde.lv).

Continue along Amatu iela to Šķūņu iela (Barn Street). On your right there is a camel-coloured building with white decoration, an excellent example of Riga's Jugendstil (art nouveau). Note the sculptures of a boy reading (at roof level) and of frogs (by the entrance). The nearby billiards/snooker hall was once the site of St Catherine's Church, built between the 14th and 15th centuries.

Riga Dome Church
If you turn right out of Amatu iela, past Zirgu iela, you come to the cathedral square, Doma laukums. The square is dominated by the cathedral, the Dome church (Rigas Dome – the word comes from the German *Dom*, meaning cathedral) or St Mary's Cathedral, as it is sometimes referred to, the largest church in the Baltic States (open for visitors Tuesday–Friday 13.00–17.00 and Saturday

10.00–14.00). The foundations of the church were laid in 1211 and consecrated in 1226. It was modelled on the cathedral at Rattenburg at the instigation of Albert, the Bishop of Riga, although he did not live to see his plans come to fruition. The original church was cruciform, but was extended in the 15th century; the central nave was heightened to let in more light, and three chapels were added. Two towers were envisaged, but only one was actually built over what is now the main entrance. It burned down in 1547 and was replaced in 1595. That tower was replaced again in 1775–76 due to fears about its structural soundness (fears prompted by the collapse of the tower of St Peter's). The old tower was 132m high, the tallest in Europe; the new one was much smaller at 90m.

Like many of Riga's churches the Dome became a Protestant church in the Reformation, and much of its elaborate interior decoration was destroyed in 1524 and the church lost its original name of St Mary's. Thus all that remains today as decoration are the tombs of merchants, all purchased, the price set by reference to closeness to the high altar. A whole chapel was devoted to the Tisenhausen family: note the plaque for Mary Tisenhausen who died in 1611, and the stained glass donated by the family in the 19th century and made in Munich in 1893. One depicts the Tisenhausen family with the Virgin Mary and angels, the other Bishop Albert, the founder of the church. In the neighbouring chapel stained glass depicts Walter von Plettenberg reading the edict proclaiming religious freedom and pledging protection from the Catholic bishops (1525). On the north side there is more modern stained glass (by E Tode, 1902) depicting the life of St Martin, the life of St George and the lives of the apostles, Peter and Paul. The three stained-glass windows above the altar depict stories from the Old and New Testaments.

The pulpit, the work of the wood carver Tobias Heincs, dates back to 1641. The angel that surmounts it was added much later in 1817 and is the work of the sculptor, Imhof.

The organ of the Riga Dome is world famous: indeed for many people the church is known as a concert hall and in particular for its organ recitals rather than as a place of worship. The first organ was installed in the 16th century, but the present instrument was built in 1884 by the firm of Walcker & Co of Ludwigsburg, Germany. It was first used at an inaugural recital and service on January 31 1884 when it was played by three organists, including the cathedral organist, Wilhelm Bergner. It was rebuilt and restored in 1981–84 by the Dutch organ builders, Flentrop Orgelbouw bv Zaandam. With four manuals and a pedal board, 6,718 pipes and 124 stops, it is large even by cathedral standards; indeed when it was first built it was the largest instrument in the world. The organ case is older than the organ itself: the work of Jakob Raab, it dates back to the 16th century, although the baroque decorations were added later in the 17th century.

The tower of the Dome was used as a lookout post. The watchman would send messages down to the guards on the ground below by means of a wooden ball. (The tower of the town hall was used in the same way.) Now the tower is dominated by a huge weathercock, the predecessor of which can be seen in the church itself where it was placed after 390 years of service in the open air.

Although the Dome is still used for concerts, it now also operates again as a place of worship. The first service in recent times was held there on October 9 1988 to mark the founding of the Popular Front (*Tautas Fronte*). The box office for concert tickets is in the church porch. For details of concerts see the posters in the church or consult *Riga This Week*, *Riga Guide* or *Riga in Your Pocket*. They generally take place on Wednesdays and Fridays. Services are held at 08.00 every day and at noon on Sundays.

Close to the main entrance and away from the main square, is the **Cross-Vaulted Gallery of the Dome**, the cathedral cloister and courtyard now in the final stages of restoration. This is open daily during the summer months from 10.00–17.00 for a small admission charge.

The cloister itself is a remarkable Romanesque masterpiece, with impressive ornamentation of twining flowers and leaves. Restoration has been in progress since the mid 1980s but is not yet complete. Displayed within the cloister is an assortment of items, including the original weathervane from the Dome spire, a cockerel some six feet tall, originally constructed in 1595 but replaced by a replica in December 1985; a plaster copy of the statue of Peter I, the original of which stood between 1910 and 1914 where the Freedom Monument now is; and a three-foot-high stone head, unearthed in the cloister in 2000. This last exhibit is still somewhat of a mystery. Originally found in 1851 near Salaspils (just outside Riga), the stone was then lost for almost 150 years. It is possible that the head served as an idol for the Livs, the group of people who have lived on what is now Latvian territory for over 20 centuries. Records exist of the worship and making of idols in Latvia as late as the 16th to 18th centuries, but to date no other idol has been found with such strange and expressive features.

Around the Dome
Just off Doma laukums, Tirgoņu iela (Traders' Street) has a number of bars and restaurants. Behind the Dome is Jauniela (New Street): the Pūt, Vējiņ! is a good

HERDER
Johann Gottfried Herder was born on August 25 1744 in Mohrungen in what was East Prussia where he attended the University of Königsberg (now Kaliningrad), studying first of all medicine but soon turning to theology. He was influenced by the philosopher Kant and the critic Hamann. He came to Riga in 1764 and remained there until 1769, teaching history, geography and German at the Dome School and preaching at a number of churches, mainly in the outlying suburbs of the city, but also in the Dome. (His final sermon, we know, was preached in St Gertrude's, since the text survived Herder's death.)

During his time in Riga Herder wrote two major works, *Fragmente über die neuere Deutsche Literatur* (*Fragments on Recent German Literature*) and *Kritische Wälder* (*Critical Woods* – the strange title comes from Quintilian's *Sylvae*). In his *Fragments* Herder formulated his ideas on language, society and folk song. During his time in Riga he collected 78 Latvian folk songs, *dainas*, which were found in his manuscripts after his death but some of which found their way into his collection of songs and ballads from many countries, *Stimmen der Völker* (*Voices of the Peoples*) which appeared in 1778–79. For Herder, the folk song was the most natural form of human expression, as a person's mother tongue was his most natural means of communication (an idea he propounded in his *Ideal der Schule*, his thoughts on education prompted by his teaching experience in Riga).

He left Riga to travel to France. After spending some time in Strasbourg he took up an appointment as chief pastor in Weimar where he died on December 18 1803.

The statue in his honour was unveiled on August 25 1864, the 120th anniversary of Herder's birth. It is a copy of a statue in Weimar by Ludwig Schaller and was restored in 1959.

place to eat and drink (there is a bar downstairs and a good restaurant upstairs).

The building at 8 Doma laukums is the Latvia Radio Building. It and the nearby Finance Ministry recall the architectural style of Nazi Germany and were built during the time of the Latvian president, Kārlis Ulmanis. The Radio Building was one of the buildings that was barricaded in 1991 by demonstrators resisting communist sympathisers; bullet holes in the building offer a grim reminder of the fighting. Doma laukums was heavily guarded and occupied by people lighting bonfires and erecting tents. From time to time radio staff would appear on the balcony of the Radio Building to announce the news to the people gathered in the square below. It was from the same balcony that President Gorbunovs proclaimed independence in August 1991.

Opposite the Radio Building is Rīgas Fondu Birža, the Riga Stock Exchange, a green and brown building with ornate statues. It was built in 1852–55 in Venetian style to a design by the architect Harald Bose. It fell into disuse during the Soviet occupation, during the 1990s was again occupied by a bank, but is at present empty.

Herder Square

If you leave Doma laukums passing the main door of the cathedral with the Radio Building behind you, you come into Herdera laukums, Herder Square. This small square is dominated by the statue of the German critic, writer and theologian, Johann Gottfried Herder, which stands on a small green.

Turning out of Herdera laukums you come to Palasta iela (Palace Street). The building that was once the clergy enclosure of the abbey attached to the Dome is now the **Museum of History and Navigation of the City of Riga** (Rīgas Vēstures un Kuģniecības Muzejs). Founded in 1773, this is the oldest museum in Latvia. It was originally set up to house items from the private collection of Nicolaus von Himsel (1729–64) whose portrait by an unknown artist hangs in the ground-floor exhibition hall. The main permanent exhibition traces the development of Riga from its beginnings to 1940. It does so by reference to maps, plans, pictures and objects of all kinds from the everyday life of the city's inhabitants. The second main permanent exhibition is devoted to the history of navigation from ancient times to the present day. Open daily 10.00–17.00 except Monday and Tuesday.

Peter I's Palace

Further on in Palasta iela at Number 6 stands a tiny building in which the Russian tsar, Peter I, kept his personal carriage when he visited Riga.

Just beyond it at Number 9 is what used to be Peter I's Palace, from which Palasta iela derives its name. Peter I bought this house from a local merchant called Henaberg and is said to have been especially fond of it because he was able to indulge in his hobby of gardening there, on either the terrace or the hanging garden on the roof. When he lived here in the 18th century it was possible to see the harbour from the windows of the palace (before it was moved further from the centre of the city). In 1745 the palace was rebuilt to designs by Rastrelli, the architect better known in Latvia for his work on the Rundāle Palace. In 1886 it became the Russian school and until recently functioned as a Russian cultural centre.

Old Town: Walk two

Our second walk in the Old Town starts from the Riflemen's Square (Strēlnieku laukums). This large open area used to be a market square, then the site of the town hall of Riga. The most distinguished building is the Blackheads' House, rebuilt in 1999.

The Blackheads' House

The Blackheads' House (Melngalvju nams), one of Riga's most important monuments, was restored in 1999. This magnificent house (really a building made up of two houses connected by an enclosed courtyard), with its Dutch Renaissance façade (1620), dated back to 1334 but was destroyed in World War II. The 'Blackheads', first mentioned in 1413, were an association of unmarried merchants who lived in Riga and Reval (Tallinn). Originally a loose association, they grew to become a powerful force. It is believed that they got their unusual name from their black patron saint, St Maurice. The first floor of the building was used for shops and businesses; the guildhall of the association occupied the second floor; the upper floors were used for storage and warehousing.

The huge step-gable was 28m high and highly decorated with statues of people and animals. The building was topped by a large figure of St George which acted as a weather vane. A statue of Roland used to stand in front of the building. A popular figure in the Middle Ages, and especially in Germany, the Roland statue in front of the house was originally erected in 1897 and restored in 1999.

The interior is now a museum. Particularly impressive is the assembly hall on the first floor. You can also visit restored rooms on the ground floor and tour the old foundations in the basement. The museum is open daily 10.00–17.00 except Monday. Buy your ticket in the ground-floor souvenir shop before entering the building.

The Riga tourist information office is now housed in part of the Blackheads' House.

Next to the museum entrance there is a café. Try its Vecriga coffee (coffee with balsams). Opposite the Blackheads' House is the newly restored **town hall** (Rātsnams).

Riflemen's Memorial

The present name of the square comes from the Memorial to the Latvian Riflemen which was erected in 1970 to commemorate the valour of the Latvian Rifle Regiment during the civil war. The Riflemen formed Lenin's bodyguard during the 1917 Revolution. Plans to change the square provide for the statue to be removed and replaced by something more politically neutral.

Occupation Museum

The ugly, rectangular black building behind the memorial was also built in 1970 and used to be a museum devoted to the exploits of the regiment. Now it is the **Museum of the Occupation of Latvia** (Okupācijas Muzejs) which contains a permanent exhibition devoted to the history of Latvia during the Soviet and Nazi occupations from 1940–1991. Founded in 1993, the museum exhibits photographs and documents, maps and artefacts dealing with the period and contains a replica of a barracks room from a Soviet *gulag*. There are explanatory booklets for each part of the exhibition in Latvian, Russian, English and German. Open May–September daily 11.00–18.00; October–April closed Mondays.

Riga's bridges

The traditional bridge with the large lantern-like lights is the Akmens tilts (Stone Bridge) which replaced the long pontoon bridge that spanned the river before World War II. A more elegant example of 20th-century architecture is the dramatic modern bridge, the harp-like Vanšu tilts, which crosses the river to the north.

Mentzendorff House

Leave the square by turning into Grēcinieku iela (Sinners' Street) and taking Kungu iela (Gentleman's Street). On the corner of Grēcnieku iela and Kungu iela there is an impressive building called the Mentzendorff House (Mencendorfa nams). The house once belonged to a rich Riga merchant family and is now a museum of life in the 17th and 18th centuries. Open Wednesday–Sunday 10.00–17.00.

Walk down Kungu iela past the Mentzendorff House to Mārstaļu iela. Number 21 Mārstaļu iela is (or will be, once restored) a fine example of baroque domestic architecture and was built in 1696 for another wealthy citizen of Riga, Dannenstern and his family. Nearby at Number 19 is a plaque to George Armisted (1847–1912), a Scot who was Lord Mayor of Riga City. (If you are travelling more widely in Latvia, you can see the manor house he built, Jaunmoku Pils, just outside Tukums.)

Reiter House

The red house at Number 2 Mārstaļu iela is the **Reiter House** (Reitera nams), built in 1682 for another wealthy Riga merchant, Johann von Reiter, and now used for conferences and exhibitions.

Turn right into Audēju iela (Weaver Street) and then right again into Vecpilsētas iela (Old Town Street). The buildings at Numbers 10 and 11–17 are good examples of some of the 20 or so medieval warehouses of the Old Town. On the corner opposite the Italian restaurant is the house from which the **Latvian Popular Front** operated in the late 1980s and which is now a small museum (page 124). Return to Audēju iela and continue walking away from Mārstaļu iela. The street is normally packed with shoppers, but if you have chance glance up over the door of Number 3. Next to the German motto 'God protect our coming in and coming out' you will see storks on a nest. Storks are a striking feature of rural Latvia, where the 10,000 or so pairs that arrive annually are welcomed by local people as bringers of good luck. You will find the stork motif throughout Latvia, including in the ballroom decoration at Rundāle (page 206).

Convent Courtyard

Turn left into Rīdzene iela, alongside the Centrs shopping centre, then left again into Teātra iela (Theatre Street), which brings you to Kalēju iela. Just off Kalēju iela is a passage leading to the **Konventa Sēta**, an area of beautifully restored historic buildings between Kalēju iela and Skārņu iela. The 17th-century warehouses and other buildings in this area had fallen into complete decay (the area used to be known as 'the dead town') but have now been restored with the aid of German investment.

The history of the Konventa Sēta goes back, like so much of Riga's history, to the 13th century when a castle was built on this site by the Knights of the Sword. The Convent of the Holy Spirit (from which the area then took its name) was also established here, and in due course a number of almshouses and other institutions settled nearby. Eventually commerce superseded religion and the buildings began to be replaced by warehouses. Each warehouse had its own name, but because of the associations the area had with the convent, many were given names with the word 'dove' in them (the dove being a symbol of the Holy Spirit, the third person of the Trinity). The former St George's Chapel became known as 'the white dove', and the building next to it 'the grey dove' and so on. Many of these traditional names have been revived as part of the restoration. One house called Campenhausen recalls the Riga councillor who founded a house for elderly ladies here. The so-called 'grey sisters' building once served as accommodation for the nuns of the convent.

In 1989 talks began between Latvian and German architects and builders about restoring the derelict area. Before long a German-Latvian joint venture firm,

REHO, was formed and the reconstruction of the Konventa Sēta began. The restored complex of buildings reopened in December 1996. A major part of the Konventa Sēta is taken up by the Konventa Sēta hotel, a modern three/four-star hotel occupying a number of the restored buildings.

Porcelain Museum

The newly opened **Porcelain Museum** (Rīgas Porcelāna Muzejs) is also here. The museum opened to acclaim in 2001 and is the only porcelain museum in the Baltic States. Riga has a long history of making porcelain, starting with the opening of the Kuznetzov factory in the first half of the 19th century, and the 6,000 exhibits reflect the many types of porcelain, from prestigious tea sets to crockery for everyday use, which have been made in the city from the mid 19th century to the present day. One room is devoted to items from the Soviet era, including vases and statues of Lenin, Stalin and other leaders. By far the most dominant item is a 2m-high red and gold vase made to celebrate Riga's 700th anniversary in 1901. Open 11.00–18.00 except Mondays.

St John's Courtyard and Church

Close to the Konventa Sēta at the end of Teātra iela there is a part of the city wall. An archway in Kalēju iela leads to Jāṇa Sēta (John's Courtyard), a cobbled courtyard with the city wall on one side and a bar, café and restaurant forming the other sides of the quadrangle.

A second arch leads out of the courtyard to St John's Church (Jāṇa baznīca). Built in 1234 for the Dominicans by Bishop Nicholas, the oldest surviving parts of the church are the main door and porch. The original chapel became too small, so in 1330 it was expanded by the addition of a red-brick nave with a choir and apse covered by a tiled roof and decorated with a small tower which still survives. As a result of renovation work in the 15th and 16th centuries the meshed vaulted ceilings came into being. The 35m-high nave dates from the 15th century. The baroque altar is 18th century, the work of J E Meier and K E Apelbaum, and has sculptures depicting the *Crucifixion* and SS Peter and Paul. The altar painting, *The Resurrection*, is the work of the Riga artist, A Stiling. Several paintings of the *Passion* and of the apostles decorate the organ loft. The stained glass is 19th century. The organ is a gift from the town of Uddevalla in Sweden; the old organ, which dated from 1854, was given to the church of Cesvaine in Vidzeme.

The façade was restored in 1924–26 under the supervision of the architect E Laube. On the outside, at the altar end of the church, is a statue of St John the Baptist (the patron saint of the church), and nearby is one of Salome, the daughter of Herodias who married Herod Antipas, her dead husband's brother. St John preached against the marriage, as a result of which Herodias persuaded Salome to dance for her husband and seek as her reward the head of John the Baptist.

The history of this church again reflects Riga's turbulent past. The Dominicans were ousted in the Reformation, and for some time after 1523 the church was used as stables by the mayor of Riga, Shulte, then as an arsenal, until in 1582 the Polish king, Stephen Bathory, seized it and handed it over to the Jesuits. However, in due course it was returned to the Lutheran Church, and is still used as a place of worship, primarily by the Lutherans, but also on occasions for ecumenical services.

The façade overlooking Skārņu iela is decorated with two stone faces which are said to be the faces of two monks. One explanation for their being there is found in the story that they represent two monks who were immured at the time the church was built; the other is that they were put there as an early elocution aid - the monks were supposed to shape their mouths in the same way as the stone monks, thereby improving their own qualities as preachers. The church is open Tuesday–Friday 10.00–17.00.

Ekke's Convent
Skārņu iela (Butchers' Street) got its name from the shops that were located in this part of Riga in medieval times. Number 22, next door to St John's Church, is a house known as Ekes konvents (Ekke's Convent). It is believed to have been built in 1435 as a guesthouse for travellers. However, in 1592 Nikolaus Ekke, a mayor of Riga, acquired the building and turned it into a home for widows of members of Riga's small guild. Now the building houses a tea shop.

St George's Church/Museum of Decorative and Applied Arts
Further along Skārņu iela, next to Number 10, the old white building with brick-lined windows is St George's Church (Jura baznīca). It was the first stone church and possibly the oldest building in Riga, built at the beginning of the 13th century and generally dated at 1202 or 1204 when it was part of a castle (Wittenstein Castle) belonging to the Knights of the Sword. The castle was destroyed in 1297 after which it became a church until the Reformation, before falling into disuse. In 1989 it became part of the **Museum of Decorative and Applied Arts** (Dekoratīvi Lietišķās Mākslas Muzejs) which specialises in applied art from Latvia and abroad from the 19th century onwards. Open 11.00–17.00 every day except Monday.

St Peter's Church
On the other side of Skārņu iela stands one of Riga's most famous and distinctive churches, St Peter's (Pētera baznīca). It is a large red-brick church with a simple, light interior decorated by coats of arms. The main entrance is located on Vecrigas laukums (Old Riga Square). The original church that was built here in 1209 was

RIGA AND BREMEN
Opposite Ekke's Convent in the shadow of St Peter's there is a modern statue of some animals called *The Town Musicians of Bremen*. Based on an old German tale, it is a gift from the city of Bremen to the people of Riga and marks a long association between the two cities. Some historians believe that merchants from Bremen settled in Riga as long ago as the 12th century, since there is reference in an old chronicle to some Bremen merchants drowning in a storm in the Daugava estuary in 1158. Whether or not that is true, there were certainly trading links between Riga and Bremen in the 12th and 13th centuries and missionary activity as well: Meinhard was consecrated as Bishop of Livonia by Hartwig II; Meinhard was succeeded by Berthold who in turn was succeeded by Albert who was also from the Bremen area.

The Bremen notary, Johann Renner, settled in Livonia in the 16th century and occupied various official positions in Riga between 1554 and 1561. He wrote one of the early historical accounts of Livonia. A later mayor of Riga, Johann Grote, was also born in Bremen (in 1654) but died in Riga in 1732.

Trade between the two Hanseatic cities grew in the 18th and 19th centuries to such an extent that Bremen established its own consulate in Riga in the 1800s, and in 1924 a Latvian consulate was opened in Bremen.

Relations between the two cities were broken off during World War II, but the old friendship was re-established when a twinning agreement was entered into in 1985.

wooden and, unusually, was built not by foreigners but by the largely Christian Liv people of Riga. No record remains of the original church which was rebuilt in 1406, although the reconstruction process went on until the end of the 15th century. A steeple was erected in 1491 but collapsed in 1666 causing considerable damage and killing the inhabitants of a neighbouring building. A replacement was completed in 1690 by the Strasbourg architect, Bindenschu, and was, in its time, the tallest in the world. However, this too was damaged by fire caused by lightning in 1721. The tsar, Peter I, was in Riga at the time of the incident and ordered the steeple and spire to be restored yet again. Reconstruction was completed in 1746 under the supervision of Johann Wulbern. His steeple stood for 195 years until it was destroyed along with the rest of the church by German mortar fire in 1941, ironically on June 29, the feast of St Peter.

The latest reconstruction work began in 1963 and was completed by 1973. The present steeple, 123m high, is a steel replica of its predecessor. It conceals a lift which takes visitors up to two viewing platforms that provide wonderful panoramas of the city. (The lift starts from the gallery in the tower and is open from 10.00–18.00 except on Monday; price Ls1.50.) For many years St Peter's was the tallest building in Riga until Intourist built the Hotel Latvijā which was about a metre higher.

In 1352 Riga's first clock was installed in St Peter's. One of the church's finest objects was a marble pulpit by the Italian, Giovanni Baratta, but it was destroyed in the fire of 1941 along with the German oak altar, the wooden pews and a magnificent organ.

Many of Riga's churches have cockerels as weathervanes, and St Peter's is no exception. A golden weathercock has topped the spire for 200 years. The symbol has a special significance for this church, since it recalls how the apostle Peter denied Christ three times before the cock crowed.

After restoration, St Peter's functioned initially only as a museum and concert hall, although now it has begun to be used again for church services.

There are two famous stories associated with St Peter's. The first is the story of the blue guard. The blue guard was a civilian volunteer unit formed in the 18th century to guard prominent citizens of Riga. One is supposed to haunt St Peter's. An old man bet two young men that they would not dare to spend the night of the feast of St Andrew in the church and prove that they had been there by hammering a nail into the altar. On St Andrew's night the two youths entered the church just before midnight, but at the stroke of midnight the old man and his witnesses who were waiting outside the church heard a terrible cry. The people outside soon broke into the church and one of the young men managed to escape through the main door. However, his friend was found hanged from the nail, a victim of the ghost of the blue guard.

The second story concerns Johann Heinrich Wulbern, the steeple builder. There was a tradition that when a new building was being topped off, the architect would go to the top and throw down a glass which was supposed to shatter, the number of shards representing the number of years for which the building would stand. Unfortunately, when Wulbern threw down his glass it was caught by a passing hay cart and therefore suffered only a minor crack. Nothing came of this evil omen, but the glass is preserved in the Museum of History and Navigation.

On leaving St Peter's, return to Skārņu iela and then turn right into Kaļķu iela. This last part of our walking tour of Old Riga will bring you back to the Hotel de Rome and a sign that Riga is now a thoroughly 21st-century consumer-oriented city: opposite the hotel and almost in the shadow of the Freedom Monument is Riga's first McDonald's.

Art nouveau
Although the majority of art nouveau buildings are in the New Town (see page 118) there are some in the Old Town as well. There are examples at Smilšu iela (Number 8, the cake shop; Number 6, a bank; and Number 2); Skūnu iela (Number 4 and 12–14); there is an imposing doorway opposite the Pūt, Vējiņ! restaurant in Jauniela. The attractive Flower House, with paintings of pharmaceutical plants on the outside walls, is at the corner of Mazā Monētu iela and Mazā Jaunava, just behind the Rolands Hotel.

New Town walk, including art nouveau
The Old Town and New Town are separated by the city canal (pilsētas kanāls) which runs through a series of parks and gardens. The canal follows the line of part of the old city wall which was demolished in the 19th century. Through the centre of the parks, separating the Old Town from the New Town, is Brīvības bulvāris (Freedom Boulevard), a pedestrianised street that is also the site of the Freedom Monument.

Freedom Monument
The Freedom Monument (Brīvības piemineklis) dominates the centre of Riga. Known locally as 'Milda', it was erected in 1935 and paid for by public subscription. It stands over 350m and is the tallest monument of its kind in Europe. It was designed by the Latvian architect Kārlis Zāle and consists of a tall granite column surmounted by a 9m-high figure of a woman holding three golden stars above her head. The three stars represent the three cultural regions of Latvia – Kurzeme, Vidzeme and Latgale. Engraved in gold letters on the base are the words *'Tevzēmei un brīvībai'* ('for fatherland and freedom'). Also decorating the monument is a sculpture of Lāčplēsis, the bear slayer, his long hair covering his bear ears (see pages 216 for more about Lāčplēsis). The monument was dedicated on November 18 1935, the 17th anniversary of the declaration of independence.

Nowadays the base is often surrounded by flowers, frequently red and white, reflecting the colours of the Latvian national flag. Flowers were forbidden during the Soviet era; indeed the Soviet authorities had contemplated removing the monument altogether, since it served as a focus of Latvian nationalist aspirations, but thought better of the idea, fearing demonstrations and reprisals. Instead they erected a statue of Lenin. The two monuments stood back to back for decades, Lenin facing east towards Moscow, the Freedom Monument facing west. Lenin has now disappeared, but the Freedom Monument remains.

Laima clock
Close to the Freedom Monument (on the Old Town side of the park) stands the Laima clock, another well-known landmark and a popular meeting point. Laima is the name of a well-known chocolate manufacturer and the Latvian word for happiness or good luck (there was an ancient deity of that name – see page 30).

National Opera
Southwest of the Laima clock is a fountain, the Nymph of Riga, which dates back to 1888. It stands in front of the stately National Opera, the home of Riga's opera and ballet companies. Originally built as a German theatre, this impressive building (classical on the outside, baroque on the inside) can be seen from anywhere in this central parkland area. See page 38ff.

The parks
The parks on either side of the Freedom Monument were laid out in 1853–63. The one through which Brīvības bulvāris runs is the Bastejkalns Park, so called after the

17th-century bastion that once stood here and formed a vital part of Riga's defences.

If you walk through Bastejkalns Park you will come across a set of engraved stones near the bridge that crosses the canal (most are on the New Town side, one is on the Old Town side of the canal). On the night of January 20 1991 Black Beret forces loyal to Moscow attempted to capture a number of government buildings including the Ministry of the Interior on Raiņa bulvāris, the street running alongside the canal on the New Town side. Several Latvians were shot, some say by sniper fire from the rooftops. The stones preserve the memory of five victims: Gvīdo Zvaigne, a cameraman who was filming events; Andris Slapiņš, a cinema director and cameraman; two militiamen, Sergejs Kononenko and Vladimirs Gomanovics; and Edijs Riekstiņš, a student.

The park also contains monuments to the writer, Rūdolfs Blaumanis, the composer Alfrēds Kalniņš, and the researcher, Keldys.

Next to Bastejkalns Park is Kronvalda Park with its monuments to the Latvian writers Edzus and Upitis. Also set in this park are the Riga Congress House (Rigas kongresu nams) and the Riga Council Building (Rigas dome).

National Theatre
Close to the canal on Kr Valdemāra iela is the National Theatre. It is a small theatre with seating for only 890. It was here that Latvia declared independence on November 18 1918. A concert is held here every year to commemorate the event.

University
At the New Town end of Brīvības bulvāris, on Rainis bulvāris, stands the main building of the University of Riga, a Gothic building with elements of the Romanesque. It stands on the site of the ancient Rīdzene River, long since channelled underground, and was originally used by the Riga Polytechnical Institute. It features a stone staircase divided into three parts, the centre section of which is traditionally used only by graduates.

On Merķeļa iela, the street behind the university and alongside Vermanes Park, is the impressive **House of the Riga Latvian Society** (Rigas Latviešu biedrība). The society was founded in 1868 at a time when Latvian was fighting to become a widely acknowledged language but the current building, with paintings on the façade by Jānis Rozentāls, dates from 1910. Just opposite, say hello to the engaging **statue of Kārlis Padegs**, an artist whose scandalous paintings were the talk of Riga in the 1930s. You can see one of his paintings, *Madonna with a Machine Gun*, in the State Museum of Fine Arts.

Esplanade Park
The Esplanade Park is the second major park in the town centre. It is also the location of a number of important buildings in the New Town.

The Academy of Art (Mākslas akademija) is a fine example of neo-Gothic architecture. In front of it there is a statue by Burkards Dzenis (1936) of Jānis Rozentāls, the founder of the Latvian Realist school of painting. Next to the Academy is the **State Museum of Fine Arts** (Valsts Mākslas Muzejs), built in 1905 by Wilhelm Neumann in German baroque style, which houses a collection of 17,000 paintings. It used to have a superb collection of paintings from all parts of Europe, including works by Ingres, Sir Edwin Landseer, Caspar David Friedrich and works by early German, Dutch and Italian masters. However, after World War I its director, Vilhelms Purvītis (himself a prominent landscape painter), began to concentrate on Latvian art, and now it exhibits works of almost exclusively Latvian and Russian origin. Inevitably, there is a great deal of work by Rozentāls (his portrait of the singer Malvine Vignère-Grīnberga painted in the last year of his life is particularly well known), but the majority of paintings are by artists whose names will be known only to experts in Latvian and Russian art. There is a portrait of the Russian writer Turgenev (painted in 1869) by A Gruzdins (1825–91), a bust of the Russian composer Mussorgsky by Teodors Zaļnkalns (1876–1928), a portrait of Kārlis Zāle (the designer of the Freedom Monument) by Ludolfs Liberts (1895–1959) painted in 1934 and showing a relaxed Zāle smoking a cigarette, and a picture of the old harbour when it was located closer to the Old Town by Jānis Roberts Tilbergs (1880–1972). Latvia's best-known woman painter is Alexandra Belcova (1892–1981). Several of her portraits are on show. The museum also has a notable collection of paintings of the Himalayas by the Russian artist and explorer Nicholas Roerich (1874–1947). Open 11.00–17.00 every day except Tuesday; May 1–Oct 1 open 11.00–19.00 Thursdays.

Also in the park is the **monument to Jānis Rainis**, one of Latvia's most famous writers and translators (see page 218).

Orthodox Cathedral

The Russian Orthodox cathedral, with its distinctive domes surmounted by Orthodox crosses, was built in 1876–84 to designs by Roberts Pflugs and Jānis Baumanis. During the Soviet years it was used as a planetarium and for scientific lectures. Now it has been handed back to the Orthodox Church, and has been magnificently restored.

Opposite the cathedral, the large government building is the Ministru kabinets, the Cabinet Office.

Reval Hotel Latvijā

The skyline of the New Town is dominated by what used to be the huge Soviet-built Hotel Latvijā but is now a modern hotel, refurbishment having been completed in May 2001. With its 27 storeys, it is still the tallest building in the country and has become something of a landmark, although many of Riga's inhabitants used to regard the original hotel as an eyesore. It took about 20 years to complete. There is a story about a travel guide who was asked by someone in her group what the huge building site was. She told the person concerned and bemoaned the inefficiency of Soviet construction. The story got back to her boss who reprimanded her for her disloyalty. The next time she was asked the same question, by which time building was at a more advanced stage, she simply replied, 'I don't know what it is, but things move fast here: there was nothing there the other day.' The travel writer, Colin Thubron, describes a stay there in the 1980s in *Among the Russians*:

> The hotel itself conformed miserably to expectation. It was huge,
> charmless, exhibitionist. Latvians joke that these tourist ghettos are made of
> 60 per cent glass, 30 per cent ferro-concrete and 10 per cent microphones.
> All their minor fittings, all those things by which a civilization may be
> gauged by archaeologists after it has gone, were wretchedly poor. When I
> turned on the light-switch the electricity made a scuttling like rats along
> the curtain rails, then died. The furniture was of black-varnished pine; the
> shower curtains chiffon-thin. The lukewarm water which trickled from the
> shower was augmented by surreptitious leaks in other places, and the rain
> had enfiladed the double-glazed windows to stream down the frames.

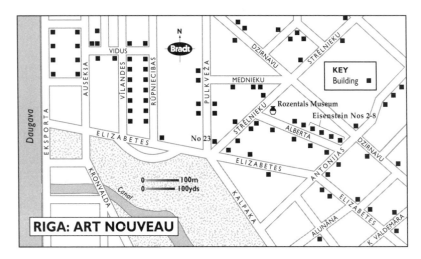

The new Reval Hotel Latvijā has no traces of this former description. It has been fully renovated and offers all the usual facilities of international hotels. Even if you are not staying there, a ride to the Skyline Bar on the 26th floor, using the glass lift, provides wonderful views over Riga.

Art nouveau

If you turn left along Elizabetes iela along the front of the Hotel Latvijā, you come to Antonijas iela on the right; this in turn takes you to Alberta iela. The streets in this area are known for two architectural features. There are a number of traditional wooden buildings here, including some on Brīvības iela itself.

ART NOUVEAU IN RIGA

Riga has one of the largest collections of art nouveau buildings in the whole of Europe. Around one-third of all the buildings in central Riga were built in this style between around 1896 and 1913. Even within this relatively short time various sub-styles can be distinguished: eclectic art nouveau, perpendicular art nouveau and from 1905 the distinctively Latvian National Romanticism.

Art nouveau (or Jugendstil as it is known in German) originally developed in Germany and Belgium towards the end of the 19th century and spread rapidly throughout Europe as far as Spain and Hungary. Its original decorative elements – birds, animals, shells, elaborate flower motifs are typical – were in stark contrast to the academic styles of the late 19th century. Philosophically, art nouveau introduced the concept that everything useful should be beautiful; the outside of a building for example should be suited to the function of the building. As the style spread throughout Europe individual countries developed their own variations.

The style which developed in Riga was influenced mainly by German, Austrian and Finnish architects, but the approach also has distinctive elements drawn from Latvian cultural traditions and construction techniques. Most of the architects who designed Riga's art nouveau buildings were trained at the Riga Polytechnical Institute; almost 90% were Baltic Germans, but the 10% or so of native Latvian architects built about 40% of the new buildings.

There are also some of Riga's finest examples of art nouveau or Jugendstil in the surrounding streets. Wandering around these areas, and remembering to look up to the very top of the buildings, gives an idea of the range of styles and the sheer inventiveness of many of the architects. Some of the most memorable buildings are the work of Mikhail Eisenstein (1867–1921), father of film director Sergei of *Battleship Potemkin* fame. These include **10b Elizabetes iela**, with its monumental faces, and the well-restored building at 41Strēlnieku iela, now occupied by the School of Economics. Numbers 2, 2a, 4, 6, 8 and 13 Alberta iela are also his work. Number 4 is of particular interest. With lions dramatically astride the turrets, it was for several years the home of Eisenstein. At Number 12 Alberta iela, designed by Konstantīns Pēkšens, is the **Jānis Rozentāls and Rūdolfs Blaumanis Memorial Museum** (see below). The museum is an interesting record of the life of these artists, but even if you do not visit the museum, it is worth looking into the entrance and admiring the elaborate staircase leading up to it.

Other buildings of note in this area include the block at the corner of Strēlnieku iela and Elizabetes iela (21a) which has a plaque to commemorate the architect and diplomat Mārtiņš Nuksa (1878–1942), 23 Elizabetes iela, with the motto 'Labor vincit omnia' ('Work conquers all'), Numbers 3 and 14 Ausekļa iela, and Number 3 and 4 Vidus iela.

While Eisenstein's buildings are in the eclectic art nouveau style, the buildings in the New Town shopping area reflect a greater diversity of styles. Examples of perpendicular art nouveau can be seen at 49–51 Terbātas iela, the work of E Laube, and at 61 Lāčplēša iela (architect Rudolf Dohnberg). Examples of the much heavier National Romanticism style can be seen at 15–17 Terbātas iela, the work of Pēkšens and Laube, and at 62 Brīvības iela, again the work of Laube.

There are also some art nouveau buildings in the Old Town (see page 115).

The most extravagant art nouveau buildings are in Alberta iela. Six of the apartment blocks here (Numbers 2, 2a, 4, 6, 8 and 13) were designed by Mikhail Eisenstein. Close by, Elizabetes iela is also rich in art nouveau buildings, including the former studio of the painter Jānis Rozentāls, now a museum. The building was designed in 1904 by Konstantīns Pēkšens (one of the most prolific art nouveau architects, responsible for over 250 buildings). The spectacular murals lining the circular staircase inside the building bear witness to the fact that art nouveau was not limited to building exteriors, but also included interior design, furniture, china, glassware and book design.

After the revolution of 1905 a distinctively Latvian variation of art nouveau developed, known as National Romanticism. Keen to promote national awareness at a time of oppression, architects sought to use traditional Latvian folk art elements and to use the language of the indigenous art of wooden construction. Natural building materials were used, and typical elements were steep roofs, heavy structures and the use of ethnographic ornamental motifs. Some examples include Brīvības iela 47, Terbātas iela 15–17 and Kr Valdemāra iela 67, all built by Eižens Laube (together with K Pēkšens in the case of the school building at Terbātas iela 15–17). See also the photograph of an art nouveau doorway in the Old Town (opposite page 86).

Jānis Rozentāls and Rūdolfs Blaumanis Memorial Museum

Further examples of some of the area's finest art nouveau houses are to be found on Alberta iela, including the house at Number 12, designed by K Pēkšens, Flat 9 of which is now the Jānis Rozentāls and Rūdolfs Blaumanis Memorial Museum (Jāņa Rozentāla un Rūdolfa Blaumaņa Memoriālais Muzejs). The museum is reached from an entrance in Strēlnieku iela. Take the elaborate staircase in the rather neglected hallway to the top floor and ring to gain admission. Good photographs of Alberta iela can be taken from the Rozentāls Museum.

Jānis Rozentāls (1866–1916) was born, the son of a blacksmith, in Kurzeme. In spite of the fact that he enjoyed only a rudimentary education, he studied at the St Petersburg Academy of Arts from which he graduated in 1894. He painted some 300 portraits, landscapes and altarpieces and did a large amount of book illustration as well as producing essays and criticism. He and his wife ran Riga's most famous salon. He moved to Helsinki at the beginning of World War I and died there on December 26 1916 where he was initially buried. However, his remains were removed to be reinterred in the Meža cemetery in Riga (see page 132) in 1920.

Rozentāls's wife, Elija Forsele-Rozentāle (1871–1943) was born in Finland. After studying at the Helsinki Music School and in Paris, Rome and Milan she went on to become a renowned mezzo-soprano. She met her husband-to-be when she came to Riga to sing in November 1902. They married in 1903 and lived in the flat that is now the museum together with their children, Laila, Irja and Miķelis. She too is buried in the Meža cemetery.

The painter Rūdolfs Blaumanis rented a room in the flat and lived there between 1906 and 1908.

The museum was established in 1973. The living rooms contain pictures, photographs and artefacts connected with the life of its inhabitants. The studio and other rooms on the top floor are an art school and are used to exhibit works by the students who range from young children to mature painters. Open 11.00–17.00 every day except Tuesday and Wednesday.

Alexander Nevsky Church

The Alexander Nevsky Church on the corner of Brīvības iela and Lāčplēša iela is named after the 13th-century Russian prince who was canonised by the Russian Orthodox Church in 1547 for his efforts to preserve Orthodoxy in Russia against the Germans whom he defeated at Lake Peipus (now in Estonia) in 1242. His story is now famous because of the film made by Eisenstein in 1938 with music by Prokofiev.

St Gertrude's Church

St Gertrude's Church, just off Brīvības iela in Ģertrūdes iela, is a large red-brick church built in 1863–67 to designs by J D Felsko. The plain interior and pleasing woodwork and gallery are typical of many Latvian churches.

Vērmaņu Gardens

Bounded by Elizabetes iela, Kr Barona, Merķeļa and Tērbates iela, the Vērmanes dārzs (as the gardens are called in Latvian) is the most popular of Riga's central parks. Opened in 1817, it was named in honour of the woman who donated the land to the city. Originally it was a refuge for residents of Riga who could not get out to the countryside. It soon acquired attractions, including a bronze fountain cast in Berlin, a playground, an ice rink, a sundial and the first rose garden in Riga. It has an open-air theatre and statue of Krišjānis Barons, the writer and poet, and Mihails Tāls, the chess champion (see page 28).

Berga Bazārs

Not far from the Vērmaņu Gardens, just behind the Jāņa Sēta bookshop in Elizabetes iela, is the Berga Bazārs. This area was originally developed in the late-19th/early-20th century by the builder and property developer, Kristaps Bergs (1840–1907) as a combination of commercial, residential and retail properties: the architect was Konstantīns Pēkšēns (1859–1928). The area fell into disrepair during the Soviet period, but reconstruction began in 1992 when ownership was restored to Bergs's great-grandchildren. The development has a new hotel (the Berga Bazārs), cafés, shops, including one selling hand-made chocolates, and restaurants.

Central Station, the market and the Academy of Sciences

If you take Raiņa bulvāris past the university it eventually brings you to the railway station. The first station was built here in 1861 and was known as the Orel or Dvinsk station. A second station, Tukums station, served Kurzeme. In 1888 a chapel called the Chapel of Thanksgiving was erected next to it to give thanks for the fact that the tsar's family escaped with their lives from a train crash near Borki in Kharkov. It was demolished in 1925. A new station was built between 1957 and 1960 but this has recently been replaced by a large station-cum-shopping-centre complex.

Beyond the station (under the railway bridge) is the Central Market (Centrāl tirgus). In the 19th century this area was full of what used to be called 'red warehouses' (some still stand), so called after the colour of the bricks used to build them. The modern market buildings consist of five large pavilions, each one originally designed to deal with a different product. Each one is 12m high and covers an area of 75,000m², and was built in 1930 to a design intended for Zeppelin hangars. Apart from the formal market, the area around the hangars is full of stalls selling all manner of food, clothing and other goods.

If you continue along Gogoļa iela to Turğeneva iela you come to an excellent example of Soviet architecture of the Stalin era in the form of the Academy of Sciences building. Built in 1957, its nickname, 'Stalin's birthday cake', reflects its ornateness. Similar buildings can be found in Moscow and Warsaw. The Communist hammer and sickle motifs close to the top are now difficult to see.

MUSEUMS

Riga has a huge number of museums, most of them of a high standard. They tend to be closed on Mondays and sometimes Tuesdays, so if you have a particular interest you should plan your trip carefully.

Monday opening

The only museums open on Monday are the State Museum of Art, the Motor Museum, the Open Air Ethnographic Museum, 'Jews in Latvia', the Sports Museum and the Museum of the Occupation (in summer only).

In general museums open at 10.00 or 11.00 and close at 17.00. In summer, a few of the museums stay open until 19.00, usually on Wednesday or Thursday. These include the State Museum of Art, the Arsenal Museum of Art, the Museum of Decorative and Applied Art, the Museum of Natural History, the History Museum and the Photographic Museum.

Which, if any, museums you visit, obviously depends on your personal interests. The most commonly visited museums include the Open Air Ethnographic Museum, the Museum of the Occupation, the Motor Museum, the State Museum of Art, the Jānis Rozentāls Memorial Museum and the adjacent art nouveau houses, and the Blackheads' House.

Jāņa Akurātera Museum 6a O Vāciesa iela, Pārdaugava; tel: 761 9934 (across the Daugava River from the Old Town, see page 130). The wooden house was the home of Jānis Akurāters (1876–1937), the popular Latvian writer, rifleman and later director of the Radio Service in Riga. Right up to his death, he wrote poetry and novels, his best known being *Kalpa zena vasara* (*The Young Farmhand's Summer*) and *Degosa sala* (*The Burning Island*). Open Wed–Sat 11.00–17.00.

Arsenal Museum of Art (Mākslas Muzejs Arsenals) 1 Torņa iela; tel: 721 3695. The museum has a reserve of 12,500 pictures, sculptures etc by Latvian artists who emigrated after 1945. Exhibitions are held on the ground floor and paintings by children displayed on the first floor. Open 11.00–17.00 every day except Mon; May 1–Oct 1 open until 19.00 Thu.

State Museum of Art (Valsts Mākslas Muzejs) 10a Kr Valdemāra iela; tel: 732 4461. The museum, built in 1905 by Wilhelm Neumann in German baroque style, houses a large collection of mainly local works of art and is a must for anyone interested in 19th- and early-20th-century Latvian art. Art by non-Latvian artists is less prominent, but the museum does have a notable collection of paintings of the Himalayas by the Russian artist and explorer Nicholas Roerich (1874–1947). In addition to the permanent collection, the museum also holds frequent exhibitions of works by more modern or contemporary artists. At the entrance is a small area selling postcards of some of the paintings and greetings cards of Old Riga. Open 11.00–17.00 every day except Tue; May 1–Oct 1 open until 19.00 Thu. Admission Ls1.20. Tours in English Ls5.

Aviation Museum Riga Airport – to the right of the terminal; tel: 720 7482. The museum contains Soviet helicopters and planes of various ages, including almost all the models of the Soviet MiGs, which can be viewed in detail when the museum is open, or over the wall, if it is closed. Allegedly open 10.00–17.00; closed Sat and Sun, but phone to check before visiting.

Krišjānis Barons Memorial Museum (Krišjāņa Barona Memorialais Muzejs) 3–5 Kr Barona iela; tel: 728 4265. The museum is the flat (Number 5) occupied by Krišjāņa Barons (1835–1923), the Latvian poet and folklorist who is best remembered as the collector of Latvian oral literature, *dainas,* traditional four-line songs. Exhibits recreate his life and work through documents and photographs. Information is available in English; examples of folk music and videos can also be purchased. Open 11.00–18.00; closed Mon and Tue. Admission Ls0.40.

The Blackheads' House (Melngalvju nams) 7 Ratslaukums; tel: 704 4300. Open 10.00–17.00 every day except Mon. Admission Ls1. See page 110.

Cinema Museum (Rīgas Kino Muzejs) Krāslavas 22; tel: 722 0282. The building, which is in the old Russian working-class district of Riga, used to house the secret printing press used by the communist newspaper, *Cīņa* (*Battle*). You can still visit the secret passages underneath the building and view the model printing presses. Open 12.00–17.00 every day except Mon.

The Cross-Vaulted Gallery of the Dome (see page 107). Open 10.00–17.00 every day May–Oct.

'Dauderi' Latvian Cultural Museum (Latvijas Kultūras Muzejs) 30 Sarkandaugavas iela; tel: 739 2229. This museum is housed in an elegant red-brick house and was built from 1897–98, and contains a vast collection of memorabilia related to the recent history of the country brought together by Gaidis Graundiņš, a Latvian living in Germany. Open 11.00–17.00; closed Mon and Tue.

Museum of Decorative and Applied Art (Dekoratīvi Lietišķās Mākslas Muzejs) 10–20 Skārņu iela; tel: 722 2235. The museum opened in 1989 in the restored Jura baznīca (St George's Church) in the Old Town. The exhibits include tapestries, pottery, glasswork and sculpture, and the old churchyard has been transformed into a sculpture garden. Open 11.00–17.00 every day except Mon; open until 19.00 Wed.

Museum of Fire-fighting (Ugunsdzēsības Muzejs) 5 Hanzas iela; tel: 733 1334. This unusual museum is appropriately housed in an art nouveau fire station built in 1912 and contains displays depicting the history of fire-fighting in Riga. The engines displayed go back to 1899 and include a Chevrolet from America. Open 10.00–16.30; closed Mon and Tue. Admission Ls0.20.

Latvian Museum of Foreign Art (Latvijas Ārzemju Mākslas Muzejs) 3 Pils laukums; tel: 722 6467. Housed in part of Riga Castle, the museum consists of three floors of paintings, sculptures, drawings and ceramics by artists from Germany, Holland, France and Belgium. There are almost no works of great distinction. Open 11.00–17.00 every day except Mon. Admission Ls1.20.

Latvian History Museum (Latvijas Vēstures Muzejs) 3 Pils laukums; tel: 722 1357. This museum, part of the castle complex, traces the history of Latvia and Latvian culture from 9000BC to the present day. Each room takes a different and unrelated theme. A hat exhibition opened in 2002. Open 11.00–17.00; closed Mon and Tue; open until 19.00 Thu. Admission Ls0.70; free on Wed.

'Jews in Latvia' Museum 3rd floor, 6 Skolas iela; tel: 738 3484. This small but moving museum is devoted to the history of Jews in Latvia, from the first records of Jewish families living with full civil rights in Piltene in the mid-16th century, through growing discrimination in the 19th and early 20th century, to the destruction of the synagogues in Riga, Jelgava and Liepāja in 1941 and the terrible sufferings subsequently imposed by both the Nazis and the Soviets. Open 12.00–17.00 Sun to Thu. Admission free.

Museum of Riga's History and Navigation (Rigas Vēstures un Kuģniecības Muzejs) 4 Palasta iela; tel: 735 6676; www.vip.lv/museums/riga. The main permanent exhibition traces the development of Riga from its beginnings to 1940. It does so by reference to maps, plans, pictures and objects of all kinds from the everyday life of the city's inhabitants. The collection is weak on the medieval period but particularly strong on 1920–40, showing how affluent and diverse life was for a reasonable number of people at that time. The exhibition also includes many models of ships that have been connected with Riga from the 10th century to the present day. Open 11.00–17.00; closed Mon and Tue. Admission Ls1.

Mentzendorff House (Mencendorfa nams) 18 Grēcinieku iela; tel: 721 2951. The former residence of a wealthy Riga merchant family this house is now a museum devoted to life in Riga in the 17th and 18th centuries. Open 10.00–17.00 every day except Mon and Tue, when open by prior arrangement for groups. Admission Ls1.20. Guided tours in English Ls3.

Motor Museum (Rīgas Motormuzejs) 6 S Eizenšteina iela; tel: 709 7170. The museum houses an acclaimed collection of over 100 motor vehicles, including cars which once belonged to Soviet leaders. See page 126. Open 10.00–18.00 Tue to Sun; open until 15.00 Mon.

Latvian Museum of Natural History (Latvijas Dabas Muzejs) 4 Kr Barona iela; tel: 722 6078. The museum has permanent exhibitions of geology, zoology, entomology, anthropology, and environmental protection. It also has an exhibition concentrating on the River Daugava and the effect of the construction of the hydro-electric power station on the river basin. Open 10.00–17.00; closed Mon and Tue; open 12.00–19.00 Thu. Admission Ls0.60.

Museum of the Occupation of Latvia (Okupācijas Muzejs) 1 Strēlnieku laukums; tel: 721 2715; www.occupationmuseum.lv. This museum, housed in an exceptionally ugly rectangular building, contains a permanent exhibition devoted to the history of Latvia during the Soviet and Nazi occupations of 1940–91. See page 110. Open 11.00–18.00; Oct 1–May 1 closed Mon. Admission free.

Open Air Ethnographic Museum (Latvijas Etnogrāfiskais Brīvdabas Muzejs) Brīvības gatve 440; tel: 799 4515. A visit to the beautifully constructed Open Air Ethnographic Museum will help you understand some of the more distinctive elements of Latvian history and tradition. The site includes farms, churches, windmills, houses, fishermen's villages and many other buildings, set in a huge pine forest next to Lake Jugla. Brought together from all parts of Latvia, some buildings date back to the 16th century. See page 126. Open 10.00–17.00 every day. Admission Ls1.

Latvian People's Front Museum (Latvijas Tautas Frontes Muzejs) Vecpilsētas 13–15; tel: 722 4502. This is a small, recently opened museum in the former offices of the popular movement which contributed so much to the regaining of Latvian independence. It displays pictures of the movement's leaders and the demonstrations leading up to independence and also shows how the office looked in its period of struggle. Open Tue 14.00–19.00; Wed–Fri 12.00–17.00; Sat 12.00–16.00. Admission free.

Pharmaceutical Museum (Farmācijas Muzejs) 13–15 Riharda Vāgnera iela; tel: 721 6828. Part of the Paul Stradin Museum of the History of Medicine, this branch is housed in a beautifully renovated 18th-century house in the Old Town. It has an extensive collection of documents, samples of medicine manufactured in Latvia and many other pharmacy-related items which non-visitors would be hard put to imagine. The interior of a 19th-century chemist's brings it all to life. Open 10.00–16.00 Tue to Sat.

Latvian Photographic Museum (Latvijas Foto Muzejs) 8 Mārstaļu iela; tel: 722 7231; www.culture.lv/photomuseum. The basic exhibition is of cameras and pictures from 1839 to 1941, including many of historic events such as the 1905 revolution and World War I. An interesting exhibit is dedicated to the Minox 'spy camera', invented by Walter Zapp, who was born in Riga in 1905 (page 28). The cameras were made in Riga between 1938 and 1943 and have been used ever since by spies, real and imagined, including by Sean Connery in *You Only Live Twice*. Open Tue, Fri and Sat 10.00–17.00 ; Wed and Thu 12.00–19.00; closed Sun and Mon. Admission Ls1.

Riga Porcelain Museum (Rigas Porcelāna Muzejs) Kalēju 9–11, in Konventa Sēta courtyard; tel: 750 3769. Riga has a long history of making porcelain, starting with the opening of the Kuznetzov factory in the first half of the 19th century, and the 6,000 exhibits reflect the many types of porcelain, from prestigious tea sets to crockery for everyday use, which have been made in the city from the mid 19th century to the present day. Visitors can see demonstrations of porcelain manufacturing and for Ls3 can take part and decorate mugs themselves. Open 11.00–18.00 every day except Mon.

Latvian Railway Museum (Latvijas Dzelzcela Muzejs) 2–4 Uzvaras bulvāris; tel: 583 2849 (just across the river from the Old Town, 5 minutes beyond the Akmens Tilts bridge). The museum dates from 1994 and is run by Latvian Railways. During its short life it has accumulated a wide range of materials going back about 100 years, including signals, timetables, track and above all, steam engines. Railway enthusiasts may be interested to know there is another branch of the museum at Jelgava (one hour by bus from Riga), which concentrates on railway safety and training. Open Wed–Sat 10.00–17.00. Admission Ls0.50.

Jānis Rozentāls and Rūdolfs Blaumanis Memorial Museum (Jāņa Rozentāla un Rūdolfa Blaumaņa Memoriālais Muzejs) 12–19 Alberta iela; tel: 733 1641. The museum commemorates the life and work of two of Latvia's most famous artists: Rozentāls lived here from 1904–15; Blaumanis only for two years. See page 119. Open 11.00–18.00; closed Mon and Tue. Admission Ls0.60.

Latvian Sports Museum (Latvijas Sporta Muzejs) 9 Alksnāja iela; tel: 721 5127. This has a unique collection of bicycles, including a collapsable Peugeot built in 1915 and used during World War I and an English Raleigh lady's bicycle dating from 1895, as well as more conventional exhibits. It is housed in an attractive 17th-century warehouse. Open Mon–Fri 11.00–17.00; 11.00–17.00 Sat.

Paul Stradin Museum of the History of Medicine (P Stradiņa Medicīnas Vēstures Muzejs) 1 Antonijas iela; tel: 722 2656; www.mvm.lv. Located in the New Town on the corner of Antonijas iela and Kalpaka iela, this museum is the creation of the Latvian doctor and surgeon, Paulis Stradiņš (1896–1958), who collected the majority of the exhibits over a period of 30 years and presented them to the city of Riga. The exhibits, which include medical instruments, books and papers, cover a wide range of topics, from Riga during successive plague epidemics to how the human body copes with eating in space. Open 11.00–17.00 every day; closed Sun and Mon and the last Fri of each month.

Latvian War Museum (Latvijas Kara Muzejs) 20 Smilšu iela; tel: 722 8147; www.karamuzejs.lv. The museum is located in the Powder Tower (see page 102). During the Soviet occupation this museum was devoted to demonstrating how Latvia became a revolutionary Soviet state. Now it is a mainstream war museum with collections of army uniforms and other exhibits devoted to the military history of Latvia. Open May–Sep 10.00–18.00 every day except Mon and Tue; Oct–Apr 10.00–17.00 every day. Admission Ls0.50.

Theatre Museum (Eduarda Smiļģa Teātra Muzejs) 37–39 Smiļģa iela, in Pārdaugava (page 129); tel: 761 1893. This museum is housed in the building where theatre director and actor Eduards Smiļģis (1886–1966) lived for all but five years of his life. Although his personal theatre here could have accommodated an audience, he always rehearsed in strict privacy, totally on his own. This theatre was modelled on the Daile Theatre in central Riga. The collections comprehensively cover the history of the Latvian theatre, not only in Riga but also in Ventspils and in Liepāja. Open 11.00–18.00; closed Mon and Tue; open 12.00–19.00 Wed.

Museum of Writing, Theatre & Music (Rakstniecības, Teātra un Mūzikas Muzejs) 2 Pils laukums; tel: 721 1956. The former Rainis Museum, founded in 1925 and devoted to Latvian literature, has recently been rebranded as the Museum of Writing, Theatre & Music. Permanent exhibits include photographs, manuscripts and texts relating to the history of Latvian literature from its earliest times right up to the 20th century. Unfortunately, all the information (except for a short pamphlet) is in Latvian. Open 10.00–17.00; closed Mon and Tue. Admission Ls0.40.

OUTSIDE THE CENTRE

Outside the main tourist areas, Riga offers many possibilities for interesting visits and walks. These include visits to the Ethnographic Open Air Museum, the Motor Museum, walks in the Moscow District, the Pārdaugava area (the left bank of the River Daugava) and the Mežaparks, cemeteries and zoo. Brief descriptions are given below, but visitors with time to explore, and a good Riga map, will find lots more sites and views of interest.

Ethnographic Open Air Museum

The Latvian Ethnographic Open Air Museum (Latvijas Etnogrāfiskaja Brīvdabas Muzejs, 440 Brīvības gatve; tel: 799 4510; fax: 799 4178) is located on the outskirts of Riga by Lake Jugla about 12km from the city centre. The only way of getting there by public transport is to take the number 1, 19 or 28 buses from the city centre to the stop just by the road leading to the museum (the stop bears the name of the museum, so is easy to spot). Established in 1924 (although it opened in 1932 with only six buildings) the museum now covers 100 hectares and depicts traditional ways of life from the 16th to 19th century. It consists of reconstructions of old farmsteads and traditional houses, windmills, fishing villages and exhibits; on occasions there are also demonstrations of traditional crafts. Note the traditional *dore*, hollowed tree trunks standing on stone bases used for beekeeping, the pub, *krogs*, and windmills; the Usma church is still used for services on Sundays as well as for weddings.

The museum has an excellent self-service restaurant in a traditional wooden building close to the entrance which serves typical Latvian food and drink. You should allow at least two hours for a visit, and you could easily spend a half or even a whole day here. Open daily 10.00–17.00.

Motor Museum

The Motor Museum (Rīgas Motormuzejs, 6 S Eizenšteina iela). is located to the east of the Old Town about 8km from the centre along Brīvības gatve. It can be reached by taking the number 15 bus, but this does not run from central Riga

WOODEN BUILDINGS

Although still not very well known internationally, Riga's wooden buildings have aroused a great deal of interest locally in recent years, and with justification. Wooden architecture developed over many years in Riga, almost until World War II, long after most countries in Europe had turned away from it. In the post-war period, when wooden buildings in many countries were destroyed, buildings in Riga were left intact, mainly because of the lack of housing under Soviet occupation. Since the restoration of independence there has been a trend among wealthier people to buy and renovate some of these lovely buildings, most of which had fallen into disrepair.

The oldest surviving wooden buildings are from the middle of the 18th century and are in Pārdaugava (the opposite bank of the river from the Old Town). The best-preserved example from the 18th century is perhaps the Hartman House (Hartmaṇa muižiṇa) at 28–30 Kalnciema iela (west of the intersection with Slokas iela). Another example is 28 Daugavgrīvas iela, although most buildings from this period are still in poor condition. A well-preserved example from the early 19th century is the Blok House (Bloka muižiṇa) on the corner of Vienības gatve and Altonavas iela south of (alight at the Pansionāts stop in Mežciems). The number 14 or 18 trolleybuses go from Brīvības iela and Čaka iela respectively to Gaiļezers Hospital, about 500m from the museum. The museum is not easy to spot: look out for a modern red-brick-and-glass building. The entrance is reached via a bridge from the car park. It is an acclaimed collection of over 100 motor vehicles, including cars which once belonged to the Soviet leaders, Stalin, Khrushchev and Brezhnev, and to Erich Honecker, the leader of the former German Democratic Republic. Wax figures of some of these former politicians and motor enthusiasts help to liven up the displays: Stalin sits in his armoured ZIS 115 (said to have done 2.5km to the litre), Brezhnev at the wheel of his crashed Rolls-Royce, and Gorky stands next to his 1934 Lincoln. The museum has a good café, toilets and a shop selling souvenirs. Open 10.00–18.00 Tuesday–Sunday and 10.00–15.00 on Monday.

Moscow District walk

You can either walk to the Maskavas district or take tram number 7 from the stop opposite the National Opera on Aspāzijas bulvāris. The route takes you past the Central Market and along Maskavas iela to the **Maskavas district** (Maskavas Forštate), so called because it was a Russian area in earlier times (Maskva = Moscow in Russian) and the road to Moscow passed through it. For many years it was inhabited mainly by Russians and Jews and, although this is no longer the case, it continues to attract a high proportion of people of non-Latvian origin. The area is a quiet haven where it is easy to imagine yourself here 100 years ago: the streets are still cobbled, many of the houses wooden, trees and parks plentiful and the number of cars typically very few.

If you have come by tram, get off at Mazā Kalna iela (two stops after coming under the elevated road). The area near the junction of Maskavas iela and Mazā Kalna iela used to be known as Krasnaja Gorka (Red Hill) and was where the Russian population of Riga came to celebrate the first Sunday after Easter, a traditional Orthodox feast day. The traditional Russian name is barely remembered now, but the tradition remains alive in the name of the nearby street, Sarkanā iela (Red Street). Walk up Mazā Kalna iela as far as you can go, noting the

Torņakalns station. Large houses such as this had a country atmosphere about them, although they were situated on one of the main roads into Riga. Unfortunately very few examples still exist.

An easily accessible area where wooden buildings abound is the Maskavas district, and in particular Maskavas iela. If you take tram number 7 from the stop opposite the National Opera you will go through the Central Market and emerge a little later on Maskavas iela (see above). Most of the wooden houses here are from the end of the 19th and beginning of the 20th century. Typically they are large two-storey residences, some with gables and cornices. At 149–53 Maskavas iela, near Maskavas dārzs (park), for example, you can see a row of such houses.

Wooden buildings are also scattered around the New Town. At the time when art nouveau was in fashion, many Latvian architects were interested in building in wood as well as in stone. Examples can be found at 100 Brīvības iela (in the courtyard, designed in 1899 by K Felsko), on Ernesta Birznieka-Upīša iela, near the station, and at many other locations. Inside some of the wooden buildings, some fine interiors and staircases have survived.

See also Mežaparks (page 130) and Jūrmala (page 133) for examples of wooden buildings.

JEWISH RIGA

The only **synagogue** that now operates in Riga is in Peitavas iela. The site of what used to be the main synagogue (the **Choral Synagogue**) on the corner of Dzirnavu iela and Gogoļa iela is marked by a memorial (not a very impressive one) consisting of parts of the old synagogue set in a sort of park. A plaque records the destruction of the synagogue on July 4 1941 and the masscre of the Jews who were forced into it before it was set on fire. Number 29 Dzirnavu iela was also the site of a Jewish school until 1940. It opened again in 1989 as the only recognised Jewish school in the country.

There is a **Jewish Museum** and community centre (page 123) at 6 Skolas iela, a short walk from the Reval Hotel Latvijā, which deals with the history of Jewish life in Latvia since the 18th century and the revival of Jewish life in the country since independence.

A number of **plaques** in Riga commemorate influential Jews in Latvia. At 2a Alberta iela a plaque marks the house where Sir Isaiah Berlin, 'the British philosopher', lived from 1909–15. At 6 Blaumaņa iela there is a plaque for Marks Razumnijs (1896–1988), a Jewish poet and playwright.

On Ķīpsala (Kip island) is the **house of Jānis Lipke** (1900–87) who sheltered 53 Riga Jews in his house on the island during World War II. As their number grew, two large cellars were dug to conceal them, and 43 survived the war.

On the outskirts of Riga are a number of sites which also may be of interest. **Rumbula**, 10km outside of Riga off Maskavas iela, is a site where some 25,000 Jews from the Riga ghetto were murdered in 1941. **Biķernieki mežs**, also close to Riga, is a similar site. A memorial was recently dedicated to the victims here by the Latvian president. To get there take bus number 14 from Brīvības iela to Biķernieku mežs. Finally, **Salaspils**, 20km south of Riga, was a Nazi camp where many thousands of people, including Jews, were killed (page 141).

For information on the Jewish ghetto, see below.

traditional 'shops' on the left (holes in the wall), and you will come to the **Russian Orthodox Church of St John the Baptist** at the edge of the **Ivan Cemetery** (Ivana Kapi). Turn right out of the church and then right along Daugavpils iela. A left turn along Jēkabpils iela leads through two parks, formerly cemeteries, **Klusais dārzs** (Quiet Garden) to the left and **Miera dārzs** (Peace Garden) to the right. Each has a church in its ground: St Francis, a Catholic church in the latter, and All Saints, a Russian Orthodox church in the former. At the edge of the park turn left down Katoļu iela as far as Maskavas iela.

It was in this area that the **Jewish ghetto** was established in 1941. In August 1941 the Rigan citizens who lived in the district were moved to locations closer to the centre of the city, and by October an area of about 750m² had been formed, taking in Lāčplēša iela, Maskavas iela, Ebreju iela (Jews Street) and Daugavpils iela. The total Jewish population of the ghetto was about 30,000. The men in the ghetto who were fit to work were put to forced labour; the others were taken to Rumbula Forest on November 30 1941 and systematically murdered by German guards with the assistance of a significant number of Latvian collaborators. Other Jews were brought in to replace those murdered, only to suffer the same fate in the forests of Biķernieki or in Dreiliņi. The total number of people killed in this way has never been finally ascertained, but estimates indicate it to be around 50,000. On November 2 1943 the Riga ghetto was closed following the Warsaw ghetto uprising, and the few remaining inhabitants were shot or transported to concentration camps. No trace of the ghetto remains today, although there is a Jewish cemetery (Ebreju kapi) not far away between Tējas iela and Lauvas iela.

A left turn along Maskavas iela, followed by a right turn into Grebenščikova iela leads to the **Church of the Old Believers** (page 31), the glittering dome of which you can see from a distance. The area beyond the church and close to the river has seen considerable development in recent years. The large Mols shopping centre now stands on the riverbank and its buildings dominate the environs. Before crossing to it, you may like to visit the **Armenian Apostolic Church** (at the time of writing being restored) on Kojusalas iela. From in front of the shopping centre you can take a shuttle bus back to the station, close to the Central Market.

Left bank walk

Pārdaugava is the name for the area on the 'left bank' of the Daugava, the part of Riga that lies on the river bank opposite the Old Town, where about a quarter of the city's total population lives. It consists of a number of areas, such as Torņakalns and Āgenskalns, which have long since been swallowed up into Riga but which in places retain something of the atmosphere of small provincial towns. It began to be inhabited only after the building of bridges across the Daugava (an iron bridge in 1871 and a pontoon bridge in 1896). Gradually it grew into an area of about 120km^2 of industrial and residential development. At present the northern area in particular, close to the approaches to Vanšu brige (Vanšu tilts), is undergoing a further renaissance, as hotels and offices spring up. Particularly controversial is the *Saules Akmens* (Sun Stone) high-rise office complex built for Hansa Bank on Ķīpsala island, which has been criticised by UNESCO's world cultural heritage committee, among others, for being too tall for its location.

You can approach the area on foot by crossing the Akmens tilts (Stone Bridge) from the Old Town. If you prefer, take the number 2, 4 or 5 trams from 11 Novembra krastmala to the second stop after the bridge across the river. After crossing the river you come to Uzvaras bulvāris (Victory Boulevard) and the **Latvian Railway Museum** (page 125). The road leads on to **Uzvaras Parks** (Victory Park), so called to commemorate the liberation from German occupation, with its huge **Soviet War Memorial**. If you are interested in the theatre, you could take Bāriņu iela, the right fork through the park after Slokas iela, continue a little way beyond the park until you come to Eduarda Smiļģa iela, where you will find the **Theatre Museum (Eduarda Smiļģa Teātra Muzejs)** at number 37–39. The smaller **Arkādijas Parks** (Arcadia Park) was created in 1852 by the Prussian consul-general, Wehrmann (Vērmans). Next to it, **Mary's Pond** (Māras dīķis) is a popular place of recreation. It derives its name from the mill attached to St Mary's Church which was acquired by the city of Riga in 1573. The pond is probably the old mill pond and is sometimes referred to as Mary's mill pond (Māras sudmalu dīķis).

At the edge of Arkadijas Parks is Torņakalns railway station (you can also travel here directly, one stop on the railway from the Central Station). On June 14 2001 a **Monument to the Victims of Communist Persecution (Represēto piemineklis**) was unveiled to commemorate the 60th anniversary of one of the largest deportations of Latvians to Siberia. The work of Latvian sculptor Pēteris Jaunzems and the architect Juris Poga, it caused some considerable controversy. If you continue to walk along the road next to the railway lines away from central Riga, you will come shortly to Torņakalns's **Lutheran Church** (Lutera baznīca).

The church was opened in 1891 some years after a local pastor had decided to raise funds for a new church to commemorate the 400th anniversary of Martin Luther's birth in 1483. The architect was Johannes Koch (1850–1915), who also worked on fashionable apartment blocks in the New Town. Just beyond the church Torņakalna iela crosses the railway lines on a viaduct designed in art nouveau style. This was the first concrete construction in Riga: according to contemporary reports, many people were afraid to walk across it.

Close by (cross the viaduct, continue to the end of Torņakalna iela and turn right into Vācieša iela) is a museum that commemorates and was formerly the home of a Latvian writer, the **J Akurātera Memorial Museum** (page 122). Alternatively, turn the other way along Torņakalna iela, walk past the cemetery and right into Vienības gatve. Very shortly, at the corner of Altonavas iela, you will see the **Blok House** (Bloka muižiņa), a well-preserved example of an early 19th-century wooden building. Return to the corner of Torņakalna iela and cross into Satiksmes iela and then left on to Jelgavas iela. The bath house along here has a traditional sauna (under Ls2 per person) and also serves food and *kvass* (see page 63). From here you can easily make your way back to Torņakalns station for the return journey to central Riga.

Mežaparks, cemeteries and zoo

The Mežaparks area in the northeast of Riga lies on Ķīšezers (lake) and includes a park, which is the site of Riga Zoo as well as the immensely large Lielā estrāde (large stage), a stadium which can hold up to 20,000 singers and 30,000 spectators and is used for the annual Song Festival. The area also includes a spacious residential sector, which claims to be Europe's first garden city. To visit Mežaparks, take tram number 11 from K Barona iela to the Zooloģiskais dārzs (Zoological Park) stop, a trip of around 20 minutes. The route also takes you past the main cemeteries.

The first houses and streets here were built in Kaiser's Park, as it was then called, in 1902 but the area was gradually extended over the next 30 or so years. In its heyday it included art nouveau, functionalist and art deco family houses, all individually designed and all set in spacious green gardens. Between them, the individual gardens boasted around 100 species of trees and shrubs, many of them rare. The majority of owners were Baltic Germans, most of whom left Latvia from 1939 onwards. Under the Soviet occupation the houses, originally intended for one family, were turned into multi-occupancy dwellings and gradually fell into disrepair due to lack of money for their upkeep. Over the last few years, many of the properties have been restored, although some are still in various stages of neglect, and the area is now once again one of the most sought-after areas of real estate in Riga.

The best way to see the area is just to wander along some of the streets to the east of Koknese prospekts. An interesting circular route would take you from the tram stop along Ezermalas iela, right into E Dārziņa iela, right again into V Olava iela, left down Jāņa Poruka iela, right into Vēlmas iela, left into Sigulda iela, left along Koknešes prospekts, a short detour into Visbijas prospekts, returning again to Koknešes prospekts, left along Pēterupes iela, continuing into Hamburgas iela and finally back along Ezermalas iela to the tram stop.

Some houses which may be of interest include the richly decorated Villa Adele at 9 Hamburgas iela, now the residence of the German ambassador; the plain house at 14 Jāņa Poruka iela, an attempt to create a distinctly Latvian style of functionalism; 25 Hamburgas iela, a decorated art nouveau mansion built on top of what used to be a sand dune, and the mansard roofs, verandas and terraces of houses designed around 1911 by architect Gerhard von Tiesenhausen at 2, 4 and 6–8 Visbijas prospekts.

Riga Zoo

Riga has had a zoo since 1912. Covering an area of 16.4 hectares it has 2,500 animals and 400 species. It is known for its bears (brown and polar bears are represented), Galapagos turtles and Amur tigers. Rides on horseback or in carriages are alternatives to walking. It is at 1 Meža prospekts in the forest of the Mežaparks and is open from 10.00–18.00 every day.

Riga's cemeteries

Riga has three cemeteries that are worth visiting, if time permits, since they reflect something of the history of Latvia and present a number of architectural styles. They are all close to one another in an area directly south of Mežaparks and can be reached by public transport.

The Brothers' Cemetery

The Brothers' Cemetery (Brāļu Kapi) or Cemetery of Heroes on Aizsaules iela can be reached by taking the number 4 or number 9 buses from Brīvības iela heading east (bus stops in front of the Hotel Latvijā or at the central bus station) or the number 11 tram from the stop by the National Opera.

The Brothers' Cemetery is a fascinating ensemble of architecture and sculpture in attractive natural surroundings. It was planned in 1915 when thousands of Latvians were dying in the fight against the Germans in Kurzeme, and the same year the first fallen soldiers were buried here. It took 12 years to complete the cemetery, the overwhelming part of the work being done between 1924 and 1936. There are approximately 2,000 graves in Brāļu Kapi, 300 of them simply marked 'nezinams' ('unknown'). On March 25 1988 a memorial service for the victims of the years of the Stalin terror was held here, organised by the Latvian Writers' Association, and 10,000 people attended.

In Latvian folklore the oak symbolises masculine strength, while the lime tree symbolises feminine love; both of these powerful symbols are used extensively in the cemetery. The Latvian coat of arms appears over the entrance gate, while on both sides there are sculptured groups of cavalrymen. An avenue of lime trees leads to the main terrace. In the centre an eternal flame burns, flanked by oak trees. Beyond it is the cemetery itself, bordered by trees, shrubs, bushes and walls decorated with the coats of arms of all the Latvian regions and towns.

Especially moving are the Ievainotais jatnieks (The Wounded Horseman) and Divi brāļi (Two Brothers) sculptures. At one end of the cemetery stands the figure Māte Latvijā (Mother Latvia) who looks down in sorrow at her dead, a wreath to honour her fallen sons in one hand, in the other the national flag. The sculptures are the work of Kārlis Zāle who is himself buried here.

The cemetery was allowed to fall into neglect during the Soviet period, but was restored in 1993 and has since then become a focus of Latvian national feeling.

Rainis Cemetery

The Rainis Cemetery (Raiņa Kapi), Aizsaules iela, can be reached by taking the number 11 tram from Vērmanes Gardens/Merķeļa iela or the number 4 or 9 buses from the main bus station. Latvia's best-loved writer, Jānis Rainis, died on September 12 1929 and was buried here three days later. The cemetery was renamed in his honour. An avenue of silver birch leads to his grave which is marked by a red granite sculpture. Around the monument there is a semi-circular colonnade entwined with ivy.

Alongside Rainis lies his wife, the poet Aspāzija (Elza Rozenberg who died in 1943). The cemetery is also the resting place for a great number of Latvian writers, artists and musicians, many of whose graves are decorated with a creativity to match the life it is designed to commemorate.

Woodlands Cemetery

The Woodlands Cemetery (Meža Kapi), also on Aizsaules iela, was designed by G Kufelts, the director of Riga's parks, in 1913. Numerous political and government figures from the period of Latvia's first independence are buried here, including the former president, Jānis Čakste, and the government ministers, Zigfrids Meierovics and Vilhelms Munters. In addition, a number of Latvian artists, writers, poets and scientists lie here, among them Jānis Rozentāls, Anna Brigadere and Paulis Stradiņš. In April 1988 Latvia's leading human rights activist, Gunārs Astra, was buried here. Astra was sentenced to seven years' imprisonment followed by five years' internal exile by the Soviet regime in December 1983 for the crimes of possessing recordings of radio programmes, photo negatives and subversive books and for writing a manuscript of a personal nature. In his final words to the court he delivered an impassioned speech against the Soviet regime including these words:

> I fervently believe that these nightmare times will end one day. This belief gives me the strength to stand before you. Our people have suffered a great deal but have learned to survive. They will outlive this dark period in their history.

Riga's coat of arms

Near Riga 6

A number of places can be reached easily from Riga and are suitable for day trips. They include Rundāle, Sigulda, Cēsis and Salaspils, but Jūrmala is the closest place of any size.

JŪRMALA

In a sense, Jūrmala is not a place at all but a name: Jūrmala is the Latvian for 'seaside' or 'by the sea' and is in reality the collective name given to a number of small towns and villages along the Gulf of Riga about 25km from Riga. The name Jūrmala was officially recognised in 1959 as the name for this collection of towns stretching about 30km along the coast west of the Lielupe River. Long ago, the Lielupe flowed east into a smaller river, the Buļļupe, which in turn flowed into the Old Daugava River as it joined the Gulf of Riga. As a result of major flooding in about 1456 the Lielupe broke through to the gulf, as did the Daugava; consequently, both rivers now flow directly into the gulf. The Old Daugava River and the place where the original Riga fortress stood are now a swamp.

History

Jūrmala has been a resort since the end of the 18th century. Up until then the area was little more than a number of small fishing villages, although a certain amount of industry has also been important to the area: in the 17th century copper, lime and glass were all produced there, and the port at Kaugurciems was an important outlet for the export of locally produced goods. However, in the late 18th and early 19th centuries the area became popular with visitors, and summerhouses began to appear. The first hotel in the area was built in 1834 in Dubulti; in 1870 the first sanatorium (the Marienbāde in Majori) was constructed; and in 1877 the railway line to Tukums was completed, opening the area up to greater numbers than ever before. Mixed bathing was permitted in 1881. The sea air, mild climate, spa water and medicinal mud also made the small, growing towns along the coast a favourite with convalescents, so Jūrmala also gained a reputation as a health resort. The number of visitors rose from about 18,000 in 1873 to 60,000 by 1914.

World War I put a major brake on this development – battles were fought at Sloka and close to Ķemeri and Tīrelpurvs. However, after the war a town was formed out of ten of the villages, the railway bridge was rebuilt and a major road constructed, thereby improving access. Jūrmala began to grow again, and by 1925 it was experiencing an influx of about 100,000 visitors every year.

The resort was developed even further under the Soviet occupation: hotels, convalescent homes, sanatoria and pioneer camps were built from 1945 onwards, transforming Jūrmala into one of the most important holiday resorts in the Soviet

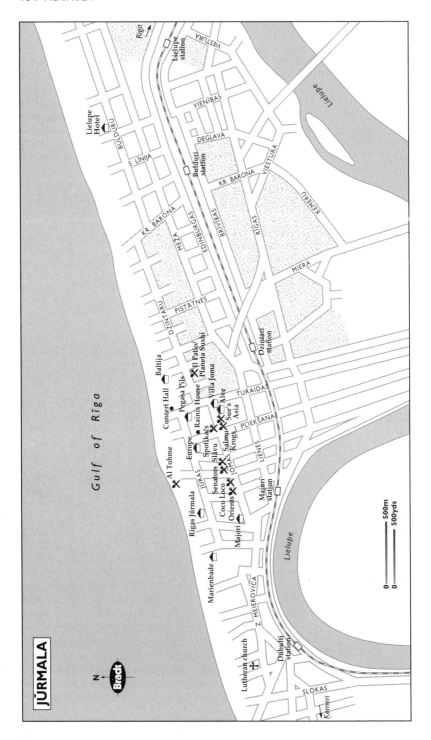

Above The New Castle at Sigulda (RR)
Right Room stove at Rundāle Palace (TH)
Below Rundāle Palace (TH)

Above Beach
resort at Jūrmala
in summer (MW)

Below The Baltic
Sea can remain
frozen through
to April (TH)

Union, attracting over 250,000 visitors a year. The area was also industrialised, bringing pollution, in particular from the paper mill at Sloka.

Jūrmala today
The beautiful 30-odd kilometre stretch of beach is virtually unspoilt and is the major attraction of Jūrmala. The gulf waters which had become polluted with sewage and waste from the Sloka paper factory have been cleaned up: the introduction of sewage treatment plants and the closure of the factory mean that the sea is now cleaner than it has been for many years. As a result, swimming has become possible again (the EU Blue Flag was awarded in 2000), and the beaches and woods are ideal for long walks. Sometimes pieces of amber can be found, particularly after a storm. However, the closure of the Soviet-operated factories and the almost complete downturn in tourism from the former Soviet Union have made for new problems: many of the medical centres have closed, and many hotels have found it hard to survive.

But things have started to improve again, albeit gradually, and while some parts of Jūrmala remain a little run-down, many of the hotels have undergone (or are undergoing) refurbishment. Much work has been done to redecorate the many summerhouses that give the town its distinctive feel. In 1997 the government declared the area around Ķemeri, at the far end of Jūrmala, a national park.

The most popular spots are Lielupe (named after the river), Dzintari (which literally means 'pieces of amber') and Majori.

In hot weather there are often mosquitoes, and in summer a species of tick is found here from which it is possible to contract encephalitis (see page 58).

Getting there
You can get to Jūrmala from Riga by train, bus, taxi or car. It can also be reached by boat in summer. There are frequent trains from the central railway station in Riga. It takes about 20 minutes from Riga to the first stop at Lielupe, although not all trains stop there. However, all trains do stop at Majori (about 40 minutes from Riga). Trains are most frequent between May and October (one every ten to 20 minutes) and run from about 05.00–23.00. Note that there is no one station called Jūrmala – it is probably best (unless you have a specific goal) to get out at Majori.

During the summer there are frequent buses from the bus station. Taxis leave Riga from a special taxi rank just outside the station. There is also a comfortable minibus connection between Jūrmala and Riga, running every 20–30 minutes.

On Saturdays and Sundays in summer the *Jūrmala* leaves from 11 Novembra krastmala, just next to Vanšu bridge, at 11.00, arriving in Jūrmala at 13.00. The return trip leaves Majori at 17.00, arriving in Riga two hours later. The boat trip costs Ls3 one way for adults and Ls1 one way for children between six and 12 years old. For further information; tel: 957 8329; fax: 734 6515.

Jūrmala is only a 20–30-minute drive from Riga. However, as you approach Jūrmala you must pull into the lay-by at the toll point and buy a special ticket before entering the area by car. Tickets cost Ls1 a day.

Accommodation
Jūrmala is undergoing a great deal of development and the number of accommodation possibilities, particularly in small guesthouses, is growing constantly. In the summer season, booking in advance is advisable.

Alve 88a Jomas iela, Majori; tel: 775 5951; fax: 775 5972; email: alve@navigator.lv; www.alve.times.lv. A stylish hotel, with lots of wood and glass, and 10 spacious and airy rooms, on the main street in Majori. Spa programmes, including detoxification and relaxation, are offered, with a steam bath, spa bath, thalassotherapy and body wraps available in the spa centre. Convenient location, but can be noisy on summer weekends. Double rooms from Ls45.

Camping Nemo 1 Altbalss iela, Vaiveri; tel: 773 2350; fax: 773 2349; email: nemo@nemo.lv; www.nemo.lv. Spaces for tents and caravans at the Nemo Water Amusement Park, right next to the beach in Vaivari. Open in summer only (May–Sep). A two-person chalet costs Ls12 per night.

Eiropa (Europe) Hotel 56 Jūras iela, Majori; tel: 776 2211; fax: 776 2299; email: hoteljuras@apollo.lv; www.hoteljuras.lv. Opened in 2004, an elegantly restored art nouveau house with 19 rooms, including some suites, and only 50m from the beach. Prices include not only breakfast, but also use of the sauna and fitness room. Double rooms from Ls70.

Kurši Guesthouse 30 Dubultu prospekts, Dubulti; tel: 777 1606; fax: 777 1605; email: kursi@angstceltne.lv. Offers self-catering apartments, mostly on 2 floors, and all with a private shower, toilet, kitchenette and satellite TV. For long stays there are substantial discounts, and if you fancy a 'romantic weekend' package, the guesthouse offers a special deal with a candlelit dinner and use of a sauna. Ls35–66 a day.

Lielupe Hotel 64–68 Bulduru prospekts, Bulduri; tel: 775 2755; fax: 775 2694; email:lielupe@lielupe.lv. A concrete-block hotel 500m from Bulduri station and 200m from the beach. At the time of writing only half the rooms have been modernised with private bathroom, satellite TV and phone, so if you choose to stay here make sure you have one of these. The advantages of the hotel are the many facilities on hand, including a concert/film hall seating 300, indoor and outdoor swimming pools, indoor and outdoor tennis courts, sauna and massage, fitness studio and solarium; you can also organise horseriding. Double rooms cost from Ls63 a night.

Majori 29 Jomas iela, Majori; tel: 776 1380; fax: 776 1394; email:vmajori@mail.bkc.lv. Recently refurbished, this is probably one of the better hotels in the area. The art nouveau building, with a green roof and tower, is in the centre of Majori about 250m from the sea. Do not confuse the hotel with the much smaller boarding house of the same name on Smilšu iela. The hotel rooms are pleasantly decorated and all have private bathrooms, a telephone and cable TV. Double rooms cost Ls48–63.

Pegasa Pils 60 Jūras iela, Majori; tel: 776 1149; fax: 776 1169; www.pegasapils.lv. A beautifully restored art nouveau mansion, originally built in 1900, and now offering double rooms and suites with balconies 50m from the beach in Majori and very close to the Dzintari Concert Hall. All the rooms are comfortably furnished and are equipped with AC, a minibar, telephone and satellite TV. The hotel also has a restaurant, sometimes with live music. Double rooms from Ls75.

Youth Hostel of the Latvian University Fund (Jauniešu viesnīca) 52–54 Dzintaru prospekts, Dzintari; tel: 775 1873; fax: 722 8661; email: luf@latnet.lv. The hostel has 20 double rooms with shared showers, toilets and kitchen. Double rooms Ls12.

Eating and drinking

By far the widest choice for eating is along Jomas iela in Majori, where you can find everything from pizza to high-class fish dishes. The best plan is just to stroll along the street and see what takes your fancy. In the unlikely event that nothing does, there are some excellent hotel restaurants too, which are happy to serve non-residents. In summer, most restaurants are open from 12.00 to 23.00, although a few, including Al Tohme, Orients and Coco Loco, claim to stay open until the last guest leaves. If you are visiting in winter, note that most restaurants are open only for lunch. Prices in general tend to be slightly lower in Jūrmala than in Riga: expect to pay Ls4–6 for a main course in most restaurants. All the restaurants listed here accept credit cards.

Al Tohme 2 Pilsoņu iela, Majori; tel/fax: 775 5755. A rare find, not only because the restaurant is right next to the beach and has views of the Gulf of Riga, but also because it is Lebanese and serves Middle Eastern food. You can also enjoy a *nargile* (waterpipe) as you relax in the stone-mosaic-decorated interior.

Coco Loco Jomas iela 37, Majori; tel: 776 1464. A mixture of Jamaican and European food in a relaxed atmosphere, just off Jomas iela. Never without music.

Il Patio, Planeta Sushi 2 Dzintaru prospekts, Dzintari. After their success in Riga, these two restaurants, owned by the same Russian company, have now opened in Jūrmala. Unusually you can order from both menus, starting with sushi and finishing with an Italian ice-cream.

Kūriņš 47 Kauguciema iela, Kauguri; tel: 773 6598. The restaurant is in a wooden building in the style of a traditional Latvian fisherman's house, and is located directly on the beach at Kauguri. It offers Latvian specialities, as well as mainstream European dishes. On summer weekends there is traditional Latvian country music from 22.00 on Fridays until early in the morning.

Orients 33 Jomas iela, Majori. Specialises in Russian and Caucasian meat dishes but also serves seafood and oriental dishes. A lively place with exuberant interior décor and live music in the evenings.

Pegasa Pils 60 Jūras iela, Majori; tel: 776 1169. In the newly restored art nouveau hotel Pegasa Pils, this restaurant is classy in atmosphere and in quality of food. The dishes are international and the service excellent.

Salmu Krogs 70–72 Jomas iela, Majori. A large summer restaurant with a wide choice of grilled fish and meat. A popular place on summer evenings, partly due to its prices, which are lower than many in Jūrmala.

Senators 55 Jomas iela, Majori; tel: 781 1161. A restaurant and bars, with interior and exterior seating, next to the Slāvu Restorans. Enjoy pizza, ice-cream or beer in pleasant surroundings.

Slāvu Restorans 57 Jomas iela, Majori; tel: 776 1401. You cannot miss this large restaurant halfway along the main street in Majori. There is seating both indoors and on the terrace and a wide choice of dishes, including many Russian specialities such as caviar and dumplings. Prices are reasonable, at around Ls4.70 for a main course and Ls1.50 for desserts.

Spotikačs 77 Jomas iela, Majori. A restaurant which specialises in Ukrainian food and drink, including well-known dishes such as chicken Kiev and drinks such as fruit-flavoured vodka. You can sit outside, or in an attractive wooden building with painted bird and flower motifs on the walls. Also in Riga.

Sue's Asia 74 Jomas iela, Majori; tel: 775 5900. An extensive choice of Indian, Chinese and Thai dishes in an exotically oriental setting. Also in Riga.

Villa Joma 88a Jomas iela; tel: 775 5971. This green wooden building with an unusual interior décor is the restaurant of the Hotel Villa Joma but is extensively patronised by non-residents. The menu has a wide range of international dishes, including attractions such as duck with caramelised apple and orange sauce, and enticing desserts such as wild berry pie with ice-cream and berry sauce.

Tourist information

Jūrmala Spa and Tourist Information Centre (Jūrmalas Kurorta un Tūrisma Informācijas Centrs), 42 Jomas iela, Majori, Jūrmala, LV-2015; tel: 776 4276/776 2167; fax: 776 4672; email: jurmalainfo@mail.bkc.lv produces an excellent brochure with up-to-date details of hotels including prices. You should also consult this office for guided tours, information about healthcare and medical facilities in Jūrmala, and hotel reservations.

Activities

Most people go to Jūrmala to enjoy the beaches or walk in the dunes and forests. The beaches near Majori and Dubulti tend to get crowded in the short summer season. If you prefer quieter beaches, try Lielupe, at the Riga end of Jūrmala. If you would like to be more active, you can hire a bike, play tennis, go riding, learn to windsurf or kitesurf, visit churches and museums, or spend some time birdwatching.

Bicycle hire
ABS Nomas Grupa Ltd 24 Jūras iela, Majori; mobile tel: 613 3334; email: velo_abc@one.lv
Bicycle and Tourist Equipment Rental 100 Dubultu prospekts, Jaundubulti; tel: 776 7464
Rental 21 Mellužu prospekts, Melluži; tel: 776 7899. Roller-skates also for hire.

Sports
Bowling At the Bowling Club Rio-Rio inside the 'Grateka' sports and recreation centre, 49 Meža prospekts, Bulduri; tel: 77 54481; email: fitlains@delfi.lv; www.grateka.lv
Horseriding Try the Riders' Club 'Cavalcade', Horse Riding Therapy Centre, 61 Asaru prospekts, Vaivari; tel: 776 6151; mobile: 941 5916. Horses can also be hired via the Neptuns restaurant, 1 Kolkas iela, Jaunķemeri; tel: 773 7951.
Swimming Nemo Water Amusement Park 1 Atbalss iela, Vaivari; tel: 773 2350; fax: 773 2349; email: nemo@nemo.lv; www.nemo.lv. Swimming pools, water slides and saunas. Admission Ls2.50. Open daily 10.00–22.00 in summer.
Tennis At lots of hotels and also at the Sports Centre 'Concept' 36 Vienības prospekts, Bulduri; tel: 714 9911.
Windsurfing and kitesurfing Equipment rental and training available at Burusports 1 Piejūras iela, Pumpuri (at the beginning of Upes iela); tel: 920 7123; email: windguru@kite.lv. Open daily Jun1–Aug 31 10.00–20.00.

The towns of Jūrmala
If you take the train from Riga, the first stop just before Jūrmala is Priedaine, south of the Lielupe River and a short distance from the coast. There is little to see here.

Lielupe is close to the mouth of the river from which it takes its name. The station, built in 1913, is typical of the wooden architecture that became popular in this area at the end of the 19th century. Lielupe is the home of a well-known but modest yacht club (turn right out of the station along Mastu iela). The cemetery in Lielupe is well known as the site of the graves of a number of Latvian writers and artists.

Nearby at **Buļļuciems** you can visit the Jūraslīcis Open Air Fishery Museum (Jūraslīcis brīvdabas muzejs, 1 Tīklu iela; tel: 775 1121), a modest complex of 19th-century wooden buildings. To find the museum watch out for the black anchor on a small pillar of stones, just beyond the Kulturnams in the centre of the village. Tīklu iela takes you to the museum. Open 10.00–18.00.

Before World War I **Dzintari** (from the Latvian *dzintars* meaning amber) was called Edinburg in honour of the marriage between the Russian Grand Duchess Marie and the then Duke of Edinburgh; indeed, one of the main roads through the town is still called Edinburgas prospekts. It is also known for its open-air concerts which take place between May and September on the stage next to the Dzintari Concert Hall (Dzintaru Koncert Zāle), a National Romantic-style building, on the seafront at the end of Turaidas iela. Dzintari was where the Chautauqua Conference took place in September 1986: a delegation of 270 Americans held talks with Soviet leaders about the illegal incorporation of Latvia into the USSR.

THE MOUNTAINEER
Then friends depart, first one and then the other,
And solitude grows with each passing year.
Now no companion walks with you like a brother,
No hillside flower blooms to bring you cheer.

The peak is lost in mountain height,
Eternal stillness turns your heart to stone.
No place remains for rest or for respite
A shield of ice entombs your soul like ore,
While earthly longing burns in flesh and bone.

Jānis Rainis (1865–1929)

An **Exhibition of Old Machinery** is at 11 Turaidas iela, Dzintari; tel: 926 3329. Luckily, this museum is more interesting than its name implies. It is mainly a collection of old transport (cars, bicycles etc), although there are also some radio sets. One of the exhibits, a motor carriage called 'Victoria', was owned by the Russian Tsar Nikolas II and dates from 1907. **The Latvian Museum of Prison History** (6–14 Piestātnes iela, Dzintari; tel: 941 6038), deals with penal history from the Middle Ages to the present. Visits by appointment only.

Majori is the main centre of the Jūrmala area. It was here that the writer, Jānis Rainis (1865–1929), had his summerhouse (at 5–7 J Pliekšāna iela) in which he lived with his wife, the poet Aspāzija, from 1927 until his death on September 12 1929. In 1949 the house was made into a museum in honour of both of them, the **Rainis and Aspāzijas Memorial Summer House** (as it is now called). The room in which Rainis worked has been left intact: his books, papers and even the woven blanket which his mother made for him all remain; a similar room contains the remaining effects of his wife. The third room was used by their housekeeper. The room on the ground floor is used for lectures and readings. Open 11.00–18.00 every day except Monday and Tuesday.

The **Jūrmala Museum**, 27–29 Tirgoņu iela, Majori, houses art exhibitions and deals with local history. Open Wednesday–Sunday 11.00–17.00.

Jomas iela is the main street and is now a pedestrian zone. It is here that most of Majori's cafés and shops are to be found. Note the monument to Rainis and Aspāzija in the square next to the Jūrmala culture centre; erected in 1990 it is the work of the sculptors Z Fernava-Tiščenko and J Tiščenko. At the end of the street there is a small square close to the railway station. In it stands a statue of Lāčplēsis (the bear-slayer), the subject of the famous epic poem by Andrejs Pumpurs (see page 216 for more about Lāčplēsis).

The **Hotel Majori** (29 Jomas iela) is an important example of architecture of the so-called school of historicism. Built between 1923 and 1925 it is the work of the architect Medlingers. It has recently been restored.

The former Rācenis spa (Rāceņa peldiestāde) at 1 Pilsoņu iela, a two-storey wooden house built in 1914, is also typical of local building styles and has recently been renovated. The pavilion with terrace overlooking the sea (1 Tirgoņu iela), also the work of Medlingers, is another example of the wooden housing that is characteristic of Jūrmala.

The Catholic church of Our Lady (Dievmātes katoļu baznīca) on Pilsoņu iela, built in 1889, is also an example of traditional wooden architecture. It was formerly a gym; the tower was added this century.

Dubulti is the next stop on the coastal railway. It is here that the Marienbāde Sanatorium was built in 1870. It was restored in the 1940s and is noted for its tower and open gallery (43 Z Meierovica prospekts). Not far from it (at 20 Meierovica prospekts) is the two-storey summerhouse in which Aspāzija lived from 1933 to 1943. It is now a branch of the local museum. It is open Tuesday, Wednesday, Thursday and Saturday 11.00–16.00 and Monday 14.00–19.00.

The Lutheran church at Dubulti, with its art nouveau elements, plain interior and wooden gallery, used as the Jūrmala Museum of History and Art during the Soviet era, is one of the largest churches in Latvia and is a well-known landmark, visible from the Daugava River. The Orthodox church (Sv Kņaza Vladimira pareizticigā baznīca), 26 Strēlnieku prospekts, dates back to 1896 and contains some pleasing icons.

Jaundubulti's only special attraction is the Ludis Bērziņš Memorial Museum (27 Poruka prospekts; tel: 776 0244), a two-storey summerhouse built in 1929 which was the home of the Latvian theologian, teacher, folklorist and writer, Ludis Bērziņš (1870–1965) who lived here from 1934–44. Open Tuesday–Friday 11.00–17.00 and Saturday 12.00–16.00.

The next towns on the coastal route are **Pumpuri** and **Asari**. The station at Asari, currently being restored, is the work of P Feders, a leading Latvian architect of the early 20th century. The cemetery at Asari at 85 Kāpu iela is again a place where a number of leading Latvian citizens are buried. In 1928 an additional cemetery was established by the coast and in it lie the bodies of 247 soldiers who fell in World War I and in the struggle for independence. At Kaugurciems you can see the memorial to those killed in the battles for independence of 1918–20. It was erected in 1934 on the site of the battle of May 18 1919, destroyed in World War II and rebuilt in 1989.

Slightly inland lies **Sloka**, the site of the infamous cellulose and paper factory that contributed so heavily to pollution in the Jūrmala region. The Latvian artist Egle is buried in the cemetery here, as are the Latvian riflemen who fell in the battles for independence fought here in 1915 and 1919.

After Sloka the railway line bends further inland away from the coast and takes you on to the town of **Ķemeri**. The spa here (Ķemeru peldiestāde at 28 E Dārziņa iela – closed at present) was famous for its medicinal mud cures. The classical-style spa building dates from the 1920s. The Ķemeri Hotel, a sanatorium for many years, is also in the classical style. Built between 1933 and 1936 it is known as the 'white castle' or the 'white ship'. The interior of the hotel was elegant and spacious, the exterior simple yet imposing. The work of E Laube, it ranks as one of the finest examples of architecture from the first period of Latvian independence. Empty for many years, the building has recently been bought by Kempinski Hotels and Resorts who plan to reopen it as a 150-room hotel, the Kempinski Kemeri Palace, in early 2005.

The small Lutheran church in Andreja Upīša iela, built in 1897, is a good example of neo-Gothic architecture of the school of historicism. Note the monument to the 80 riflemen buried in the cemetery at Vēršupīte; also the work of E Laube, it was erected in 1926.

Ķemeri Park, created by the landscape gardeners K H Wagner and A Zeidaks, is an attraction of this pleasant town. It contains a number of delightful pavilions in classical style and 12 bridges across the Vēršupīte, each in a different style (the park buildings are all the designs of the Latvian architects F Skujiņš and E Laube). It also contains the Orthodox Church of SS Peter and Paul, built in 1893 in the style of the wooden churches of northern Russia. A number of Russian soldiers killed in World War I are buried here.

Ķemeri National Park

Ķemeri was established as a national park in 1997. It covers an area of about 40,000 hectares, about 50% of it forest, 30% bog or marshland, 10% water and 10% agricultural land. About a quarter of all recorded fauna in Latvia can be found here and over half of Latvia's bird species, including the rare sea eagle and black stork. Also to be found here are beavers which play an important part in the ecology of the area. The park is accessible to the public only by personal application. For further information contact the Information Centre of Ķemeri National Park (Meža Maja, Ķemeri; tel: 77 30078; fax: 77 30207; email: nationalparks@kemeri.gov.lv). To get there take a train to Ķemeri station. Alternatively you can take bus number 6 from Sloka or bus number 11 from Lielupe. If you go by car, follow the signs to Jūrmala and continue on the A10 towards Ķemeri.

SALASPILS

To reach Salaspils by car take the A6 south towards Ogre and look out for the large granite sign 'Salaspils 1941–44'. To go by train, take the train heading southeast for Ogre, Lielvārde or Aizkraukle and alight at the Dārziņa stop. (A single ticket costs Ls0.28.) Then follow the footpath for about 15 minutes. The tourist office advises that visitors do not walk this footpath alone.

First mentioned as a settlement in 1186, Salaspils is a place associated with war, death and destruction. The Battle of Salaspils of 1605 delayed the Swedes from gaining a foothold in Latvia. Some 12,000 Swedes under the leadership of Charles IX attacked a Lithuanian unit of about 4,000 men but were repulsed: only about a quarter of the Swedish army managed to retreat to their ships in Riga. Now, however, it is remembered largely as the site of the Nazi concentration camp, Kurtenhof. Built in 1941 during the Nazi occupation of Latvia in World War II, the camp operated for three years. In 1944, as the Red Army approached Riga, the camp guards and administrators ordered the inmates to exhume and burn the thousands of bodies buried at the camp; it then was burnt to the ground by the retreating Nazis in an attempt to hide the atrocities committed there. Over 100,000 men, women and children, most of them Jews, were put to death here, among them Austrians, Belgians, Czechs, Dutch, French, Latvian, Polish and Soviet citizens. Today, lines of white stones mark the perimeter of the camp.

The Salaspils Memorial, which now dominates the site of the former camp, was erected in 1967 to honour those who died there. A huge concrete wall in the shape of a long beam marks the position of the former entrance; symbolising the border between life and death, it bears the words of the Latvian writer, Eižēns Vēveris (a prisoner at Salaspils): '*Aiz šiem vārtiem vaid zeme*' ('Beyond these gates the earth moans'). You can actually walk the length of the wall on the inside – there is a door at each end. A series of steps takes you through a number of gloomy rooms, giving the impression of a mausoleum. There is also a small exhibition with photographs of the camp. The seven sculptures which stand in the grounds behind the wall evoke the suffering but also the spirit of defiance and resistance of those imprisoned and killed.

The stillness of Salaspils is broken only by the ticking of an underground metronome beneath the altar-like structure located to the left as you enter the grounds. The noise of the ticking is a reminder of the lives spent and ended here. A narrow path leads through the woods to the place where the prisoners were executed.

OTHER PLACES NEAR RIGA
Rundāle Palace and Mežotne

Rundāle Palace is about 77km south of Riga to the west of Bauska and can easily be visited by car or by coach. Consult your hotel or one of the tour organisers mentioned on page 77 for details of coach trips. For more information about Rundāle, see page 206.

Mežotne is a recently restored palace, close to Rundāle, where it is possible to stay overnight.

Sigulda and Turaida

Sigulda and Turaida can easily be visited in a day from Riga by train, bus or car, or you can take a coach trip. For information about tours, consult your hotel or one of the tour organisers mentioned on page 77. For further information about Sigulda and Turaida, see *Chapter 7*. There is a good bus service from Riga.

Cēsis

There are day trips by coach to Cēsis. Consult your hotel or one of the tour operators mentioned on page 77 for further information. For information on Cēsis, see *Chapter 7*. There is also a good bus service from Riga.

Kurzeme and Latgale

There are also coach trips to the countryside of Kurzeme and Latgale. For further information ask at your hotel or consult one of the tour organisers mentioned on page 77.

European lime, Tilia europaea

Vidzeme

Vidzeme is the name of the area to the east of Riga extending to the border with Estonia in the north and east of Latvia. It contains some of Latvia's most famous towns as well as much of the country's most attractive countryside. After Riga and its immediate environs, it is probably the second most popular destination in Latvia.

The north of Vidzeme consists of sandstone plateaux and the northern plain. Rivers and lakes abound, as do woods and forests of birch, pine and spruce. It is a hilly farming area with large open areas of fields and meadows.

Central Vidzeme's Uplands contain the highest point in Latvia, the 310m Gaizins Hill. The Uplands of eastern Vidzeme extend north into Estonia, their highest point being Suur Munamägi in Estonia, 317m above sea level. The landscape here is pretty: grassy hills, fields of wild flowers, misty lakes, dense pine forest and lush meadows.

Along Vidzeme's northern border with the Baltic, grazing pastures often run into the sea. Sigulda, 53km to the east of Riga, is the start of the Gauja National Park and the site of Turaida Castle, the best reconstructed stone castle in Latvia. Further northeast, around 80km from Riga, lies Cēsis, with its old castle ruins and elegant parks. Winding through Vidzeme is one of Latvia's largest and most picturesque rivers, the Gauja; the area through which it passes is known for its sandstone caves.

MAIN ATTRACTIONS
The main attractions for visitors to Vidzeme are the towns of Sigulda and Cēsis and the nearby Gauja National Park. Travellers along the Via Baltica between Riga and Tallinn will also pass through Vidzeme along the route which runs along the Baltic coast.

HISTORY
North Vidzeme was inhabited by Livs and Latgals who are known to have lived in the area from 500BC. The region was part of Latgale until the 13th century when the south and east came under the rule of the Bishop of Riga and the rest of the region became the State of the Livonian Order. When the Livonian Order collapsed in 1561, Latgale and Vidzeme became part of the Duchy of Pārdaugava and were thus under Lithuanian rule until the region was taken over by Poland. After the Swedish–Polish War it fell under Swedish rule in 1628. The period of Swedish rule continued until 1721. This was a time of peace and progress for the region: schools were established, and laws were passed which gave limited rights and freedoms to the peasants. Under Russian rule, Livonia continued to be governed as a separate province until the unification of Latvia more or less within its current borders at the beginning of the first period of independence.

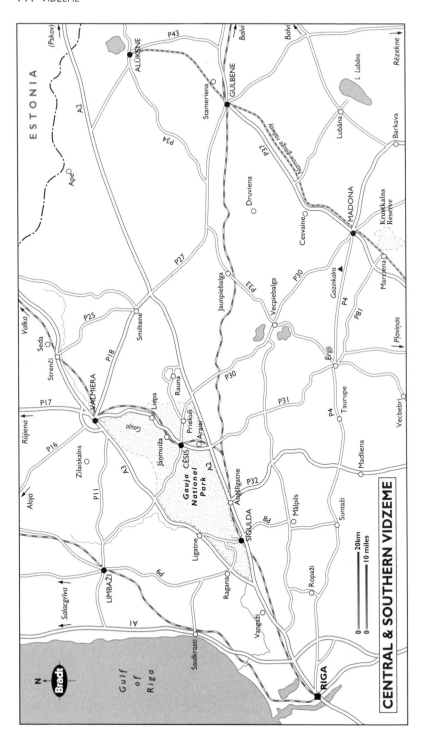

CENTRAL & SOUTHERN VIDZEME

GETTING AROUND

The most convenient way of visiting Vidzeme is by road transport. Although most of the towns can be reached by bus, and some by rail, country areas in the national park and the Uplands are not well served by public transport.

By car

Vidzeme is served by three main roads that form the basis of obvious routes for the visitor. The first runs from Riga, through Sigulda, Turaida, Cēsis, the Gauja National Park and on to Valmiera and finally Valka on the Estonian border. The area covered by this route is likely to be the main goal of any visitor for whom time permits only one trip outside the capital. The second route takes one north out of Riga, through Saulkrasti and along the coast to Salacgrīva and Ainaži, then back towards Riga again via Mazsalaca and Limbaži. The third route cuts through the south of Vidzeme and heads southeast out of Riga through the towns of Madona, Gulbene and Alūksne before doubling back to Riga through Jaunpiebalga.

By bus

Most of the main towns in Vidzeme can be reached by bus. Buses leave Riga bus station for Sigulda every 30 minutes between 07.00 and 21.30 and take one hour. To Cēsis the journey takes two hours, and buses leave at 08.05 (except Sunday), 09.00, 09.30 (except Saturday), 10.00 (except Sunday), 11.00, 12.00, 13.10, 14.00, 15.00, 16.00, 16.45, 18.05, 19.00, and 20.30. Buses to Valmiera leave Riga every 30–40 minutes between 07.30 and 22.20 and take around two and a half hours.

There are also buses every day between Cēsis and other towns in the region, including Alūksne, Ainaži, Jaunpiebalga, Madona, Rūjiena and Valka.

If you want to head along the coast, buses are the only possibility north of Saulkrasti. Buses to Tallinn and Pärnu in Estonia follow this coastal road. From Riga to Saulkrasti takes around one hour, and to Salacgrīva almost two hours.

By train

There are regular trains to Sigulda (around 14 a day), to Cēsis (five a day) and to Valmiera (four a day), which take around the same time as the bus. Prices are very low: in late 2004 Ls0.71 to Sigulda, Ls1.10 to Cēsis and Ls1.37 to Valmiera.

Trips along the coast can be done by train as far as Saulkrasti, but the line then heads away from the coast to Limbaži, Rūjiena and finally Mazsalaca. Only one train a day, however, goes as far as Mazsalaca.

SIGULDA AND TURAIDA, CĒSIS, THE GAUJA

Take the A2 out of Riga following signs in the direction of Sigulda (and ultimately Pskov in Belarus). The first town worth a visit is Sigulda itself.

Sigulda

Sigulda is about 53km northeast of Riga (about 45 minutes by car from Riga). It is an attractive town which feels spacious and elegant, and is a good centre for sporting and outdoor activities. It is also the administrative centre of the Gauja National Park.

Sigulda has long been a major trading centre. Until the 13th century it was a stronghold of the Liv tribes whose ruler, Kaupo, was the first to convert to Christianity. In 1207 it became divided, and the land on the right bank of the Gauja fell under the aegis of the Bishop of Riga; the left bank was ruled by the Knights of the Sword, who built a stone castle known by the name Segewald from which the name of the modern town is derived.

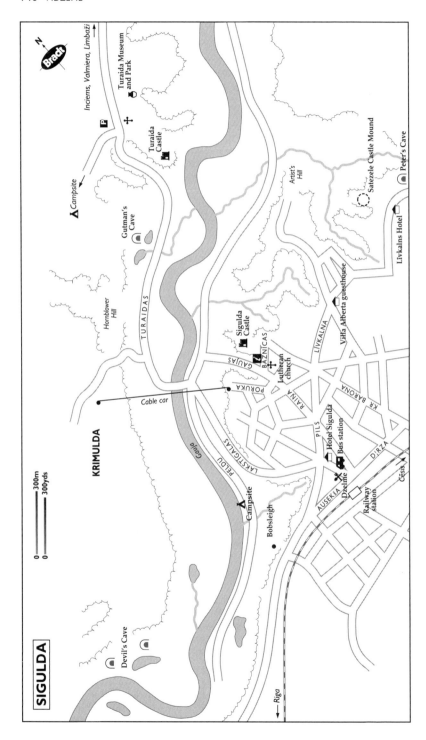

SIGULDA

N

0 ___ 300m
0 ___ 300yds

Inciems, Valmiera, Limbaži

Turaida Museum and Park

Campsite

Turaida Castle

Gutman's Cave

Hornblower Hill

T U R A I D A S

Artist's Hill

Satezele Castle Mound

Peter's Cave

Livkalns Hotel

Sigulda Castle

BAZNICAS

Lutheran church

GAUJAS

PORUKA

Villa Alberta guesthouse

LIVKALNA

KR BARONA

Cable car

KRIMULDA

RAINA

PILS

Hotel Sigulda

Bus station

DIRZA

Gauja

PELDU

LAKSTIGALAS

AUSEKLA

Dzelme

Railway station

Cesis

Campsite

Bobsleigh

Riga

Devil's Cave

The Knights of the Sword remained in control of Sigulda until 1562 when the town fell to the Poles. They were briefly ousted by the Swedes in 1601, but regained the area from the Swedes after less than a year. The retreating Swedish forces burnt the castles of Turaida and Krimulda as they left. This period of instability did huge damage to the town: by 1613 only five families remained in occupation. In 1652 Sigulda fell again to the Swedes who retained control until their defeat in the Great Northern War in 1710. Russia took over, and Sigulda began to thrive once more.

The construction of the railway connecting Riga and Valka in the 19th century opened Sigulda up, and visitors began to come from St Petersburg and Warsaw. Soon Sigulda became a favourite holiday resort for the rich.

It was accorded full municipal status in 1928. After World War II Sigulda became a regional centre, and in 1953 it incorporated its neighbours, Turaida and Krimulda. Its importance as a centre of tourism was consolidated further when it became the administrative centre of the Gauja National Park in 1973. Its castles and scenery make it worth a visit at any time of year, and in winter it is a major centre for winter sports.

Accommodation

The most central hotel is the **Sigulda** (6 Pils iela; tel: 797 2263; fax: 797 1443; email: hotelsigulda@latnet.lv; www.hotelsigulda.lv) which has been renovated and extended recently; all the rooms are spacious and comfortable. The **Aparjods** (1 Ventas iela; tel/fax: 790 2455; email: aparjods@aparjods.lv; www.aparjods.lv) is just off the A2 behind a garage, on the right as you approach Sigulda from Riga by car, and has 15 rooms at prices from Ls27–50. All rooms have satellite television and some of the suites have jacuzzis. The **Livonija** (55 Pulkveža Brieža; tel: 297 3066; fax: 797 2347; email: hotel.livonija@lis.lv) has singles from Ls14 and doubles from Ls18 (breakfast is Ls2 extra). The **Līvkalns** (Pēteralas iela; tel: 797 0916; fax: 797 0919; email: livkalns@livkalns.lv; www.livkalns.lv) is a small traditionally built eight-room hotel, attractively situated on the edge of Sigulda close to the path leading to Peter's Cave. It offers doubles at Ls28, and has a sauna with swimming pool. Off the A2, if you continue past the Aparjods towards the lake, Ancīšu diķi, you come to a relatively new hotel, the **Santa** (tel: 770 5271; fax: 770 5278; email: hotelsanta@vide.lv; www.hotelsanta.lv). It is an attractive modern hotel with a good restaurant, sauna and small pool. Another option is the recently opened **Villa Alberta** guesthouse (10a Līvkalna iela; tel: 797 1060; fax: 797 1061; email: villaalberta@apollo.lv; www.zl.lv.villaalberta) which has its own sauna and restaurant. Single rooms are from Ls22 and doubles from Ls25.

There is a **campsite** on Peldu iela by the river (1 Peldu iela; tel: 797 3724; email: janis@makars.lv; www.makars.lv). Ls1 per tent, plus Ls1 per person; and also one near Turaida (see page 150).

Eating out

Aparjods (1a Ventas iela; tel: 770 5242) has a restaurant which is open to non-residents. It serves traditional Latvian food in a setting which echoes a medieval Latvian farmhouse. The food and ambience are excellent and include many local ingredients. The **Santa** likewise offers very acceptable food. In the centre of town, the restaurant at the **Hotel Sigulda** serves a range of local and international dishes. There are several other possibilities in the town centre, including various cafés on Pils iela.

Tourist information

The tourist information office is at 3 Baznīcas iela; tel: 797 1335; fax: 797 1372; email: info@sigulda.lv. Open May–October 10.00–19.00 and November–April 10.00–17.00.

What to do

Just off Gaujas iela, J Poruka iela leads to the Sigulda boarding point of the **cable car** across the Gauja valley to Krimulda. It departs every hour on the hour between 10.00 and 12.00 and then every half-hour until 18.30 and takes you at a height of 80m across the Gauja river valley from Sigulda to Krimulda. On the Krimulda side of the valley you can visit the ruins of Krimulda Castle. The old Teutonic castle of Krimulda was built from 1255–73 and was used as a residence for visiting dignitaries. It was destroyed in the early 17th century and little of it remains today. In the other direction (to the south) is Krimulda Palace or Manor House. Built in 1854 in Russian style, it is now a sanatorium for children. You can also go **bungee jumping** from the cable car site (price Ls15 per jump; Ls13 for second jump). It is generally possible from May to October on Saturdays and Sundays from 18.30, but it is best to check; tel: 644 0660; www.lgk.lv. Short **air observation flights** operate at the weekends from 11.00 until the last client. Flights last six to eight minutes and cost Ls7 for adults and Ls5 for children. They depart from Krimulda, near the Turaida to Ragana road. For further details; tel: 968 9636.

When weather conditions permit, you can also go up in a **hot-air balloon** and float above Sigulda and the surrounding area. Contact the Traveller's Club Altius; email: altius@altius.lv for more details.

One of Sigulda's most famous sights is the tower of the artificial **bobsleigh run** which plunges into the Gauja valley, one of only 13 in the whole world. It was built in 1986 by Yugoslav engineers and was used by the Soviet bobsleigh team for training. It is 1,420m long and can be visited (generally open 12.00–17.00 on Saturdays and Sundays; to check opening times tel: 797 3813) and used. Amateurs can use a sort of rubber raft instead of a real sleigh; it holds six people and can reach a speed of 60km/h. Rides cost Ls3 per person.

Boat trips on the river and canoeing can be arranged through Makars Travel Agency (2 Peldu iela; tel: 924 4948; fax: 797 0164; email: janis@makars.lv; www.makars.lv). Prices range from Ls4 per person for an hour's boat ride to Ls39 for a three-day canoe trip, camping en route.

Račkalni and Inčukalna parish also offer a number of outdoor sports possibilities. You can hire canoes, rubber boats, rafts, tents, sleeping bags and **quad bikes** from them; tel: 797 7277; fax: 797 7251; email: info@ramkalni.lv; www.ramkalni.lv.

If you are in Sigulda in winter, you can hire **skis and snowboards** from Burusports (1 Mazā Gāles iela; tel: 797 2051).

What to see

If you arrive in Sigulda by train you will get off at the small but impressive **station**; the work of Professor P Feders, it was built in 1925, and when it was first opened was regarded as one of the finest examples of railway architecture in the Baltic region.

The station is close to the town centre with its hotels, restaurants, cafés and a few shops. Raiņa iela takes you towards the river valley and Turaida. Just past the road junction at the end of Raiņa iela where Gaujas iela begins, on the right-hand side is the **Lutheran church** which dates back to 1225. Numerous alterations (the last in 1930) have left little now to attest to the antiquity of the site. Its white walls are typical of the style of many Baltic Protestant churches. It is set in an attractive park.

Close to the church is a **statue dedicated to Krišjānis Barons** (1835–1923), one of Latvia's best-known poets and folklorists. Barons is remembered today primarily for the work he did in preserving the *dainas* (see page 42), traditional four-line songs which he collected by advertising in newspapers. He was sent tens of thousands of examples, which he collected and catalogued. The cabinet that he used to store and file them has been classified as a national treasure and can be seen at his museum in Riga (see page 122). He began to publish his collection of *dainas* in 1894. It eventually ran to six large volumes containing about one and a half million songs.

Nearby, just past the National Park Administration offices, is the so-called **New Castle** (Jaunā pils) or Writer's Castle (Rakstnieku pils). Built from 1875–81 in the style of a medieval castle, the New Castle was really a sort of manor house but became a sanatorium for convalescing heart patients in 1953. You can still walk in the grounds, but the building is closed to the public. In the courtyard in front of the house is a **monument** to the Latvian writer and philologist, **Atis Kronvalds** (1837–75).

The site of the New Castle was once occupied by some of the fortifications of the castle of the Knights of the Sword. Behind it you can still visit the ruins of the **Knights' Castle** which dates back to 1207–26. The original fortifications occupied two hilltops separated by a deep moat, surrounded by fortress walls containing several watchtowers and connected by underground passages. In spite of its formidable appearance and location, the castle was not effective and was overrun, destroyed and then rebuilt on several occasions. It was largely destroyed in the Northern War of 1700–21. All that remains today are two of the watchtowers and the walls of the main keep. On the same site there is an open-air stage that is used for theatre and concerts. Beginning here is a walk that takes you along the edge of the Gauja valley and offers wonderful views down to the river itself.

On the outskirts of Sigulda are a number of sites of natural beauty. On the Sigulda side of the Gauja is the so-called **Artists' Hill** (Gleznotāju kalns). It can be reached by following Līvkalna iela northeast out of the centre of Sigulda. The top of the hill is about 93m above sea level and you can see for about 12km. The hill is called the Artists' Hill because it was a favourite spot of the painters Feders, Rozentāls and Purvītis.

A short distance from the Artists' Hill is a free-standing sandstone cliff. Yet further on is the **Satezele castle mound** (Satezeles pilskalns), all that now remains of a fortress built by the Livs in the 13th century. Satezele is the old name by which Sigulda was known. It was from here that King Dabrel led the first revolt against the German Knights.

Pētera ala (**Peter's Cave**) is reached by climbing down the steep steps from the Artists' Hill and following a footpath leading west, away from the town. The cave itself is to be found on the southern bank of the Vējupīte River, a tributary of the Gauja. Its name remains something of a mystery, some saying that it is named after the son born to a young woman in the cave, others claiming it is named after a peasant who hid there during the Northern War.

To the southwest of Sigulda, just off the main Riga to Sigulda road and not far from the bobsleigh run, is the so-called **Tsar's Throne** (Ķeizara krēsls), another hill that offers splendid views over the Gauja valley and surrounding countryside.

Festivals

Sigulda is the centre for a number of events and festivals. Hot-air ballooning is popular (see above), and the hot-air balloon festival, which is generally held in or around May, attracts thousands of visitors each year. There is an international opera festival in Sigulda in July. The festival, which started in 1993, is an important cultural event for the whole country and attracts singers from around the world. In December there is also a bobsleigh festival.

In 2007 Sigulda will celebrate 800 years since its foundation: the town is already preparing events to mark 'Sigulda 800' that year.

Turaida

Turaida is around 6km from Sigulda, across the River Gauja. It is possible to walk, but be warned that the last part is uphill. To visit Turaida by bus, take one of the frequent buses (approximately every 20 minutes) which leave from outside Sigulda railway station and travel up Turaida iela to Turaida. If you leave Sigulda by car, go via Gaujas iela and the bridge and you will then come to the Turaida road (Turaida iela).

Accommodation

There are no hotels or guesthouses in Turaida but the ample possibilities in Sigulda make this unnecessary. There are, however, campsites. One called **Gravzaķi** is located about 1.5km along the road leading away from the reservation alongside the car park. Follow the signpost. Like most campsites, it offers almost no facilities, but there is a café/shop at the Turaida car park.

What to see

You can drive straight to Turaida or stop on the way to visit some caves. To visit, stop at a car park on the right as you drive towards the castle. The paths on the other side of the road (a tunnel runs under the road from the car park) lead to an open area where you will see the caves.

Gūtman's Cave (Gūtmaņa ala), Latvia's largest and most popular cave, is 18m deep, 12m wide and 10m high. Located at the base of Taurētāju kalns (**Horn Blower Hill**), a hill used by the Latgals as a lookout post against invading enemies, the cave is actually a grotto that was eroded by a small underground spring and the waters of the Gauja River before the river changed its course by almost half a kilometre at the end of the 18th century. The water in the cave is said to have magical powers, bringing health and happiness to those drinking it. The name of the cave comes from the German Gutman, either the name of a real person or the German for a good man who is rumoured to have lived in the area and healed the sick with the aid of water from the cave. The walls are covered with countless inscriptions, the oldest dating back to 1668.

There are two other caves nearby. In one, discovered in 1957, 1,932 guns were found. Another, Viktora ala (**Victor's Cave**), is said to have been hollowed out by a man called Viktors Heils (who may have been real or a legendary figure) so that his beloved, Maija, could watch him work in the garden in Sigulda.

There is not really a town of Turaida any more, although a signpost on the road implies that you are leaving Sigulda and entering a different place. As you come up the hill leading away from the river valley and past the caves you come to a car park on the left and opposite it is the entrance to the **Turaida Museum Reservation** (tel: 971 1402; fax: 297 1797; email: turaida@lis.lv; www.turaida-muzejs.lv). The reservation is a large park of about 45 hectares through which a series of paths leads you to Turaida's monuments and attractions. Open 10.00–17.00, and 10.00–18.00 in the summer months.

The earliest reference to Turaida is in 1207. Albert, the Bishop of Riga, ordered a stone castle to be built here in 1214 to replace a former Liv-built wooden fortress that had been destroyed by fire in 1212. The castle was originally named Friedland (literally 'land of peace' in German); only later did it get the name Turaida ('the garden of God', from 'Tura' meaning God and 'aida' meaning garden in Livonian). It soon became an important military stronghold and was also used as a residence for the local bailiff and for the garrison of the Livonian province.

In the 15th century the Livonian Order took Turaida Castle and adapted it to firearms, but it was recaptured in 1487 and remained under the control of the bishopric until 1561 when Livonia fell to the Poles.

In the 18th century, by which time Turaida had lost its military significance, part of the castle was demolished and the materials were used in other buildings, notably the manor house. In 1776 the castle was again destroyed by fire, and only portions of the walls survived.

Restoration work began in the 1950s. The original stone castle had high stone walls and five towers. The main tower and large sections of the castle walls have now been restored. You can climb the tower which offers excellent views of the river and over the rest of the reservation. However, a great deal of work remains to be done, and whilst the castle looks magnificent as you approach it and is worth a visit, only a specialist is likely to want to inspect it in detail. The 'Tornis' (tower) gallery exhibits the work of Latvian artists and jewellery for sale during the summer. In addition there is an exhibition of Liv garments of the 11th–13th centuries.

Between the entrance to the reservation and the castle, just above the footpath, you can see the so-called church mound with its wooden church. The present building dates back to 1750 and is a listed building, being a fine example of Latvian traditional style. Originally it was a rectangular log construction, but now only the upper part is wooden, the lower part being clad in plaster for stability and protection. It ceased to function as a place of worship in 1965 but was rededicated in 1991. Inside there is a baroque altar and some beautifully carved wooden pews. The church was formerly surrounded by a traditional cemetery. Now only one grave remains, that of the legendary Maija, the 'Rose of Turaida'. The grave (inscribed simply 'Turaidas Roze 1601–1620') is a common visiting place for newly weds, partly because of its romantic associations, partly because it is customary in the Baltic States for newly married couples to visit some cultural monument. Fundamentally, however, the story of the Rose of Turaida is a grim one, that of a young woman who chose death rather than enforced marriage or rape.

The story of Maija goes back to 1601 and the Polish–Swedish Wars. Turaida was under siege from Swedish troops who had penetrated into the Gauja valley. After three days of fighting, the Poles were defeated and the castle fell into the hands of the Swedish troops. After the battle, the clerk of the castle was wandering around the battlefield, looking for wounded soldiers. He came across a young girl and took her home with him, naming her after the month of May, the month in which the battle ended and the girl was found. The young girl grew up into a beautiful woman, attracting a great deal of attention from the men of the area. However, the man to whom she was attracted was Viktors Heils, the gardener of the castle. She would observe Viktors from a cave where he and she often met.

Unfortunately for the couple, two Polish army deserters, Adams Jakubovskis and Pēteris Skudrītis, had taken up residence in Turaida and Jakubovskis had also fallen in love with Maija. He began to press Maija to marry him, but she turned him down. With the help of his fellow soldier, Jakubovskis planned to abduct the girl: they sent her a letter, purportedly coming from Viktors asking her to come and meet him at the Gutman Cave on August 6 1620. When she arrived at the cave, the two Poles blocked her exit. Maija resisted the advances of Jakubovskis who tried to force himself on her, tearing her clothes. To distract him, Maija said she would give him the scarf she was wearing around her neck (a gift from Viktors): she claimed it had magic properties, and could protect its wearer from an enemy sword. To prove it she invited him to attack her with his sword. Believing her,

Jakubovskis struck a blow to Maija's neck, severing her head from her body. The two Poles fled the town.

That night Viktors found her body. Unfortunately for him, an axe (or in some versions of the story a knife) belonging to him was found in the cave, and before long he was charged with murder and found guilty. However, just before he was due to be executed, a repentant Skudrītis returned to the town and told the true story of Maija's capture and how she had procured her own death rather than betray her lover. Jakubovskis had been so horrified at the girl's self-inflicted death that he had hanged himself.

Viktors was released, buried his beloved, and planted a lime tree on her grave. A tree still grows on the grave, although it is now old and deformed as a result of a fire in 1972.

Whether the story of Viktors and Maija is a legend or true remains a matter of controversy. In the middle of the 19th century some documents (see *Reports on Court Proceedings and Punishments in Vidzeme and Kurzeme*, Jelgava/Leipzig, 1848) were discovered in the vaults of Riga Castle, among them one telling of the murder of a young woman called Maija in the Gutman Cave in circumstances similar to those in the story of the Rose of Turaida. The Latvian writer Rainis based his play *Mīla stiprāka pār nāvi* (*Love is Strong as Death*) on the tale.

Behind the church on a hill lies the **Sculpture Park** known as **Jelgavkalns**. The site of the park was once an ancient Liv settlement. Dedicated in 1985 to Krišjānis Barons to mark the 150th anniversary of his birth, it is the setting for a number of works by the Latvian sculptor Indulis Ranks, each one depicting an aspect of Latvian folklore from the *daina* folk songs which Barons collected. Although the folk-song tradition in Latvia is very ancient, it was only in the 19th century that the National Awakening movement revived interest in it. Krišjānis Barons spent a summer in Sigulda and Turaida, and often walked on the hills close to Turaida Castle, hence the site of the park. The sculptures do not refer directly to particular songs or legends, but rather allude to them in a general way.

The rest of the reservation area is taken up mainly by buildings connected with the Turaida estate, the origins of which go back to the 16th century. To the left of the entrance is the old estate or manor house with its ponds, sheds and outbuildings. Before World War I there were more than 30 buildings on the estate which had 28 breeding ponds and prosperous farmland. After World War II most of it was included in a collective farm, and many of the old buildings disappeared. However, some have now been restored, and one can visit, in addition to the old and new estate manager's houses, the cowsheds, smithy, bath house and other agricultural buildings.

There are guided tours of the reservation on offer. For information; tel: 297 1797. In the summer there are exhibitions and folk-song festivals. The Festival of Roses takes place each year in July, and Liv Day, which celebrates Livonian culture, takes place on the last Sunday in August.

If time permits you may care to visit **Krimulda Church**, about 5km from Turaida on the road with the car park opposite the reserve (P7). It dates back to 1205 when the region was Catholic. The original church was destroyed and the present building is mainly 17th century. The 46m tower was restored in 1924.

Just before you reach the church you will see a sign, Izjāde ar Zirgiem. A farm here offers horseriding.

Līgatne

It is not the town of Līgatne which tourists come to visit, but Līgatnes mācību un atpūtas parks, the **Nature and Educational Park** (tel: 415 3313), located close to

LĪGATNE NATURE & EDUCATIONAL PARK

n
coming from the A2 and follow the signs. You have to buy a ticket to visit the park in which wild animals such as bears, deer, beavers, European bison, foxes and elk live in large fenced-off enclosures of natural habitat. A particular attraction is the brown bear enclosure. Bears had vanished from Latvia by the turn of the century, but now some have immigrated from Estonia, and a few (the numbers are still counted in tens) have been settled in Latvia since the 1970s. There is also a lynx enclosure. Wild lynx live in all parts of the country, but are rarely seen as they hide deep in the woods and forests and are still hunted. A winding, hilly, single-track road leads you through the park to observation points from which the animals can be seen. No feeding is allowed. The park is open 09.30–18.00 (closes 16.30 Monday).

Another interesting feature of Līgatne is the **Pasaku taka** (fairytale trail), a trail through the woods taking you past about 80 wooden sculptures of the characters in Anna Brigadere's tale, *Maija and Paija*. It took 29 sculptors to make them all. Started in 1986 to mark the 125th anniversary of Anna Brigadere's birth in 1861, it was completed in 1988.

There are a number of other trails. On **Cepurīšu kalns** (Little Hat Hill) there is a tower which offers a view over about a third of the Gauja National Park. There are several outcrops of sandstone, among them Gaviļu iezis, Jumpravas iezis and Katrīnas iezis.

Along the banks of the Gauja there are many sandstone caves and rock formations. The highest sandstone rock is **Zvārtas iezis** (46m) near the little village of Kārļi (see page 159 for more information about this rock and the area around it). From Līgatne drive northeast to Kārļi, home of the oldest fishery in

Latvia, along the Amata River, a tributary of the Gauja. Lush and winding, the Amata is picturesque in the summer, but during the winter becomes shallow and dries up. About 4km south of Kārļi you come to a dirt road which leads to Zvārtas iezis. Here there is a large open area away from which a number of paths lead, including steps which take you to the top of a hill from which there is a wonderful view of the Amata. Canoeing trips along the Amata are popular, as are hikes through this beautiful part of the national park. Of the many hiking trails in and around the Amata valley, the all-day hike along the left bank of the river is a favourite. It starts from the bridge in Kārļi and ends at the bridge in Cēsis.

Āraiši

From Zvārtas iezis head southeast back to the main Vidzeme highway and follow it on to Cēsis. This will take you past the road leading to Āraiši. Āraiši (about 7km from Cēsis) is the site of a reconstructed lake fortress, resting on huge log platforms or rafts in the middle of a lake. This provided a degree of protection from enemies, and in about the 10th century was used in particular by the Latgalian tribe. It was not easy to live in such a village, since walking over the large logs could be difficult. The Āraiši village was established over a period of about 200 years. The people were short, so the buildings appear rather hutch-like to the modern visitor. Two or three families lived in each house, and there were 22 houses in all. Each had a clay floor with seats running around the walls. The house of the chief could be distinguished by the crossed end logs. Today only a few of the houses have been reconstructed. In summer actors re-enact village life at the time Āraiši was inhabited. It is possible to hire a traditional dugout boat to visit the site. The site (tel: 419 7288) is open May 1–November 30 daily 10.00–18.00.

Nearby stand the ruins of **Āraiši Church** which dates back to 1225. In the Middle Ages the main castle in the area was at Cēsis, the one in Āraiši being used mainly for storage. Next to it is the Āraiši Church, and across the road there is a large windmill which has been refurbished and can sometimes be visited.

Cēsis

The small town of Cēsis lies in the centre of the Gauja National Park, about 90km northeast of Riga. It is about an hour's drive from Riga or can also be reached by train. Although its population is only about 20,000, it is one of the oldest and prettiest towns in Latvia. Its winding streets, castle ruins and gardens make it a favourite spot for painters. It has a well-known music school and has also produced a number of Latvia's top mathematicians. In summer it hosts an open-air opera festival. It is also famous for its beer: the Cēsis brewery has been a feature of the town for many years. In 2006 Cēsis will celebrate its 800th anniversary. For information about the many special events that are being planned see www.cesis.lv.

History

Numerous castle mounds and archaeological excavations attest to the age of the settlements here. In the 11th century Riekstukalns was the site of a fortress. During the 12th century, Livs from the Venta River moved here to live alongside the local Latgals. By 1206 Cēsis had become an important trading centre on the road between Riga and Tartu (Dorpat), and in 1209 the Knights of the Sword built a stone castle alongside the wooden one on the Riekstukalns. In time this castle came to be one of the strongest in the area and the headquarters of the Knights. The year 1281 saw the building of a Gothic stone church, today called the Jāņa baznīca (St John's) located at 21 Torņa iela. Because of its strategic location on the Gauja River, Cēsis quickly developed

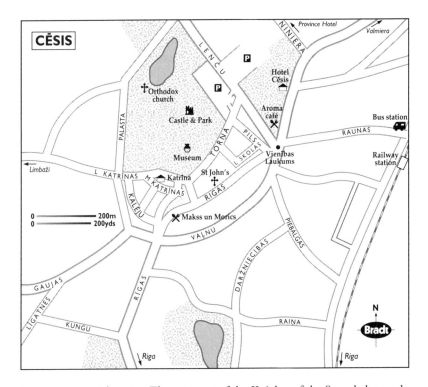

into a commercial centre. The presence of the Knights of the Sword also made it politically important. In 1383 Cēsis joined the Hanseatic League, and for centuries it stood as a powerful medieval town surrounded by thick protective walls. Then in 1577 came the horror of Ivan the Terrible, who had decided to cut a path from Russia to the Baltic Sea and laid siege to Cēsis. One story tells how Ivan's troops had the town surrounded, and the citizens knew they could not hold out much longer but, nonetheless, they raised the flag (with its ram emblem) every morning in defiance of the Russian invader. Unfortunately, there were underground passages beneath the castle and a traitor told the Russians of their existence, thereby enabling Ivan's troops to win. One legend claims that some of the citizens of Cēsis were so terrified of falling into the hands of the Russian troops that they took refuge in a cellar filled with gunpowder and blew themselves up rather than surrender. A century later, in 1671, a great fire burnt down the entire town. During the Northern War, Cēsis passed from the hands of one conqueror to another and the castle was destroyed by the Russians in 1703. This time no effort was made to rebuild it, although in the late 1700s a new castle was built beside it. In 1777 the castle estate was acquired by Count Sievers who built a house on the site of the eastern part of the original castle, thereby joining the end wall of the castle and the tower. During the War of Independence (1918–20) Cēsis was the scene of a decisive battle (June 19–23 1919) fought and won against German forces under the command of General von der Goltz by a combined Latvian–Estonian regiment, led by General Johannes Laidoner. By the 1930s, Cēsis had developed into a tourist centre and still is today, visited for its own sake and because of its location at the heart of the Gauja National Park.

THE BATTLE OF CĒSIS

The remnants of the German Landeswehr troops, including the so-called Iron Division left over from the end of World War I, were supposed to help Latvia to repel the Bolshevik forces still occupying parts of the country. In February 1919 a German general, Count Rudiger von der Goltz, was put in command of this army of 10,000 men, the largest fighting force in Latvia. However, the count and his Baltic-German landlord cohorts had other plans, which included restoring the Russian and German monarchies. Latvia and the other Baltic peoples were to become German subjects.

On April 16 1919, German troops in Liepāja staged an uprising against the provisional government of Ulmanis who was forced to flee and take refuge in a ship under the protection of British warships. Von der Goltz formed a puppet government headed by the Latvian clergyman, Andrievs Niedra.

German troops invaded Riga on May 22 1919. By then the Latvians and Estonians had concluded a defence treaty. The Germans were expected to head east to pursue the Bolsheviks, but instead they went north to fight the Estonians and Latvians, a move that brought strong condemnation from Western allies.

The Estonian army under the command of Johannes Laidoner had recently defeated Bolshevik troops in eastern Estonia (Estonian troops would capture Jēkabpils and Krustpils on June 5). He gave the Germans an ultimatum to advance no further. The Germans ignored it. On June 6 they occupied Cēsis (Vonnu in Estonian). On June 19 battle started between the Germans on one side and 5,500 Estonian and 1,500 Latvian troops on the other. The fierce fighting ended on June 24 when the Germans were forced to retreat. This was a major turning point in the battle for Latvian independence. The victory at Cēsis allowed Ulmanis and his government to return to Riga in triumph.

Under the terms of the peace negotiated, the defeated German troops were supposed to leave Latvia, but von der Goltz ignored orders and remained on Latvian soil to regroup his forces, and it was only in December that the Latvian army, with assistance from allies, was able to force the Germans out.

Accommodation

The best hotel in Cēsis is the **Hotel Cēsis** (1 Vienibas laukums; tel: 412 0122; email: dlg@danlat-group.lv; www.danlat-group.lv). Located on the main square right in the town centre, it is a Danish–Latvian joint venture. It backs on to the Maija Park and is a short walk from the castle. The food in the restaurant is excellent but regrettably the hotel gives priority to groups, and being a guest does not guarantee a place in the restaurant. The staff will arrange sightseeing and tours, car hire, fishing and canoeing. The hotel has 41 rooms; singles cost Ls30 and doubles Ls42 a night. Another good option in Cēsis is the **Katrīna** (8 Mazā Katrīnas iela; tel: 410 7700; fax: 410 7701; email: hotelkatrina@apollo.lv) in an attractively renovated early 20th-century building in the centre of the town. Prices are Ls24 for a single and Ls32 for a double. A third option, close to the Maija Park, is the **Province** (6 Niniera iela; tel: 412 0849). Rooms here are available at Ls17 for singles and Ls28 for doubles. A cheaper possibility is the **Mārtiņš** guesthouse

(9 Rīta iela; tel: 412 3678; email: martins@martins.apollo.lv), a well-maintained guesthouse on the outskirts. Single rooms cost Ls8 and doubles Ls18. For budget travellers the **Piparini** youth hostel (52–54 Dzirnavu iela; tel: 910 5015); beds cost Ls2-4. There are also many campsites throughout the Gauja National Park.

Eating out
The best restaurant is in the **Hotel Cēsis** (but see above). It is especially good for game. Also part of the Hotel Cēsis is the **Café Popular**. Located in the basement, it serves traditional Baltic food. Both the **Katrīna** and the **Province hotels** also have cafés. Apart from the hotels, the possibilities are relatively limited. **Makss un Morics** (43 Rīgas iela; tel: 412 4367) has an attractive ambiance and extensive menu (unfortunately only in Latvian), and the **Aroma** coffee shop (4 Lenču iela) offers coffee and snacks.

Tourist information
The tourist information centre is at 1 Pils laukums; tel: 412 1815; email: info@cesis.lv; www.cesis.lv.

The town
The town centre is an open square (Vienības laukums) from which the main streets radiate. The brewery, which dates back to the 19th century, is on Lenču iela between the Cēsis Hotel and the castle. If you walk down Lenču iela there is a small park on the right. Turn left into the cobblestone road which leads to the Old and New castles. The New Castle (which dates from the 18th century) is a pink building with a white tower and the former seat of the Sievers family. Now it houses the **Cēsis Museum of Art and History** (open 10.00–17.00, the Exhibition House Monday–Saturday 10.00–12.00). Near the entrance a recent monument commemorates those who suffered and died during the period of 'Communist terror' from 1940–91. The tower offers a panoramic view of Cēsis. Next to it are the ruins of the stone castle. The park below it, which was laid out in 1812, has a small lake and fountain. In the Museum Garden (9 Pils iela) is a forge for making traditional jewellery (Seno Rotu Kalve), run by Daumants Kalniņš, a well-known authority on ancient Latvian art (tel: 915 8436; email: daumants@softhome.net; www.kalve.times.lv). Visitors can watch jewellery being made according to traditional techniques, learn about the history of Latvian jewellery, and can even participate in the process, and of course purchase brooches, bracelets and other items.

If you make your way around the castle you come to Lielās Kātrīnas iela. The house at Number 14 is the one in which Andrejs Pumpurs (the author of the Lāčplēsis epic) lived and worked. If you continue along the street you come to the 13th-century Jāņa baznīca, St John's Church (21 Torņa iela), with its many tombs of members of the Livonian Order, priests and knights. It also has an altarpiece by one of Estonia's leading painters, J Kelers. It is not yet fully restored, although the tower is often open and can be visited for Ls0.50. Occasional organ recitals are given.

The old centre of the town is a conservation area. The main street, Rīgas iela, is full of historic buildings. Number 7 Rīgas iela is the former town hall and guardhouse (built in 1767); 16 Rīgas iela is a medieval guildhall (1788); the former music and singing club, the Harmonija building, is at Number 24 – it dates from the early 18th century and now houses a museum dedicated to the composer Alfreds Kalniņš (1879–1951); and the Princešu nams (a house also dating from the early 18th century) is at Number 77. The Maija Park was established in the 1800s by the grandfather of the poet Eduards Veidenbaums (1867–92). Veidenbaums was born in Cēsis and is buried in the nearby Liepa cemetery. There is a museum dedicated to his life, 'Kalači', Liepa (tel: 419 5309), a simple house containing manuscripts and other items.

A number of famous Latvian writers and artists were born in Cēsis or spent part of their lives here. Apart from Veidenbaums, Pumpurs and Kalniņš, they include Auseklis (1850–79), Reinis Kaudzītes (1839–1920) and Poruks (1871–1911).

Cēsis is also generally credited with being the city where the Latvian national flag was created. According to legend, Latvian troops seeking to repel foreign invaders lost their chieftain on the battlefield. They wrapped the dying man in a white flag captured from the enemy in a previous battle. The Latvian warriors gathered around their dying leader who told them they must continue to defend their homeland and drive the enemy away. His body was removed from the flag which was soaked in blood everywhere except the centre where the chief had lain. Enraged by his death, his warriors tied the maroon and white flag to a spear, attacked the invaders, and drove them from their land. Chronicles mention 1279 as the date when this event occurred. The flag was banned during the period of the Soviet occupation. Cēsis was the first city in Latvia to fly it again in 1987.

Near Cēsis

Six kilometres east of Cēsis, **Priekuļi** is known as a centre of agricultural studies and for its agricultural museum.

If you head down Lenču iela out of Cēsis and follow the signs for about 5km you come to **Ērgļu klinits** (Eagle Cliff). Although there are no direct footpaths leading to it, if you walk through the fir and birch woods towards the Gauja River you will see an observation platform. At the bottom of the steps there is a small beach of yellow sand 100m long and about 20m wide. The area around here is popular for walks.

From Cēsis you can also take the main road north in the direction of Valmiera. If you do, you will come to a crossroads at which you turn right towards **Liepa**. Liepa has a number of sandstone caves. In the cemetery you can visit the grave of Eduards Veidenbaums (1867–92), one of Latvia's best-known poets. Three kilometres from Liepa, at Kalači, is Veidenbaums's house with the little barn in which he wrote so much of his verse. Veidenbaums spent most of his life here, and the house is now a **museum** (tel: 419 5309). Open May 15–October 15 10.00–18.00 every day except Wednesdays .

Just before you get to Valmiera you come to **Kauguri**, the scene of a peasant uprising in 1802. The peasants lost, but the rebellion was the start of a movement to improve living conditions under the ruling Germans.

A few kilometres east of Priekuļi is the village of **Rauna** on the Rauna River. Its main claim to fame is its castles. The Teutonic one dates back to the 13th century, and Rauna grew up around this once impressive structure which was considered the most ornate of all the castles controlled by the Bishop of Riga. It was destroyed during the Northern War and only ruins now remain. The church at Rauna also dates back to the 13th century and remains an important archaeological site, although it has been rebuilt several times over the centuries. Rauna also has the Tanis castle mound, the site of a Latgal settlement. It is said to date back over 2,000 years. About 2km outside Rauna is the attractive Rauna waterfall and a saltwater mineral stalactite cliff, the only one of its kind in Latvia. Nearby is the house where Jānis Cimze (1814–81), the musician and founder of the Latvian national choir, was born.

Gauja National Park

The Gauja National Park (see map, page 160) begins about 50km to the northeast of Riga and covers an area of some 900km², around 100km long and 10km wide along the Gauja river valley. Most of the park is accessible to the public, although part of the area on the left bank of the Gauja River where the Amata River branches off is protected. The Gauja itself flows through a wooded valley. The sandstone forms strange shapes and cliffs, and there are numerous caves, some dating back to prehistoric times. About 47% of the area is forest. There are estimated to be about 900 species of plants, 200 species of birds and 48 species of mammals in the park. The area has been settled by Livs and Latgalians since prehistoric times and more recently it was conquered by the Knights of the Sword. It was traditionally important for trade because of the route to the sea via the Daugava.

Cēsis is the ideal town from which to make excursions into Latvia's most popular national park. It can be visited by car, but is also easily accessible on foot and by bicycle. In fact, many of the sand-based paths and tracks which cut through the area are more easily travelled on foot or by bicycle. Camping is allowed, but only in designated areas.

If you are walking or travelling around by any other means in the Gauja National Park, buy the Jāņa Sēta map of the park (1:100,000).

The Gauja area is not just renowned for its natural beauty but also because it is a major winter sports centre. Riding is a popular way of exploring the region, as is canoeing on the river. Especially attractive is the trip beginning from Cēsis heading south to Āraiši lake and the area around Zvārtas iezis.

There are innumerable opportunities to walk along and above the Gauja River itself, and at various points there are campsites, although care should be taken to ascertain which are in operation before setting out on any trip. One of the most picturesque stretches is that between the bridge just north of Līgatne and Cēsis, a distance of about 20km.

Zvārtas iezis (where there is ample parking) is also a good starting point for walks, providing you head northwards (downstream).

The tourist offices at Cēsis, Sigulda, Gulbene and Valmiera can help you with local contacts for hiking, cycling, horseriding, boating and skiing in and around the Gauja National Park.

The **Makars Travel Agency** (1 Peldu iela, Sigulda – see page 148) also organises many such activities.

Valmiera

The P20 through Cēsis which is off the main Riga–Pskov road, 20km from Sigulda, continues to Valmiera at the northern end of the national park. If you go by train you should note that the station is a long walk from the town. Valmiera's historical importance is due to its location on the Gauja River, which made it a city of some commercial importance and earned it membership of the Hanseatic League. The town was named in the early 13th century after Prince Vladimir of Pskov (Wolmar in Latvian). Banished from Pskov, Vladimir found favour with the Bishop of Riga who invited him to rule the newly occupied settlement in the Tālava region. In 1283 a stone castle was built to ensure German control over the Talavians. It stood until 1702, and today you can still see its remains (which are fenced off). Valmiera was an important trading centre, since it was situated on the busy road leading to Tallinn, Pskov and Novgorod. In 1802 a major peasant revolt took place at nearby Kauguri. In 1917, the American journalist, John Reed, author of *Ten Days that Shook the World*, lived in Valmiera.

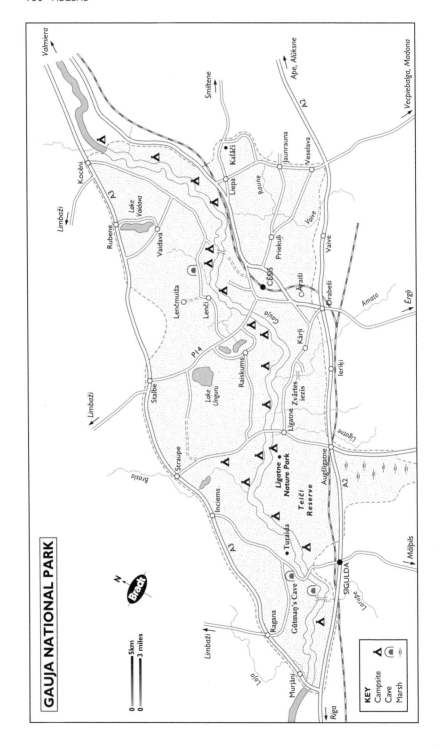

GAUJA NATIONAL PARK

KEY
Campsite
Cave
Marsh

Accommodation

The **Hotel Wolmar** (16a Terbātas iela; tel: 420 7301; email: wolmar@valm.lv; www.wolmar.lv) is the largest hotel in the town and offers singles from Ls19 and doubles from Ls25. The **Motel Pakavs** ('Horseshoe') (5 Beātes iela; tel: 428 1050) is smaller but satisfactory. Single rooms Ls15; doubles Ls22. The new **Naktmājas Hotel** (15 Vaidavas iela; tel: 420 1200; email: info@naktsmajas.lv; www.naktsmajas) offers 39 rooms on the edge of the town and is primarily a business hotel. There is also a small guesthouse, **Luca** (2 Lucas iela; tel: 945 6899). Double room Ls18. There is also a **youth hostel** (25c Ausekļa iela; tel: 420 7537) and another, the **Eži** (1 Valdemara iela; tel: 420 7263). Bicycles can also be hired here and activities arranged. Nearby campsites include **Baiļi** (tel: 422 1861) at Baiļi in Kauguru parish, **VPIC** (12 Purva iela; tel: 945 4186) and **BMX Parks** (tel: 928 3494).

Another option fairly close to Valmiera is the **Dikļi Palace Hotel** (contact Dikļi Pils, Dikļu pagasts, Valmieras rajons; tel: 420 7480; email: pils@diklupils.lc; www.diklupils.lv). Formerly a manor house northwest of the town, it is now a 30-bedroom luxury hotel and is an excellent example of the way in which Latvia is now using its listed buildings to promote tourism.

Eating out

There are restaurants at the **Motel Pakavs** and at the **Hotel Wolmar**. There are several cafés in the centre of town, primarily on Stacijas iela. The **Mazais Ansis** (at Rubene, 10km out of Valmiera on the A3; tel: 424 8400) is a lakeside complex, including a restaurant with traditional Latvian cuisine, a bar and children's play areas.

Tourist information

The tourist information office is located at 10 Rīgas iela; tel: 420 7177; email: tic@valmiera.lv.

What to see

Number 1 Varoņu laukums is an interesting landmark. Constructed in 1752 this building is Latvia's oldest pharmacy (*vecā aptieka*), and functioned for over 200 years until it closed in 1965. At 2 Bruņinieku iela the **Simona Church** (St Simon's Church) built in 1283 and reconstructed in 1729, was used for concerts during the Soviet era until the revival of the parish during *glasnost*. Since 1989 it has been used again for religious services. From the tower there is a fine view of Valmiera and the River Gauja. The red-brick **Orthodox church** with its blue towers is also in the centre of town. Other sites include the **sculpture park** (with its collection of work from Estonia and Latvia) and the so-called **Bachelor's Park** with its old manor house. In summer you can go boating on **Lake Dzirnezers**. The **theatre** is one of the best known in Latvia.

At 3 Bruņinieku iela, beyond the church, you will find the **Museum of Local Studies** (Valmieras novadpētniecības muzejs). It stands on a site once occupied by a castle of the Livonian Order. It is devoted to the history of the area and also contains works by the local painter R Vītols. Behind the museum is an attractive park that leads down to walks by the river. In front of it there is a statue called 'The Boys of Valmiera'; it takes its theme from a popular Latvian novel by Pāvils Rozītis about Valmiera and the students who attended the teachers' academy here. Open Monday–Friday 10.00–17.00 and Saturday 10.00–15.00.

Even though Valmiera is located in what is primarily an agricultural region, the town itself has developed industrially and become a centre for the manufacture of fibreglass. In 1996 the University College of Northern Latvia was established there in

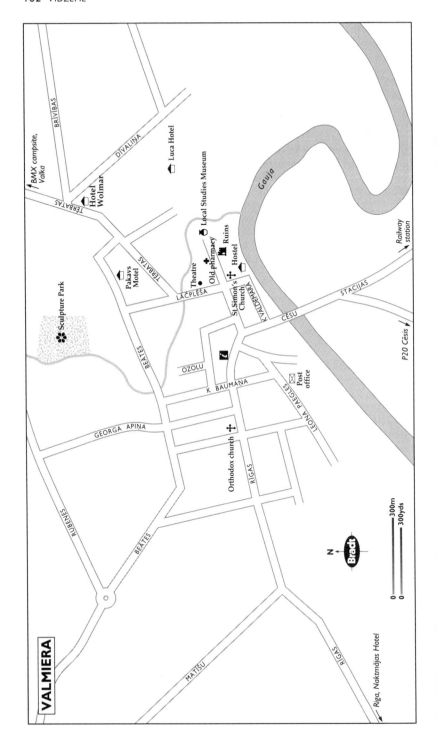

partnership with the University of Lillehammer in Norway. That, together with the fact that Valmiera has a music school, makes it a major Latvian centre for education.

Near Valmiera
From Valmiera you may wish to head a few kilometres northwest to Zilaiskalns (**Blue Hill**). Rising 127m above sea level, the hill has an observation point from which you can see **Lake Burtnieki** (see page 167), and even as far as Cēsis. The hill was said to have a magical spring whose waters healed many ailments. Some claim the Liv hero, Imants, is buried here. Not far from Zilaiskalns is **Dikļi** where, in 1818, the first Latvian-language play, *Laupītāji* (a translation of Schiller's *The Robbers*) was performed in the threshing barn at Zundu House. The barn still stands. Dikļi was also the place where the first Latvian Festival of Song and Dance was held in 1864. There is a museum devoted to the festival and the manor house is now a hotel (see page 161).

Strenči
The A3 continues towards Strenči, about 20km from Valmiera. The section of the Gauja River between Valmiera and Strenči is particularly attractive, especially the part about 4–5km before you reach Strenči. In 1998 the traditional raftsmen's festival was revived on this stretch of the Gauja (it takes place in May each year).

Valka
Thirty kilometres northeast of Strenči, on the border with Estonia, lies the town of Valka. Valka was divided in 1920 when the Latvian–Estonian border was established. The part of the town that lies in Estonia is called Valga. Buses and taxis do not cross the border, and shops do not accept currency from the 'other side'. There is an exchange office at the crossing on the outskirts of the town, but not in the town centre. The existence of Valka as a settlement can be traced back to 1286. It was badly destroyed in the Polish–Swedish wars but became a district town towards the end of the 18th century and developed further when the railway arrived at the end of the 19th century. The teacher and composer, Jānis Cimze (1814–81) lived here. His body lies in the cemetery at Valka, but his name also lives on in the form of the J Cimze Music School in Seminãra iela.

Accommodation
On the Estonian side of the border is the **Säde Guesthouse** (Jaama pst 1, Valga 68204; tel: 764 1650; fax: 766 1017) which has 52 beds, with prices below US$8 per person per night. A new hotel at Kuperjanovi 63, also on the Estonian side, will be opening early in 2005.

Tourist information
The tourist information office is at 3 Beverinas iela; tel: 470 7522; email: tic@valka.apollo.lv; www.valka.lv. Open in summer Monday–Friday 08.00–18.00, Saturday 10.00–16.00; and in winter Monday–Friday 08.00–17.00.

What to see
Unless you are particularly interested in border towns, there is no reason to visit Valka. It is a pleasant enough place but contains little of particular interest, at least on the Latvian side. The town's main attraction is the former seminary, about 3km from the border on the Riga road, which carries the name of its founder, Jānis Cimze (1814–81), and which is now the Valka Local History Museum (tel: 472 2198). A smaller, disused barn houses a **farming museum** and depicts former local life around the theme of the four seasons showing how the weather dictated most

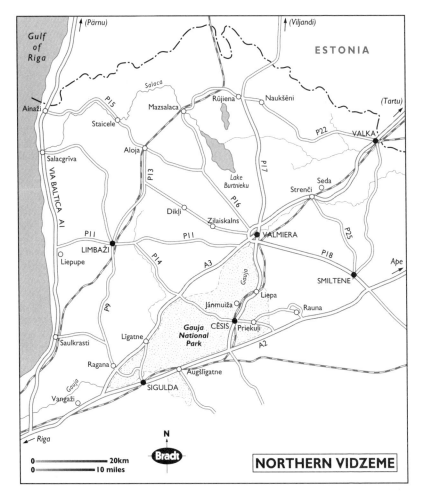

NORTHERN VIDZEME

activity. Valka is also unusual in having five cemeteries side by side: tensions between different groups were too great to allow them to be buried in the same cemetery.

From Valka a minor road leads southwest away from the Estonian border through Lugāži and Bilska to Smiltene.

Smiltene

The small town of Smiltene was first mentioned in 1359. It became a town in 1920. Its ancient castle was built in the 13th century and destroyed during the Polish–Swedish wars in the early 1600s. Like many of Vidzeme's small towns, it is now much more lively than a few years ago and has lost much of its sleepy, otherworldly feel. Just southeast of Smiltene is yet another castle mound, **Certenes**, an important settlement in the 12th century. If you are interested in natural wonders, head 5km northwest of Smiltene along the Valmiera road to the **Zauskas priedes** pines. The oldest and the largest (370 years old and 4.6m in diameter) is now dead, and only the trunk remains. Nearby at Blome there is a huge oak tree called **Ringu ozols** with a circumference of 8.4m.

Accommodation and eating out
On the outskirts of Smiltene, the **Kalna Ligzda** (Kalnamuiža; tel: 477 2173) has about 30 rooms. It also has a sauna. To get there, follow signs out of the town towards Valka and the Kalnamuiža area is signposted on your right. Another option is the **Park Hotel Brūžis** (2 Brūža iela; tel: 477 3708) situated on the edge of a small lake. Room prices Ls14–30. To reach it, continue along Dārza iela away from the centre of town and take Dakteru iela on your left; Brūža iela is on your left and you will soon see a signpost to the hotel. The food here is very acceptable.

Tourist information
The tourist information office is at 3 Dārza iela; tel: 470 7575; email: tourism@smiltene.lv. Open Monday–Friday 10.00–18.00.

BETWEEN RIGA AND ESTONIA: THE GULF OF RIGA
If you head north out of Riga on the A2 then in the direction of Salacgrīva on the A1, it eventually takes you to Pärnu just over the border in Estonia. The first town of any significance you come to, about 45km from Riga, is Saulkrasti.

Saulkrasti
Saulkrasti has been a health and holiday resort since the 19th century, although it is said that Catherine II of Russia stopped at the beach at Pabaži to swim there in the late 18th century. The modern town of Saulkrasti was formed in 1933 by merging the two villages of Peterupe and Neibāde. The name Saulkrasti was taken from the location in which the play by E Cīrulis, *Blossom Time* (*Ziedu Laiks*), was set. In 1950 the town grew further, taking in the village of Pabaži (formerly Katrīnbāde). It remains a popular resort. It has a regional studies museum (19 Skolas iela) in the house where the Latvian writer Reinis Kaudzīte lived from 1913–20, and a private museum of old bicycles (look for the penny-farthing on the main Riga road), but otherwise its attraction lies entirely in its location on the coast.

Accommodation
The **Saulkrasti** (72 Ainazu iela; tel: 795 1960) is beside the sea in parkland. Another option is the **Hotel Sunbeach** (72 Ainazu iela; tel: 795 1733). The **Maija** (3 Murjāņu iela; tel: 795 1372) is also a hotel. There is also a guesthouse, **Pabaži** (7 Mednieku iela; tel: 795 1885). There are campsites at **Incupe** (82 Rīgas iela; tel: 295 1247) and **Juras priede** (56 Upes iela; tel: 295 4780).

Liepupe
Further north through the pine forest lies Liepupe (the river and town have the same name). To your right along the riverbank you will see the ancient castle mound which many historians believe was once the powerful Liv city of Metsepole. Liepupe was the home of the enlightened 18th-century thinker, Garlibs Merkelis who advocated the emancipation of the Latvian serfs from their German and Russian landlords.

There is a pretty stretch of coastline between **Vitrupe** and **Rankulragu** near **Tūja**. It is here that you will find Latvia's longest sandstone outcrop, known as the red cliffs. For 2km the wind and sea have shaped these cliffs, forming caves and unusual shapes. An easy walk along the beach takes you from Vitrupe south to Tūja, a distance of about 18km. Part of the coastline is a nature reserve.

Accommodation and eating out

Near the road sign marking the 72nd kilometre marker is the motel **Casablanca** (tel: 921 6654; www.moteliscasablanca.com). There is a campsite at Tūja (tel: 924 7992) and another at Salacgrīva.

Salacgrīva

Further north again is the town of Salacgrīva, once a prosperous Liv fishing village and now Latvia's fourth largest port. As long ago as the 5th–6th centuries there was a Liv settlement called Saletsa at the mouth of the River Salaca. In 1226 the Knights of the Sword built a castle here which survived until the 17th century when it was razed to the ground by war. Salacgrīva became important as a shipbuilding town in the 19th century but only acquired official municipal status in 1928. In 1960 it opened up when it was connected to Riga by the Riga–Tallinn highway. Five kilometres from Salacgrīva is Akmeņu sala (**Rock Island**), an island in the sea; and north of the town (near Ainaži) are the **Randu pļavas**, an area of meadow which runs down to the sea and is known for bird migration and nesting. It is also home to some 37 endangered plant species.

Nearby, on the banks of the Svētupe River, are the caves (**Lībiešu upurala**) where the Liv people made sacrifices. The Salaca and Svētupe rivers provide good fishing (check locally for regulations).

The administrative centre of North Vidzeme Biosphere Reserve is at 10a Rīgas iela; tel: 407 1408. This reserve, created in 1997, covers the Vidzeme coast of the Gulf of Riga and the area around the Salaca River, including Lake Burtnieku, and contains important woodland and coastal habitats.

Accommodation

The Hotel Brize (7 Valmieras iela; tel: 935 5995; www.brize.lv) is just 400m from the sea. Its 18 rooms cost Ls15–50.

Ainaži

Ainaži is the last town on this road before the Estonian border. The name comes from the Liv word *annagi*, meaning lonely. For centuries the area near here was barely inhabited: it consisted mainly of forest and marshland, and only a small coastal strip was settled. The people lived from fishing and other maritime work. However, the town of Ainaži began to grow when two brothers who had prospered from fishing, Miķelsoni and Veides, purchased the manor of Ainaži from Count Mellin for 68,000 roubles in 1868. It became the site of Latvia's first naval academy (47 Kr Valdemāra iela), and now houses the **Naval College Museum** (Ainažu Jūrskolas Memoriālais Muzejs; tel: 404 3349), a legacy of the town's shipbuilding industry which flourished in the 19th century. Among other things, the museum contains a reconstruction of a 19th-century classroom. The naval academy was founded in 1864 by the two brothers at the instigation of Krišjānis Valdemārs (1825–91) and educated over 3,000 men before it closed in 1919. The museum opened in 1969 and has exhibits dealing with the history of the naval academy, the construction of sailing ships in the 19th century and related matters. Although Ainaži remained an important port until World War II, other ports (notably at Salacgrīva and Kuiviži) developed more and the town began to lose its maritime connections. Now it is important as a transport and customs centre. Open daily in summer 10.00–16.00; closed on Sundays and Mondays in winter. Close by is the **Ainaži Fire-fighters Museum** (69 Valdemāra iela; tel: 404 3280). Open Wednesdays, Fridays and Saturdays 10.00–16.00.

Beyond the museum but before the border, Kuǧu iela leads down to a car park and the beach.

From Ainaži we head east along the P15 through **Rozēni** and **Staicele, Aloja** and **Matīši**. A few years ago Staicele announced plans to open a permanent exhibition about storks (nearby at Vecalē there is the northernmost colony of white storks in the world), but so far nothing has materialised. Staicele does however have a museum devoted to the Livs (see page 188), **Pivä lind** (14 Liela iela; tel: 403 5396). Open May 1–November 1 Wednesday–Sunday 11.00–17.00. The P16 north takes you to Mazsalaca.

Accommodation

The **Ainaži Motel** (82 Kr Valdemāra iela; tel: 407 1114) by the via Baltica (part of a garage at the southern entrance of the town) has five rooms. Rooms Ls8.50–20.

Mačkalni, near Rozēni (tel: 403 3281) is a guesthouse with ten bedrooms and a sauna, situated on the banks of the River Salaca. Rooms Ls5–10.

Mazsalaca

The only building of interest is the imposing 13th-century Lutheran church, but the area has many natural attractions, including a pretty stretch along the Salaca River, best explored on foot or by boat. In spring Mazsalaca is known for its blossom – apple and cherry – and for its lilac trees which grow along the banks of the river. This area is also visited for its caves and cliffs, especially **Skaņaiskalns**, a 35m sandstone cliff from which echoes rebound. Nearby are the Devil's Cave, the Devil's Pulpit and the so-called werewolf pine. Mazsalaca is also known as the birthplace of the composer, Adams Ore (1855–1927). Nearby is the old manor house of **Valtenburg**. Dating from 1780, it marks the beginning of a long walk to the Skaņaiskalns in Parka iela. The trip can also be made by car, but it is easier to see the wooden sculptures on the way if you go on foot.

Rūjiena

Rūjiena, about 15km from Mazsalaca, is set in similarly attractive countryside. Rūjiena can trace its origins to the 13th century. It is known for its sculptures (one of the most famous is *The Sower of Rūjiena*). The **Lutheran church** is attractive and in good condition. The school is housed in an old manor house.

Accommodation

The **Hotel Tālava** (12 Rīgas iela; tel: 426 3767) offers accommodation and has a restaurant. It is a Latvian–Swedish joint venture; the original 1939 building was renovated in 1993 and is a listed building. Rooms Ls15–25.

From Mazsalaca head south, parallel to the Salaca River which flows out of **Lake Burtnieki**, Latvia's fifth largest lake. The lake can also be reached by a short bus journey from Valmiera. Buses leave the Valmiera bus station at 07.00, 11.55, 15.55 and 18.20. The lake has two islands (Cepurīte and Enksare) and various legends are associated with it. According to one, the Castle of Light lies at the bottom of the lake and one day will rise again. The town of Burtnieki at the southern tip of the lake is known for its horses and stud farm. The Burtnieki Cup is popular with racehorse enthusiasts.

The Briedkrogs, a few kilometres out of town, used to be a pub but now houses local history exhibits.

There are various accommodation possibilities near the lake in summer. They include the **Burtnieki Guesthouse** (9 Jaunatnes iela; tel: 425 6386) which offers accommodation at Ls6, and the **Enksare** (25 Jaunatnes iela; tel: 425 6453) which has rooms at Ls8 and also has a small pool and sauna.

From Lake Burtnieki pass through **Urga** until the P13 takes you back to Aloja again. Heading south out of Aloja, the P13 takes you to Limbaži.

Limbaži

Limbaži is one of Latvia's oldest towns. Historians claim it was the centre of the Liv kingdom, Metsepole, and to this day many Livonian names still survive. The Liv fortress, Lemisiles (the name comes from the Liv and means 'large island in the middle of forest marsh'), was destroyed by the German Knights who replaced it with a stone castle in 1223. A century later the area around the castle grew into a prosperous Hanseatic town. Limbaži, however, like many Latvian towns, has suffered in Latvia's many wars. In 1602, during the Polish–Swedish Wars, the Swedish army burned Limbaži to the ground and tore down its ramparts. It is claimed that the present name of the town goes back to this time: a Swedish clergyman overheard a conversation involving the two words 'limba' and 'azi' and put them together to create a new name for the town. One-hundred-and-fifty years later, a great fire gutted the town, destroying all but four houses.

Accommodation
The best accommodation is outside Limbaži. On the P9 around 30km south of Limbaži is the **Biriņi** manor house (tel: 406 6232; email: birini@latnet.lv; www.ltn.lv/~birini). The building was designed by Riga architect Friedrich Wilhelm Hess and constructed between 1857 and 1860. The exterior is neo-Gothic but the interior predominantly neo-Renaissance. There is a pleasant walk in the park along the lake. You can also see the tomb of Count Ludwig August Mellin, built in 1814. The manor house has limited but high-quality overnight accommodation; rooms from Ls13–25 per night. Also on this road is **Igates Manor** (tel: 405 5867), again with some accommodation; rooms from Ls5–25.

Tourist information
The tourist information office is at 5 Burtnieku iela; tel: 407 0608; email: limbtic@apollo.lv. Open Monday–Friday 09.00–17.00 and Saturday 10.00–15.00.

What to see
The ruins of the old **castle** remain (7 Burtnieku iela), and the **Lutheran church** (St John's, designed by the architect Bindeschu) dates back to 1680. Between the church and the hospital you can see the remains of the 13th-century Liv moat. The **Alexander Nevsky Orthodox Church**, built in 1903, was one of the most beautiful in the country but is in need of restoration. The **Regional Studies Museum** (7 Burtnieku iela) is an interesting source of information on local history. Behind it are some castle ruins in a former manor house building that was once a post office. It is open Tuesday–Saturday 10.00–17.00 in winter; 10.00–18.00 in summer. Also nearby are the lakes of Lielezers and Dūņezers. Limbaži is also known as the birthplace of the composer, Kārlis Baumanis, who wrote the Latvian national anthem, *Dievs Svētī Latviju* (*God Bless Latvia*). There is a **monument** to Baumanis in Jūras iela. Unveiled in 1920, it is the work of G Šķilters.

Not far from Limbaži at Dunte it used to be possible to visit **Münchausen's Museum** (Minhauzena Muzejs – the address is simply 'Krogi', Dunte; tel: 240 2033), housed in a former pub (*krogs*). Since this building burnt down in 2000 the contents, mainly items relating to the history of the Liepupe district, have been housed in the Liepupe parish administration building (tel: 402 0142), which can be visited on Wednesday–Sunday 10.00–16.00. Also nearby is the **Emīls Melngailis Memorial Museum** (Emila Melngaiļa Memoriālais Muzejs, Vidriži; tel: 405 5849) which commemorates the life and work of the composer and folklorist Emīls Melngailis (1874–1954). Open May 15–October 15 10.00–18.00; closed Sunday, Monday and Tuesday. There are two other museums in the area. **Leons Paegle Memorial Museum** (Leona Paegles Memoriālais Muzejs, Vidriži; tel: 406 2264), is located in a house called 'Lauči' in which the poet Paegle (1890–1926) was born. Open May 15–November 1 Wednesday–Saturday 10.00–18.00. The **Museum of the Bārda Family** (Bārdu Dzimtas Muzejs 'Rumbiņi') is in a house called 'Rumbiņi' in Pociems which celebrates the lives of Fricis Bārda (1890–1919) and his wife Paulina (1890–1983), both important figures in Latvian literature. Open May 15–November 1 Wednesday–Saturday 10.00–18.00.

There are two routes back to Riga, the first by taking the P11 back to the coast in the direction of Tūja, then heading south again on the A1; alternatively you can take the P9 from Limbaži to Ragana, from there taking the A3 and A2 back to Riga.

SOUTHERN VIDZEME: MADONA, PIEBALGA, ALŪKSNE

The P4 out of Riga leads east into southern Vidzeme. About 110km from Riga you come to the Vidzeme Upland (Vidzemes Augstiene).

Taurupe

About 90km from Riga you come to Taurupe, a small town made famous by Mārtiņš Krieviņš (1909–88) who wrote a novel about landless families leaving the town for Russia, where they founded a colony also called Taurupe. It was also the birthplace of Vilhelms Purvītis (1872–1945), one of Latvia's greatest nature and landscape artists.

Ērgļi

The area near Ērgļi is a favourite with skiers (a special train runs from Riga to Ērgļi during the season). About 3km out of Ērgļi at Braki, the farm on which the Latvian writer Rūdolfs Blaumanis lived is now an outdoor museum, the **Rūdolfs Blaumanis Memorial Museum** (Rūdolfa Blaumaņa Memoriālais Muzejs; tel: 487 1569). The house (named 'Braki') in which he wrote most of his works still stands as does the granary, the threshing barn and sauna, all renovated to the condition they were in during Blaumanis's lifetime. You can walk in the gardens and birch grove. Much of what you see served as the setting for many of his works. Blaumanis himself is buried in the old cemetery of Ērgļi by the Ogre River. Open daily in summer 10.00–18.00. Six kilometres away, near Lake Pulgosnis, a modest collection of old houses and barns forms a museum dedicated to the four Jurjāņi brothers, all of them well-known Latvian musicians.

Accommodation

Hotel Ergli 31 Rīgas iela; tel: 486 0666; www.erglihotel.lv. Rooms from Ls15.

Gaiziņškalns

Gaiziņškalns, between Ērgļi and Madona, is the highest point in Latvia, 312m above sea level. Tucked away among other hills, it does not appear high, but from the observation point on the summit you can get some fine views of the forests and lakes of Vidzeme. This is a favourite place for cross-country skiing (skiers generally lodge in private houses). The roads here are unmade.

RŪDOLFS BLAUMANIS

Rūdolfs Blaumanis was born in 1863 and is perhaps (after Jānis Rainis) Latvia's best-known writer. His depiction of the lives of ordinary people and the deep emotions that run beneath apparently placid exteriors, and his understanding of traditional rural concerns, won him a special place in Latvian cultural life. His theme of conflicting moral values and the often difficult relationship between men and women is exemplified in his play, *The Indrans*, which deals with the emotional upheavals and tensions attendant on a father handing over his farm to his son and daughter-in-law. One of his best-loved comedies is *Skroderdienas Silmačis* (*A Tailor's Days in Silmeci*) which is often performed at midsummer festivals. His novels, *The Wader in the Marsh* and *Hoar Frost in Spring*, are generally classified as naturalist in style, but Blaumanis also had a gift for the mystical, best illustrated in his verse and in his one-act play, *Saturday Night*. He is particularly admired for his mastery of poetic form. He died in 1908.

Madona

Madona is located about 50km from Ērgļi. Heavily bombed during World War II, it is now a new town with a population of about 10,000. In fact even its name is new: until 1926 it was called Birži. It is a pleasant town, but there is little to detain the traveller here.

Accommodation

Hotel Madona 10 Saieta laukums; tel: 486 0666. Fairly basic accommodation; with café and sauna. Rooms Ls10–40.

From Madona you can head northwest into the heart of the Vidzeme Upland. Take the P4 west, then after about 13km the P30 in the direction of Cēsis.

Piebalga

There are records of people settling here as far back as 1318. Now there are two distinct places, Vecpiebalga (Old Piebalga) and Jaunpiebalga (New Piebalga). The original Piebalga was an estate until the late 18th century when the manor separated from the rest of the estate. Both pieces of land were given to Prince Sheremetyev by Tsar Peter I and remained in his family until the early part of this century.

You cannot visit Vecpiebalga without hearing about *Mērnieku laiki (The Times of the Land Surveyors)*. This classic Latvian novel was written in the 1800s by two brothers, Matīss Kaudzīte (1848–1926) and Reinis Kaudzīte (1839–1920), known simply as 'brāļi Kaudzītes' (the Kaudzīte brothers). The novel became so popular that the names of some of the characters in it have become part of the Latvian language. The pub (*kalna krogs*) that figured prominently in the book is on the road to Ērgļi, and the place where the ball in the novel took place is by Lake Inesa. There is even a statue of Liene, the heroine of the novel, in the old cemetery – flowers are often to be found at her feet – and, of course, one of her creators. Kalna Kaibēni, the Kaudzītes' house in which the two men laboured for 20 years to produce their masterpiece, has, inevitably, been turned into a museum. The **'Kalna Kaibēni' Kaudzīte Brothers' Memorial Museum** (Brāļu Kaudzīšu Memoriālais Muzejs 'Kalna Kaibēni'; tel: 416 8216) claims to be the oldest literary museum of its kind in Latvia. Established in 1929, it has preserved the rooms in which they worked and lived and the garden which they tended as they were in the lifetime of the two writers. There is also a workshop, granary and bath house that can be visited. Open May 15–October 15 every day 10.00–17.00.

The countryside around Vecpiebalga is attractive, but in Vecpiebalga itself there is little to see: a castle mound marks the site of what was once yet another castle of the Knights of the Sword, and the school (founded in the 17th century), housed today in a building dating back to 1864, is the place where a number of famous Latvian figures received their first education (among them the writer Kārlis Skalbe). Skalbe (1879–1945) lived in a house, 'Saulrieti', in Incenos, just outside Vecpiebalga. Now Saulrieti (the name means 'sunset') is the **Kārlis Skalbe Museum** (Kārļa Skalbes Muzejs 'Saulrieti'; tel: 416 4252) and contains items relating to Skalbe's life and that of his wife, Lizbete, the translator. Open May 15–October 15 every day 10.00–17.00 except Monday and Tuesday. Nearby in Kaikasos there is a museum dedicated to another writer, Antons Austriņš (1884–1934). The **Antons Austriņš Memorial Museum** (Antona Auštriņa Memoriālais Muzejs) is at 'Kaikaši', Vecpiebalga. The house is again the one in which the writer lived, but it also contains an unusual collection of images of the sun collected by Austriņš's daughter, Mudīte. Nearby, Lake Alauksts is a popular place where singing and dancing events are often held, especially on midsummer night's eve. Open May 15–October 15 every day 10.00–17.00 except Monday and Tuesday.

Between Vecpiebalga and Jaunpiebalga, down an avenue of lime trees, is the **'Jāņskola' Emīls Dārziņš and Jānis Sudrabkalns Museum** (Emīla Dārziņa un Jāņa Sudrabkalna Muzejs 'Jāņskola'; tel: 416 2354) housed in the building in which the composer, Emils Dārziņš, was born in 1875. On the ground floor there is an exhibition devoted to the Latvian poet, Jānis Sudrabkalns (1894–1975). Open May 15–October 15 every day 10.00–17.00 except Monday.

Southeast of Madona, **Lake Lubāns** on the border between Vidzeme and Latgale, was once the largest lake in the country but is now much smaller as a result of artificial deepening of the Aiviekste River; today it is only 1m deep, although it is fed by ten rivers, among them the Rēzekne and the Malta.

Northeast of Madona is the town of **Cesvaine**. The main attraction of this small place was the palace, built from 1890–97, with its distinctive red-tiled turret and strange mixture of architectural styles. Along the northern façade of the palace are the remains of the castle of the Bishop of Riga dating back to the 14th century. Unfortunately the castle was severely damaged in a fire in December 2002.

Gulbene

Gulbene is of interest to railway enthusiasts because it is the location of a narrow-gauge railway. Completed in 1903, it runs from Gulbene to Alūksne through some beautiful hilly countryside.

The station, built from 1925–26, is the work of the architect P Feders. Generally, however, Gulbene is a run-down town offering little of interest to the traveller. Apart from Feders's station, which is worth visiting because of its size and the quality of its restoration, the only significant buildings are the Lutheran church (13 Brīvības iela) and the few remaining buildings on the Vecgulbene (Old Gulbene) Estate, notably the classical White Palace (Baltā pils; at 12 Brīvības iela), the Red Palace (Sarkanā pils; at 1 Parka iela), which is now a primary school, and the Old Granary (at 9 Brīvības iela), which houses the Gulbene Museum of History and Art (Gulbenes Vēstures un Mākslas Muzejs; tel: 447 3098). Open Monday–Friday 10.00–16.00; Saturdays 10.00–13.00.

THE GULBENE–ALŪKSNE NARROW-GAUGE RAILWAY

This is the last section of narrow-gauge railway still in use in Latvia. It runs for 33km through lovely scenery between the two towns, stopping at a number of small places en route. It is part of the Stukmaņi to Valka railway, originally built in 1903. There are three return journeys every day, leaving Gulbene at 06.00, 13.25 (working days and Saturdays only), 10.00 (Sundays and holidays only) and 18.00, and returning from Alūksne at 07.50, 15.20 (working days and Saturdays only), 12.00 (Sundays and holidays) and 19.50. The journey, by diesel locomotives and carriages built in the 1960s and 1980s, lasts 1½ hours. An adult ticket costs Ls0.64 one way. For more information, see www.banitis.lv/eng.

Avoid staying in Gulbene if you can, as the accommodation it offers at present is primitive. However, the Hotel Gulbene (271 O Kalpaka iela; tel: 447 3128) says it plans to restore its rooms by 2005.

Not far from Gulbene at **Druviena**, the **Druviena Old School** (Druvienas Vecā Skola; tel: 444 4550) is a small museum, in the former school building, devoted to the work of the poet Jānis Poruks, the critic Kārlis Egles, the historian Rūdolfs Egles, and the bibliographer Jānis Misiņš. It is said that the countryside here was a great inspiration to Poruks. The museum is open April 1–September 30 every day 10.00–17.00 except Monday.

After Gulbene you can head northeast to Alūksne or east/southeast to Balvi on the P35.

Balvi

Balvi is located attractively near two lakes, Lake Balvi (Balvu ezers) and Lake Perkoni (Pērkoņu ezers). It has a pleasing two-tower Catholic church (**Holy Trinity**) which dates back to 1805 and a somewhat starker **Lutheran church** built in 1905. Note also its **Memorial to the Partisans** (Latgales partizānu pulka kritušiem karavīriem), a large statue in the heroic style by the architects A Jansons and K Jansona (1938). **The History and Art Museum** (Balvu Vēstures un Mākslas Muzejs) at 5a Vidzemes iela; tel: 452 2034) was established in 1989 and contains exhibits relating to the art, culture and history in and around Balvi. Open Monday–Friday 08.00–17.00; closed Saturday and Sunday.

Accommodation

Balvi Hotel 14 Tautas iela; tel: 452 2307. A modest hotel, with restaurant, centrally located near the Lāča Dārzs park; 25 rooms.

Stāmeriena

Between Gulbene and Alūksne lies the small town of **Stāmeriena**. The romantic manor house was mainly built in the 1850s and 1860s, and retored after a major fire in 1905. The owner, Boris von Wolff, often entertained the Italian writer Giuseppe di Lampedusa (author of *The Leopard*) there, and its picturesque location between two lakes makes it popular with visitors. Also worth visiting is the Orthodox church, built by von Wolff for his mother. Nearby at Kalncempji, the **Museum of Local Studies** (Kalncempju Novadpētniecības Muzejs Ates Dzirnavās; tel: 434 4542), housed in an old mill (Ates mill), contains objects relating to the history of farming and life in the area. Open daily 09.00–17.00 except Tuesdays. Nearby is the **Vonadziņi** guesthouse, on the shores of Lake Ludza (1 Skolas iela, Stāmeriena; tel:

924 2551; www.vonadzini.lv). The guesthouse has 16 rooms and a restaurant, various recreational facilities including a children's playground and beach volleyball, and is built in traditional style with a thatched roof.

Alūksne
Alūksne lies in the northeastern corner of Latvia close to the border with Estonia and is one of the prettiest towns in Latvia. It is also the terminus for the Gulbene–Alūksne narrow-gauge railway. The Knights of the Sword tore down the wooden fortress built by the inhabitants on an island in the lake and replaced it with a stone castle in 1342, naming it Marienburg. It in turn was destroyed by the Swedes in 1702, and then the whole city was demolished by the Russians in the Northern War. Archaeological studies are now being undertaken on this historic site (Marienburgas pils). In the town there is a manor house (also referred to as the new palace), built in 1861 by the German Baron Vietinghof whose family remained there until 1918 but which now houses the **Museum of Local Studies and Art** (Alūksnes Novadpētniecības un Mākslas Muzejs; tel: 432 1363). Founded in 1959, it contains exhibits relating to the history of Alūksne and the surrounding area and a collection of oil paintings by Leo Kokles. Open every day 10.00–17.00 except Sunday and Monday. In the park there is a pavilion named after Alexander I of Russia who stopped in Alūksne after travelling through France and Germany having defeated Napoleon's armies.

Alūksne's main claim to fame is being the home of Ernst Glück who lived here from 1683–1702. Glück, a Lutheran clergyman and teacher of German descent, was the first to translate the Bible into Latvian. Two huge oak trees stand in the back garden of his house at 15 Pils iela, a long, low wooden building, a 5–10-minute walk from the church: Glück planted one when he completed his translation of the New Testament in 1685 and the other when he completed the Old Testament in 1689. They are marked by a stone inscribed 'Glika Ozoli' (Glück's oaks). There are some examples of his work in the church. Glück also founded the first school in Alūksne in 1683. The **Ernst Glück Museum of the Bible** (Ernst Glika Bībeles Muzejs; tel: 432 3164) now occupies Glück's former house at 25 Pils iela. Open Wednesday–Saturday 12.00–17.00 and Sunday 13.00–15.00.

Glück's adopted daughter, Marta Skrovronska, a Lithuanian peasant, was another famous person from this town. In 1702 the Russian general, Sheremetyev, captured Alūksne, and Glück and his daughter were taken prisoner. Sheremetyev took Marta back to St Petersburg where she became the mistress of Prince Menshchikov, a close friend of the tsar, Peter I. Before long she became Peter I's consort, and in 1712 converted to Orthodoxy, took the name Catherine, and married the tsar. Thus she became Catherine I, Empress of Russia, and reigned from 1725–27.

The **Lutheran church** is the work of Christoph Haberland. The site on which it was constructed was swampy so foundations of 2,000 oak tree piles had to be laid before it could be built. It was completed in 1788. Those with an interest in modern architecture may like to take a look at the Catholic **Church of St Boniface**, opened in 2004. It is on Helenas iela, parallel to Pils iela.

Tourist information
The tourist information office is at 8a Dārza iela; tel: 432 2804; email: tic@aluksne.lv.

Accommodation
Disappointingly there are no real hotels in Alūksne but if necessary you could stay at **Ierullā guesthouse** (2b Lielā Ezera iela; tel: 432 1757). Other options are

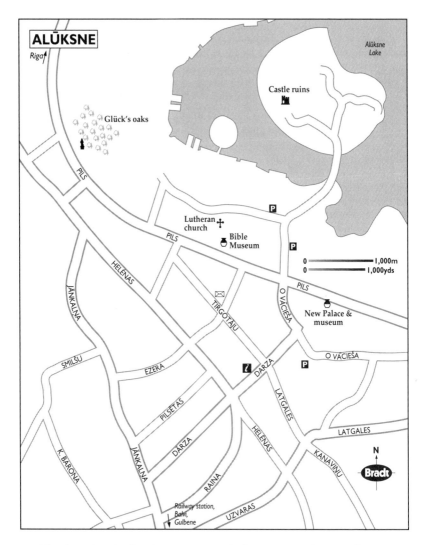

outside the town in locations mentioned above, or at the **Hotel Araji** in **Jaunanna**, on the P43 around 11km south of Alūksne (tel: 430 7099; email: mail@hotel-araji; www.hotel-araji.com) which offers rooms from Ls7–20 and has a wide range of facilities including saunas and horseriding.

Kurzeme

Kurzeme is the name of the region comprising western Latvia. It extends from the Gulf of Riga in the north to the Lithuanian border in the south, and from the Baltic coast in the west to beyond Tukums in the east. A separate kingdom (the Duchy of Kurland, as it was known in German, Courland in English) for many years, Kurzeme to some extent retains a distinct identity.

Kurzeme is one of Latvia's least-populated regions. Although it includes two large towns, Liepāja and Ventspils, it is largely rural, and much of its charm lies in the mixture of thick forest and very gently rolling meadowland inland, and in its unspoilt sandy beaches both along the Gulf of Riga and the Baltic coast. The climate is the wettest in Latvia; the Baltic Germans used the phrase 'Kurland weather' as shorthand for rain and wind. The only consolation is that its winters are the warmest in the country.

MAIN ATTRACTIONS
The coastline and villages around Cape Kolka, some of them home to the Livs, are unspoilt and picturesque. Inland, the area around Kandava and Kuldīga is particularly pretty, and has some facilities for canoeing, walking and other outdoor pursuits. For birdwatchers Lake Engure is Latvia's prime location, while the Slītere reserve further north is also well populated with a wide variety of species. Both Ventspils and Liepāja are sizeable ports with a growing number of attractions and close to unspoilt beaches on the Baltic coast.

HISTORY
Kurzeme had a separate history from the rest of Latvia for several centuries, when as the Duchy of Kurzeme it prospered greatly and even had overseas colonies. It began, however, in the same way as the other parts of Latvia, inhabited by native tribes, the Cours (*Kurši* in Latvian, and *Kuren* in German) until the German knights invaded in the 13th century. The leader of the Cours, Lamekins, held out against the knights, becoming a Christian and making a separate agreement with the Pope. This strategy only succeeded until 1267, when Courland was finally conquered.

When Livonia was taken over by Ivan the Terrible when the Livonian Order collapsed in 1561, Gotthard Kettler, the last master of the Order, managed to keep control of Kurland and part of what is now Zemgale. This area became known as the Duchy of Kurland and owed allegiance to Poland. Under Duke Jakob (see page 15) the duchy became a significant regional power, even annexing Tobago and an island in the mouth of the River Gambia in Africa. In Kurland itself, the duke's craftsmen worked throughout the region producing baroque masterpieces for Kurland's churches. Ships were built at Liepāja, using Kurland's ample supplies of

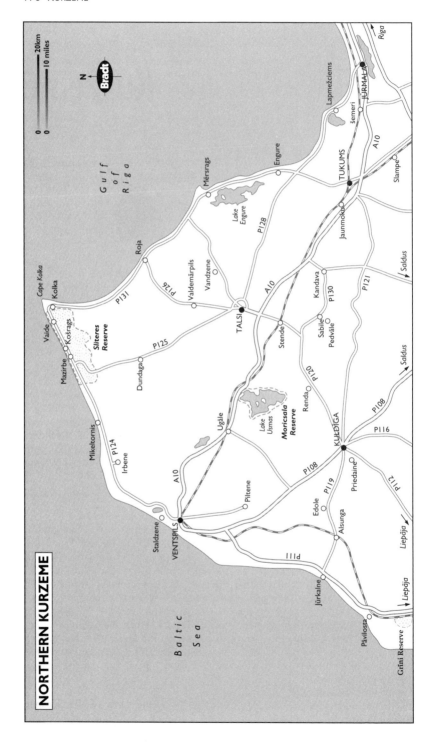

wood, and used to trade overseas. Jelgava (known then as Mitau) was the capital of the duchy, and in the course of the 18th century buildings fit for a capital proliferated there.

In 1795 however, the duchy, along with the rest of Latvia, became part of the Russian Empire, and subsequently, after World War I, part of the new independent Latvia.

The independent spirit of Kurzeme was evident again in the 20th century. When, on Germany's surrender at the end of World War II, the Red Army immediately took over the whole of the Baltic States, Kurzeme's guerrilla forces kept on resisting, keeping the Red Army at bay until May 1945. Until as late as 1957 the 'Forest Brothers', as they were known, continued their armed opposition.

A TRIP AROUND KURZEME

It is possible to make day trips into Kurzeme from Riga. The shortest would be to Tukums, which could be combined with a trip to Jūrmala, as it is on the same railway line from Riga. Private transport is by far the best way of visiting Kurzeme. The area is not particularly well served by public transport.

By car

Cape Kolka is 150km from Riga and can be reached by car in about three hours by taking the coast road. Likewise, the area around Kuldīga and Kandava could be visited by car in a day. Unless you are happy to spend all your time travelling, however, at least one overnight stay is recommended in Ventspils, Liepāja or a country town such as Kuldīga.

By bus

It is possible to go by bus from Riga to Cape Kolka; there are three departures each day, and from Kolka two daily departures to the Liv village of Mazirbe. Buses from Riga to Kandava, Renda and Sabile leave five times a day. Six to nine buses (depending on the day) run from Riga to Kuldīga and take three and a half hours, eight from Ventspils and one from Liepāja. Buses from Riga to Talsi (11 buses a day; 07.55–20.45) take three hours. From Riga to Ventspils takes four hours (14 buses a day; 06.40–22.35), and from Riga to Liepāja four hours (14 buses a day; 06.45–19.40).

By train

Tukums can easily be reached by train. Trains leave Riga station every two hours, pass through Jūrmala and arrive in Tukums in around one and a half hours.

Accommodation

There are good hotels in Ventspils and Liepāja, and rooms and chalets in several towns in the Kandava/Kuldīga inland area and at Kolka. Kurzeme also has a growing number of more interesting overnight possibilities: accommodation is available in some castles, including Jaunmoku near Tukums, and in a number of farmhouses, some of them traditional Latvian buildings (for details see *Country holidays*, page 52).

Tukums

Tukums, 65km west of Riga, is an ancient Liv settlement, whose name derives from the Liv (Finno-Ugric) words *Tukku magi*, meaning a row of hills. Despite these origins, nothing remains from this early date, apart from the castle mound.

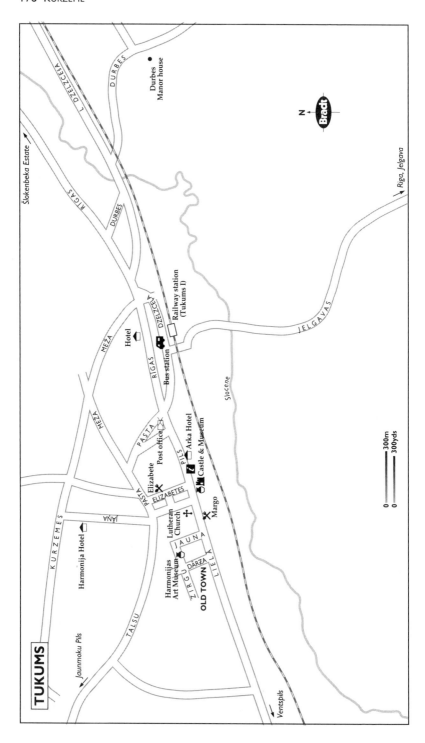

Tukums suffered badly from bombing during World War II and large Soviet army houses and two airfields were subsequently set up in the area. Until the early 1990s the area was off limits to travellers and had no hotel. Recently, however, Tukums has been making efforts to make the most of its heritage and is now a pleasant small town with some attractive buildings.

Accommodation and eating out

Within Tukums itself, the newest possibility is **Harmonija** (3a Jāņa iela; tel: 312 5775; email: info@harmonija.lv; www.harmonija.lv). It has rooms at Ls12–13, as well as a sauna and swimming pool. The **Arka Hotel** (9 Pils iela; tel: 312 5747; email: ervins@arka.apollo.lv; www.infoline.lv/arka) is right in the centre of town and has rooms costing Ls10–48.50. More interesting possibilities are outside Tukums itself. These include **Jaunmoku Pils** (tel: 310 7126; email: jaunmoku_pils@lvm.lv; www.lvm.lv) (see below) where rooms cost Ls5–35 per night. The **Šlokenbekas Muiža** (see below) (tel: 314 4319; email: lejaskrumi@kopideja.lv) also has accommodation in an attractive setting, with a sauna and swimming pool. Rooms Ls20.

Tukums has a number of cafés, including **Margo** (1 Lielā iela) and **Elizabete** (12 Elizabetes iela). Coffee and cakes are available at the Arka Hotel at 9 Pils iela. Restaurants include Karē at 25 Pasta iela, Alus pagrabs at 9 Pils iela (the Arka hotel) and Tvists at 4 Talsu iela.

Tourist information

The tourist information office at 3 Pils iela (ground floor) (tel: 312 4451; www.tukums.lv) can help in booking tours and accommodation in Kurzeme.

What to see

The town is small and can easily be visited on foot. If you would like to see the town and surroundings by bike, however, you can hire bikes from **Velo Divi** (2 Talsu iela; tel: 312 2798). Within the town itself, the **Local History Museum** (tel: 312 4348) is housed in the tower of the castle of the Livonian Order, built from 1277–1306, and now adjoining the attractively pedestrianised main square (Brīvības laukums). Open Tuesday–Saturday 10.00–17.00 and Sunday 10.00–18.00; closed Monday. Nearby, on Brīvības laukums, is the **Lutheran Church of the Holy Trinity** (Sv Trīsvienības), dating from 1644, with a weathercock on its steeple.

Tukums **Old Town** includes Harmonijas iela, Dārza iela, Zirgu iela, Jauna iela, Talsu iela and Lielā iela. The wooden architecture characteristic of the area dates back to the late 19th and early 20th century. Cobbled streets and lighting were restored in 2002. Within this area is St Stephen's Catholic Church (built in 1897) and the **Tukums Art Museum** (Tukuma Muzejs; 7 Harmonijas iela; tel: 318 2392), well known within Latvia for its collection of Latvian 20th-century art. Open Tuesday–Saturday 10.00–17.00 and Sunday 11.00–16.00; admission Ls0.20.

Just outside the centre is **Durbes Pils** (tel: 312 3694), a manor house originally built in the 17th century, but reconstructed in the 1820s in the classical style. It houses the exhibition 'The Latvian and his master', a collection of everyday items. The manor house was given to the poet Rainis but later turned into a sanatorium. It is set in attractive landscaped parkland. Open Tuesday–Saturday 10.00–17.00 and Sunday 10.00–18.00; closed Monday.

Five kilometres east of Tukums is the Šlokenbeka estate (**Šlokenbekas Muiža**; tel: 314 4319). Built at the end of the 15th century, it has recently been restored and houses various exhibitions about transport and roads in Latvia. The gate, portals and weathervanes are original. Open Monday–Friday 08.00–12.00 and 13.00–17.00; Saturday and Sunday by appointment only.

Also fairly close to Tukums, 5km west along the A10, is **Jaunmoku Pils** (tel: 310 7125/6; email: jaunmoku_pils@lvm.lv), another manor house, built in 1901 by the industrialist George Armisted to commemorate the 700th anniversary of the founding of Riga. Armisted, a Scot, was Riga's last mayor before World War I. The manor house is huge and worth a visit to see the tiles painted with pictures of Riga and Jūrmala, as well as the building itself. Several rooms have been restored for use as a hotel. Open 10.00–18.00 except on Monday. At **Kaive**, slightly northwest of Tukums, is an ancient oak (Kaives dižozols), reputedly the thickest in the Baltics, with a diameter of 10m. Although only one branch has survived to the present day, the oak continues to grow.

From Tukums you can either head for Talsi and then on to the coast, or visit the country area between Kandava and Kuldīga. To reach the Kuldīga area, continue along the A10 from Tukums towards Talsi for around 24km and then take the P130 on your left to Kandava.

Kandava

Kandava is one of the country's oldest towns. Its name derives from a Liv word meaning 'a place by the water's edge'. The Abava River splits the town in two and is spanned by the oldest stone bridge in Latvia. Originally built in 1873, it was reconstructed in 1938 and again in 1996. The main part of the town is up the hill from the river, and includes a recently restored square where the fire station figures prominently: most of Kandava's wooden structures were burnt down in several fires during the 19th century, and the present buildings date mostly from the end of the 19th century and the early 20th century.

Accommodation and eating out

In Kandava town centre, the **Pils** (7 Pils iela; tel: 912 0805) is a good basic hotel with rooms costing from Ls15–20. On the road 9km from Sabile in the direction of Renda, the **Plosti Tourist Centre** (tel: 3123237; email:plosti@plosti.lv; www.plosti.lv) offers two- or three-room apartments from Ls6–35, and has a café and restaurant; it is also possible to camp here. At **Pedvāle** there is a guesthouse, **Firkpedvāle** (tel: 325 2249) with beds at Ls5 per night; you can also camp there. Meals in the café are good value. In **Sabile** there is a hostel, **Kurzemes Šveice** (70 Ventspils iela; tel: 325 2249) with beds from Ls2 per night. You can also hire boats for trips on the river. The **Imulas** guesthouse is just outside Sabile heading towards Kandava, near the crossroads to Pūces (tel: 312 3647; email: imulas@imulas.lv; www.imulas.lv). It has 15 rooms costing from Ls15–35, and also has a bar, café and sauna.

What to see

Behind the fire station is **Plague Hill** (Mēra kalniņš), an ancient burial ground where victims of the plague are thought to have been buried in the 18th century. Also in the centre of town is a **Lutheran church** (1736), containing a pulpit and other furniture made by Duke Jakob's craftsman Johans Mertens (1696–1737). The remains of a castle and gunpowder tower, originally built by the Livonian Order, can be seen off Lielā iela on the way to the old town. Remains of a fortress, occupied during the 12th and 13th centuries, can also be seen outside the town, about 1km from where the Kandava road meets the A10 Tukums–Talsi road. Also just outside the town, about 1km southwest of the centre, is the **sulphur springs**

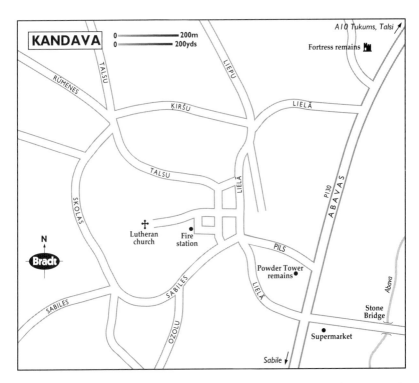

marsh, where at various times lime kilns and health resorts have been situated. Today the area is of most interest in June and July when it is covered with a rare species of yellow flowering bush; if you visit, beware of the snakes that are also attracted to this strange habitat.

If you arrive by train, note that the station is about 7km north of the town. At the station there is a memorial commemorating the 200 people from Kandava and nearby who were deported from there to Siberia on March 25 1949.

Continuing on the P130 from Kandava towards Sabile, you will pass through a picturesque area, popular with hikers. Around 17km from Kandava is the **Plosti Tourist Centre** (see above), where you can hire boats to sail on the Abava. You can go horseriding nearby. You can also walk around the area and visit the **Devil's Stone** and **Devil's Cave** (Velna akmens/Velna ala). This is an ancient place of worship, used more recently at the turn of the century as a place where Latvians hid from the Russians. Legend has it that the devil, angry with the local people, wanted to block the Abava. He carried a huge stone to the river, but just then a cock began to crow. In fear, the devil threw down the stone and hid in a nearby cave which he never left again. The stone is on the left bank of the Abava and the cave a little further up the steep slope.

If you would like a longer walk, a 10km trail starts and ends at the tourist hostel. Walk along the road towards Sabile for around 1km, then turn left and cross over the river towards the Amula watermill. At the watermill, head west again to the Imula River and then follow the river south to the castle ruins. From here the trail leads east to the Amula River and then north along the river to the Devil's Stone and the Devil's Cave. Finally, cross a ford over the Abava River and return to the tourist hostel. The hostel can provide advice and maps.

Sabile

Sabile, like Kandava situated on the banks of the Abava River, is a small cobblestoned town flanked by rolling hills. Here too the Cours built a castle. Although nothing remains of the castle, stones from the building were used to repair the Lutheran church in the 17th century, prior to its full reconstruction in 1876. Inside, the wood carvings and candelabra (1692) are of high quality. The altarpiece is by a German painter, Wolf, and may have been brought here from Dresden. Graves dating from the earlier Livonian period can be seen along the banks of the Abava.

Sabile appears in the *Guinness Book of World Records* for another of its traditions – its vineyards, supposedly the world's most northerly. Since the 16th century, grapes have been grown on the Sabile Wine Hill (Sabiles vīna kalns), and during the Middle Ages wine was exported to various European markets. Wine-making was halted for many years but began again in 2003 when around 150 litres of red wine were made. In 2004 the harvest was even smaller due to heavy frost in spring. The small quantities made means that it is currently impossible to buy Sabile wine, but if you are passing through you may be able to sample a little at the Wine Cellar in the Culture House (kultūras nams) in Sabile, at 16 Ventspils iela.

About 4km west of Sabile, and signposted from the road, is the **Abavas Rumba**, literally the Abava waterfall. Further along the river, about 12km from Sabile, are **Māras Kambari**, sandstone caves named after Māra, the ancient Latvian earth goddess. It is said that pagans performed sacrificial rites here and that later, in the Middle Ages, bandits used the caves as a base from which to raid merchant ships sailing along the Abava.

Around 1.5km from Sabile, and signposted from the town centre, is Pedvāle, an open-air museum with sculptures, paintings and other exhibits. It is possible to stay here overnight, as well as play minigolf or go horseriding. You can have a guided tour of Pedvāle for Ls10. For more information, see www.pedvale.lv or tel: 325 2249.

From Sabile, it is possible to head west to Kuldīga or north to Talsi.

Talsi

The approach road to Talsi with its view of the lake and the town behind it creates a very attractive picture of this small town. It is situated 118km from Riga in the hilly central part of the north Kurzeme Uplands, and near two lakes, Talsi and Vilku, and is a good base for exploring northern Kurzeme. Narrow streets wind along the slopes above the lakes, and the old houses, parks and gardens are reflected in the waters of the lakes. It is a pleasant place to walk around (Lielā iela goes more or less from one end to the other and has many small cafés and bars).

Originally a Liv settlement, the Cours arrived in Talsi in the 10th century and built a fortress here, around which a town sprang up and became the centre of the state. When the Knights of the Order of Livonia arrived they too built a fortress close to Talsi. Battles with Poles, Swedes and Russians in the 17th and 18th centuries, the Black Death in 1657 and 1710, and a large fire in 1733 badly damaged the Livonian inheritance. Talsi also suffered during the Napoleonic Wars, when the town was invaded by the French army, and during the 1905 revolution, when punitive expeditions attacked the town with cannons, killing many inhabitants and burning down many houses.

Accommodation and eating out

In the town itself is the **Talsi Hotel** (16 Kareivju iela; tel: 323 2020), a large Soviet-era hotel, largely renovated. Rooms cost from Ls12–40. Outside Talsi, 5km from the town on the Riga–Ventspils road is **Motel Mikus** (tel: 329 2226),

Left Statues at Salaspils, site of a former Nazi concentration camp (SC)

Below left One of many works at the Sculpture Park, Turaida (RR)

Below The 'Two Brothers' sculpture in Riga's Brothers' Cemetery (SC)

Above Waterfall at Kuldīga, said to be one of the widest in Europe (SC)

Left Cēsis Castle (SC)

Below Gauja National Park (RR)

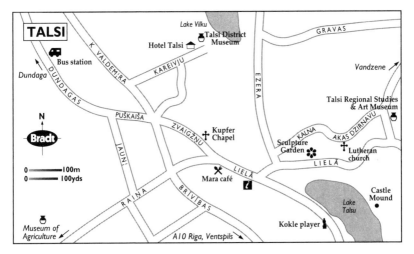

with a small restaurant, and double rooms costing Ls12–18. In Talsi, most eating possibilities are on Lielā iela and Brīvības iela, including **Māra** (16 Lielā iela).

Outside Talsi at Vandzene is the **Hotel Rezidence** (tel: 329 1170; email: residence@apollo.lv; www.hotelrezidence.lv). The hotel has a pleasant garden and lake, and serves good food in a pub-style ambiance. Rooms cost Ls18–34.

Tourist information
The tourist information office is in the People's House (Tautas nams) at 19–21 Lielā iela; tel: 322 4165; www.talsi.lv.

What to see
The **castle mound**, 32m above sea level, is one of the largest in Kurzeme. Archaeologists digging here in the 1930s found silver coins from 12th-century England and 11th-century Cologne among more than 3,000 antiquities, together with remains of at least three oak castles which had once stood here. The site rises to the east of Lake Talsi. To the west of the lake on Fabrikas iela is a monument erected in 1996 as a memorial to Latvia's freedom fighters and known as **Koklētajs**, meaning the *kokle* player, the *kokle* being a traditional Latvian musical instrument similar to a harp. The **Lutheran church** dates mainly from the 18th century. Between 1802 and 1836 Karl Amenda worked here as a priest. This priest and musician is now best known for helping to raise Mozart's children after the composer's early death, and as a friend of Beethoven (in Beethoven's words 'My true, sincere, loving, good-hearted, noble friend'), to whom Opus 18, No 1 is dedicated. Amenda's grave is about 3km from Talsi, near Sukturi. From the graveyard you can see Maitajmuizas ezers (lake). Beyond the trees in the distance lies Lake Engure, Latvia's third largest lake. Also worth a brief look is the **Kupfer Chapel** (Kupfera kaplīča) on Zvaigžņu iela, built in 1806, with a wooden double grave, in Latvian decorative style but with a German inscription, in the grounds. The Talsi Sun on the outside wall of 25 Lielā iela, across the square from the tourist information office, depicts light and sun in ancient Kurši (the Latvian tribe from which the name Kurzeme derives) symbols. The **Talsi District Museum** (Talsu Novada Muzejs, 19 Milenbaha iela; tel: 323 2213; email: talsi.muzejs@apollo.lv) was built as a palace in 1885, and was restored in 1996. Open 11.00–17.00 in summer and

KRIŠJĀNIS VALDEMĀRS

The writer Krišjānis Valdemārs was, together with Atis Kronvalds, one of the most important figures in the National Awakening movement. Born in 1825, he was influenced by Stender. In 1853 he published 300 stories, short stories and riddles, many of them translations, but always adapting the foreign material to Latvian circumstances.

Valdemārs was not just a writer but also a social, economic and political thinker. He was responsible for setting up a newspaper, *Pēterburgas Avīzes* (The *St Petersburg Gazette*), which was published between 1862 and 1865 but was closed down by the Russian authorities. It played a major part in the revival of Latvian national consciousness. Valdemārs used the columns of the newspaper to advertise for folk literature on behalf of Barons whose work in preserving the Latvian heritage he encouraged: it was he who asked Barons and Fricis Brīvzemnieks to embark on a systematic collection of Latvian folklore in 1867. Valdemars also played a key role in establishing the Ainaži Naval College (see page 166). He died in 1891.

10.00–16.00 in winter. There is also a **Museum of Agriculture** (Lauksaimniecības Tehnikas Muzejs, 11 Celtnieku iela; tel: 329 1343) with displays of 19th- and 20th-century farming vehicles and equipment. Open Monday–Friday 09.00–17.00.

Northeast of Talsi just off the road between **Vandzene** and Valdemārpils is another of the **large rocks** (Vandzenes lielais akmens) which are dotted over this region of Latvia. A little further on, close to the entrance to Valdemārpils is a **Forestry Museum** (Meža muzejs; tel: 320 0491) with an exhibition describing Latvia's forestry industry. Open May–October Tuesday–Saturday 09.00–19.00. Close by is **Valdemārpils**, known until 1926 as Sasmaka, when it was renamed in honour of Krišjānis Valdemārs, a leading spirit in the National Awakening movement, who was born in the area. A large granite block depicting the head of Valdemārs stands in the main square. The church, built in 1646, has some attractive wood carvings, and is currently being restored. There is a small but pleasant guesthouse, **Vidi**, in Valdemārpils (tel: 327 6100) with eight rooms and prices from Ls8.

Just off the road between Valdemārpils and Cīruli is the **Lauma Nature Park** (Laumu dabas parks; tel: 640 3240; www.laumas.lv). The park has a number of attractions, including a bee trail, a botany trail, bicycle rental and biking trails. Open May 1–September 30 10.00–18.00; admission Ls1.

Dundaga

Continuing north you will come to Dundaga, 37km from Talsi, with its somewhat surprising attraction: a huge statue of a crocodile. A gift of the Latvian consulate in Chicago, the statue arrived in 1995 to commemorate Arvīds Blūmentāls, a Latvian from Dundaga who emigrated to Australia during World War II, lived in the outback hunting crocodiles and, it is said, was the model for the hero of the film *Crocodile Dundee*. The crocodile lurks at the corner of Talsu iela and Dinsberga iela.

Accommodation

There are several guesthouses in the area, including the **Pūpoli** (tel: 324 0100; email: pupoli@dundaga.apollo.lv), with eight beds.

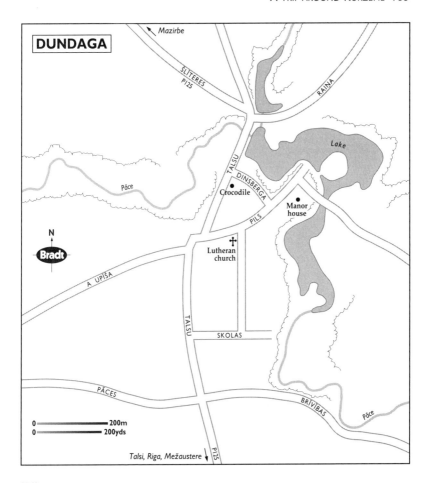

What to see

Apart from the crocodile, Dundaga's main claim to fame is its **castle/manor house**, dating from 1249 but many times restored (its current appearance dates from just before World War I), which was used for many centuries as a store for food awaiting delivery to customers in Riga. The manor house (tel: 324 2093) is at the end of Pils iela overlooking the lake. It is open May 15–October 31 Monday–Friday 09.00–16.00, Saturday and Sunday 11.00–16.00. The **Lutheran church**, also on Pils iela, is also worth trying to have a look inside. Built in 1766, its tall spire was extended in 1897. The furniture is rococo and the altarpiece, *Easter Morning*, was painted in 1912 by the well-known painter Jānis Rozentāls.

Jānis Einfelds, a young Latvian, has written a short story entitled *Dundaga Mornings*, the opening sentences of which capture some of the charm of this small town:

> Summer shimmered like something about to overflow. Milk ran in streams. In the lakes and ponds, ducks fluttered around and the local boys went swimming in the raw. Among the reeds, past their feet, slid fish, eternally inaudible, expressing the essence of the depths.

New Latvian Fiction – see *Appendix 3*

In **Mežaustere**, on the P125 6km south of Dundaga, the **Kubalu School Museum** (Kubala Skolas Muzejs; tel: 324 3751) in the Kubalu school built in 1842, has rooms preserved in their 19th-century state, and relics of the life of the writer and translator Ernests Dinsberģis (1816–1902). Open May 1–October 31 Monday–Friday 09.00–18.00 and at weekends by appointment; telephone for exact opening hours.

Fifteen kilometres north of Dundaga is one of Latvia's oldest nature reserves, **Slītere National Park** (Slīteres Valsts Rezervāts). The area includes forests, dunes, swamps and beaches and runs along the Baltic Sea coast south from Cape Kolka. Within the area it is possible to see a wide variety of flora, and animals such as moose, deer, wild boar, lynx and wolves. It is also home to some protected rare birds, including the black stork. Birdwatchers will be particularly interested in seeing the large number of birds which gather at Cape Kolka during the spring migration. The reserve is open May 1–October 31 Wednesday–Sunday 10.00–18.00. For further information, contact the park office at 3 Dakterlejas iela, Dundaga; tel: 324 2542; email: slitere@mail.bkc.lv; www.slitere.gov.lv. Information is also available from Slītere lighthouse north of Dundaga up the P125; tel: 324 9211.

The coastal road

A coast road leads all the way from Riga to Cape Kolka, where the Gulf of Riga meets the Baltic Sea. The drive along the coast takes you through a succession of small fishing villages and large expanses of pine forest. The road is never far away from sandy white beaches, often completely deserted.

Lake Engure

Lake Engure, 2km north of the small village of Engure, is an important bird reserve. It is Latvia's third largest lake, but is suffering from a number of environmental problems. The name Engure comes from the Liv word *anger*, meaning 'eel', but ironically eel are no longer found here. Chemical fertilisers have meant that the lake tends to become overgrown with reeds: in summer the water becomes too hot for fish, while in winter they can suffocate under the ice. As a result some species, including eel, bream and salmon have disappeared from the lake. Despite this, some fish, such as perch, pike and roach, survive, and the lake remains rich in bird and insect life.

The lake is particularly well known for ducks, geese and swans. Mute swans have been nesting here since 1935 and the population has now increased to around 100 pairs. The rare grey heron, which normally nests in tall trees, breeds in the reed beds around the lake. Cranes can be seen here at migration periods, and the rare black stork is also to be found here. If you are lucky, you may even hear the boom of bitterns or little bitterns echoing through the winter mists. In total around 97 bird species have been observed in the reserve and around 60 species regularly breed here.

It is possible to drive down tracks from the coastal road to the lake, but if you want to do serious birdwatching you should visit the Ornithological Centre or the Krievrags observation tower; tel: 316 1198.

Accommodation

Accommodation in the area is limited. There are two campsites in and around Mērsrags: **Kāpas** (tel: 612 6205) and **Bebri** (tel: 988 5002), and a holiday cottage **Apsīši** on the west side of the lake (tel: 942 0181).

Roja

Beyond Engure, 120km north of Riga, lies the small coastal town and port of Roja. Its **Museum of Maritime Fishing** (Jūras un Zvejniecības Muzejs, 33 Selgas iela;

tel: 326 9594; email: rojatic@inbox.lv) traces the history of the Roja Naval College and Latvian shipbuilding. It also contains exhibits about Krišjānis Valdemārs who was strongly influenced by his early visit to Roja. Open May–October Tuesday–Saturday 10.00–18.00, and November–April Tuesday–Saturday 10.00–17.00. The **Zitari** guesthouse (57 Selgas iela; tel: 326 9256; fax: 326 9151) also offers modern accommodation. The **Roja Hotel** (6 Jūras iela; tel: 323 2226; email: rojahotel@inbox.lv; www.rojahotel.lv) on the northern edge of the town has single/double rooms from Ls10–33, and a 24-hour café.

Cape Kolka

Continuing ever onwards you will finally arrive at Kolka where the surfaced road ends. The village itself is a typical coastal village. It has a new restaurant/bar/hotel complex, the **Zitari** (tel: 327 7145) on the left as you enter from the south, with double rooms for Ls20 and one luxury room for Ls40. There is also a bed and breakfast, **Ūši** (tel: 327 7350) with two rooms at Ls10. To visit Cape Kolka continue through the village until you come to a T-junction. Take the track to the right and after 400m you will come to a car park, where, in summer, you will have to pay to leave your car. A short walk through the pines and past a coastguard station leads down to the beach and to the spot where the Gulf of Riga meets the Baltic Sea. Note that it is dangerous to swim at this point, although further along in either direction it is said to be safe. On the edge of the dunes you cannot fail to see a large orange sculpture, the Sun Sign. A similar sculpture, this time red and called Zāle Saule (Grass Sun), can be seen in a field near Strazde, south of Talsi. A little way off the coast you can see an island with a lighthouse – this is the Sõrve Peninsula on Saaremaa. Close to Cape Kolka at Zītare is the **Liv Centre** (tel: 327 7267), a collection of Liv artefacts (see below). Open Tuesday–Saturday 09.00–17.00.

The Livonian Coast

If you have headed north along the Gulf from Riga, you will have been travelling along the Līvõd Rānda (the Livonian for Livonian coast) soon after leaving Roja. This is an area which extends from Roja to Lužņa, north of Ventspils on the Baltic coast, and is made up of 14 fishing villages. The oldest and most characteristic villages are on the Baltic Sea coast south of Cape Kolka. In 1991 Latvia passed a law to protect the culture and national identity of the people living in this area, the Livonians, who have lived for over 20 centuries by the Baltic Sea in what is now Latvia. Over the centuries their numbers have dwindled and today only a few remain, with only around 20 people still speaking the ancient Liv language. Latvia's recent law makes it mandatory that their social and economic infrastructure be strengthened and Livonians may now give their nationality as Livonian on their passport, and 120 have done so. Many homes along the Livonian coast do not have telephones; the first lines were only connected in 1996.

If you visit some of the villages along the northern coast, you will experience at first hand the quiet life which still persists amid the natural beauty of the sea and the forests. Most villages, including for example **Vaide** and **Košrags**, have simple wooden houses, and Vaide has elk bones hanging from the street signs. **Mazirbe**, 18km south of Kolka, houses the **Livonian People's House** (tel: 324 8371), which contains a small collection of photographs and traditional Livonian costumes. It is open Wednesday–Sunday 11.30–18.00. Interested linguists can obtain a copy of the Livonian-language newspaper *Līvli*. A Liv festival is held in Mazirbe on the first Saturday in August. At Miķeļbāka, close to **Miķeļtornis,** south on the road towards Ventspils, is the tallest lighthouse in the Baltics, built in

> ## LIV CULTURE LIVES?
> Members of the Liv population are making great efforts to try and ensure that their language and culture do not disappear completely. In addition to publishing the newspaper *Līvli*, a selection of Livonian poetry, including verses by the contemporary poet Valts Ernstreits, has been prepared for publication, and scholarships for students of Livonian descent (Ls15 per month) are available. Research into national costumes and traditional ways of life is being undertaken, and in September 1998 the first ever Livonian Culture Day took place in Riga. The Liv language is related to Finnish and some links between Livs and Finns have recently been revived. A Livonian–German dictionary was published 60 years ago and Livonian–Latvian dictionaries also exist. For English speakers, here are just a few starters: *rānda* – coast; *rai* – chair; *vodāgist* – breakfast; *tarā* – garden.

1894 and reconstructed in 1957, which the attendant may open for you to climb and survey the surrounding area.

Ventspils

The bustle and ostensible prosperity of Ventspils's centre comes as something of a jolt after wandering along the timeless byways of rural Kurzeme. Ventspils is the first of Latvia's larger provincial towns to thoroughly modernise its centre, thanks to the money it has earned from its oil transit facilities. The image of Ventspils as something of a boom town is, however, quite new. Only a few years ago it was known as one of the most polluted and environmentally hazardous places in Latvia. There were even reports that gas masks had been distributed to children to protect them against the results of seemingly frequent industrial accidents. Today, these are distant memories: air pollution in Ventspils is now lower than in other cities and towns in Latvia. Visitors will be struck by the way the old town has been restored, the roads renewed and investment put into sports and leisure facilities, as well as by the prevalence of sculptures, mainly on or near Ostas iela, the riverside promenade, for example the seated figure of Valdemārs (see page 184) by M Polis, the water sculpture called *Drops* by G Panteļejevs, and the curiously named *Mental Meteorites* by O Feldbergs.

There are ferries between Ventspils and Nynäshamm in Sweden five times a week (tel: 360 7358; email: ferry@mullerbaltic.lv; www.mullerbaltic.lv) and between Ventspils and Travemünde in Germany twice a week (tel: 360 7337; email: ventlines@latfinn.com; www.ventlines.lv).

Accommodation and eating out
Dzintarjūra (literally 'amber coast') 26 Ganību iela; tel: 362 2719; www.dzintarjura.lv. A large renovated Soviet hotel, with single rooms costing Ls20–28 and doubles Ls32–60.
Hotel Ostiņa 32 Dzintaru iela; tel: 360 7810; email: hotel.ostina@apollo.lv. Located near the Seamen's Centre on the right bank, the hotel has singles from Ls13–21 and doubles at Ls21–40 including breakfast.
Olympic Centre Ventspils 33 Lielais prospekts; tel: 362 8032; email: viesnica@ocventspils.lv; www.ocventspils.lv. The hotel has 2- and 3-bed accommodation at Ls10–16 per room.
Vilnis 5 Talsu iela; tel: 366 8880; www.vilnis.lv. A modern business hotel situated in the port area on the north bank of the Venta; a shuttle bus takes guests to the city centre every 10 minutes. With 54 rooms; singles from Ls25 and doubles from Ls75.

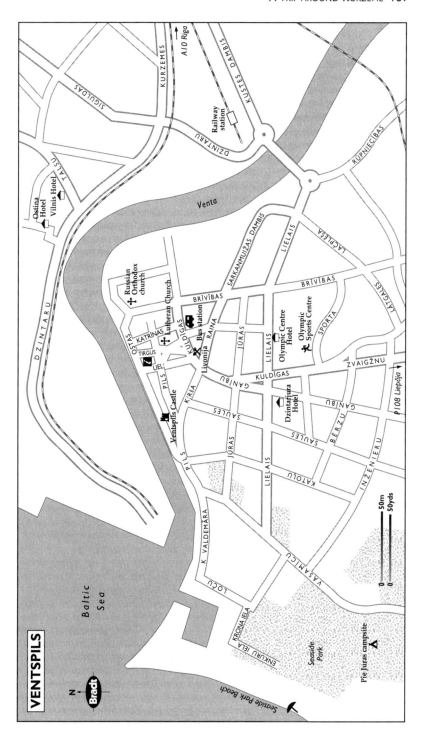

The most central campsite is **Pie Jūras** (Seaside Camping) camping site, next to the Open Air Museum (56 Vasarnicu iela; tel: 362 7991; email: camping@ventspils-lv; www.camping.ventspils.lv). Cabins with two rooms, WC, shower and kitchen cost from Ls10–20 per day. A large number of other campsites are located along the coast, including **Liepene Kempings** (tel: 369 2223; email: rukis@fix.lv), around 10km north of the town on the coast road to Kolka, which offers accommodation in wooden chalets by the sea at prices from Ls2.50–15 per person.

Apart from the restaurants in the Dzintarjūra and Vilnis hotels, the main restaurant in the town is **Livonija** (13 Kuldīga iela; tel: 362 2287). It has a dining room upstairs, with an extensive menu, and a bar downstairs, as well as an outside terrace in summer and a disco at weekends. The restaurant at the castle, **Melnais Sivēns** (Black Piglet) (17 Jāņa iela; tel: 362 2396), is convenient and pleasantly located. A large number of other cafés and restaurants can be found in the area near the Livonija.

Tourist information
The tourist information office is located at 7 Tirgus iela; tel: 362 2263; www.ventspils.tourism.lv.

What to see
In the old town you can see most of the sights by walking along Pils iela and making a few detours. Just east of this street, in Skolas iela, which becomes Plosta iela, is an attractive **Russian Orthodox church**, built in 1901 with an impressive 'onion' tower. On the corner of Skolas iela and Tirgus iela are the oldest houses in Ventspils, dating from the 17th century. The first building of note directly off Pils iela, heading from the east, is the **Lutheran church** on Tirgus iela, built in 1835 by Tsar Nicholas at a cost of 86,686 gold roubles. A portrait of him hangs in the church. A little further west on the bank of the Venta is the restored **Ventspils Castle** (tel: 362 2031). The castle, originally dating from the 13th century, has metamorphosed over the centuries from a tower protecting the mouth of the Venta to a Lutheran church and, between 1825 and 1950, a prison. Today it houses the **Museum of Ventspils**, where modern digital exhibitions trace the history of the town. It also includes the Black Piglet, a medieval-style castle tavern. Open daily May 1–October 31 09.00–18.00 and November 1–April 30 10.00–17.00. Next to the castle is the building of the **Free Port of Ventspils Authority**, originally built as a hotel, and reconstructed in 1998, winning a prize for the best reconstruction of the year awarded by the Union of Latvian Architects. Close by, at 1 Jāņa iela, is a business centre housed in an innovative modern ship-like building.

A highlight of a visit to Ventspils is a trip to the **Seaside Park Museum** (Piejūras Brīvdabas Muzejs, 2 Riņķa iela; tel: 362 4467). The exhibits, which are explained clearly in English, include fishing boats, fishermen's houses, displays about the Baltic Sea etc. Open May 1–October 31 Tuesday–Saturday 09.00–18.00 and November 1–April 30 10.00–17.00. A narrow-gauge steam train, built in 1916, runs around the edge of the museum area at weekends May 1–October 31 12.00–17.00. In summer too there are demonstrations by blacksmiths, weavers and other traditional craftsmen. To get to the museum take the number 6 bus from the town centre.

The source of Ventspils's prosperity is its ice-free port. The main port area is along the Baltic Sea north of the Venta but ships can be seen right along the Venta, starting from in front of the castle. In 1996 Ventspils handled about 80% of the 45 million tonnes of cargo handled by Latvian ports, making it not only the largest port in Latvia but the 12th largest in the whole of Europe. You can see more of the town's river activities by taking a trip on the *Hercogs Jēkabs* (*Duke Jakob*), a modern river boat which makes 45-minute trips along the River Venta. It leaves from the old town riverfront near the castle (tickets are available from the nearby kiosk at the intersection of Ostas and Tirgus iela) approximately every two hours in summer.

It is possible to swim in the sea close to Ventspils. The beaches are extensive and there are places where you can often find amber, particularly after a storm. Swimming is not a health risk in most places north and south of the city: since 1999 the Ventspils beach (a 1.2km stretch near the yacht port) has been awarded Blue Flag status. The most popular beach area, 2km south of the city, can be reached by bus number 10 which runs along Lielais prospekts from the Dzintarjūra hotel. If you prefer a less natural environment, Ventspils now has an Aqua-Park with three swimming pools and various chutes and games (19 Medņu iela; tel: 366 5853; www.ocventspils.lv). Open daily May–September 19.00–22.00. The **Ventspils Olympic Centre** also offers a wide range of sporting facilities, including a swimming pool, a skating rink and tennis courts, as well as a café. You can find it at 7–9 Sporta iela, off Kuldīgas iela about 500m south of the crossroads with Lielais prospekts; tel: 362 2587. Opening hours are 09.00–23.00.

Up the coast from Ventspils at Irbene is the **Ventspils Centre of Radio-astronomy** (Ventspils Starptautiskais Radioastronomijas Centrs), situated in a former Russian army town, the houses and flats of which have been abandoned eerily in the forest. Two parabolic radio telescopes still operate from here, an RT 16 and an RT 32. The RT 32 is a parabolic antenna and is the largest in northern Europe and the eighth largest in the world. In the 1970s and 1980s, when the whole area was closed to the public, RT 32 and two smaller dishes and a communications centre formed *Zveolsdoshka* (meaning 'Little Star'). It is claimed that Little Star was used during the Cold War by the KGB to spy on data transmissions between Europe and the USA. During the 1990s RT 32 was restored by a group of Latvian scientists from the Latvian Academy of Sciences, who converted it from military to scientific use. If you would like to go on a visit from Ventspils you can organise an excursion with a guide by phoning 368 2541. To reach Irbene, drive north from Ventspils up the P24 beyond the road to Ovīši and take the unmarked right turn immediately after a small electricity sub-station.

From Ventspils it is only a 55km journey inland on the P108 to Kuldīga, another highlight of Kurzeme. Alternatively you may like to continue on down the coast the 125km to Liepāja. If you head for Kuldīga, you can make a short diversion to Ēdole (head south off the P108 at Bungas).

Ēdole Castle

Built 1267–76, very little of the original castle now remains. It was rebuilt in Gothic style around 1840 but was largely destroyed in a fire in 1905. Many legends are associated with the castle. One is the story of how a lord's son killed his brother near the castle walls. The blood of the murdered brother kept reappearing on the walls of the castle, until finally a fireplace was built. Later, when some workmen tried to break down the wall, they were mysteriously killed. Since that time, the wall has been left intact.

Kuldīga

If you have time to visit only one of Kurzeme's old towns, it should probably be Kuldīga. Prettily located on the Venta River and its tributary the Alekšupīte, it is much better preserved than many of the old towns and retains Renaissance, baroque and Gothic-style buildings, as well as some picturesque gardens. These factors have made it a popular choice for Latvian film-makers. Kuldīga was an important centre for the Cours before the invasion of the German knights, and later, under its German name of Goldingen, became a stronghold of the Knights of the Sword, and, towards the end of the 16th century, the first capital of the Duchy of Kurland. Although plundered in the Polish–Swedish and the Northern wars, it survived better than other towns in Kurzeme. By the 1930s, Kuldīga had become a popular holiday spot, and it remains so today.

Accommodation and eating out
Jāņa Nams Hotel 36 Liepājas iela; tel: 332 3456; fax: 332 3785. A very pleasant family-run hotel, with restaurant and sauna. Rooms cost Ls11–20.
Kursa Hotel 6 Pilsētas laukums; tel: 332 2430; fax: 332 3671. A Soviet-era hotel with rooms from Ls10 (singles) and Ls12 (doubles). The accommodation is basic but clean and the hotel includes a café and bar.

Both the hotels above have restaurants. Other cafés include the **Namiņš** (25a Kalna iela) and the **Venta** (1 Pilsētas laukums). There are also many other eating and drinking possibilities on Liepājas iela.

Tourist information
The tourist information office is in the old town hall at 5 Baznīcas iela; tel: 332 2259; email: tourinfo@kuldiga.lv.

What to see
The town hall square (Rātslaukums) is a good place to begin a walking tour. If you prefer to explore by bike, you can rent a cycle at Samiņš shop (1 Liepājas iela; tel: 680 3381). The 'new' **town hall** (now a library) was built in 1860 in Italian Renaissance style, but you can still see the original 17th-century **wooden town hall** across the square at 5 Baznīcas iela. Number 7 on the same street is the oldest residential building in Kuldīga, built in 1670, reconstructed in 1742 and renovated in 1982. Close to the square on the north side of Liepājas iela is a large 18th-century **granary**, recently reconstructed.

If you now turn off Liepājas iela into Raiņa iela you will come to **Holy Trinity Roman Catholic Church** (Svētās Trīsvienības katoļu baznīca), consecrated in 1649. The interior is mostly 18th century, but the *Madonna and Child* dates from the 14th century, and the altar was a gift from Tsar Alexander I in 1820. If you go back to the square and walk down Baznīcas iela you will come on your right to another church worth visiting, **St Catherine's Church** (Svētās Katrīnas baznīca), at 33 Baznīcas iela. Mentioned as early as 1252, the present structure was built in 1866. The wooden altar and pulpit date from 1660, and, like the altarpiece in St Anne's at Liepāja, are the work of Duke Jakob's woodcarver, Nicolai Soffrens. Also on Baznīcas iela, Number 17 is a house which used to belong to the mayor of Kuldīga and where the Swedish king, Charles XII, stayed in January 1702 during the Great Northern War.

Baznīcas iela leads on over the Alekšupīte River. Close to the bridge is a **watermill** and ahead of you is the site of the castle of the Livonian Order, strategically positioned between the Alekšupīte and Venta rivers. Also ahead of you is a strikingly restored pink building, the local court (*tiesa*). Behind the court building is a pleasant café/restaurant, the Namiņš.

If you head left after crossing the Alekšupīte, the road leads to a **brick bridge** (1874) over the Venta. Before the bridge, a path, Pils iela, takes you through the park alongside the **castle ruins**. The castle was originally built in 1242; during the

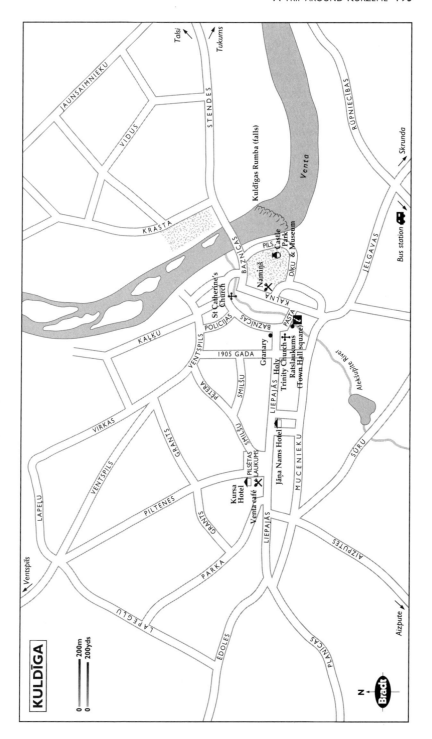

KULDĪGA

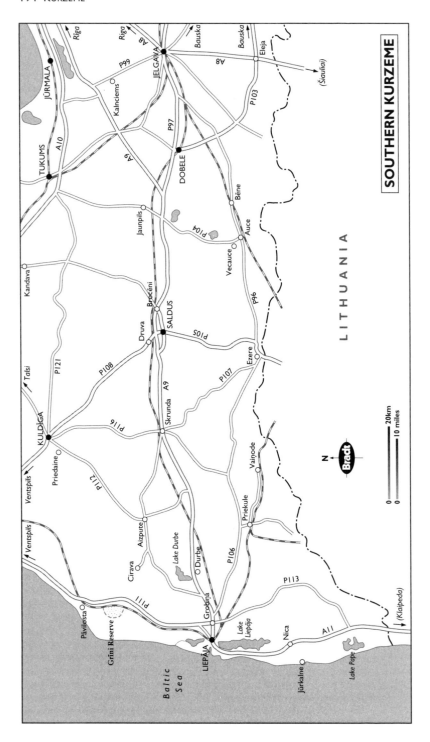

SOUTHERN KURZEME

16th and 17th centuries the dukes of Kurland used it as one of their residences, but like many buildings in Latvia it was destroyed during the Great Northern War. The area where it stood is now a park and small sculpture garden. At 5 Pils iela is the **Kuldīga District Museum** (Kuldīgas Novada Muzejs; tel: 332 2364). Open every day 11.00–17.00 except Monday.

As you walk along Pils iela you should have a clear view to your left down towards the Venta and the **Kuldīgas Rumba**. Although normally translated as waterfall, the 'fall' is less than two metres high. It does, however, extend the full breadth of the river, and is said to be one of the widest waterfalls in Europe. The area near the Rumba is a picturesque spot, popular for picnics, swimming and fishing.

The Venta has its source in northwest Lithuania and extends for around 350km before reaching the Baltic Sea at Ventspils. Its former strategic importance is clear from the number of castles that were built along its banks. Around 2.5km north of Kuldīga is all that remains of one of the oldest, the mound where once stood the fortress built by Lamekins, the Cour, ruler of much of this area before the arrival of the German knights in the 13th century.

Aizpute

Between Kuldīga and Liepāja is the small town of Aizpute. The old area of the town has a number of wooden houses; ruins of a castle built by the Knights of the Sword can still be seen; and close to them the church, originally built in 1254 and reconstructed in 1733. Nearby, 5km south at Bojas, a former summer residence of the German Baron Behr (just off the P115), is the Forest Museum (**Meža Muzejs Boju Pili**). The museum (tel: 344 8067) covers the history of forestry and hunting. Open daily May 15–September 15 Tuesday–Sunday 10.00–17.00, and September 16–May 14 Monday–Friday 10.00–14.00.

Liepāja

Liepāja is Latvia's third largest city. It has yet to experience investment on the scale of Ventspils, although like Ventspils it is an ice-free port. Although some buildings are still run-down, many have been renovated and Liepāja is making a real effort to become an attractive tourist centre.

Although there were probably dwellings here well before the arrival of the Livonian Order in the 13th century, Liepāja was not officially recognised as a town until 1625, when it changed its name from Līvciems to Liepāja (from *liepa* meaning lime tree). Like most Latvian towns, it has had a difficult history: it was attacked by Charles XII of Sweden during the Northern War in 1701 and then devastated by Napoleon's army on its way to Moscow in 1812. With the arrival of the railway in the early 19th century and the deepening of its harbour, Liepāja began to expand in earnest. By 1869 an undersea cable linked it with Copenhagen; in 1889 it became the first city in the Russian Empire to have trams; in 1906 a passenger service to New York began to operate. It was designated a naval port in 1890 by Tsar Alexander III, a status held until 1994.

During the War of Independence, the national government of Kārlis Ulmanis fled to Liepāja after most of Latvia was invaded by the Bolsheviks. In April 1920 the government even had to shelter on a British warship off Liepāja, before being able to return and finally win back all of Latvia.

If you arrive by train or bus, you will need to cross the canal into old Liepāja to see most of the sights. Tram number 1, the only tram in the city, leads directly from Rīgas iela outside the station into the old town. If you arrive by car and want to park in the centre you will need to feed the parking meters at the rate of Ls0.40 for two hours.

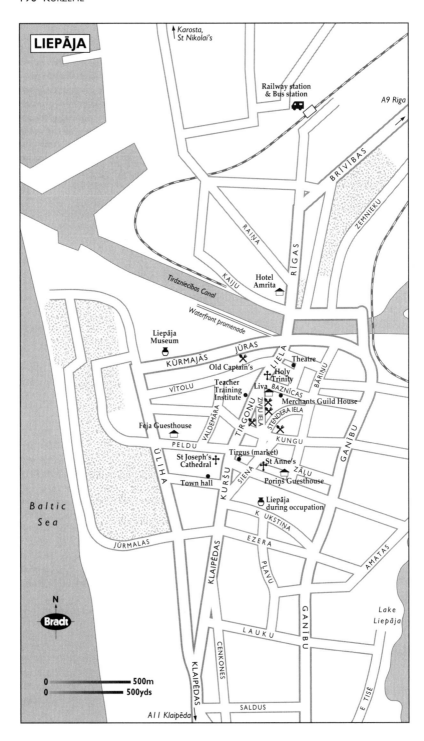

LIEPĀJA

Karosta,
St Nikolai's

Railway station
& Bus station

A9 Riga

BRĪVĪBAS

ZEMNIEKU

RAINA

RĪGAS

KAIJU

Tirdzniecības Canal

Hotel
Amrita

Waterfront promenade

Liepāja
Museum

KŪRMAJĀS

JŪRAS

Old Captain's

LĪVA IELA

Theatre

BĀRIŅU

Holy
Trinity

VĪTOLU

Teacher
Training
Institute

Līva

BAZNĪCAS

TIRGOŅU

ZIVJU IELA

Merchants Guild House

STENDERA IELA

GAŅĪBU

Feja Guesthouse

VALDEMĀRA

PELDU

KUNGU

ŪLIHA

St Joseph's
Cathedral

Tirgus (market)

KURŠU

SIENA

St Anne's

ZĀLU

Town hall

Poriņs Guesthouse

Baltic
Sea

Liepāja
during occupation

K UKSTIŅA

JŪRMALAS

KLAIPĒDAS

EZERA

PĻAVU

AMATAS

N

Bradt

GAŅĪBU

Lake
Liepāja

LAUKU

CENKONES

E TISĒ

0 ━━━━━ 500m
0 ━━━━━ 500yds

KLAIPĒDAS

SALDUS

A11 Klaipēda

Accommodation and eating out

The **Līva** (11 Lielā iela; tel: 342 0102; email: info@liva.lv; www.liva.lv). A former Soviet hotel which has been renovated. Prices range from around Ls7 for economy rooms to Ls45 for business-class rooms. A better bet is probably the **Hotel Amrita** (7a Rīgas iela; tel: 340 3434; email: info@amrita.lv; www.amrita.lv), although prices are high for provincial Latvia. Opened in 1997 it has 83 modern rooms and a restaurant, **Oskars**. Single rooms cost Ls40; doubles from Ls65. Liepāja also has a number of attractive guesthouses, including the **Feja** (9 Kurzemes iela – entrance on Peldu iela; tel: 342 2688; email: feja.hotel@apollo.lv; www.feja.lv), which is family-run, with single rooms Ls12–30 and doubles Ls20–24. It also has a restaurant. An alternative guesthouse is the **Poriņš** (5 Palmu iela; tel: 915 0596; email: porins@apollo.lv), located in a quiet street close to the centre. Rooms cost Ls15–24. There is also a youth hostel, **K@2** (2 Katedrales iela, Karosta; tel: 34 57154; email: info@karosta.lv). North of Liepāja and just south of Pavilosta there is a campsite, **Ievlejas**.

Apart from **Oskars** in the Hotel Amrita, possibilities for eating include the **Old Captain's House** (Vecais Kapteinis, 14 J Dubelšteina iela; tel: 342 5522), Latvia's first **Rock Café** (18–20 Stendera iela; tel: 348 1555) and the **Senču Sēta** (13a Stendera iela; tel: 342 6360), an attractive restaurant with a garden.

Tourist information

The local tourist information centre is situated on the ground floor of the Hotel Līva (tel/fax: 348 0808; email: ltib@apollo.lv). Open 09.00–17.00; closed Saturday and Sunday.

What to see

A walking tour of the city could start with a visit to Holy Trinity Church (**Svētās Trīsvienības baznīca**) on the corner of Baznīcas iela and Lielā iela. Built between 1742 and 1758, this Lutheran church is known for its wooden carvings and for its organ. The organ was rebuilt in 1885 and was until 1912 the largest in the world. If you are in Liepāja on a Saturday in summer you will probably be able to hear the organ at one of the church's regular recitals. In the surrounding streets there are many buildings of historical note, although most are awaiting restoration. Opposite the church, for example, at 10 Lielā iela, is a building which originated as a **merchant's house** but was rebuilt in the 1880s to house a bank. At the front is a statue, the Roman god Mercury, the patron of travellers, merchants and moneychangers. The building at 3 Baznīcas iela was built between 1878 and 1880 as the **Merchants' Guild House**. Like many of the buildings in old Liepāja, it was designed by M P Berči, the city architect for over 30 years at the end of the 19th century. The symmetrical façade of the building and the rich decoration of the columns are typical of his work. This building now serves as part of the **Liepāja Theatre**. The main theatre building is at 4 Teātra iela. Although built between 1912 and 1915 for German-language productions, performances in Latvian started in 1917. The theatre company is still well known within Latvia.

Heading south along Lielā iela you will pass the Līva hotel on your left and the vast **Teacher Training Institute** (Liepājas Pedagojas Akadēmija) on your right. Lielā iela then leads into Tirgoņu iela, a pedestrian street with several cafés. Between Kuršu iela and Kuršu laukums is the market, one of Latvia's largest and oldest. The so-called siena tirgus (**hay market**) has existed since the early 18th century; until the beginning of the 20th century local people came here to buy and sell hay, firewood, flax and livestock. Close to the market are two notable churches: **St Joseph's Cathedral** (Sv Jāzepa katedrāle) at 13 Rakstvešu iela is open

07.00–19.00 each day, and **St Anne's Lutheran Church** (Sv Annas baznīca) at 5 Kuršu laukums. The present cathedral dates from 1894 to 1900 and has an impressive painted interior. St Anne's is well known for its magnificent baroque altar, carved in 1697 by one of Duke Jakob's woodcarvers, Nicolai Soffrens. At 24 Kungu iela is an old Liepāja hotel, one of the oldest buildings in the town, where Peter the Great once stayed.

Liepāja Town Hall (Pilsētas Dome, 6 Rožu iela) is an imposing building, constructed in 1889 originally as a court: the basement contained prison cells until World War II. Just inside the entrance is a small café. Beyond the town hall on the north side of J Čakstes laukums (square), note the well-restored art nouveau building, now a school. You can also visit an exhibition of **Liepāja during the Occupation** (7–9 K Ukstiņa iela; tel: 342 0274). Open Tuesday–Sunday 10.00–18.00.

The west side of the old town adjoins a large park and beach area. You can reach this by heading west along Peldu iela from close to the market, or by walking along the canal (K Zāles laukums) and then along Jūras iela and Kurmājas prospekts. Both routes will take you past buildings of faded splendour. At 16 Kūrmājas prospekts is the **Liepāja Museum** (tel: 342 2327), again designed by Berči. Open June–August Wednesday–Sunday 11.00–18.00; September–May Wednesday–Sunday 10.00–17.00. The **park**, developed between 1870 and the early 1900s, was a sophisticated resort area in its heyday. Tree-lined walks, fountains, summerhouses, and various medicinal baths, including mudbaths with mud from Lake Liepāja, delighted visitors. The park and beach area is still attractive for walking, and the beach here has recently been awarded a Blue Flag.

Like Ventspils, Liepāja is in the process of creating a waterfront promenade with sculptures. Although still in the early stages, the promenade can be visited on the canal bank behind Jūras iela. Liepāja also has an ice rink.

Some way from the centre in the north of Liepāja is the old **military harbour** (Karosta). At the end of the 19th century this area was developed with a fort, barracks and administrative buildings, designed to protect the Russian Empire. Later, during the Soviet occupation, the harbour became a major naval base for the USSR. Today most of the area is abandoned and desolate, but the old Jūras katedrāle (Cathedral of the Sea), now **St Nikolai's Orthodox Church**, remains resplendent with its golden onion domes. At the **Karosta prison** (4 Invalīdu iela) you can watch, and participate in, a performance of *Behind the Bars*, every evening. For exact details, call the tourist office. The area is best reached by car, but is also accessible via minibus number 3 from Lielā iela; alight at the Atmodas stop.

Some 60km north of Liepāja is **Jūrkalne**, a beach with cliffs which contrasts with the flatness of Jūrmala, and where you can swim from the beach. The traditional Grass Day (Zāļu Diena) is celebrated in Jūrkalne each year during the weekend of the second week in August. On the Friday and Saturday various events are organised, including concerts, markets and dances.

From Liepāja it is only about 60km to the Lithuanian border. At **Nīca** there is a motel, the Nicava, on the A11 (tel/fax: 353 4162). It is an attractive hotel set in an old park overlooking a pond. Between Nīca and the border is **Lake Pape** (see page 9). This reserve is good for birdwatching – 271 bird species have been recorded – and there are also nature trails of 9km and 26km. To book a visit to the ornithology station telephone 920 3235 or email: jbaumanis@email.lubi.edu.lv.

Skrunda

If you return to Riga along the A9 from Liepāja, you will pass through the towns of Skrunda and Saldus. Skrunda is best known for the early warning radar station installed here by the Soviet defence forces to track possible nuclear attacks from the West. Although most of the Soviet forces left Latvia in 1994, a special agreement was reached to allow Russian personnel to remain at Skrunda until 1998. The final troops left, amid much Latvian rejoicing, in August 1998.

An annual rock festival is held at Skrunda in May. At the time of the festival in 1995, during celebrations to mark the fifth anniversary of independence, a tower at the military base was blown up, invoking great displeasure from Moscow.

The Skrunda ponds are known to attract rare European waterfowl.

Saldus

Located about halfway between Liepāja and Riga, Saldus is a pleasant place for a short stop. The scenery around Lake Ciecere is delightful and the town itself has a long history, although most of the existing building is recent. The painter Jānis Rozentāls lived here from 1900–01 and the house where he lived is now a museum, the **Jānis Rozentāls Museum of History and Art** (Jāņa Rozentāla Saldus Vēstures un Mākslas Muzejs, 22 Striķu iela; tel: 388 1603). Open Wednesday–Sunday 10.00–16.00. You can also see one of his paintings in the church.

There is a hotel, the **Kalnsētas** (24 Kalnsētas iela; tel: 382 3849; email: ojars@kalnasetas.apollo.lv). Between Saldus and Dobele at Blidene, on the A9, there is a modern hotel, **Motelis Fricis** (tel: 383 2530).

Jaunpils

Around 30km east of Saldus, and north of the A9 is Jaunpils, a small town traditionally known for its cows (most of Latvia's brown cows come from the area) but recently trying to market itself as a gateway to Kurzeme. The castle, built in 1301 as a fortress for Knights of the Livonian Order, has been fairly well preserved, and the church, built in 1592, has a noteworthy altar and pulpit. Some accommodation is available in the castle, but booking is advisable (tel: 944 7859; email: info@jaunpilspils.lv; www.jaunpilspils.lv).

South of the A9, and close to the Lithuanian border, is the town of **Auce** (in the Dobele region and strictly speaking in Zemgale). Auce suffered badly during World War II, both in battles with the Nazis and the Soviets. The nearby manor house, Vecauce, is now an Academy for Agricultural Studies; the large gardens are open for visits.

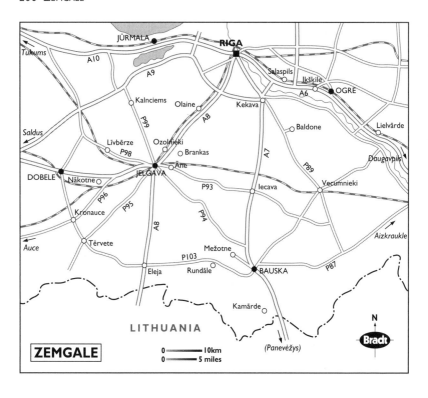

Oak, Quercus robur

Zemgale

Zemgale is the smallest of Latvia's four regions. It lies south of
Riga and west of the Daugava River, extending south
to the Lithuanian border. Its proximity to Riga
means that all parts of the region can be visited on
day trips from the capital.

Just as the River Daugava dominates Latgale,
Latvia's second longest river, the Lielupe, which simply means 'large
river' in Latvian, flows through the centre of Zemgale. The Lielupe
starts at Bauska, where two rivers originating in Lithuania, the Mūsa and Mēmele,
meet up close to the castle. It then flows north through Jelgava to Jūrmala and on
into the Bay of Riga.

The region's position on the main route between Riga and the Lithuanian
capital Vilnius means it is readily accessible and relatively well served by public
transport. The main road from Riga to Vilnius, the A7, leads directly from Riga to
Bauska, and is a main bus route. The railway goes to Jelgava.

The scenery in Zemgale is not spectacular. For many centuries, however, the
region has been the most prosperous in Latvia, mainly due to the port at the mouth
of the River Lielupe and the fertile land throughout most of the area. Before the
war, Zemgale provided most of Latvia's food, and even today visitors will be struck
by the high number of working farms. Traditional farm buildings remain a feature
of the area. Typically these buildings had separate rooms for owners and serfs
(peasants in this area were only given their freedom in the period 1811–19) and a
built-in fireplace with chimney and hearth.

MAIN ATTRACTIONS

For the majority of visitors to Latvia, there are two main reasons to venture into
Zemgale: to visit the impressive baroque palace and buildings at Rundāle, designed
by Rastrelli, and the Livonian castle nearby at Bauska. Two additional attractions
are the baroque palace built at Jelgava, also under the supervision of the Italian
architect Rastrelli, and housing the family vault of the Dukes of Kurland, and the
recently restored palace of Mežotne, close to Bauska, which is now a country
house hotel.

HISTORY

Zemgale's history, like that of all of Latvia, has been a succession of invasions,
battles and changing rulers. The Zemgal tribes (or Semigallians as you will
sometimes see them referred to) were Baltic people (like the Latgals and Cours,
their neighbours to the east and west), and are mentioned in Scandinavian records
as far back as AD870. During the 12th and 13th centuries Zemgale was divided into
seven districts, each with at least one fortified castle, but ruled by a single leader.
When the German crusaders began their attacks on what is now Latvia, the Zemgal

tribes initially welcomed them but, having seen their actions, became their fiercest resisters and were the last of the Latvian regions to surrender to them in 1290. After this defeat around 100,000 Zemgals left, settled in Lithuania and played a role in helping the kingdom of Lithuania carve out its massive empire in the 14th century, stretching into present-day Russia and as far as the Black Sea.

After the crushing of the German rulers in 1561, Zemgale became part of the Duchy of Kurland (now Kurzeme), a semi-independent area, and enjoyed relative prosperity, particularly under the rule of Duke Jakob in the 17th century. Jelgava (known then in German as Mitau) became the capital of the duchy and a major Baltic town. The 18th century, however, saw further changes with the start of Russian rule, the strengthening of the privileges of the Baltic-German ruling classes and the growing problems of the native peasants. The culture of rural Zemgale remains to some extent the product of this clash between a western European culture of land ownership, copied principally from the Germans, and native Latvian traditions with their pagan ethos; peasants, for example, were given surnames only in 1835.

A TRIP AROUND ZEMGALE
By car
If you are staying in Riga, you will be able to visit Bauska, Rundāle and Jelgava in a one-day round trip. From Riga to Bauska takes around one hour, from Bauska to Rundāle 20 minutes, from Rundāle to Jelgava an hour, and back to Riga under an hour. If you want to make an overnight stop, there are hotels in Bauska and Jelgava, but Mežotne Palace is by far the most appealing option (see opposite).

By bus or train
Trips to Bauska and Jelgava are easy. Buses leave Riga for Bauska every 30–40 minutes between 06.00 and 22.30 and take one and a half hours, and long-distance buses from Riga to Vilnius, Kaunas and Panevėžys in Lithuania also stop in Bauska. The best way to get to Jelgava is by train. Trains leave Riga Central Station at least every hour between 05.38 and 23.14 (returning from Jelgava between 05.15 and 22.21) and take around 50 minutes. The price for a one-way journey is Ls0.59. There are also buses from Riga to Jelgava, taking approximately one hour each way. Getting to Rundāle by bus requires more planning. You should first go to either Bauska or Jelgava and then take a bus to Pilsrundāle (not Rundāle). From Jelgava there are two or three buses each way every day. Services from Bauska are more frequent. Neither Bauska nor Rundāle is on the rail network.

Tours
Hotels and tour companies in Riga run day trips to Rundāle. See the list on page 77.

Riga to Bauska
If you are travelling by road, head south out of Riga (the road to Bauska is well signposted if you start from the right bank heading south and cross the Daugava River) on what becomes the A7. If you have the time and inclination, a few detours are possible before reaching Bauska. Around 3km past Ķekava, a left turn leads to **Baldone**, where you will find Latvia's oldest mineral springs and mudbath spa. The sulphide and chloride mineral water and mud from the nearby peat bog have acclaimed medicinal qualities. Further south on the A7 you will come to **Iecava**, an important industrial centre during the time when Zemgale was part of the Duchy of Kurland. In 1812 Napoleon Bonaparte is said to have rested on his way to Moscow in the grounds of the 18th-century park along the banks of the River Iecava. What is certainly true is that close to Iecava a major battle was fought

between the French and the Russians in 1812.

Six kilometres north of Iecava, on the left-hand side driving from Riga, is the **Motelis Brencis** (tel: 392 8033), a modern motel with 22 rooms, a sauna, bistro, bar and restaurant. A double room costs Ls20, including breakfast.

Just after passing the sign marking the beginning of Bauska, a road on the right is marked to **Mežotne**. The village of Mežotne, some 10km along the road, stands on the banks of the Lielupe River and has a manor house built in 1802 for Princess Charlotte von Lieven, a governess of the Russian Emperor Paul I and one of the ancestors of the journalist, Anatole Lieven (see *Appendix 3*). The rooms on the second floor have been restored and are generally open for visits daily 10.00–17.00 except Saturday and Sunday. A hotel was opened there in August 2001 (contact Mežotne pils, Mežotnes pag; tel: 396 0711; email:mezotnpils@apollo.lv). Prices are Ls30 for singles, Ls45 for doubles. In the grounds, which have also been restored, are several monuments of historical interest. Between the house and the river you can see, in the words of Lieven in his book, *The Baltic Revolution*, 'a monument to 11 pupils of the local high school who were deported to Siberia in 1940 when a portrait of Stalin, placed in the school after Latvia's annexation, was found floating in the Lielupe. Only two returned...'.

On the opposite side of the River Lielupe is the site of the final battle fought by the Zemgals against the German crusaders. Although they were not defeated, they realised their future was hopeless, burnt down their castle (only the mound remains), and fled to Lithuania where they resettled. A pontoon bridge used to cross the Lielupe, allowing access to the site. Currently, however, no such bridge is in existence, so the mound can only be viewed from the opposite bank.

Bauska

Bauska is a small country town (population 11,000) now known mainly for its castle. It is well worth stopping here on the way to Rundāle, both to see its sights, principally the castle, and for refreshment.

Accommodation

Hotel Bauska 7 Slimnīcas iela (close to the bus station and post office); tel: 392 4705. The hotel has 40 rooms, each with a toilet and bath. Facilities are basic. Rooms Ls5–24.

See also **Mežotne**, above.

Eating out

In the centre of Bauska various cafés are located on the square opposite the museum at Rātslaukums, on the left off Kalna iela just after entering Bauska from the north. The bistro in the Hotel Bauska (7 Slimnīcas iela; tel: 392 3037) is open from 09.00–23.00.

Away from the centre, there is a convenient and very acceptable café at the entrance to Bauska Castle. It is also possible to eat lunch and dinner at Mežotne.

Tourist information

There is a tourist information office at 1 Rātslaukums; tel: 392 3797; email: tourinfo@bauska.lv.

What to see

Bauska Castle (Bauskas pilsdrupas) dates from the mid 15th century and is one of the best-preserved of Latvia's castle ruins. It was originally built as a fortress by the Livonian knights but was destroyed and rebuilt several times during the 16th

and 17th centuries. Finally in 1706, in the course of the Great Northern War, Tsar
Peter I ordered his generals to raze the castle. Various sections were completely
destroyed and local inhabitants began to take apart the castle walls and use the
bricks as building materials for their houses. The castle has now been fairly
extensively restored, although work is still continuing in some areas. The various
stages of building (the original fortress of the Livonian Order from the 15th
century, the Duke of Kurland's residence from the 16th century and ramparts
from the 17th and 18th centuries) can be seen in the **Castle Museum** (Pils
Muzejs; tel: 392 3793). Entrance to the towers costs Ls0.45 and to the towers and
exhibition inside Ls0.80. Open May–October every day 09.00–19.00.

Good views of the castle and also of the two rivers, the Mēmele and Mūsa,
which merge close to the castle, can be enjoyed if you walk through the grounds
behind the castle. In summer (generally the third weekend in July) an Early Music
Festival is held in the castle grounds.

To reach the castle, head south along the main road from Riga (Kalna iela) and
turn right in the middle of the town down Uzvaras iela. The car park for the castle
is directly at the end of this street to the right. If you arrive in Bauska by bus, walk
along Zaļā iela towards the town centre and then turn left into Uzvaras iela.

If you have time to see more than the castle, you could visit the Bauska
Museum of Regional Studies and Art (Bauskas Novadpētniecības un Mākslas
Muzejs, 6 Kalna iela; tel: 396 0508) which focuses on the region's history between
1796 and 1940. The museum has recently been extended and now includes
exhibitions on Jews and Germans in Bauska, as well as an intriguing look at
hairdressing techniques in the 1950s. Open Tuesday–Friday 10.00–18.00, Saturday
and Sunday 10.00–16.00. The **Church of the Holy Spirit** (Sv Gara baznīca) is

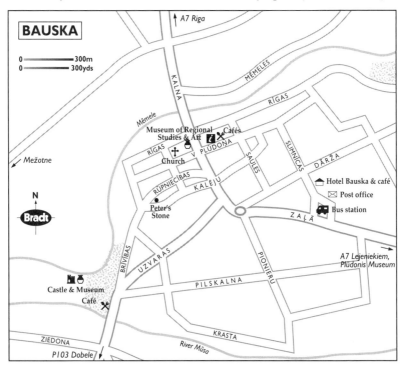

also well worth a visit (13a Plūdoņa iela). The church was built from 1591–94 in late-Gothic style but the interior is a good example of baroque and rococo decorative styles. See, for example, the altar and pulpit. The pews, the organ loft and the private box of the Schoepping family (1770) near the altar all present examples of impressive woodwork. Open June–November Monday–Friday 10.00–15.00. On the corner of Kalēju iela and Rūpniecības iela, not far from the castle, is **Peter's Stone**. It is said that, at the beginning of the Great Northern War, Peter I of Russia had dinner on this stone with the King of Poland, August II, and then competed with him in tests of strength. Legend maintains that they buried the silver spoons they used for their meals and that these are still beneath the stone.

Also near the castle on Brīvības bulvāris is a bronze statue of a Zemgallian soldier, erected in 1992. The words engraved on the monument are by the local poet Vilis Plūdonis (1874–1940). Anyone interested in Latvian literature may also want to visit the **Memorial House and Museum of Vilis Plūdonis** the house along the Mēmele River where he wrote many of his poems. To visit the museum head out of Bauska south on the A7, turn left at the border of Bauska and travel 8km to Lejeniekiem ('Lejenieki', Ceraukste; tel: 919 4975). Open May 1–October 31 10.00–18.00. From the house you can also walk for around 1km along the River Mēmele, which inspired much of his poetry, to the Plūdonis family graveyard, where the poet is buried.

BAUSKA TO RUNDĀLE

The road to Rundāle and Pilsrundāle (P103) is signposted on the right after you cross the bridge travelling south over the River Mūsa, leaving Bauska Castle behind you. If you have transport a pleasant detour is to turn sharp right at the crossroads signposted to Rundāle. This road is in poor condition but follows the riverbank closely, has excellent views of Bauska Castle and passes through pleasant countryside and parkland. Eventually it comes to a dead end.

If you follow the main road from Bauska, you will see signs on the left to Pilsrundāle after around 15km. Rundāles Pils (Rundāle Palace) is well signposted.

Rundāle

Rundāle is often billed as the most significant palace in the Baltics. Certainly most visitors will be impressed by its grand exterior, dominating the surrounding flat farmland leading down to the Lielupe River, and the 40 or so sumptuously decorated rooms which have been restored. **Rundāle Palace** (Rundāles Pils, tel: 396 2197; fax: 392 2274; email: rpm@eila.lv; www.rpm.apollo.lv) was built in the 18th century as a summer palace for Ernst Johann von Bühren (Biron in Latvian) by the Italian architect Francesco Bartolomeo Rastrelli. Rastrelli, already established as the architect of the Winter Palace in St Petersburg, began work in 1736 and took five years to finish the task. The interiors were mostly completed later, between 1763 and 1768. Among those who worked on them were Italian painters from St Petersburg and Johann Michael Graff from Berlin, whose work includes the artificial marble wall panelling and the decorative moulding in many rooms.

Why was such a lavish palace built by Rastrelli beyond the Russian borders? The link with Russia was Anna Ioannovna, a niece of Tsar Peter I who, in 1710, married Frederick, Duke of Kurland. During the 1720s Ernst Johann von Bühren, a Baltic-German baron, became her chief adviser, and some say lover also. In 1730, on the death of Peter, Anna became Empress of Russia and delegated much of the management of the empire to a group of German advisers, von Bühren among them. When von Bühren expressed the wish for a summer palace, Anna complied

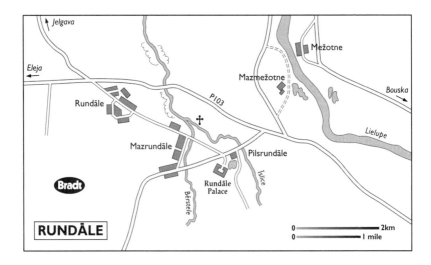

by sending Rastrelli to Kurland and providing all the necessary money and craftsmen too; nearly everyone involved in the construction – a total of 1,500 craftsmen, artists and labourers – was sent from St Petersburg. Before the palace could be finished, however, Rastrelli began work on another major project, a palace at Jelgava, seat of the Duchy of Kurland. Many of the workmen and the materials needed for Rundāle were transported to Jelgava instead. In 1740, just before Rundāle was completed, Anna died, von Bühren was forced into exile, and the building of the palaces halted. Only in 1763 when the Russian Empress Catherine II restored von Bühren to favour, did he return to Kurland and finish the work on Rundāle. The palace was finally completed in 1767, but von Bühren was only able to enjoy it for a short time until his death in 1772. When Russia annexed the Duchy of Kurland in 1795, von Bühren's son, Peter, agreed to leave taking with him some of the splendid interior items from Rundāle and installed them instead in his properties in Germany. Rundāle itself was given to another favourite of Catherine II, Subov.

Since the incorporation of Kurland into Russia in 1795, the palace has had many uses and owners. Although damaged in the Napoleonic Wars and again during World War II the exterior has been repaired and remains fundamentally unaltered from its original design. The interior has not survived so well. Parts of the castle were used as a granary after 1945, and other areas fell into severe disrepair. In 1972, however, the Rundāle Palace Museum was established and major restoration work began. Artists in Leningrad began the restoration of works of art, and they were subsequently joined by experts from Riga, Moscow and Belarus. As a result the 40 or so rooms (out of 138) restored contain many impressive, but few original, works of art. Particularly interesting are the Golden Hall (the throne room), with beautiful ceiling decoration and chandeliers, the Grand Gallery (the banquet room) and the aptly named White Hall (the ballroom), with its intricate stucco. Look out here for the storks! The palace also houses some permanent exhibitions: 'Treasures of the Rundāle Palace', with furniture, porcelain, silverware and paintings, and 'The Time of Misery', an exhibition about Lutheran churches in Latvia during the years of Soviet power.

Behind the palace, the French-style formal garden has been largely reconstructed. It is surrounded by a canal, beyond which are hunting grounds.

On the south side of the palace is a formal baroque garden, still being reconstructed. A restaurant in the palace is used for formal receptions, and is a favourite place for weddings.

The palace is open daily November–April 10.00–17.00; May, September and October 10.00–18.00, and June–August 10.00–19.00.

RUNDĀLE TO JELGAVA

From Rundāle Palace you can take the right fork immediately outside the entrance towards Rundāle village and straight back to the P103 Bauska to Eleja road. Turn left towards Eleja and then take any of a number of roads signposted to Jelgava. You can make a stop in Jelgava or return directly to Riga by continuing on the A8.

If you are interested in Latvian literature or would like to spend some time enjoying Latvia's forests, you may like to make a diversion before heading north to Jelgava and Riga. This would take you to the **Meža Ainava Parks** (Forest Landscape Park, known as the Nature Park) at Tērvete and to the **Anna Brigadere Memorial Museum** (Annas Brigaderes Memoriālais Muzejs, tel: 376 3352) within it.

Anna Brigadere was a well-known writer of children's stories, plays and poems, who spent most of her life (1861–1933) in this area, and the 11 years until her death in a house known as *Sprīdīši* (named after one of her characters), which is now a memorial museum. The museum is open daily May 1–October 31 10.00–17.00 except Mondays.

The park in which the museum stands has several distinct areas, each with evocative names. These include the **Ancient Pines Park** (Vecs Priežu Parks) which has some of the oldest and tallest pines in Latvia, Fairytale Forest (**Pasaku Mežs**)and **Dwarf Forest** (Rūķīšu Mežs).

Close to the park is the **Tērvete History Museum and Look-out Tower** (Tērvetes Senvēstures Muzejs un Skatu Tornis; tel: 989 6804). The museum contains a collection of replica Zemgallian ornaments and tells the story of Tērvete

---

A LATVIAN TALE: THE STORY OF 'SPRĪDĪTIS'

One of Anna Brigadere's best-known plays, based on a traditional folk story and often performed for children at Christmas, is *Sprīdītis* (meaning roughly the same as Tom Thumb in English). Sprīdītis is a tiny young man, 'smaller than a midget', with a lot of pluck. One day he is sleeping in the forest when he is disturbed by the local lord. Sprīdītis is annoyed and threatens to kill the lord. Amused by the daring of the tiny man, the lord says he will let Sprīdītis marry his daughter if he is able to defeat a bear. Sprīdītis takes him up and, using his cunning, manages to trap a bear in a barn. When he goes to claim his bride, the lord says he must kill 12 robbers before marrying his daughter. Again Sprīdītis uses his wits: he makes the robbers fall out and kill each other. Still, however, the lord is not satisfied, and tells Sprīdītis to drive the enemy out of his land. The tiny Sprīdītis mounts a horse, and brandishing a sword goes to meet the enemy shouting '*Varde* (frog), *varde, varde*.' Seeing this strange sight, the enemy commander thinks an angel has come down from heaven to punish him, turns on his heels and flees. For a third time Sprīdītis returns to claim his bride, and this time the lord agrees. Sprīdītis, the small man who defeated enemies far larger and far more numerous, finally triumphs – a lesson not lost sight of by Latvians during periods of occupation.

Castle, one of the most powerful castles in the Baltic region in the 13th century. Opening hours are as the Anna Brigadere Museum. It is also possible to stay overnight in rooms at *Sprīdīši*, but accommodation is very limited and fairly basic (tel: 376 3352). Costs Ls5 per person.

Continuing on the P103 towards Dobele, you will pass through the village of **Kroņauce**, where an old bridge over the picturesque River Auce has been replaced and where the riverbanks offer good picnic possibilities. Dobele itself has a two-star hotel with 25 rooms, a restaurant, café and bar: **Hotel Dobele** (2 Uzvaras iela; tel: 372 1229). Rooms cost from Ls6–25.

From Dobele drive east on the main road through Šķibe to Jelgava. Just after Šķibe you will pass a large sign on the right marking the start of Latvia's first collective farm (*kolkhoz*), *Nākotne*.

Jelgava

Although Jelgava (previously known in German as Mitau) has a prestigious history, this is not immediately apparent to visitors today. Few buildings remain from the city's heyday as capital of the Duchy of Kurland between the 16th and 18th centuries and subsequently as capital of the Russian province of the same name. Jelgava suffered more than any other city in Latvia during both world wars, and the rebuilding of the city after World War II reflects a strong Soviet influence. The city, the country's fourth largest, is now a major manufacturing centre (mini-vans, farming equipment, ceramics – including the brown ceramic bottle of *Melnais Balzāms*, Latvia's distinctive liqueur, see page 64). The main reason to visit Jelgava would be to see Rastrelli's Palace, built concurrently with the better-known Rundāle.

Accommodation

The well established **Hotel Jelgava** (6 Lielā iela; tel: 302 6193; email: hotel.jelgava@apollo.lv; www.zl.lv/hoteljelgava) has 27 rooms which have now been refurbished. Expect to pay around Ls30 for double rooms. The **Zemgale** (2 Skautu iela; tel: 300 7707) is part of a large new complex including bowling and curling facilities. Rooms cost Ls12–50. There is also a youth hostel at the university, **Universitate** (7 A Pumpura iela; tel: 302 9936) with 105 beds costing Ls2–14.

Eating out

The **Hotel Jelgava** has only a modest café. The **Krodziņš Tobago** (7 Jāņa Čakstes bulvāris) is a five-minute walk from the hotel and offers pleasant food in an enjoyable atmosphere, overlooking the river. The **Lido** (17 Lielā iela) is a large Italian bar and bistro. The **Silva** (7 Driksas iela) is a popular local bar/bistro/restaurant, which offers a good selection of cakes and ice-creams as well as larger meals. It has outdoor seating when the weather permits.

Tourist information

The tourist information office is at 37 Pasta iela; tel: 302 2751; email: rica@jrp.lv; www.jelgava.lv or www.jrp.lv.

What to see

The **palace** (Jelgavas pils) is on the eastern side of the town on the Riga road at the end of Lielā iela on a small island in the Lielupe River, and very close to the Jelgava Hotel. Recently restored, the palace functions mainly as the Latvian Agricultural University.

Like Rundāle – and for the same reasons – Jelgava Palace was built in two phases by Rastrelli, 1738–40 and 1763–72, for the use of Ernst Johann von Bühren (see

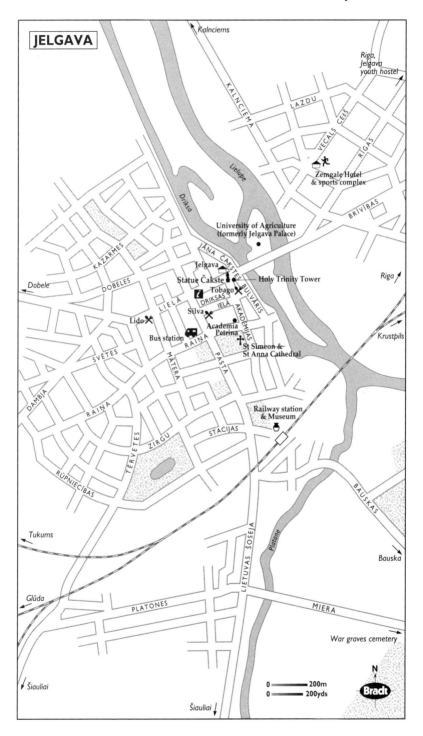

JELGAVA

Kalnciems

Riga,
Jelgava
youth hostel

KALNCIEMA

LAZDU

VECALS CEĻŠ

RĪGAS

Lielupe

Zemgale Hotel
& sports complex

BRĪVĪBAS

Driksa

University of Agriculture
(formerly Jelgava Palace)

KAZARMES

JĀŅA ČAKSTES

Dobele

DOBELES

Jelgava

Statue Čakste

LIELĀ

Tobago

DRIKSAS IELĀ

BULVĀRIS

Holy Trinity Tower

Riga

Silva

Lido

Bus station

RAIŅA

MATERA

Academia
Petrina

AKADĒMIJAS

St Simeon &
St Anna Cathedral

PASTA

Krustpils

SVĒTES

DAMBJA

RAIŅA

TĒRVETES

ZIRGU

STACIJAS

Railway station
& Museum

RŪPNIECĪBAS

BAUSKAS

Tukums

LIETUVAS ŠOSEJA

Platone

Bauska

Glūda

PLATONES

MIERA

War graves cemetery

Šiauliai

0 ——— 200m
0 ——— 200yds

N

Bradt

Šiauliai

pages 205–6 for details). After his death, only days after its completion, the palace was used less and less, although the exiled Louis XVIII of France stayed here for long periods between 1798 and 1807 and members of the tsar's family and state guests also made use of some of the apartments.

Inside the palace the main interest for most visitors is the vault which houses the **tombs of the Dukes of Kurland** (tel: 300 5617). The vault contains 21 metal sarcophagi and nine wooden coffins, with members of the House of Kettler and the von Bühren family entombed between 1569 and 1791. A display in the vault contains full details, as does an English guide, *The Family Vault of the Dukes of Kurland*, published by the Rundāle Palace Museum and available at the museum and from the tourist office. Open May–October 10.00–16.00 except Sunday, and November–April except Saturday and Sunday.

Also of interest in the centre of Jelgava is **St Simeon and St Anna Cathedral** (Sv Sīmaņa un Annas pareizticīgo katedrāle), on Raiņa iela, an Orthodox church, the exterior of which has been magnificently restored. The church was originally built to allow Anna Ioannovna to practise her religion freely after her marriage to the German Friedrich Wilhelm, and was designed by Rastrelli. It was rebuilt in 1892 and then badly damaged in World War II. Although a decision was taken to blow it up, in the end it was renovated in its present striking style. The church also houses an altarpiece painted by Jānis Rozentāls. Only the tower of the Holy Trinity Lutheran Church (Sv. Trīsvien baznīca), begun in the late 16th century but not completed until the late 17th century, now survives. The church, formerly one of the largest and most beautiful buildings in Jelgava, was destroyed in 1944 and was never rebuilt. Funds have now been collected to rebuild the tower and this work is currently under way. Another building of note is the **Academia Petrina** (10

JĀNIS ČAKSTE

Jānis Čakste (1859–1927) was the first president of Latvia. He was born in a small village in Zemgale, Lielsesava, and went to secondary school in Jelgava before studying law at Moscow University. In 1888 he began work as a lawyer in Jelgava and was actively involved in local life for several years. In 1905 he played a role in drafting plans for Latvia's autonomy and the following year was elected to the Russian State Council (Duma) as a representative from Kurzeme. After the dissolution of the Duma he joined other deputies in encouraging citizens to withhold payment of taxes and to refuse to send recruits to the tsar's army. As a result he was sentenced to three months' imprisonment. In 1915 Čakste moved to Tartu in Estonia and founded, with other Latvians, the Latvian Refugees' Central Committee, becoming its chairman in 1917. The following year the People's Council of Latvia elected Čakste as president and he headed the Latvian delegation at the Paris Peace Conference. Late in 1919 he returned to Latvia and was elected as president under the provisional rules of the Latvian state. The first Saeima (parliament) in 1922 elected him formally as the first president of Latvia, and he was elected again by the second Saeima in 1925. Čakste died in Riga in1927.

Several streets in Latvia are named after the first president, including the Jāņa Čakstes gatve in Riga. His memorial museum (Auči) is in the Sidrabenes district southeast of Jelgava and just north of Stalgene (tel: 305 5736). Open Friday 11.00–17.00. There is also a memorial plaque on the outside wall of Sesava church, as well as the monument in Jelgava.

Akadēmijas iela; tel: 302 3383) which now houses the local history and art museum but has been famous since Theodor Gotthus discovered the chemical laws of photography here in 1818. Open Wednesday–Sunday 10.00–17.00.

Railway enthusiasts may be interested in the **Latvian Railway Museum** (Latvijas Dzelzceļu Muzejs, 3 Stacijas iela; tel: 584 2494) which has branches in various parts of Latvia but its main exhibition is here in Jelgava. At the main site close to the railway station are exhibits including photographs, technical equipment and historic documents. You can also see rolling stock from the 19th century and other items at the Jelgava locomotive depot fairly nearby at 30 Prohorova iela. Open Wednesday–Saturday 10.00–15.00.

Three of Latvia's presidents have attended school in Jelgava, including **Jānis Čakste**, the first Latvian president of state (see box opposite). On November 14 2003 Latvia's current president unveiled a **monument to Čakste** by sculptor Arta Dumpe in Trīsvienības laukums (Trinity Square) on Lielā iela, close to Holy Trinity tower.

British visitors may also be interested to visit a small **British War Graves** cemetery on the outskirts of Jelgava. The cemetery, which is part of the Nikolaja Cemetery, commemorates 36 soldiers and sailors who died during World War I, mostly in the spring and summer of 1917. The men died as German prisoners of war in a number of hospitals on what is now Latvian territory, and their remains were relocated to Jelgava in 1924. The British Bed of Honour was sanctified on November 9 1924, with the participation of the executive British envoy Mr P Leigh-Smith, British and Latvian clergy, Jelgava city authorities and several public organisations and school representatives. To get to the cemetery, from Jelgava railway station take Lietuvas Šoseja away from town, turn left at the first crossroads into Miera iela and continue to a roundabout where the cemetery is signposted (first exit into Bauskas iela).

Ash, Fraxinus excelsior

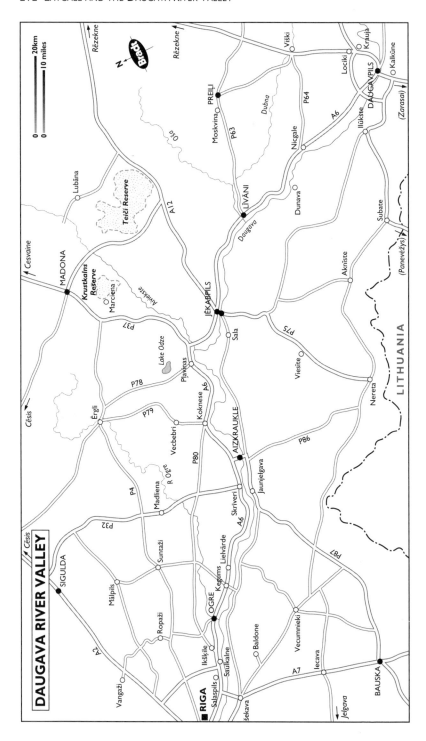

Latgale and the Daugava River Valley

Latgale is the least visited of Latvia's four regions, and also the poorest. Situated in the southeast of the country, it includes Daugavpils, Latvia's second largest city, 218km from Riga and close to the borders with Belarus and Lithuania. Any trip to Latgale from Riga, by road or rail, is likely to follow the Daugava River.

The Daugava River, Latvia's longest, flows from its source in Russia through Latgale, dividing Zemgale and Vidzeme before flowing out into the Gulf of Riga. The Latgale Uplands include Latvia's largest lakes and some of its prettiest scenery.

Latgale's position on the border with Slav cultures has had a strong influence on its development. Although the traditional architecture and costumes are of Latvian origin, it is easy to distinguish the influence of countries such as Poland, Russia and Belarus. Because of its tangled history, Latgale manages to be at once Latvia's most Russified area and the centre of Catholicism for the whole country. Most of the towns are predominantly Russian and most of the language you will hear will be Russian. Latgalian, a regional dialect quite different from Latvian, is still spoken in a few rural areas. Life in the country areas sometimes seems locked in a different era: it is common to see horses working in the fields, and people drawing water from wells.

MAIN ATTRACTIONS

The Latgale Upland, a region of lakes northeast of Daugavpils, is among Latvia's most beautiful areas. In summer it offers numerous possibilities for canoeing, walking and other outdoor pursuits. Other features of more specific interest include the Roman Catholic shrine at Aglona, the vast hydro-electric dams along the Daugava River and the statue of Māra, a Latvian symbol of independence, in Rēzekne. The area is also well known for its ceramics and pottery tradition.

HISTORY

The Latgals, like the Zemgals and Cours, were a Baltic tribe who arrived in the area during the early centuries AD and drove out the Livs and Estonians who had previously lived there. By the 12th century the Latgals had divided the area into four districts, each with its own towns fortified by castles. In 1561, Latgale became part of the Duchy of Pārdaugava and was under Lithuanian rule until 1569, when it was taken over by Poland. The region remained in Polish hands for just over two centuries. During this time Polish landlords, officials and peasants came to the area, reinforcing the Catholic tradition in Latgale. At the same time, Old Believers, who were being persecuted in Russia, fled to Latgale. In 1772, however, Latgale was swallowed up by Belarus, part of the Russian Empire, and Russian officials, merchants and peasants came to settle. By the end of the 19th century the shortage of land was such that many native peasants left for other areas of Russia. Almost 100 Latgal villages were set up in Siberia.

Up to the end of World War I Daugavpils and the area to the north remained part of the Russian province of Vitebsk, rather than the Latvian provinces of Livland and Kurland. After independence, many Poles and Russians returned to their native countries, while many Latvians moved to Latgale from other areas of the country. After World War II, the position was reversed, with many Latgals moving away from the area as the number of Russians, Belarussians and Ukrainians settling in the towns increased. As a result, the population in Latgale today is extremely diverse: in 1990 43% of the population was Russian, 42% Latvian, 6% Belarus, 5% Polish and 4% other groups including Ukrainians.

A TRIP AROUND LATGALE
If you have only a short time to spare, several options are available. A trip along the Daugava River from Riga to Daugavpils is possible in one day, although, depending on the time of year, this does not leave much time for sightseeing on the way.

By car
If you travel by car, you can vary the route by travelling south on one bank and returning north on the opposite bank. One way takes around three hours by car. If you would like to travel around the Latgale Upland and enjoy some of the scenery there, you will need more than a day. Travel other than by car is difficult.

By train
The journey to Daugavpils takes three and a quarter to four hours one way from Riga. Trains leave Riga at 07.05, 15.20 and 17.25 and return from Daugavpils to Riga at 06.14, 07.20 and 18.00. Various stops are made along the way, including at Aizkraukle and Jēkabpils. A one-way journey from Riga to Daugavpils costs Ls2.32.

By bus
Buses from Riga to Daugavpils take around four hours and leave Riga seven times a day between 10.00 and 20.20. If you are approaching the area from other parts of Latvia, there are bus services several times a day from Jēkabpils, Rēzekne and Krāslava, and several times a week from Cēsis and Valmiera.

Accommodation
Accommodation in the area is limited. The only sizeable hotel is in Rēzekne. The old Soviet hotel in the centre of Daugavpils is due to reopen, fully renovated, in 2005 and promises international-standard accommodation. There are also acceptable hotels in Jēkabpils. There are various small private hotels along the A6 and the A12 and many private houses offering accommodation in the Latgale Upland. In summer there are also many possibilities for camping in this area.

RIGA TO DAUGAVPILS
If you are travelling by road, head south out of Riga along the A6. This road leads directly to Daugavpils, following the course of the Daugava, and then on to the Belarus border. If you are travelling by public transport and alight before Daugavpils, check when the next bus or train is expected to come along, or you may find yourself stranded for quite a while.

The highlight of the trip is likely to be a number of extremely pleasant views of the river. Once you leave Riga, the only town of any size you will pass through is Jēkabpils. Other points of interest may be the series of hydro-electric plants and dams built during the Soviet occupation, for historians a number of ruined castles and mounds, and for anyone interested in Latvian literature the house of Jānis Rainis, now a museum.

Heading south from Riga, the following places are worthy of note and are listed in the order in which you will pass them:

Salaspils is on your left as you leave Riga (see page 141).

Dole was once an island in the Daugava, but now, connected by land to the riverbank, is the site of the first of several hydro-electric plants and dams you will pass on the way to Daugavpils. The Dole island is also the site of the Daugava Museum which deals with the history of the people who settled in towns near the river. The exhibits and displays show the history of trade, fishing and river life. The museum is open every day between 11.00 and 17.00 except Tuesday.

Saulkalne If you look across to the opposite bank of the river here, you can see Nāvessala (the Island of Death). During World War I, German soldiers were kept at bay here for two years by local forces, before defeating the Latvians by the use of gas, one of the first cases of its kind in the war.

Ikšķile The remains of the first church built in Latvia and the first stone building in the whole of the Baltics, the Church of St Mary (1185) can be seen from the riverbanks. The remains now stand on an island, created when the Riga hydro-electric plant flooded the banks of the Daugava.

Ogre was a popular health resort in the 19th century, and is still one of Latvia's greenest towns. Its relatively dry climate and views of the river attracted wealthy citizens from Riga, particularly after the opening of the Riga to Daugavpils railway in 1861. The town of Ogre lies at the mouth of the river of the same name. The name of the river comes from the Russian *ugor*, meaning eel. It is said that the river gained its name from the occasion when Catherine I, wife of Tsar Peter I, asked her cook to serve smoked eel. Servants were dispatched to search for the fish, and found some at the mouth of the river subsequently named Ogre. Today little remains of this affluent past, apart from a few restored sanatoria. The **local history museum** is at 3 Kalna prospekts (tel: 502 4345).

Ķegums The Daugava's first hydro-electric station (signposted as HES) was built between 1936 and 1941. The plant still supplies electricity to Riga, Jelgava and the surrounding area.

Lielvārde is well known in Latvia as the site of the last battle of the legendary hero, Lāčplēsis (meaning 'bear-slayer'). At the stone castle, built in 1205, the ruins of which can still be seen on the banks of the Daugava, Lāčplēsis fought the evil Black Knight (see pages 216–17). During the Soviet period, the name of the hero was given to a large collective farm *(kolhoz)* close to Lielvārde. The *kolhoz* signs can still be seen on the A6 just south of Lielvārde. The entrance to a park and a sign to **Andrejs Pumpurs Museum** (tel: 505 3759; email: muzejs@lielvarde.lv) is close to one of these signs as you are leaving the town heading south. Pumpurs (1841–1902), author of an epic describing Lāčplēsis's exploits (1888), was also a well-known poet. Every year on September 22, Pumpurs's birthday, plays are staged in the park. At any time of the year you can see wooden sculptures illustrating themes from the story outside the museum. The large rock in front of the museum is known as Lāčplēsis's bed. The rock was moved from an island in

LĀČPLĒSIS, THE BEAR-SLAYER

The story of the mythical hero Lāčplēsis is known to all Latvian children. Tales of his exploits and his dramatic death have been handed down as folk stories from generation to generation. There is even a bravery award, introduced after the liberation of Riga in November 1919, known as the War Order of Lāčplēsis. Lāčplēša Day, when Latvia's war heroes are honoured, is commemorated on November 11 every year. Visitors to Latvia can hardly fail to hear his story and see references to his life in monuments, street names, museums – and a beer brand.

There are many variations; even the hero's name has changed from the original Lāučausis (meaning 'bear's ears') to Lāčplēsis (meaning bear-slayer or, in some translations, 'bear-tearer'). The basic story goes something like this. Once upon a time, a very long time ago, a baby was abandoned in the forest by his parents. A kindly bear found the baby and brought him up as her own. (Another version says Lāčplēsis was actually the son of a human father and a bear mother, which is why he had a bear's ears.) The baby grew into a man with a huge physique and the strength of a bear, Lāčplēsis. Despite being abandoned by his parents, Lāčplēsis was well disposed towards humans and did all he could to protect them from the dangers of the natural world. His amazing strength saved a lot of people from death and destruction, although the same strength and clumsiness also sometimes caused a lot of trouble. As Lāčplēsis's fame spread beyond Latvia, other giants began to be envious of his reputation. Among them the Black Knight, a giant with three heads, was particularly annoyed by Lāčplēsis, and, having discovered the only part of the hero which was vulnerable (his ears) set out for Latvia to try and kill him. The two giants met on the banks of the Daugava, at what is now Lielvārde, and fought an epic battle. Lāčplēsis managed to cut off two of the Black Knight's heads, and the Black Knight cut off one of Lāčplēsis's ears.

the Daugava when the Ķegums hydro-electric plant was built; before that Pumpurs is supposed to have sat on the rock while writing about Lāčplēsis. The museum is open Wednesday–Sunday 10.00–17.00.

Skrīveri has a large tree park (dendroloģiskais parks) close to the river. In summer you can also take a boat across the Daugava to **Jaunjelgave**. This once prosperous town, the oldest in the Aizkraukle district, suffered badly in the Napoleonic Wars and in World War I, and has also been affected by successive floods. The house where the writer Andrejs Upītis (1877–1970) lived for several years is now a museum.

Aizkraukle is a new town built in the 1960s to house workers at the hydro-electric station opened close by on the Daugava in 1965. Strangely, the hydro-electric station is known as Pļaviņas, the name of a town to the south, as the plant was originally going to be built there and most of the workers moved to the plant from Pļaviņas. To add to the confusion, the town of Aizkraukle was called Stučka during the Soviet occupation, before being renamed in 1991. To see the hydro-electric station follow the signs to Aizkraukle from the A6 and then look for signs marked HES. The plant was the most powerful one built during the Soviet occupation. You can appreciate its size not only from the riverbank but also by driving through a tunnel in the plant itself to the opposite bank of the Daugava. The **Hotel Pērse** (6 Lāčplēša iela; tel: 512 3034) has accommodation for 40 and modern facilities as well as a café. Rooms cost Ls5–25.

Neither could strike the decisive blow, however, and finally both fell into the river, never to be seen again. The Latvian people lost not only Lāčplēsis but also the champion of their freedom. Without Lāčplēsis they were easily conquered. It is said that on the day that all evil disappears from Latvia a castle of light will rise from the river where he fell.

Over the years many prose versions of the story were written, but the best known today is the first one written as an epic poem by Andrejs Pumpurs in 1888. At a time when Latvia was trying to forge a clear national identity, Pumpurs set out very consciously to mould a story which the Latvian people could be proud of in a form, the epic poem, which was considered the highest level of folk creation. In a sense he was trying to 'invent a tradition'. To do this, he grafted on to the original folk story real historical elements and characters, including the Teutonic Knights, and suggested that Latvia would be able to overcome its 19th-century occupiers, just as Lāčplēsis had overcome so many enemies.

Another well-known adaptation of the story is the play *Fire and Night*, completed by Jānis Rainis in 1911. This play brings in Laimdota, the hero's true love, who in traditional versions lived in Koknese, close to Lielvārde on the Daugava. More recently, Māra Zālīte wrote a rock opera, *Lāčplēsis*, in 1988. Again the classical story was used for contemporary needs: Lāčplēsis's ears were made to indicate his openness to listen to the Latvian people's growing calls for independence.

Despite the fact that all the written versions of the Lāčplēsis story indicate that he had bear's ears, you will look in vain for clear visual representations. Artists and sculptors have considered that they would make their national hero a laughing stock if they gave him furry ears. The Freedom Monument in Riga depicts Lāčplēsis with long hair, so his ears cannot be seen. Other representations put the ears on his helmet, rather than directly on his head!

Koknese If you have become interested in the legend of Lāčplēsis through your visit to Lielvārde, you may also like to visit Koknese, the town where the hero's true love Laimdota lived. The town is also thought by some to be the centre of the ancient state of Jersika, given by treaty to the Germans in 1209. Whether this is true or not, a castle has existed here, destroyed and rebuilt many times, since the 12th or 13th century. Finally destroyed, like so many of Latvia's castles, during the Great Northern War in 1701, only ruins remain. These have survived the flooding following the opening of the hydro-electric station, but water now covers some of the castle and is damaging its foundations. Other natural features in the area, including the Staburags cliff, the Pērse waterfall and several castle walls and ruins have disappeared underwater. Despite this, the area remains a tourist destination for Latvians, and the castle view is a favourite one for photographers. The **Motelis Kalna Salas** (tel: 513 8422), a small modern house with a few rooms for accommodation, is on the main road just south of Koknese. Rooms cost Ls12–15.

Pļaviņas The main road now bypasses Pļaviņas, because of its frequent spring floods. The centre still has many typical buildings dating from Latvia's first independence period.

Mežezers is located 4km off the main road (signposted to the left 1km south of Pļaviņas heading towards Daugava) on the banks of Lake Odze.

There are a number of acceptable cafés on the A6 near the Daugava, all offering good value for money and clean facilities. These include **Kante** (The Edge) in Lielvārde, **Ragalu Krogs** near Koknese, and **Velniņš** (The Little Devil) near Stukmaņi, 5km west of the road junction leading to Pļaviņas.

Jēkabpils

Jēkabpils now lies on both banks of the River Daugava, having swallowed up the previously separate town of Krustpils on the right bank in 1962. Although small (population 31,000), Jēkabpils is the largest town between Riga and Daugavpils, and is a good place for a refreshment stop. If time permits you may also like to spend an hour or so walking around the centre (a circle taking in Pasta iela and Brīvības iela) where there are a number of attractive houses and churches, including the traditional 19th-century houses at 77, 83 and 87 Pasta iela. The town centre is on the left bank of the river, and there are several cafés along Brīvības iela, close to the main square. On this street you can also see the **St Nicholas Church** (Svēta Nikolaja), built in 1774. Across the street from the church is the town's oldest building, a two-storeyed house which has survived intact for several centuries. The open-air section of the History Museum (see below) (6 Filozofu iela; tel: 523 2501), includes 19th-century buildings and household items typical of the surrounding area, as well as a windmill dating from 1820. Open Wednesday–Sunday 10.00–17.00. On the right bank, in what was previously **Krustpils**, you can see the remains of a castle built in 1237. This is now the **History Museum** (216 Rīgas iela; tel: 522 1042). Open in summer Monday–Friday 09.00–17.00, Saturday and Sunday 10.00–15.00; October–May Saturdays only. In the park by the pond with the mill (214 Rīgas iela) is the castle chapel. The castle was originally surrounded by houses decorated with crosses (*krusti*), from which the town derived its name. The name of Jēkabpils, incidentally, commemorates Duke Jakob of Kurland (see page 15), and dates from the time when, following the collapse of the Livonian state in 1561, Kurland took control of the west bank of the Daugava. At that time goods travelling along the river were unloaded at Salas krogs (the site of the present-day Jēkabpils) and had to be carried overland to Jaunjelgave, due to rapids on the river.

Accommodation

There are two acceptable hotels in Jēkabpils: the **Hercogs Jēkabs** (182 Brīvības iela; tel: 523 3433), an attractive red-brick house backing on to the river, where rooms cost Ls5–30, and the less-attractive **Daugavkrasti** hotel (2 Mežrūpnieku iela; tel: 523 1232), slightly outside the main centre, which offers rooms at Ls12–18.

Just outside Jēkabpils on the A6 going south is the **Ceļinieks** (Traveller) **Hotel** (33 Rīgas iela; tel: 522 1708) with 20 beds, a sauna and restaurant. It is clean and comfortable, but fairly basic. Rooms cost Ls3.50–5.

Tourist information

The tourist information office is at 3 Vecpilsētas laukums; tel: 523 3822; email: jektic@apollo.lv.

From Jēkabpils you can either continue on the right bank of the Daugava directly to Daugavpils, or, if you want to visit the house of Jānis Rainis, stay on the left bank and follow the signs in Jēkabpils to Dunava and the Jānis Rainis Museum.

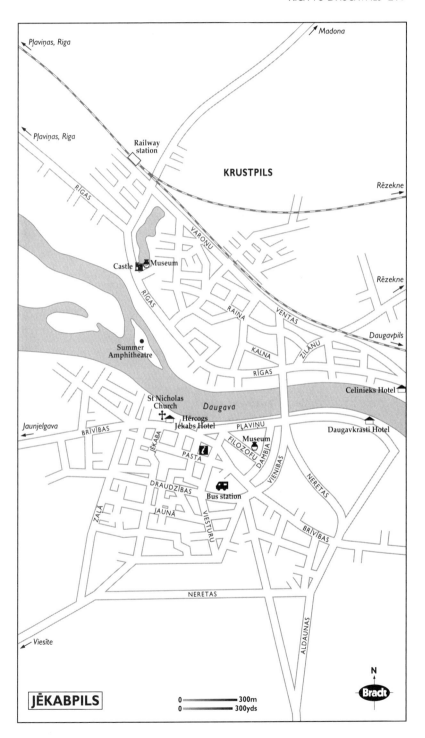

Pļaviņas, Riga

Madona

Pļaviņas, Riga

Railway
station

KRUSTPILS

Rēzekne

RĪGAS

VAROŅU

Castle Museum

Rēzekne

RAIŅA

VENTAS

RĪGAS

Daugavpils

Summer
Amphitheatre

KALNA

ZĪLĀNU

RĪGAS

Celinieks Hotel

St Nicholas
Church

Daugava

Jaunjelgava

BRĪVĪBAS

Hērcogs
Jēkabs Hotel

PĻAVIŅU

Daugavkrasti Hotel

JĒKABA

Museum

FILOZOFU

DAMBJA

PASTA

VIENĪBAS

NERETAS

DRAUDZĪBAS

Bus station

ZAĻĀ

JAUNĀ

VIESTURU

BRĪVĪBAS

NERETAS

Viesīte

ALDAUNAS

N

JĒKABPILS

0 ——— 300m
0 ——— 300yds

Bradt

JĀNIS RAINIS

Jānis Rainis was born Jānis Pliekšāns (he took the name Rainis as his *nom de plume*) in 1865 in Tadenava, the son of a prosperous farmer. He was a precocious child with a gift for languages, and by the time he finished school was familiar with the classical languages and had a good knowledge of German, Russian, English and French. At the age of 15 he produced a translation of Pushkin's *Boris Godunov*.

He studied law in St Petersburg and practised for a while as a lawyer after returning to Riga. However, his interest in literature and politics soon prevailed. He became involved in the New Movement (Jaunāstrāva), but was exiled to Pskov and Slobodski because of his left-wing political views. He took an active part in the uprisings of 1905–07 but was forced to flee to Switzerland when they were put down.

He returned to Latvia in 1920 and served as minister of education in the Kārlis Ulmanis government from 1926–28 but withdrew from public life, disappointed at Ulmanis's lack of radicalism. He spent his last years in Jūrmala in what he himself described as his 'third exile' until his death in 1929.

His work had enormous influence on Latvian literature and on the shaping of Latvian national consciousness; his name is found everywhere, especially in street names. Philosophically, his ideas were shaped by Hegelian dialectics: he saw life in terms of opposites, the conflict between which leads to synthesis or resolution. In one of his most famous plays, *Joseph and his Brothers*, he examines the conflict between Joseph, the dreamer, and his brothers, whose concerns are rooted in the practical world of animal husbandry, and that between Israel and Egypt. Joseph's brothers abandon him in a pit, but he survives to become a powerful figure, Nofer, in the court of the pharaoh. His starving brothers come to Egypt looking for food. At first Joseph plays with their fate, but in the end a mystical reconciliation occurs – the world of dreams redeems the harshness of reality and conflict.

Rainis is also known as a poet: his first collection of verse was published in 1903, but his best-known verse is contained in his second volume, *Gals un sākums* (*Beginning and End*). His translation of Goethe's *Faust* is compared by Latvians to the original German. He is buried in one of Riga's major cemeteries which now bears his name. (See page 131.)

His wife, Aspāzija, the pen name of Elza Rozenberg (1868–1945) was a major poet in her own right. Her name is commemorated in the boulevard that runs through the centre of Riga.

Dunava

Dunava is 50km or so south of Jēkabpils, and the small village contains the house, named Tadenava, built by Jānis Rainis's father shortly after his son's birth on September 11 1865. Although he spent only his first four years here, the poet, according to his writings, retained a vivid impression of the sun from his life at Tadenava. The museum (**Raiņa Muzejs 'Tadenava'**; tel: 525 2522) is open from May 15–November 1 daily 10.00–17.00 except Monday.

Between Ilukste and Daugavpils lies an area in which tens of thousands of Germans, Latvians and Russians died in the autumn of 1915 as the Germans tried to capture the fortress at Daugavpils. Much fighting occurred between the two lakes **Svente** and **Ilga**. Lake Svente is the deepest in Latgale. Its name is derived from the

Lithuanian word for holy (*sventjos*) and dates from 1435 when Lithuanian troops defeated the Knights of the Livonian Order on the banks of the nearby River Pikraca.

Līvāni

If you proceed down the right bank of the Daugava from Jēkabpils, you will pass close to Līvāni, a town once famous for its glass products. If you are interested in the Old Believers you could leave the main road at Līvāni and head towards Preiļi on the P53. Just before Preiļi you come to **Moskvina** with its Old Believers Preaching House (tel: 533 5342), the oldest preaching house in Latvia with 200 icons, bells and chandeliers.

Daugavpils

Although Daugavpils is Latvia's second largest city, it is relatively small (population 113,000) and has little of specific interest to attract visitors. Its strategic position on the Daugava has meant that it has had a long and troubled history, not to mention many names: it was known as Dünaburg by the Germans, as Dvinsk by the Poles and as Borisoglebsk by the Russians. The town expanded rapidly in the post-war era as Russian workers were brought in to work in large factories, often serving the needs of the whole Soviet Empire. Most of these industries have collapsed since Latvia regained its independence, but many of the Russian workers and their descendants have remained. Today under 15% of the population is Latvian, and many of the signs you will see, and the language you will hear, will be Russian. The demise of local industry after independence had a very adverse effect on the local economy, giving the town a grey and depressed atmosphere from which it is now making valiant and partially successful efforts to recover.

Accommodation

The old Soviet hotel which used to dominate the town centre is currently being completely renovated. It plans to reopen in 2005 as the **Park Hotel Latgola** (46 Ģimnāzijas iela; tel: 542 0932; email: hotel@hoteldaugavpils.lv; www.hoteldaugavpils.lv). When it does, doubles will cost Ls40–65; all will have satellite TV and internet access, and the hotel will have a restaurant and bars. Until the hotel reopens choice is restricted to a number of relatively small hotels and guesthouses, including the **Verina** (44 Ģimnāzijas iela; tel: 542 2190), rooms Ls25–70; the **Rebir** (19 Vienības iela; tel: 542 1857), rooms Ls22–30; and **Leo** (58 Krāslavas iela; tel: 542 0003), rooms Ls20–40, in an attractively restored old building.

About 15 minutes' drive from the town towards Rēzekne is a four-star motel, **Stalkers** (6 Katlakši, Visķu pag; tel: 547 9221). Singles cost Ls17; doubles from Ls34.

Eating out

Eating possibilities remain fairly poor in Daugavpils. **Gubernators** (in a basement at 10 Lāčplēsa iela; tel: 542 2455), is probably the best option. It offers a wide range of Latvian and international dishes at very reasonable prices in a pub-style ambiance. Most of the other eating and drinking possibilities are on Rīgas iela, the main pedestrian street leading from the railway station into the centre of town. Of these, the largest and maybe the most pleasant is the **Vēsma** bar/bistro/self-service café. The **Leo** hotel also has a restaurant.

Tourist information

The tourist information office is at 22a Rīgas iela; tel: 54 22818; email: tourinfo@daugavpils.apollo.lv.

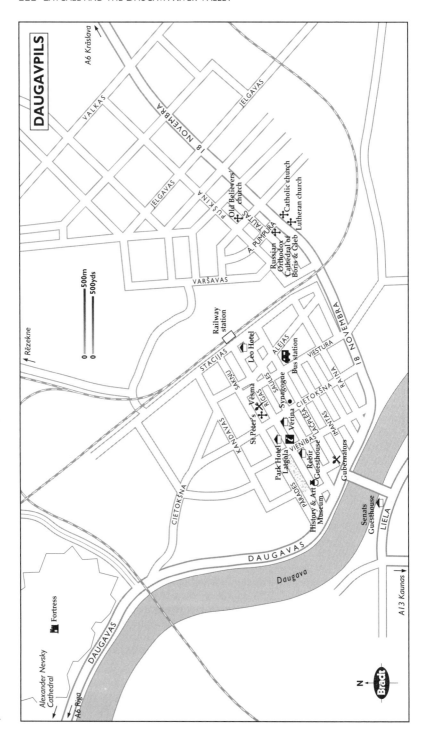

MARK ROTHKO
Mark Rothko (1903–70), one of the world's best-known Abstract Expressionist painters, was born in Dvinsk (now Daugavpils) on September 25 1903 and lived there until his family moved to Portland, Oregon, in 1913. His works, many of which consist of stacked blocks of deep colours, can now be seen in the Tate Modern in London, the Guggenheim in New York and in many other museums in North America, Europe and Japan. Although widely recognised as a major artist in America and western Europe, Soviet lack of interest in Western art meant that his work was largely unknown in Latvia until recently. The year after Latvia regained its independence, however, interest was awakened in Daugavpils when James Breslin, a biographer of Rothko, visited the city. Since then the Daugavpils History and Art Museum (see below) has striven to awaken local, national and international interest by setting up a permanent exhibition and initiating an education programme for local schools. The museum now has a special room, the Rothko Hall, with a highly evaluated permanent exhibition of 30 high-quality Rothko reproductions, produced in Vienna. All are printed on canvas and most are the same dimensions as the original paintings. The museum also owns a further 11 reproductions, to be shown in rotations. A plaque commemorating Rothko can also be seen nearby on the banks of the River Daugava.

What to see
The centre of town is compact. If you arrive at the railway station you can walk directly down the pedestrianised **Rīgas iela** (once Lenina iela), Daugava's most prestigious shopping and entertainment street. Rīgas iela leads past **St Peter's Catholic Church** (Sv Pētera) into the main square, with its new shopping centres. Continue walking away from the station along the side of the **park** with its monument to the Russians who died liberating Daugavpils from the Germans in 1944, and you will come to the **History and Art Museum** (8 Rīgas iela; tel: 542 2709) with its new Rothko Hall (see box). Open Tuesday–Saturday 11.00–18.00. Beyond this are the banks of the Daugava. A pleasant walk north along the bank will bring you, after 2km and just beyond the railway bridge, to the fortress (**cietoksnis**). The Russians started to build the fortress in 1810, and in 1812 it was used as a base from which to repel Napoleon's army as it headed towards Moscow. More recently the fortress was occupied by Soviet soldiers. Since they left in 1993 some of the ex-army accommodation has been used to house local citizens, mainly pensioners. There is currently talk of turning it into a hotel and leisure complex.

Beyond the railway is the **Hill of Churches,** an area which includes four impressive religious buildings: the **Russian Orthodox Cathedral of Boris and Gleb** (2 Tautas iela), originally built in 1655 and restored in 1905 and containing some magnificent icons, the **Catholic Church of the Immaculate Conception** (11a A Pumpura iela on the corner of 18 Novembra iela) built in 1902, the nearby **Lutheran Church of Martin Luther** (68 18 Novembra iela), which is currently being restored, and the **Old Believers Church** (on the corner of Tautas and A Pumpura iela) built in 1928, with its hundreds of icons and candles.

The **Russian Orthodox Cathedral of Alexander Nevsky** is around 3km from the centre beyond the fortress, on Garnizona kapos, and a small, but beautifully restored Russian Orthodox church is situated just opposite the tourist information office in the centre of town. The cathedral is regularly open to visitors.

BEYOND DAUGAVPILS
Aglona
Aglona lies around 48km from Daugavpils, and is reached via the A13 towards Rēzekne and the P62 (on your right 39km from Daugavpils). Buses depart several times a day from Daugavpils, and you can also go directly by bus from Riga (buses leave on Monday, Wednesday and Friday at 16.00 and take around four and a half hours).

A vast white basilica dominates the surrounding scenery, and its grounds occupy a huge area. It was not always so. Aglona developed as a centre of Catholicism in Latgale at the end of the 17th century. The basilica and abbey buildings were constructed between 1768 and 1800 in the forest between two lakes. With the strong growth of Catholicism in this part of Latvia after the end of the Soviet occupation, Aglona once again became a major focus for Catholic pilgrims. In particular, every year on the Feast of the Assumption (August 15) crowds come, not only from Latgale and Latvia, but from abroad too, to celebrate. The decision of Pope John Paul II to visit Aglona in summer 1993 led to a major refurbishment programme for the basilica and the abbey buildings and to the creation of a vast courtyard in front of the basilica. The large podium from which the Pope spoke still stands here, commanding a wonderful view of the lakes around the church. The church building itself is not of particular interest and is generally closed.

Rēzekne
Although smaller than Daugavpils, Rēzekne likes to see itself as the main cultural centre of Latgale, 'the heart of Latgale'. The town has a long history – a Latgal castle stood here from the 9th century – but suffered particularly badly in World War II when bombing by the Soviet air force destroyed around 65% of all its buildings. Like Daugavpils, Rēzekne was an important centre of investment for Soviet industrial growth and the town expanded rapidly. Today over 50% of the population is Russian.

Railways have played an important role in Rēzekne's development since 1861 when the first rail connection from St Petersburg opened. People from Rēzekne started to leave the provincial town to find more lucrative work in St Petersburg, while inhabitants of the Russian capital began to come to Rēzekne in summer to relax in the attractive scenery. The opening in 1904 of the Moscow to Ventspils railway made Rēzekne an important railway junction and, unhappily, was the reason for the particularly heavy bombing in 1944. The town still has two railway stations, and the main street, Atbrīvošanas aleja, leads south from Rēzekne II in the direction of Rēzekne I.

Accommodation
Hotel Latgale (98 Atbrīvošanas aleja; tel/fax: 462 2180), the best, and most modern, hotel in Latgale with 157 rooms, has a restaurant, bar and café. Rooms cost Ls7–20 a night. There is also a new hotel just off the A12 near Viļāni, **Pie Kaupra** (tel: 466 2314), 28km from Rēzekne heading towards Jēkabpils.

Eating out
You will find a very acceptable café/restaurant (Little Italy; 100 Atbrīvošanas aleja) in the northeast corner of the main square, up a concrete staircase. Other cafés are situated along the main street and on Latgales iela.

What to see
Rēzekne's most famous monument, the **statue of Māra**, is in the main square on Atbrīvošanas aleja, about 1km south of Rēzekne II. The monument was originally

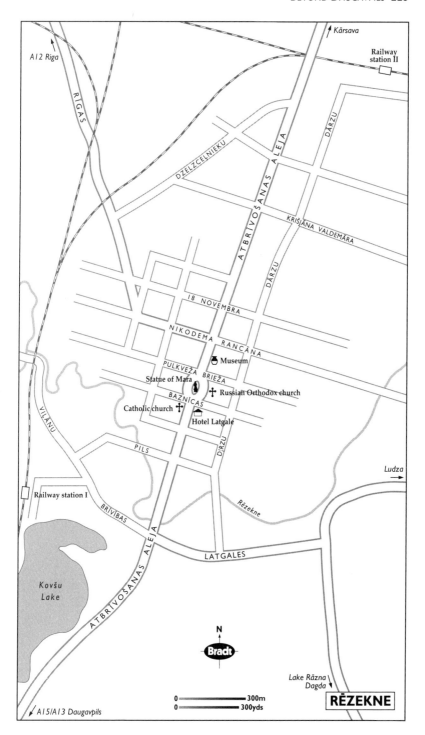

Kārsava

A12 Riga

Railway
station II

RIGAS

DZELZCEĻNIEKU

ATBRĪVOŠANAS ALEJA

DĀRZU

KRIŠJĀNA VALDEMĀRA

18 NOVEMBRA

DĀRZU

NIKODEMA RANCĀNA

PULKVEŽA BRIEŽA

Museum

Statue of Mara

Russian Orthodox church

BAZNĪCAS

Catholic church

Hotel Latgale

VILĀNU

PILS

DĀRZU

Ludza

Railway station I

BRĪVĪBAS

Rēzekne

ATBRĪVOŠANAS ALEJA

LATGALES

Kovšu
Lake

N

Bradt

Lake Rāzna
Dagda

0 ———— 300m
0 ———— 300yds

RĒZEKNE

A15/A13 Daugavpils

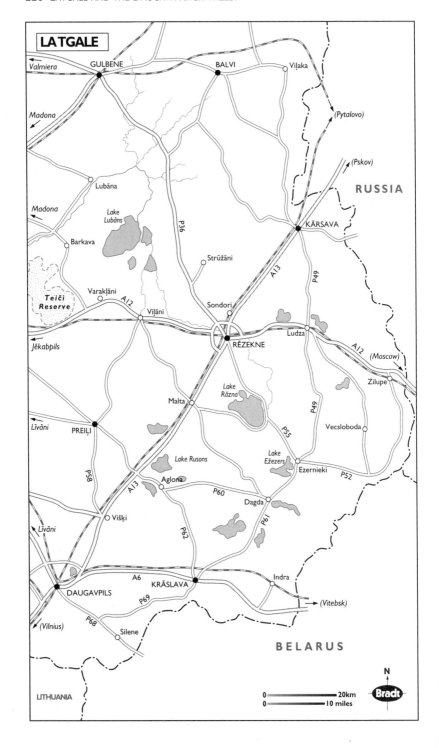

LATGALE

Valmiera GULBENE   BALVI   Viļaka

Madona   (Pytalovo)

                                                         (Pskov)

                                                    RUSSIA

        Lubāna

Madona   Lake
             Lubāns   KĀRSAVA

     Barkava

                              Strūžāni

     Varakļāni
Teiči   Sondori
Reserve   Viļāni

Jēkabpils   RĒZEKNE   Ludza

                                                    (Moscow)

                                                      Zilupe
                        Lake
                        Rāzna
              Malta

Līvāni   Vecsloboda
    PREIĻI

                   Lake Rusons   Lake
                                      Ežezers
              Aglona   Ezernieki
                        P60
Līvāni   Dagda
              Višķi

                    A6   KRĀSLAVA   Indra
DAUGAVPILS

                                              (Vitebsk)
(Vilnius)
         Silene
                                    BELARUS

LITHUANIA   N

                    0   20km   Bradt
                    0   10 miles

erected in 1939 to celebrate the liberation of Latgale from foreign rulers. It was removed twice during the Soviet occupation, but re-erected in 1992 at a ceremony which attracted Latgalians from around the world. The female figure of Māra is brandishing a Christian cross in her right hand, even though she is known in Latvian mythology as an earth-mother goddess. The inscription *Vienoti Latvijai* means United Latvia.

Around the same square are **two churches** (one Russian Orthodox and one Catholic) and the Hotel Latgale. Heading north along the main street you will come to the **Latgale History Museum** (Latgales kultūrvēstures muzejs, 102 Atbrīvošanas aleja; tel: 462 2464) which specialises in displays of local pottery. Open Tuesday–Friday 10.00–17.00, Saturday 10.00–16.00; closed on Sundays.

The Latgale Upland

Latvians often call Latgale 'the land of blue lakes', and in the area south and southeast of Rēzekne you will find a huge number of lakes, ranging from small ones, often hidden from view behind screens of trees, to Latvia's largest lake, **Lake Rāzna**, which covers an area of over 50km². Most of the lakes are clean and relatively shallow; in summer they are ideal for swimming. Fishing is popular here, as it is throughout Latvia; in winter it is a common sight to see keen anglers cutting a hole in the ice and casting their line down through to the water below. Canoeing is also possible.

Apart from Lake Rāzna, which incidentally only became Latvia's largest lake after the Soviets drained some of the water from Lake Lubāns, northwest of Rēzekne, the area around **Lake Ežezers** (literally 'hedgehog lake') is one of the prettiest in this part of the country. Another lake worth visiting is Lake Rušons, just north of Aglona. The colours of the water and the vegetation surrounding the lake and on the islands are some of the most beautiful in Latvia. Although called Latgale Upland, the hills are still relatively low, the highest point being **Lielais Liepukalns** (289m), just north of Lake Ežezers.

From the church in **Pasiene**, south of Zilupe near the Russian border, there are fine views over the border on to the Russian plains. If you would like to see three countries, rather than just two, you can proceed further south towards Skaune. Seven kilometres to the northeast by the banks of the **Zilupe** you will come to a place where one road leads to Russia, another to Belarus and a third back through Latvia.

Apart from Rēzekne and Daugavpils, the only towns of any size in this area are Ludza and Krāslava. Until World War I **Krāslava** was a major trading centre in this part of the Baltics. The Catholic church (3 Puškina iela), built in 1767, was built as a cathedral for the Bishop of Latgale. **Ludza** suffered badly from a fire in 1938 and from subsequent war damage. It has a museum of local studies (2 Kuļņeva iela; tel: 572 3931). Open Monday–Saturday 09.00–17.00 and Sunday 10.00–17.00. The street is named after a Russian major general who fought against Napoleon and who was born in the house which is now the museum. A plaque in Hebrew on Mazā Ezerkrasta iela commemorates the victims of the Ludza ghetto.

In Ludza you can stay at the clean but basic **Ezerzeme** (44 Stacijas iela; tel; 572 2490), which has rooms in various stages of renovation. Prices from Ls5.70 for a basic single to Ls24 for a decent renovated room.

Tourist information

Ludza Rural Tourism Agency is at 42-II Baznīcas iela, Ludza; tel: 570 7202; email: kondrate@one.lv; and 13 Brīvibas iela, Krāslava; tel: 562 2201; email: ep@kraslava.vp.gov.lv.

228

KEY TO STANDARD SYMBOLS ◯ Bradt

—·—·	International boundary	⊞	Historic building
·····	District boundary	⛫	Castle, fortress
-----	National park boundary	†	Church, cathedral
▫	National park	∴	Archaeological or historic site
✈	Airport (international)	✡	Synagogue
✈	Airport (other)	☪	Mosque
✝	Airstrip	⊛	Stadium
⛴	Helicopter service	⊛	Football stadium
▬	Railway	⚑	Golf course
·····	Footpath	▲	Summit
⛴	Passenger ferry	△	Boundary beacon
⛴	Car ferry	◉	Outpost
P	Car park	⤬—⤬	Border post
🚌	Bus station etc	⌂	Rock shelter
→	One-way	⊶	Cable car, funicular
M	Underground station	⌣	Mountain pass
⛽	Petrol station or garage	○	Waterhole
⛺	Campsite	☀	Scenic viewpoint
⬆	Hut	❀	Botanical site
⚲	Bar, wine bar	♣	Specific woodland feature
✗	Restaurant, café etc	⛉	Lighthouse
⌂	Hotel, inn etc	�‍	Marsh
✆	Telephone	🐟	Fishing sites
@	Internet café	🦅	Bird nesting site
✚	Hospital, clinic etc	⌇	Waterfall
⚱	Museum	✳	Source of river
✉	Post office	⬈	Beach
i	Tourist information		
$	Bank	*Other map symbols are sometimes shown in*
⚱	Statue, monument	*separate key boxes with individual*
🐘	Zoo	*explanations for their meanings.*

Appendix 1

LANGUAGE

It is unlikely that you will have communication problems in Riga. Many people, particularly young people, speak English. However, it is always good to be able to say at least a few basics in Latvian. *Labu laimi!* (Good luck!) For general information on the Latvian language, see pages 32–4 and 59.

Pronunciation

The Latvian alphabet is as follows:

a/ā, b, c, č, d, e/ē, f, g, ǧ, h, i/ī, j, k, ķ, l, ļ, m, n, ņ, o, p, r, s, š, t, u/ū, v, z, ž

Consonants

The letters b, d, f, g, h, k, l, m, n, p, s, t ,v and z are almost identical to their English counterparts in pronunciation. Other consonants are pronounced as follows:

c as ts
č as ch in 'chalk'
ǧ as the dj sound in 'during'
j as y in 'yes'
ķ as the tj sound in 'Tuesday'
ļ as the lli sound in 'million' (or the gl in Italian)
ņ as the ni sound in 'onion' (or ñ in Spanish)
š as sh in 'show'
ž as s in 'vision'
r is trilled

Vowels

The short and long vowels are:

a as the o in 'hot'
ā as in 'father'
e as in 'bet'
ē as the a in 'bare'
i as in 'pit'
ī as the ee in 'feet'
u as the oo in 'foot'
ū as the oo in 'food'
The ai combination is pronounced as the i in 'bike'
The ei combination is pronounced as ey in 'hey'
The letter o is a diphthong as in the r-less pronunciation of 'pour'
ie is pronounced as in the r-less pronunciation of 'beer'

Some useful words and expressions
Greetings
Hello	*Sveiki*
Good morning/afternoon; hello	*Labdien*
Good morning	*Labrīt*
Good evening	*Labvakar*
Good night	*Ar labu nakti*
Goodbye	*Atā*
Goodbye (cf *au revoir, auf Wiedersehen*)	*Uz redzēšanos. Visu labu.*

Basic courtesies
Please	*Lūdzu*
Thank you	*Paldies*
You're welcome (cf *bitte, prego*)	*Laipni lūdzu*
Yes	*Jā*
No	*Nē*
Excuse me	*Atvainojiet, lūdzu*
I'm sorry	*Es atvainojos* or *piedodiet*
Don't mention it	*Nav par ko*
My name is...	*Mani sauc...*

Basic communication
Do you speak English?	*Vai Jūs runājiet angliski?*
I do not speak Latvian.	*Es nerunāju latviski.*
Please speak slowly.	*Lūdzu runājiet lēnāk.*
I do not understand.	*Nesaprotu.*

Finding the way
I would like to go (by car) to...	*Es vēlos braukt uz...*
I would like to go (by foot) to...	*Es vēlos iet uz...*
Where is ... ?	*Kur ir...?*
Go straight ahead.	*Uz priekšu.*
Turn left at...	*Pa kreisi pie...*
Turn right at...	*Pa labi pie...*

Signs
Closed	*Slēgts*
Open	*Atvērts*
Entrance	*Ieeja*
Exit	*Izeja*
Pull	*Vilkt*
Push	*Grūst*
No entry	*Ieeja aizliegta*
Caution	*Uzmanību*
Danger	*Briesmas*
Parking	*Autonovietne*
No parking	*Stavēt aizliegts*
Stop	*Stāt*
Information	*Izziņu birojs*
Ladies	*Sievietēm*
Gentlemen	*Vīriešiem*
No smoking	*Smeķēt aizliegts*
Petrol	*Degviela* or *Benzīns*

Question words and phrases

What?	*Kas?*
Who?	*Kas? Kurš?* (m); *Kura?* (f)
Where?	*Kur?*
When?	*Kad?*
How?	*Kā?*
How much?	*Cik?*
What time is it?	*Cik pulkstenis?*
What time does it open?	*No cikiem ir atvērts?*
What time does it close?	*Cikos slēdz?*

Eating out

(See pages 60–4 for more information and vocabulary relating to Latvian food and drink.)

restaurant	*restorāns*
café	*kafejnīca*
I would like to order	*Es vēlētos pasūtīt*
Some more, please	*Lūdzu, vēl*
That's enough, thank you	*pietiek, paldies*
hot	*karsts*
cold	*auksts*
Bon appétit!	*Labu apetiti!*
Cheers!	*Priekā!*
coffee (with milk)	*kafija (ar pienu)*
sugar	*cukurs*
tea	*tēja*
juice	*sula*
water	*ūdens*
mineral water	*minerālūdens*
beer	*alus*
wine (red, white)	*vīns (sarkans, balts)*
bread	*maize*
butter	*sviests*
The bill, please	*Lūdzu, rēķinu*
toilet	*Tualete*

Meals

breakfast	*brokastis*
lunch	*pusdienas*
dinner	*vakariņas*

Finding a room

Do you have any rooms available?	*Vai Jums ir brīvas istabas?*
I would like a single room.	*Es vēlos istabu vienai personai.*
I would like a double room.	*Es vēlos istabu divām personām.*
How much is it a night?	*Cik maksā viena nakts?*
Is breakfast included?	*Vai brokastis ir ieskaitītas?*

Shopping

store	*veikals*
I would like ...	*Es vēlētos ...*
How much does it cost?	*Cik maksā?*
inexpensive	*lēts*

expensive	*dārgs*
open	*atvērts*
closed	*slēgts*
Do you have...?	*Vai Jums ir...?*

Locations

street	*iela*
road	*ceļš*
avenue	*avēnija prospeksveits,*
square	*laukums*
hotel	*viesnīca*
castle	*pils*
church	*baznīca*
restaurant	*restorāns*
hospital	*slimnīca*
drugstore/pharmacy	*aptieka*
cinema	*kinoteātris/kino*
theatre	*teātris*
museum	*muzejs*
post office	*pasts*
airport	*lidosta*
bus station	*autoosta*
railway station	*dzelzceļa stacija*
hill	*kalns*
lake	*ezers*
sea	*jūra*
river	*upe*
bridge	*tilts*

Emergencies

help!	*palīgā!*
quickly	*ātri*
doctor	*ārsts*
dentist	*zobārsts*
pharmacy/chemist's	*aptieka*
hospital	*slimnīca*
police	*policija*
police station	*policijas iecirknis*
telephone	*telefons*
garage (repairs)	*tehniskās apkopes stacija*
garage (petrol)	*degvielas uzpildes stacija*

Days

Note that on signs denoting opening times the days of the week are often expressed as numerals, 1 denoting Monday, 2 Tuesday etc.

Monday	*pirmdiena*
Tuesday	*otrdiena*
Wednesday	*trešdiena*
Thursday	*ceturtdiena*
Friday	*piektdiena*
Saturday	*sestdiena*
Sunday	*svētdiena*
yesterday	*vakar*

today	*šodien*
tomorrow	*rīt*

Months

January	*janvāris*
February	*februāris*
March	*marts*
April	*aprīlis*
May	*maijs*
June	*jūnijs*
July	*jūlijs*
August	*augusts*
September	*septembris*
October	*oktobris*
November	*novembris*
December	*decembris*

Cardinal numbers

1	*viens*	17	*septiņpadsmit*
2	*divi*	18	*astoņpadsmit*
3	*trīs*	19	*deviņpadsmit*
4	*četri*	20	*divdesmit*
5	*pieci*	25	*divdesmitpieci*
6	*seši*	30	*trīsdesmit*
7	*septiņi*	40	*četrdesmit*
8	*astoņi*	50	*piecdesmit*
9	*deviņi*	60	*sešdesmit*
10	*desmit*	70	*septiņdesmit*
11	*vienpadsmit*	80	*astoņdesmit*
12	*divpadsmit*	90	*deviņdesmit*
13	*trīspadsmit*	100	*simts*
14	*četrpadsmit*	110	*simtdesmit*
15	*piecpadsmit*	1,000	*tūkstotis*
16	*sešpadsmit*	1,000,000	*miljons*

Ordinal numbers

1st	*pirmais*	8th	*astotais*
2nd	*otrais*	9th	*devītais*
3rd	*trešais*	10th	*desmitais*
4th	*ceturtais*	11th	*vienpadsmitais*
5th	*piektais*	20th	*divdesmitais*
6th	*sestais*	100th	*simtais*
7th	*septītais*		

Appendix 2

PLACE NAMES

Many Latvian towns and other place names have changed over the centuries, as different rulers have imposed their own names. In particular, many Latvian towns were known under their German names until around 1920. Some of the main former and present names are listed below.

Towns

Current Latvian name	Previous German name
Aizpute	Hasenpoth
Alūksne	Marienburg
Cēsis	Wenden
Dundaga	Dondagen
Daugavpils	Dünaburg*
Dobele	Doblen
Gulbene	Schwanenburg
Jelgava	Mitau
Jēkabpils	Jakobstadt
Kandava	Kandau
Koknese	Kokenhusen
Krāslava	Kraslau
Krustpils	Kreuzburg
Kuldīga	Goldingen
Liepāja	Libau
Lielvārde	Lennewarden
Limbaži	Lemsal
Madona	Lasdohn
Mazirbe	Klein-Irben
Mersrags	Markgrafen
Mežotne	Mesothen
Nogale	Nogallen
Pasiene	Possinja
Rauna	Ronnenburg
Rēzekne	Rositten
Rūjiena	Rujen
Rundāle	Ruhenthal
Sabile	Zabeln
Sigulda	Segewold
Slītere	Schluter
Talsi	Talsen
Tūja	Taubenhof
Turaida	Treyden

Latvian	**German**
Ungurmuiža	Orellen
Valka	Walk★★
Valmiera	Wolmar
Ventspils	Windau

★ Known also as Dvinsk in Polish and Russian and additionally as Borisoglebsk in Russian
★★ The part of the town now in Estonia is known as Valga

Rivers

Daugava	Düna★
Gauja	Livländische Aa
Lielupe	Aa
Salaca	Salis
Venta	Windau

★ Also known as the Dvina where it flows through Russia

Other changes

Aizkraukle	Known as Stučka during the Soviet occupation
Madona	Changed from Birži in 1926
Valdemārpils	Previously Sasmaka; changed in memory of Krišjānis Valdemārs in 1926

THE ULTIMATE TRAVEL MAGAZINE

Launched in 1993, *Wanderlust* is an inspirational magazine dedicated to free-spirited travel. It has become the essential companion for independent-minded travellers of all ages and interests, with readers in over 100 countries.

A one-year, 6-issue subscription carries a money-back guarantee – for further details:

Tel.+44 (0)1753 620426
Fax. +44 (0)1753 620474

or check the *Wanderlust* website, which has

details of the latest issue, and where

you can subscribe on-line:

www.wanderlust.co.uk

Appendix

FURTHER INFORMATION
Further reading

Readers interested in exploring Latvia's history, literature and culture can select from a growing number of publications. In addition to guides to particular towns, for example *Riga in Your Pocket* (on the internet and available in Latvia), a number of books are widely available outside Latvia. For a general introduction to the history of Latvia and the early years of independence Anatol Lieven's *The Baltic Revolution* is so far unrivalled. For an in-depth account of the history of Latvia, two major works are available: *The Baltic States: The Years of Independence 1917–1940* and *The Baltic States: The Years of Dependence 1940–1980* (see below for details). For an interesting selection of contemporary Latvian writing, see *New Latvian Fiction*, published in 1998.

A good introduction to the troubled history of Latvia in the 20th century is *Walking Since Daybreak* by Modris Eksteins (2000). A poignant examination of memories of deportation and exile during the Soviet occupation has been conducted and published by Vieda Skultans in *The Testimony of Lives* (1998).

Visitors wanting to know more about the history of Riga or about its buildings, monuments and parks could not do better than to buy a copy of *Riga for the Curious Traveller* by Andris Kolbergs, translated into English by Anita Liepiņa and published in 2003. The detailed account covers not only central Riga but also the surrounding suburbs and gives a fascinating perspective on the development of the city. If only it had an index! *Riga The Complete Guide to Architecture* by Jānis Krastiņš and Ivars Strautmanis is a must for people seriously interested in architecture. Also of interest is *Old Riga*, a small but attractive guide with many pictures of the Old Town, written by Daiga Zariņa.

A number of beautifully illustrated and informatively written booklets were produced by the Latvijas Instituts in the run up to Riga's 800th anniversary in 2001. Titles include *Riga the City of Gardens*, an account of all Riga's parks, cemeteries and gardens, *Latvian Folk Songs, The Latvians – a Seafaring Nation, Latvian National Costumes,* and *Ecotourism in Latvia.* These can be obtained direct from the Latvijas instituts (1–3 Smilšu iela, Riga, LV–1050; tel: 750 3663; email: instituts@latinst.lv; www.latinst.lv). *The Art Nouveau Architecture of Riga* published in 1998 by the Riga City Council provides a comprehensive pictorial review of the main building styles. Pictures of buildings can also be seen at www.vip.latnet.lv/ArtNouveau.

A good airport read to put you in the mood for a trip to Riga is Henning Mankell's *The Dogs of Riga* (English version, 2001). Although locals claim they can point out inaccuracies in the descriptions of Riga, the novel creates an atmospheric reconstruction of Riga just before independence. Two well-known travel writers have written accounts of journeys in the Soviet Union, which include chapters on the Baltic states during the occupation: *Journey into Russia* by Laurens van der Post, and *Among the Russians*, by Colin Thubron.

The best bibliography on Latvia is probably *The Baltic States* by Inese A Smith and Marita Grunts (volume 161 in the World Bibliographical Series published by Clio Press, Oxford, Santa Barbara, Denver, 1993).

Addison, Lucy *Letters from Latvia* London, 1986

Andrups, Jānis and Kalve, Vitauts *Latvian Literature* Stockholm, 1954

Apinis, Peteris *Latvia, Country, Nation, State* Riga, 2000

Baister, Stephen and Patrick, Chris *Riga: The Bradt City Guide* Chalfont St Peter, 2005

The Baltic and Caucasian States (The Nations of Today). Edited by John Buchan; London, 1923

The Baltic Nations: Estonia, Latvia and Lithuania struggle towards independence. Edited by Priit J Vesilind; National Geographic vol 178 no 5

Benton, Peggie *Baltic Countdown: A Nation Vanishes* London, 1984

Bermant, Chaim *Genesis – A Latvian Childhood* London, 1998

Bilmanis, Alfred *A History of Latvia* Princeton, 1951

Chautauqua/Jūrmala 1986: a Latvian-American perspective. Edited by Ojārs Kalniņš, Rockville, 1987

Cherney, Alexander *The Latvian Orthodox Church* Welshpool, 1985

Crowe, David M *The Baltic States and the Great Powers: Foreign Relations, 1938–1940* Boulder, 1993

Dreifelds, Juris *Latvia in Transition* Cambridge, 1996

Eksteins, Modris *Walking since Daybreak* Boston, 2000; awarded the Pearsons' Writers Non-Fiction Prize.

Ezergailis, Andrew *The Holocaust in Latvia* The Historical Institute of Latvia, 1997

Fitzmaurice, John *The Baltic: A Regional Future?* Basingstoke, 1992

Flint, David C *The Baltic States: Estonia, Latvia, Lithuania* London, 1992

Gorman, Gerard *Where to Watch Birds in Eastern Europe* London, 1994

Hiden, John and Salmon, Patrick *The Baltic Nations and Europe: Estonia, Latvia and Lithuania in the Twentieth Century* London, New York, 1994

Hosking, Geoffrey *Russia, People and Empire 1552–1917* Penguin, 1998

Kirby, David *Northern Europe in the Early Modern Period: The Baltic World 1492–1772* London, 1990 and *The Baltic World 1972–1993* London, 1995

Kolbergs, Andris *The Story of Riga* Riga, 1998

Krastiņš, Jānis *The Art Nouveau Architecture of Riga* Riga, 1998

Krastiņš, Jānis and Strautmanis, Ivars *Riga The Complete Guide to Architecture* Riga, 2004

Latvia (Then & Now series) Minneapolis, 1992

Lawrence, Timothy *A Chronology of the Baltic Republics 1987–91* Manchester, 1991

Lieven, Anatol *The Baltic Revolution: Estonia, Latvia, Lithuania and the Path to Independence* New Haven, London, 1994

Mathews, W K *The Tricolour Sun* Cambridge, 1936. (Latvian verse in English translation)

Mathews, W K *A Century of Latvian Poetry* London, 1957. (Latvian verse in English translation)

Misiunas, Romualdas and Taagepera, Rein *The Baltic States: The Years of Dependence 1940–1980* London, 1993

New Latvian Fiction Review of Contemporary Fiction, Spring 1998, Normal, Illinois

Nesaule, Agate *A Woman in Amber* New York, 1994

Plakans, Andrejs *The Latvians – A Short History* Austria, 2000

Press, Bernhard *Murder of the Jews in Latvia* Boston, 1999

Rainis, Jānis *The Sons of Jacob* (trans Grace Rhys) London, 1924. (English translation of classic Rainis play)

Service, Robert *The History of 20th Century Russia* Penguin, 1998

Sinka, Juris *Latvia and Latvians* London, 1988

Skultans, Vida *Testimony of Lives* Routledge, 1998

Smith, Graham *The National Self-Determination of Estonia, Latvia and Lithuania* Macmillan, 1996

Stahnke, Astrida *Latvian Folk Tales* Riga, 1998

Stamers, Guntis *Latvia Today* Riga, 1995

Thomson, Clare *The Singing Revolution: A Political Journey Through the Baltic States* London, 1992

Thubron, Colin *Among the Russians* Penguin, 1983

Unwin, Peter *Baltic Approaches* Michael Russell, 1996

van der Post, Laurens *Journey into Russia* London, 1964

Vēveris, Ervins and Kuplais, Mārtiņš *In the Latvian Ethnographic Open-Air Museum* Riga, 1986. (Text in Latvian, Russian and English)

Virza, E *La Littérature Lettone depuis l'époque du Réveil National* Riga, undated

von Rauch, Georg *The Baltic States: The Years of Independence 1917–1940* London, 1995

von Sivers, T (editor) *Herder in Riga* Riga, 1868

Vīksne, Jānis and Vilks, Ieva *Baltic Birds 5: Ecology, Migration and Protection of Baltic Birds* Riga, 1990

Walker, Martin *The Baltic Republics* (in *Soviet Union* by Martin Walker) London, 1989

Who's Who in Latvia Riga, 1996

See www.amazon.co.uk and www.amazon.com for the latest publications.

In German

Bielenstein, Bernhard *Die Häuser aber bleiben* Jūrmala, 1998

Eckardt-Skalberg, Elfriede (trans) *Lettische Lyrik* Hannover, 1960. (Latvian verse in German translation)

Hesselink, Herman and Tempel, Norbert *Eisenbahnen im Baltikum* LOK, 1996 (covers the Baltic railways).

Knoll, Martin (trans) *Wunder und Wunden: Lyrik aus Lettland* Berlin, Riga, 1993. (Latvian verse in German translation)

See www.amazon.de for recent books in German.

Language

Moseley, Christopher *Colloquial Latvian* London, New York, 1996 (cassette available)

Pujate, G and Sosare, M *Latvian for Foreigners* Riga, 1995

English–Latvian Dictionary Latviešu-Angļu Vārdnīca Riga, 1994

Latviešu–Angļu Sarunvārdnīca Latvian–English Phrase Book Riga, 1996 (cassette available)

Maps

All the city guides have maps of central Riga on their back pages. If you need to see all the suburbs, local publisher Jāņa Sēta produces a large number of maps of Riga and the surrounding district, as well as of other towns in Latvia. You can buy these at the Jāņa Sēta shop at 83–85 Elizabetes iela, tel: 709 2288 in Riga and in many tourist offices. They also have a website www.kartes.lv. Jāņa Sēta maps can also be purchased at branches of Stanfords in the UK (in London, Bristol and Manchester).

Websites
General information

A good general site to start from for general information about Latvia is the Latvian Institute: www.latinst.lv. The site provides fact sheets on many aspects of life in Latvia, as well as a list of events throughout the year, and a long list of web links to other Latvian sites of interest; www.latviatourism.lc and www.lv provide more tourist-related information, including details of museums and hotels. The websites for the city guides are kept up to date with information about events and can be accessed at www.rigathisweek.lv and www.inyourpocket.com/latvia/en. The website of *Baltic City Papers* also provides useful tourist information, news and events listings: www.balticsww.com. Website www.muzeji.lv provides details of museums throughout Latvia, including a comprehensive listing of all museums in Riga. For detailed information on tram and trolleybus routes see www.ttp.lv and for train timetables and fares www.ldz.lv.

For current news and affairs in Riga and the whole of the Baltic States, try www.baltictimes.com, the website for the English-language newspaper. For the latest weather forecasts for Riga, www.wunderground.com/global/stations/26422.html can help. If you want to know how the economy is going, www.em.gov.lv, the Latvian Ministry of Economy site, is kept up to date. For more details about Riga and its government, consult the municipal site: www.riga.lv.

Most towns in Latvia have their own websites, sometimes only in Latvian but sometimes also in English. Try, for example, the following: **www.cesis.lv**, **www.tukums.lv**, **www.ventspils.tourism.lv** etc.

Language
www.codefusion.com/latvian/ can help you learn Latvian online
www.ectaco.com/online/diction.php3?lang=17 is an online Latvian dictionary

Specific information
www.putni.lv has detailed information on birdwatching in Latvia, including recent sightings, the best places to go and how to get there
www.opera.lv has details of the opera programme in Riga
www.gay.lv/ has information for gays and lesbians in Latvia; English site currently being constructed
www.rootsweb.com/~lvawgw/index.html can help you trace Latvian ancestors
www2.jewishgen.org/latvia/ is part of a world project helping Jewish people trace their ancestry in Latvia
www.balticshop.com is a shopping site for products from Latvia. You can also order flowers for delivery to friends or family in Latvia
http://folklora.lv has information on traditional Latvia, and includes a regularly updated list of traditional Latvian events across the country
www.Latviansonline.com, put together by Latvian expatriates in the USA and Australia, includes a lot of Latvian links and up-to-date news
www.wunderground.com/global/LV.htm for the latest information on weather in Latvia
www.virtualriga.com has some information about Riga but is mainly interesting for its pictures of Riga
vip.latnet.lv/ArtNouveau/Nouveau.htm has pictures of art nouveau buildings in Riga
www.csb.lv Central Statistical Bureau

Amber

Bradt Travel Guides

Africa by Road	£13.95	Kiev City Guide	£7.95
Albania	£13.95	Latvia	£13.99
Amazon	£14.95	Lille City Guide	£6.99
Antarctica: A Guide to the Wildlife	£14.95	Lithuania	£13.99
The Arctic: A Guide to Coastal		Ljubljana City Guide	£6.99
Wildlife	£14.95	Macedonia	£13.95
Armenia with Nagorno Karabagh	£13.95	Madagascar	£14.95
Azores	£12.95	Madagascar Wildlife	£14.95
Baghdad City Guide	£9.95	Malawi	£12.95
Baltic Capitals: Tallinn, Riga,		Maldives	£12.95
Vilnius, Kaliningrad	£11.95	Mali	£13.95
Bosnia & Herzegovina	£13.95	Mauritius	£12.95
Botswana: Okavango Delta,		Mongolia	£14.95
Chobe, Northern Kalahari	£14.95	Montenegro	£13.99
British Isles: Wildlife of Coastal		Mozambique	£12.95
Waters	£14.95	Namibia	£14.95
Budapest City Guide	£7.95	Nigeria	£15.99
Cameroon	£13.95	North Cyprus	£12.95
Canary Islands	£13.95	North Korea	£13.95
Cape Verde Islands	£12.95	Palestine with Jerusalem	£12.95
Cayman Islands	£12.95	Panama	£13.95
Chile	£16.95	Paris, Lille & Brussels: Eurostar Cities	£11.95
Chile & Argentina: Trekking Guide	£12.95	Peru & Bolivia: Backpacking &	
China: Yunnan Province	£13.95	Trekking	£12.95
Cork City Guide	£6.95	Riga City Guide	£6.95
Croatia	£12.95	River Thames: In the	
Dubrovnik City Guide	£6.95	Footsteps of the Famous	£10.95
Eccentric America	£13.95	Rwanda	£13.95
Eccentric Britain	£13.99	St Helena, Ascension,	
Eccentric California	£13.99	Tristan da Cunha	£14.95
Eccentric Edinburgh	£5.95	Serbia	£13.99
Eccentric France	£12.95	Seychelles	£14.99
Eccentric London	£12.95	Slovenia	£12.99
Eccentric Oxford	£5.95	Southern African Wildlife	£18.95
Ecuador: Climbing & Hiking	£13.95	Sri Lanka	£12.95
Eritrea	£12.95	Sudan	£13.95
Estonia	£12.95	Svalbard	£14.99
Ethiopia	£13.95	Switzerland: Rail, Road, Lake	£13.99
Falkland Islands	£13.95	Tallinn City Guide	£6.95
Faroe Islands	£13.95	Tanzania	£14.95
Gabon, São Tomé & Príncipe	£13.95	Tasmania	£12.95
Galápagos Wildlife	£14.95	Tibet	£12.95
Gambia, The	£12.95	Uganda	£13.95
Georgia with Armenia	£13.95	Ukraine	£14.95
Ghana	£13.95	USA by Rail	£12.95
Hungary	£14.99	Venezuela	£14.95
Iran	£14.99	Your Child Abroad: A Travel	
Iraq	£14.95	Health Guide	£9.95
Kabul Mini Guide	£9.95	Zambia	£15.95
Kenya	£14.95	Zanzibar	£12.95

WIN £100 CASH!

READER QUESTIONNAIRE

Send in your completed questionnaire for the chance to win £100 cash in our regular draw

All respondents may order a Bradt guide at half the UK retail price – please complete the order form overleaf.

(Entries may be posted or faxed to us, or scanned and emailed.)

We are interested in getting feedback from our readers to help us plan future Bradt guides. Please complete this quick questionnaire and return it to us to enter into our draw.

Have you used any other Bradt guides? If so, which titles? . . . .
. . . .

What other publishers' travel guides do you use regularly? . . . .
. . . .

Where did you buy this guidebook? . . . .

What was the main purpose of your trip to Latvia (or for what other reason did you read our guide)? eg: holiday/business/charity etc. . . . .
. . . .

What other destinations would you like to see covered by a Bradt guide?
. . . .

Would you like to receive our catalogue/newsletters?

YES / NO (If yes, please complete details on reverse)

If yes – by post or email? . . . .

Age (circle relevant category) 16–25   26–45   46–60   60+

Male/Female (delete as appropriate)

Home country . . . .

Please send us any comments about our guide to Latvia or other Bradt Travel Guides. . . . .
. . . .
. . . .
. . . .

Bradt Travel Guides

19 High Street, Chalfont St Peter, Bucks SL9 9QE, UK
Telephone: +44 (0)1753 893444 Fax: +44 (0)1753 892333
Email: info@bradtguides.com
www.bradtguides.com

CLAIM YOUR HALF-PRICE BRADT GUIDE!

Order Form

To order your half-price copy of a Bradt guide, and to enter our prize draw to win £100 (see overleaf), please fill in the order form below, complete the questionnaire overleaf, and send it to Bradt Travel Guides by post, fax or email. Post and packing is free to UK addresses.

Please send me one copy of the following guide at half the UK retail price

Title	Retail price	Half price
...	....	....	....

Please send the following additional guides at full UK retail price

No	Title	Retail price	Total
...	....	....	....
...	....	....	....
...	....	....	....

Sub total ....
Post & packing outside UK ....
(£2 per book Europe; £3 per book rest of world)
Total ....

Name . . . .

Address . . . .

Tel . . . .   Email . . . .

☐ I enclose a cheque for £ . . . . made payable to Bradt Travel Guides Ltd

☐ I would like to pay by VISA or MasterCard

   Number . . . .   Expiry date . . . .

☐ Please add my name to your catalogue mailing list.

Send your order on this form, with the completed questionnaire, to:

Bradt Travel Guides/LAT
19 High Street, Chalfont St Peter, Bucks SL9 9QE
Tel: +44 (0)1753 893444 Fax: +44 (0)1753 892333
Email: info@bradtguides.com
www.bradtguides.com

Index

Page references in bold indicate major entries;
those in italic indicate maps